PRE-SUASION

A Revolutionary Way
to Influence and Persuade

ROBERT CIALDINI

BOOKS

3 5 7 9 10 8 6 4 2

Random House Books
20 Vauxhall Bridge Road
London SW1V 2SA

Random House Books is part of the Penguin Random House group of companies
whose addresses can be found at global.penguinrandomhouse.com.

Copyright © Robert B. Cialdini 2016

Robert B. Cialdini has asserted his right to be identified as the author of this
Work in accordance with the Copyright, Designs and Patents Act 1988.

First published in paperback by Random House Books in 2017
First published by Random House Books in 2016

www.penguin.co.uk

A CIP catalogue record for this book is available from the British Library.

ISBN 9781847941435

Printed and bound by Clays Ltd, St Ives plc

Penguin Random House is committed to a sustainable future
for our business, our readers and our planet. This book is made
from Forest Stewardship Council® certified paper.

To Hailey, Dawson, and Leia. I never liked being bossed around by my superiors until I had grandchildren, who exposed me to the joys for all concerned.

Contents

Part 3
BEST PRACTICES: THE OPTIMIZATION OF PRE-SUASION   149

Acknowledgments

I am grateful to a number of individuals who helped make this book a reality. At the top of the list is Bobette Gorden, who lived it with me from first to last word, offering the invaluable benefits of her potent mind, inerrant ear, and loving heart. Others—Doug Kenrick, Greg Neidert, Linda Demaine, Jennifer Jordan, Gerry Allen, and Charlie Munger—read individual chapters or sets of chapters and made excellent suggestions. Still others supplied consistently helpful feedback on the entire manuscript. Nigel Wilcockson delivered a cogent overview and excellent recommendations. Andrew White showed me how aspects of the text material could be profitably augmented with information from Internet sources. Richard Cialdini and Katherine Wanslee Cialdini endured long readings of chapter drafts and yet remained sufficiently focused to respond with much appreciated observations and support. Anna Ropiecka provided great commentary from the dual perspectives of a deep thinker and a non-native English speaker, which got me to sharpen my thinking and streamline my language.

Finally, two publishing professionals warrant special note, as each deserves not only my thanks but an unalloyed recommendation to any prospective author. My agent, Jim Levine, was a godsend, steering me through the entire process with never-flagging professionalism, ethicality, and acumen. Ben Loehnen, my editor at Simon & Schuster, was a forceful in-house advocate for the project and a source of exquisite editorial counsel for the writing process; the finished product is markedly better for his involvement.

I am a fortunate man to have had the assistance of this set of individuals.

Author's Note

In 1946 W. H. Auden published a poem with a line of stern advice: "Thou shalt not sit with statisticians nor commit a social science." For a long time, even high-ranking decision makers seemed to concur, preferring to base their choices on intuition, personal experience, and anecdote. Although a name change was required in each instance (statistics is now data analytics, and social science is now behavioral science), those days are gone.

They've been replaced by an era of "evidence-based decision making" in the major institutions of society: business, government, education, defense, sports. It's an era that prizes information from big-data analysts and behavioral scientists. I have no direct knowledge of how the transformation occurred in the realm of statistical analysis, but I've been able to observe firsthand the rise in the status of behavioral science through my experiences as a social psychologist and the author of the book *Influence*.

When *Influence* first appeared, in 1984, it had little impact. Sales were so disappointing my publisher withdrew allotted advertising and promotional funds, explaining that to do otherwise would be "throwing money down a pit." Few readers were interested in what a social psychologist had to say about social influence. That ended four or five years later when sales of the book began rising, eventually to bestseller levels, where they've remained ever since. I think I know what changed to cause the upswing: the times. By then, the idea of evidence-based decision making was gaining widespread acceptance, and *Influence* offered a type of valuable evidence—from scientific, social psychological research into successful persuasion—that hadn't been available before, at least not in one handy place.

Two additional factors have played a role in the current popularity of such social psychological analysis and, by extension, of *Influence*. The first is the rise of behavioral economics, an approach to understanding human economic choices that has challenged and, in certain domains, swept away classical economic thinking. Although staking out its own territory, behavioral economics has incorporated aspects of social psychological thinking (for instance, the frequent irrationality of human conduct) and methodology (randomized, controlled experiments).

Some of my colleagues feel that behavioral economists have robbed them of credit by claiming various discoveries as their own without acknowledging existing, highly similar social psychological findings. I don't share the resentment. Although there's some overlap, it's not extensive. Moreover, if anything, behavioral economics has raised the public stature of social psychology by adopting some core features and legitimizing them in the minds of decision makers. There was a time, as recently as ten years ago, when social psychologists wouldn't be invited to international conferences on government or economic policy. Again, those days are gone.

The other contributor to the current acceptance of social psychological approaches is the newfound willingness of social psychologists to present their work (and its relevance) to the public. It's a turnabout I'd like to think that *Influence* helped produce. Before its publication, most of my colleagues didn't feel safe, professionally, writing for a popular audience. Indeed, if social psychology had been a business, it would have been known for having great research and development units but no shipping department. We didn't ship, except to one another in academic journal articles that no general reader was likely to read. An observation by the legal scholar James Boyle captures the main reason: "You have never heard true condescension until you have heard academics pronounce the word *popularizer*." That is changed today. Social psychologists, as well as myriad other behavioral scientists, are communicating with the broader community like never before in widely appreciated blogs, columns, videos, and books. In this respect, behavioral science is in a kind of Golden Age.

– —– –

Pre-Suasion seeks to add to the body of behavioral science information that general readers find both inherently interesting and applicable to their daily lives. It identifies what savvy communicators do before delivering a message to get it accepted. Their sharp timing is what is new here. Older voices have recognized the wisdom of undertaking prior action to secure subsequent success. In asserting the value of early planning, the ancient Chinese military strategist Sun Tzu declared, "Every battle is won before it is fought." Consultants are taught to gain a client's business by first attaining the status of "trusted advisor." Dale Carnegie assured us, "You can make more friends in two months by becoming genuinely interested in other people than you can in two years by trying to get people interested in you." All wise counsel. But there's a drawback: days, weeks, or months of prior activity are required.

Is it possible to enhance effectiveness not only within those lengthy time frames but also in an instant—the last instant before a communication is sent? Not only is it possible, it is established. Communicators can elevate their success by knowing what to say or do *just* before an appeal. Marcus Tullius Cicero, the Roman orator of the first century BCE, recognized the sway of certain long-standing influences on human conduct, proclaiming, "Oh, the times! Oh, the customs!" The material in *Pre-Suasion* implicates a much more immediate and manageable source of influence: Oh, the moment!

A final note concerns, fittingly, the book's endnotes. They present not only the citations for relevant scholarly work but also additional topic information intended to expand readers' knowledge of the text material in interesting directions. Accordingly, they should be viewed, in part, as places to find "color commentary."[1]

PRE-SUASION: THE FRONTLOADING OF ATTENTION

1

PRE-SUASION: An Introduction

As a kind of secret agent, I once infiltrated the training programs of
a broad range of professions dedicated to getting us to say yes. For
almost three years, I recorded the lessons taught to aspiring automobile salespeople, direct marketers, TV advertisers, frontline managers,
charity fund-raisers, public relations specialists, and corporate recruiters. My intent was to find out which practices worked time after
time. So I answered the organizations' ads for trainees or otherwise
arranged to be present in their classrooms, notebook in hand, ready to
absorb the wisdom born of long-standing experience in the business
of persuasion.

In these programs, advanced trainees were often allowed to accompany and observe an old pro who was conducting business. I always
jumped at those opportunities because I wanted to see if I could register
not just what practitioners in general did to succeed but also what the best
of them did. One such practice quickly surfaced that shook my assump-
tions. I'd expected that the aces of their professions would spend more
time than the inferior performers developing the specifics of their requests for change: the clarity, logic, and desirable features of them. That's
not what I found.

PRE-SUASION

The highest achievers spent more time crafting what they did and said *before* making a request. They set about their mission as skilled gardeners who know that even the finest seeds will not take root in stony soil or bear fullest fruit in poorly prepared ground. They spent much of their time toiling in the fields of influence thinking about and engaging in cultivation—in ensuring that the situations they were facing had been pretreated and readied for growth. Of course, the best performers also considered and cared about what, specifically, they would be offering in those situations. But much more than their less effective colleagues, they didn't rely on the legitimate merits of an offer to get it accepted; they recognized that the psychological frame in which an appeal is first placed can carry equal or even greater weight.

Besides, they were frequently in no position to tinker with the merits of what they had to offer; someone else in the organization had created the product, program, or plan they were recommending, often in fixed form. Their responsibility was to present it most productively. To accomplish that, they did something that gave them a singular kind of persuasive traction: before introducing their message, they arranged to make their audience sympathetic to it.

There's a critical insight in all this for those of us who want to learn to be more influential. The best persuaders become the best through *pre-suasion*—the process of arranging for recipients to be receptive to a message before they encounter it. To persuade optimally, then, it's necessary to pre-suade optimally. But how?

In part, the answer involves an essential but poorly appreciated tenet of all communication: what we present first changes the way people experience what we present to them next. Consider how a small procedural difference has improved the bottom line of the consulting business of a Toronto-based colleague of mine. For years, when bidding on a big project, it wasn't unusual to get price resistance from the client, who might propose a 10 percent or 15 percent reduction. That was frustrating, he says, because he never felt comfortable padding the budget to cover this kind of potential pushback on costs. If he did agree to the cut, his profit margin became so thin it barely paid to take the business. If he didn't acquiesce, he either lost the job or produced partners who were initially disgruntled because he wasn't willing to work with them on price.

Then, during one proposal meeting, he accidentally hit upon a maneuver that rid him of the problem forever. It wasn't a step-by-step attempt to specify or justify each of the expenses involved in his services; he'd long since given up on that approach, which only brought scrutiny to the bill. Instead, after his standard presentation and just before declaring his ($75,000) fee, he joked, "As you can tell, I'm not going to be able to charge you a million dollars for this." The client looked up from the written proposal he'd been studying and said, "Well, I can agree to that!" The meeting proceeded without a single subsequent reference to compensation and ended with a signed contract. My colleague claims that this tactic of mentioning an admittedly unrealistic price tag for a job doesn't always win the business—too many other factors are involved for that—but it almost always eliminates challenges to the charges.

Although he stumbled onto it, my friend is not alone in experiencing the remarkable effects of merely launching a large number into the air and, consequently, into the minds of others. Researchers have found that the amount of money people said they'd be willing to spend on dinner went up when the restaurant was named Studio 97, as opposed to Studio 17; that the price individuals would pay for a box of Belgian chocolates grew after they'd been asked to write down a pair of high (versus low) digits from their Social Security numbers; that participants in a study of work performance predicted their effort and output would be better when the study happened to be labeled experiment twenty-seven (versus experiment nine); and that observers' estimates of an athlete's performance increased if he wore a high (versus low) number on his jersey.

What's more, the potent impact of what goes first isn't limited to big initial numbers. Other researchers have shown that just after drawing a set of long lines on a sheet of paper, college students estimated the length of the Mississippi River as much greater than those who had just drawn a set of short lines. In fact, the impact of what goes first isn't limited to numerics at all: customers in a wine shop were more likely to purchase a German vintage if, before their choice, they'd heard a German song playing on the shop's sound system; similarly, they were more likely to purchase a French vintage if they'd heard a French song playing.[2]

So it's not one particular experience that guides what's done later. It can be exposure to a number, the length of a line, or a piece of music; and, as we will see in later chapters, it can be a brief burst of attention to any of a variety of selected psychological concepts. But, because this book is mainly about the things that enhance persuasion, those chapters give special treatment to the concepts that most elevate the likelihood of assent. It's important here to take note of my choice of the word *likelihood*, which reflects an inescapable reality of operating in the realm of human behavior—claims of certainties in that province are laughable. No persuasive practice is going to work for sure whenever it is applied. Yet there are approaches that can consistently heighten the probability of agreement. And *that* is enough. A meaningful increase in those odds is enough to gain a decisive advantage.

In the home, it's enough to give us the means to get greater compliance with our wishes—even from that most resistant of all audiences: our children. In business, it's enough to give organizations that implement these approaches the means to outpace their rivals—even rivals with equally good cases to make. It's also enough to give those who know how to employ these approaches the means to become better, even best, performers within an organization.

Take, for instance, one such best performer (we can call him Jim because, what the heck, that was his name) who worked for a firm whose training program I had entered to study. The company made expensive, heat-activated fire alarm systems for the home, and Jim was its top salesperson. He didn't win every sale, of course, but the likelihood that he would emerge from a sales call with a signed contract was, month after month, better than his counterparts'. After an initial period of classroom instruction, I was assigned to spend the next several days accompanying various salespeople, to learn how they approached the selling process. This always involved an in-home visit to a family that had scheduled an appointment for a presentation.

On account of his star status, I looked closely at Jim's technique. One practice stood out as central to his success. Before beginning his sales effort, he established an aura of trust with the family. Trust is one of those qualities that leads to compliance with requests, provided that it has been planted before the request is made. Despite the mountains of scientific reports and scores of books that have been written making that point and suggesting ways to achieve trust, Jim accomplished it in a fashion I've not seen in any of them. He did it by pretending to be a bit of a screwup.

The sales sequence taught to all company representatives was fairly standard to the industry. After making small talk to build rapport, the prospects (usually a couple) were given a timed ten-minute written test of fire safety knowledge designed to reveal how little they knew about the actual dangers of a home fire. Then, at the completion of the test, representatives began the active sales pitch by demonstrating the alarm system and walking prospects through a book of materials documenting the system's superiority to all others. Everyone else brought the book into the house from the start and kept it close by, ready for use. Not Jim, though. He would wait until a couple had begun taking the knowledge test, when he'd slap his forehead and say, "Oh, I forgot some really important information in my car, and I need to get it. I don't want to interrupt the test; so, would you mind if I let myself out and back into your home?" The answer was always some form of "Sure, go ahead." Oftentimes it required giving him a door key.

I watched Jim make three presentations. Each time, his "forgetfulness" surfaced in the same way and at the same point. On the drive back to the office later that evening, I asked him about it. Twice, he wouldn't give me a straight answer, annoyed that I was pressing to discover his selling secret. But when I persisted, he blurted, "Think, Bob: Who do you let walk in and out of your house on their own? Only somebody you trust, right? I want to be associated with trust in those families' minds."

It was a brilliant trick—not an entirely ethical one, but brilliant nonetheless—because it embodied one of the central assertions of this book: the truly influential things we say and do first act to *pre-suade* our audience, which they accomplish by altering audience members' associations with what we do or say next. In chapter 7, I will forward the argument that all mental activity arises as patterns of associations within a vast and intricate neural network, and that influence attempts will be successful only to the extent that the associations they trigger are favorable to change.

Jim's tactic provides a good illustration. To become a top salesperson, he didn't have to modify the features of the alarm system he was selling or the logic, wording, or style of how he portrayed it; in fact, he didn't stray from the standard presentation at all. Instead, he only had to first become associated with the concept of trust, the (intensely positive) other associations of which would then become linked to him and his advice. Even Jim's unorthodox method of connecting himself to the concept of trust was purely associative. He didn't claim to be the sort of individual—a close friend or family member, perhaps—that people let have open access to their homes. He just arranged to be treated in way *characteristic* of trusted individuals of this sort. It's noteworthy that this tactic was the only real difference I registered between Jim's presentations and those of his significantly less successful coworkers. Such is the strength of mere association.

All told, there are any of a number of first steps, besides establishing trust, persuaders can take that will make audiences more receptive to the case they intend to present. The steps can take multiple forms, and, accordingly, they've been given multiple labels by behavioral scientists. They can be called frames or anchors or primes or mindsets or first impressions. We will encounter each of those types in the remainder of these pages, where, throughout, I'm going to refer to them as *openers*—because they open up things for influence in two ways. In the first, they simply initiate the process; they provide the starting points, the beginnings of persuasive appeals. But it is in their second function that they clear the way to persuasion, by removing existing barriers. In that role, they promote the openings of minds and—for would-be persuaders like Jim—of protectively locked doors.[3]

THE BIG SAME

There's a joke I've heard influence practitioners tell about the difficulties of persuading prospects to move in a desired direction. It tracks an exchange between the sales representative of a marketing firm and a potential client who wants to bring out a new brand of frozen spinach.

Client: Do you have experience marketing new food products?

Sales rep: We have quite a lot of experience there.

Client: Does that include experience in selling frozen food?

Sales rep: Yes, it does.

Client: How about frozen vegetables?

Sales rep: We've brought several types to market over the years.

Client: Spinach?

Sales rep: Actually, yes, spinach too.

Client [*leaning forward now, voice straining in anticipation*]: Whole leaf . . . or chopped?

At business conferences, the joke produces knowing, derisive laughter from the influence professionals who hear it. Of course it was never funny the times the joke was on *them*—when they'd lost a contract or sale because a prospective customer, caught up in some detail of a difference, missed the big picture of what they had to offer. The contemptuous reaction to the joke's punch line always struck me as odd, because I had found persuasion practitioners guilty of the same kind of narrowness—not in meetings with a customer or client but in the training sessions designed to prepare them for those meetings.

It wasn't long after I began operating undercover in the training classes of influence practitioners that I encountered something curious: participants in the sessions were nearly always informed that persuasion had to be approached differently in their particular profession than in related professions. When it comes to swaying people, advertising works differently than marketing; marketing works differently than fund-raising; fund-raising works differently than public relations; public relations works differently than lobbying; lobbying works differently than recruitment. And so on.

What's more, distinctions were stressed even within professions. Selling whole life insurance is different from selling term insurance; selling trucks is different from selling cars; selling by mail or online is different from selling in stores; selling products is different from selling services; selling to an individual is different from selling to a business; selling wholesale is different from selling retail.

It's not that the trainers were wrong in distinguishing their own baili-wick from those of their professional neighbors. But this steady referencing of their uniqueness led to a pair of lapses in judgment. First, they often de-toured into distinctions of little consequence. Worse, in their emphasis on what's different among the successful persuasion professions, they didn't focus enough on an extraordinarily useful other question: What's *the same*?

This oversight seemed a serious failing because if trainees could in-deed be shown what proved convincing across the widest set of influence situations, it would help them win the day in all manner of circumstances, novel and familiar. If they could indeed be educated to understand and employ the *universal* principles that undergird effective persuasion, the details of the change they were hoping to generate wouldn't matter. They would do swimmingly whether their influence attempt involved whole-sale or retail, whole life or term, whole leaf or chopped.[4]

My goal during those times spent scrutinizing commercial training programs, then, was to discover what lies in parallel beneath all the truly superior professional approaches to influence. A driving question for me throughout that nearly three-year period was, "What do *these* approaches have in common to make them work so well?" The limited footprint of the answer that emerged surprised me. I identified only six psychological principles that appeared to be deployed routinely in long-prospering in-fluence businesses. I've claimed that the six—reciprocation, liking, social proof, authority, scarcity, and consistency—represent certain psychologi-cal universals of persuasion; and I've treated each, one per chapter, in my earlier book, *Influence*.

THE BIG DIFFERENCE

In a portion of *Pre-Suasion*, I have tried to make instructive contact with those principles again while taking an important change in direction. The earlier book was written to inform consumers how to resist influence at-tempts employed in an undue or unwelcome way. One factor that spurred me to write this book is that, although *Influence* has now appeared in mul-tiple editions and sold more copies than I could have sensibly imagined, few consumer groups ever contacted me for follow-up. But my phone hasn't stopped ringing with requests from two other types of callers: corporate representatives inviting me to speak to *their* groups and individual readers wanting to know how to become more influential in everyday interactions with coworkers, friends, neighbors, and family members. It became plain that, more than just learning how to deflect or reject it, large numbers of people are ravenously interested in learning how to harness persuasion.

In contrast to *Influence*, one aim of this book is to help satisfy that hunger directly, but with a pair of dietary restrictions. The first concerns the ethics of persuasive success. Just because we can use psychological tactics to gain consent doesn't mean we are entitled to them. The tactics are available for good or ill. They can be structured to fool and thereby exploit others. But they can also be structured to inform and thereby enhance others. Chapter 13 offers a rationale—beyond the traditional one based on the economic consequences of a damaged reputation—for why organizations should steer sharply away from unethical persuasive practices: those practices will lend themselves to the attraction and retention of employees who find cheating acceptable and who will ultimately cheat the organization as a consequence.

This book also abides by a second stipulation. Although the material should be seasoned liberally with personal illustrations and accounts, the meat of the evidence has to be scientifically based. In any effort to manage the influence process successfully, a scientifically grounded approach provides a real advantage. Traditionally, persuasion has been viewed as an elusive art; the province of those few with an intuitive grasp of how to turn a phrase just so. But something radical has happened to the study of persuasion during the past half century that permits the rest of us to benefit as fully as the born masters.

Researchers have been applying a rigorous scientific approach to the question of which messages lead people to concede, comply, and change. They have documented the sometimes staggering impact of making a request in a standard way versus making the identical request in a different, better-informed fashion. Besides the sheer impact of the obtained effects, there is another noteworthy aspect of the results: the process of persuasion is governed by psychological laws, which means that similar procedures can produce similar results over a wide range of situations.

And, if persuasion is lawful, it is—unlike artistic inspiration—learnable. Whether possessed of an inherent talent for influence or not, whether insightful about the methods or not, whether a gifted artisan of the language or not, it is possible to learn scientifically established techniques that allow any of us to be more influential.[5]

— —— —

Importantly different from *Influence* is the science-based evidence of not just *what* best to say to persuade but also *when* best to say it. From that evidence, it is possible to learn how to recognize and monitor the natural emergence of opportune moments of influence. It is also possible (but more perilous, from an ethical standpoint) to learn how to create—to make—those moments. Whether operating as a moment monitor or a moment maker, the individual who knows how to time a request, recommendation, or proposal properly will do exceedingly well.

IT'S ABOUT TIME(ING)

It's about time that I finished this book that is in one sense about timing; in fact, it's several years late. I intended to write it while away from my home university during a leave of absence at a well-known business school. There, I figured, I'd have access to knowledgeable colleagues who could help me think about relevant issues, as well as an uncluttered calendar that would allow me the blocks of time I needed to write.

A month or so before I was to relocate, I was negotiating with the associate dean about certain aspects of my visit that stood to make it more fruitful—an office near respected colleagues, secretarial assistance, telephone, parking, and library privileges—when I received a fateful call from him. It began wonderfully. "Bob," he said, "I have good news. I was able to get you the office you wanted; the computer in there is more powerful than the one you asked for; don't worry about access to a secretary, the library, parking, long-distance calls—we'll take care of all that." I was grateful and told him how much I appreciated all he'd done for me. He waited a beat and replied, "Well, there's something you could do for *me*. We've just experienced the need for someone to teach a specialized marketing class for our MBA students. I'm in a bind, and it would really help me out if you could do it."

I knew that agreeing to his request would torpedo my chances of completing the planned book during my stay because (1) I had never taught in a business school before, which meant learning a new set of teaching norms; (2) I had never taught a marketing class before, which meant developing an entire course with coordinated lectures, readings, exercises, and exams; and (3) I had never taught MBAs before, which meant, for the first time in my career, I'd be allocating much of my out-of-class activities to the questions, comments, and needs of the most relentless students known to the teaching profession: first-year MBAs.

I agreed anyway. I couldn't see any other appropriate option, not in the instant after expressing my sincere thanks for everything this moment maker had just provided. If he had asked the day before or the day after, I would have been able to say no, explaining that there was a book I needed to write during my stay. But the circumstances were different inside his privileged moment.

Because of what he had just done for me, there was no socially acceptable alternative to saying yes. (I can only be glad he didn't need a kidney.) So, owing to the demands of the moment, "yes" it necessarily was. And, yes, at the end of my leave of absence, arranged specifically to write this book, there was no book. Family members were disappointed, as were a few editors, and I was disappointed in myself.

I can see a pair of upsides to this sequence of events, though. First, instructive new research has accumulated within the domain of persuasion science, which I have incorporated into the writing. Second, the associate dean's extraordinarily effective maneuver illustrates perfectly another major assertion of this book: pre-suasive practices create windows of opportunity that are far from propped open permanently. I am confident that I would have been able to muster the resources to decline the man's request if he had made it in a separate, subsequent phone call.

When it's high time to ask. Fortunately, there are many other factors besides the effects of cannabis that increase assent if we time our requests to their presence. *Doonesbury © 2013. G. B. Trudeau. Reprinted with permission of Universal Uclick. All rights reserved.*

It's because of the only-temporary receptiveness that pre-suasive actions often produce in others that I've introduced the concept of *privileged moments.* The meaning of the word *privileged* is straightforward, referring to special, elevated status. The word *moment*, though, is more complex, as it evokes a pair of meanings. One connotes a time-limited period: in this case, the window of opportunity following a pre-suasive opener, when a proposal's power is greatest. The other connotation comes from physics and refers to a unique leveraging force that can bring about unprecedented movement. These yoked dimensions, temporal on the one hand and physical on the other, have the capacity to instigate extraordinary change in yet a third, psychological, dimension. The remaining chapters, described briefly below, show how.[6]

PART 1: PRE-SUASION: THE FRONTLOADING OF ATTENTION

Chapter 2. Privileged Moments

Chapter 2 explicates the concept of privileged moments, identifiable points in time when an individual is particularly receptive to a communicator's message. The chapter also presents and supports a fundamental thesis: the factor most likely to determine a person's choice in a situation is often not the one that offers the most accurate or useful counsel; instead, it is the one that has been elevated in attention (and thereby in privilege) at the moment of decision.

Chapter 3. The Importance of Attention . . . Is Importance

Chapter 3 explores and documents one central reason that *channeled attention* leads to pre-suasion: the human tendency to assign undue levels of importance to an idea as soon as one's attention is turned to it. The chapter looks at the effects of channeled attention in three different arenas: effective online marketing efforts, positive consumer product reviews, and successful wartime propaganda campaigns.

Chapter 4. What's Focal Is Causal

Chapter 4 adds a second reason for why channeled attention leads to pre-suasion. In the same way that attentional focus leads to perceptions of importance, it also leads to perceptions of *causality*. If people see themselves giving special attention to some factor, they become more likely to think of it as a cause. The influence-related upshots of the "what's focal is presumed causal" effect are examined in domains such as lottery number choices and false confessions in police interrogations.

Chapter 5. Commanders of Attention 1: The Attractors

If elevated attention provides pre-suasive leverage, are there any features of information that automatically invite such attention and therefore don't even require a communicator's special efforts? Chapter 5 examines several of these naturally occurring commanders of attention: the sexual, the threatening, and the different.

Chapter 6. Commanders of Attention 2: The Magnetizers

Besides the advantages of drawing attention to a particular stimulus, there is considerable benefit to holding it there. The communicator who can fasten an audience's focus onto the favorable elements of an argument raises the chance that the argument will go unchallenged by opposing points of view, which get locked out of the attentional environment as a consequence. Chapter 6 covers certain kinds of information that combine initial pulling power with staying power: the self-relevant, the unfinished, and the mysterious.

PART 2: PROCESSES: THE ROLE OF ASSOCIATION

Chapter 7. The Primacy of Associations: I Link, Therefore I Think

Once attention has been channeled to a selected concept, what is it about the concept that leads to a shift in responding? All mental activity is composed of patterns of associations; and influence attempts, including pre-suasive ones, will be successful only to the extent that the *associations* they trigger are favorable to change. Chapter 7 shows how both language and imagery can be used to produce desirable outcomes such as greater job performance, more positive personnel evaluations, and—in one especially noteworthy instance—the release of prisoners kidnapped by the Afghan Taliban.

Chapter 8. Persuasive Geographies: All the Right Places, All the Right Traces

There is a geography of influence. Just as words and images can prompt certain associations favorable to change, so can places. Thus, it becomes possible to send *ourselves* in desired directions by locating to physical and psychological environments prefit with cues associated with our relevant goals. It's also possible for influencers to achieve their goals by shifting *others* to environments with supportive cues. For instance, young women do better on science, math, and leadership tasks if assigned to rooms with cues (photos, for example) of women known to have mastered the tasks.

Chapter 9. The Mechanics of Pre-suasion: Causes, Constraints, and Correctives

A communicator pre-suades by focusing recipients initially on concepts that are aligned, associatively, with the information yet to be delivered. But by what mechanism? The answer involves an underappreciated characteristic of mental activity: its elements don't just fire when ready, they fire when *readied*. Chapter 9 examines this mechanism's operation in such varied phenomena as how advertising imagery works, how infants can be pre-suaded toward helpfulness, and how opiate drug addicts can be pre-suaded into performing an important therapeutic activity that none would consent to otherwise.

PART 3: BEST PRACTICES: THE OPTIMIZATION OF PRE-SUASION

Chapter 10. Six Main Roads to Change: Broad Boulevards as Smart Shortcuts

On which specific concepts should an audience's attention be focused for the greatest pre-suasive effect? Attention should be channeled to one or another of the universal principles of influence treated in my earlier book, *Influence*: reciprocity, liking, authority, social proof, scarcity, and consistency. There is good reason for their prevalence and success, for these are the principles that typically steer people in the right direction when they are deciding what to do.

Chapter 11. Unity 1: Being Together

Chapter 11 reveals an additional (seventh) universal principle of influence: unity. There is a certain type of unity—of identity—that best characterizes a *We* relationship and that, if pre-suasively raised to consciousness, leads to more acceptance, cooperation, liking, help, trust, and, consequently, assent. The chapter describes the first of two main ways to build *We* relationships: by presenting cues of genetic commonality associated with family and place.

Chapter 12. Unity 2: Acting Together

Besides the unitizing effect of being together in the same genealogy or geography, *We* relationships can result from acting together synchronously or collaboratively. When people act in unitary ways, they become unitized; and when such activity is arranged pre-suasively, it produces mutual liking and support. Chapter 12 provides illustrations in the forms of greater helping among strangers, cooperation among teammates, self-sacrifice among four-year-olds, friendship among schoolchildren, love among college students, and loyalty between consumers and brands.

Chapter 13. Ethical Use: A Pre-Pre-Suasive Consideration

Those using a pre-suasive approach must decide what to present immediately before their message. But they also have to make an even earlier decision: whether, on ethical grounds, to employ such an approach. Often, communicators from commercial organizations place profit above ethics in their appeals. Thus, there is reason to worry that the pre-suasive practices described in this book will be used unethically. However, chapter 13 argues against unethical use, offering data from studies indicating that such tactics undermine organizational profits in three potent ways.

Chapter 14: Post-Suasion: Aftereffects

Pre-suaders want to do more than create temporary changes via momentary shifts in attention; they want to make those changes durable. Accordingly, chapter 14 provides the behavioral science evidence for two kinds of procedures that increase the likelihood that changes generated initially will take root and last well beyond pre-suasive moments.

2

Privileged Moments

Not many people know this about me, but I'm a palm reader. At least, I used to be. As a young man, I learned palmistry to use as an icebreaker at parties. I eventually abandoned the practice, though, because as soon as I'd do a reading, a line of expectant candidates would form, denying me access to meaningful conversation and the buffet table.

Yet, during those few years, I recognized something remarkable about the palm-based information I provided: it was almost always true. My partners in the process—strangers, for the most part—were amazed by the accuracy of my depictions of their traits. "That's right!" they'd say. "How could you possibly see that?" I learned to feign an all-knowing smile to evade the question because, frankly, I was amazed too.

Not anymore. There are two general explanations for why I was correct so often. The first relies on paranormal mechanisms that can be mastered fully by only a select few; the second involves decidedly normal processes that can be commissioned by anyone. On the one hand—no pun intended, honest—it's conceivable that there is a real connection between the features of a human hand and its owner's character, history, and future. This type of explanation is often offered by purveyors of various paranormal systems. Besides the physical aspects of one's palm, the systems can be based on anything from star alignments, to body auras, to head bumps.

Of course, these differences are crucial to those who proclaim the superiority of, let's say, bumps to auras for locating the truth. However, the content-based differences don't matter. In each case, we are assured that an expert practitioner, using special information from the system, can read our personality, past, and prospects. I doubt that my palm reading feats can be interpreted in paranormal terms. Whenever submitted to close scrutiny, these systems flop.[7]

Psychic cattiness. As I learned from my palm reading days, sometimes paranormal methods can prove remarkably accurate. © 2013 Bizarro Comics. Distributed by King Features Syndicate, Inc.

Back in my palm-deciphering period, I got unmistakable indications that something was amiss with paranormal methods for characterizing people. Curious about my palmistry successes, I put elements of the system to the test, sometimes reading someone's heart line as if it were the head line—that sort of thing. None of my alterations of tightly specified practices made any difference to my level of success. For instance, whether I followed or violated the proper procedure for uncovering "the presence of a secret area of self-doubt" within my subjects, they typically responded with the same guilty nod.

On one particular evening, I was feeling out of place at a house party where I knew almost no one. Because interacting socially with strangers is one of *my* secret areas of self-doubt, I began doing palmistry as a way to fit in. I even read the home owner's palm twice, once at the beginning of the night and once when he returned a couple of hours and several drinks later, wanting to know more. In the middle of the first reading, I'd bent back his thumb and said, "You know, I can tell that you are quite a stubborn man." During the second reading, when bending back his thumb, I said, "You know, I can tell that you are quite a flexible man." After each of the opposing depictions, he thought for a second and admitted that I was absolutely right about who he really was.

What was going on? How could my readings be viewed as accurate no matter what (within reason) I claimed to see? Critics of the paranormal offer a standard explanation: palmists or astrologers or phrenologists (head bump readers) describe characteristics so widespread—stubbornness and flexibility, for example—that almost everyone can identify with them. This point is surely true, but it doesn't resolve the whole mystery. If it's so easy for people to spot their own tendencies for both stubbornness *and* flexibility, shouldn't these opposites cancel themselves out upon quick reflection? When I labeled the home owner at that party a stubborn man, why didn't he counter me then and there with the natural self-awareness of his flexibility? Why did he see the truth solely in the trait I suggested, when I suggested it?

NOT HOCUS, NOT POCUS, BUT FOCUS

The answer has to do with a common operating tendency that can alter a person's decisions dramatically. Suppose at a party I bent back your thumb slightly and, on the basis of its resistance and curvature, proclaimed you "quite a stubborn individual, someone who resists being pressured in a direction you don't want to go." I will have focused you on the trait of stubbornness, sending you down a single *psychological chute* constructed unfairly to confirm my judgment.

Here's how it would work: to test if I were right, you'd automatically begin searching your memory for times when you'd acted stubbornly—*only* for those times—and you'd almost certainly come upon a ready instance, as mulishness under pressure is a frequent personal failing. If you extended this biased search further, you'd hit on other, similar occurrences. With a blink of self-recognition, you'd likely look up at me and admit that I was on target.

Now imagine instead that I'd labeled you "quite a flexible individual, someone who, after getting new information, is willing to take it into account and adjust your position." I'd have focused you oppositely this time, sending you down a different chute: one rigged to ensure that you'd find occasions in your past when you embraced change. As a result, you'd be likely to look up from that equally biased memory search and declare me absolutely right about your fundamental flexibility.

There's a very human reason for why you'd be prone to fall for my trick. Its obtuse scientific name is "positive test strategy." But it comes down to this: in deciding whether a possibility is correct, people typically look for hits rather than misses; for confirmations of the idea rather than for disconfirmations. It is easier to register the presence of something than its absence. The great mystery novelist Sir Arthur Conan Doyle understood this tendency in crafting the anything but ordinary thinking style of Sherlock Holmes. The brilliant Holmes was as unrelenting in his attention to what didn't occur as to what did. Recall that in one of Doyle's most popular mystery stories, "Silver Blaze," Holmes realizes that a theft under investigation is an inside job (and could not have been committed by the stranger police had under arrest) because during the crime a guard dog *didn't* bark. His less intellectually disciplined counterparts, content to rely mainly on the presence rather than the absence of confirming evidence, never match his powers of deduction.

Regrettably, you, I, and most everyone else fall into the sub-Holmesian category in this regard. In a song by Jimmy Buffett, a former lover has to be informed—five separate times!—that the lack of something can convey the telling presence of something: "If the phone doesn't ring, it's me."[8]

TARGET CHUTING

If I inquired whether you were unhappy in, let's say, the social arena, your natural tendency to hunt for confirmations rather than for disconfirmations of the possibility would lead you to find more proof of discontent than if I asked whether you were *happy* there. This was the outcome when members of a sample of Canadians were asked either if they were unhappy or happy with their social lives. Those asked if they were unhappy were far more likely to encounter dissatisfactions as they thought about it and, consequently, were 375 percent more likely to declare themselves unhappy.

There are multiple lessons to draw from this finding. First, if a pollster wants to know only whether you are dissatisfied with something—it could be a consumer product or an elected representative or a government policy—watch out. Be suspicious as well of the one who asks only if you are satisfied. Single-chute questions of this sort can get you both to mistake and misstate your position. I'd recommend declining to participate in surveys that employ this biased form of questioning. Much better are those that use two-sided questions: "How satisfied *or* dissatisfied are you with this brand?" "Are you happy *or* unhappy with the mayor's performance in office?" "To what extent do you agree *or* disagree with this country's current approach to the Middle East?" These kinds of inquiries invite you to consult your feelings evenhandedly.[9]

Decidedly more worrisome than the pollster whose leading questions usher you into a less than accurate personal stance, though, is the questioner who uses this same device to exploit you in that moment—that privileged moment. Cult recruiters often begin the process of seducing new prospects by asking if they are unhappy (rather than happy). I used to think this phrasing was designed only to select individuals whose deep personal discontent would incline them toward the kind of radical change that cults demand. But now I'm convinced that the "Are you *un*happy?"

question is more than a screening device. It's also a recruiting device that stacks the deck by focusing people, unduly, on their dissatisfactions. (The truth is that cults don't want malcontents within their ranks; they are looking for basically well-adjusted individuals whose positive, can-do style can be routed to cult pursuits.) As the results of the Canadian study show, after being prompted by the question's wording to review their dissatisfactions, people become more likely to describe themselves as unhappy. In the unfairly engineered instant after such an admission, the cult's moment maker is trained to strike: "Well, if you're unhappy, you'd want to change that, right?"[10]

Sure, cult recruitment tactics can offer provocative anecdotes. But cult members, including recruiters, are known for their willingness to engage in self-delusion; maybe they're kidding themselves about the effectiveness of this particular practice. What's the hard proof that such a made moment leads to anything more than a temporarily and inconsequentially altered self-view? Could a pre-suader employ that moment to change another's willingness to do or concede or provide anything of real value?

Merchandisers value consumer information enormously. Proponents of marketing research say it serves the admirable purpose of giving the sellers the data they need to satisfy likely buyers; and, they are not alone in their high regard for the benefits of such data. Profitable commercial organizations recognize the advantages of having good information about the wants and needs of their customers or prospective customers. Indeed, the best of them consistently spend princely sums to uncover the particulars.

The prevailing problem for these organizations is that the rest of us can't be bothered to participate in their surveys, focus groups, and taste tests. Even with sizable inducements in the form of cash payments, free products, or gift certificates, the percentage of people agreeing to cooperate can be low, which gives market researchers heartburn because they can't be sure the data they've collected reflect the feelings of the majority of their target group. Could these researchers eliminate their problem by requesting consumer information in the moment following a pre-suasive single-chute question?

Consider the results of an experiment performed by communication scientists San Bolkan and Peter Andersen, who approached people and made a request for assistance with a survey. We have all experienced something similar when a clipboard-carrying researcher stops us in a shopping mall or supermarket and asks for a few minutes of our time. As is the case for the typical shopping mall requester, these scientists' success was dismal: only 29 percent of those asked to participate consented. But Bolkan and Andersen thought they could boost compliance without resorting to any of the costly payments that marketers often feel forced to employ. They stopped a second sample of individuals and began the interaction with a pre-suasive opener: "Do you consider yourself a helpful person?" Following brief reflection, nearly everyone answered yes. In that privileged moment—after subjects had confirmed privately and affirmed publicly their helpful natures—the researchers pounced, requesting help with their survey. Now 77.3 percent volunteered.

— — —

In chapter 10, we'll explore the particular psychological mechanism (a desire for consistency) that led people to become more than twice as likely to comply under these circumstances. But for now, let's derive a broader insight, one that is a major thesis of this book: frequently the factor most likely to determine a person's choice in a situation is not the one that counsels most wisely there; it is one that has been elevated in attention (and, thereby, in privilege) at the time of the decision.

This recognition allows us to think entirely differently than before about the influence process. For much of the thirty-plus years that I have been studying the ways that people can be persuaded to choose and change, my thinking has been governed by the dominant scientific model of social influence. It advises as follows: if you wish to change another's behavior, you must first change some existing feature of that person so that it fits with the behavior. If you want to convince people to purchase something unfamiliar—let's say a new soft drink—you should act to transform their beliefs or attitudes or experiences in ways that make them want to buy the product. You might attempt to change their beliefs about the soft drink by reporting that it's the fastest-growing new beverage on the market; or to change their attitudes by connecting it to a well-liked celebrity; or to change their experiences with it by offering free samples in the supermarket. Although an abundance of evidence shows that this approach works, it is now clear that there is an alternate model of social influence that provides a different route to persuasive success.

ARE YOU ADVENTUROUS ENOUGH TO CONSIDER A REVOLUTIONARY MODEL OF INFLUENCE?

According to this nontraditional—channeled attention—approach, to get desired action it's not necessary to alter a person's beliefs or attitudes or experiences. It's not necessary to alter anything at all except what's prominent in that person's mind at the moment of decision. In our example of the new soft drink, it might be the fact that, in the past, he or she has been willing to look at new possibilities. Evidence for precisely this process can be found in an extension of the Bolkan and Andersen research demonstrating that a marketer could greatly increase the chance of finding survey participants by beginning with a particular pre-suasive opener: asking people if they considered themselves *helpful*.

In a companion study, the two scientists found that it was similarly possible to increase willingness to try an unfamiliar consumer product by beginning with a comparable but differently customized pre-suasive opener—this time asking people if they considered themselves *adventurous*. The consumer product was a new soft drink, and individuals had to agree to supply an email address so they could be sent instructions on how to get a free sample. Half were stopped and asked if they wanted to provide their addresses for this purpose. Most were reluctant—only 33 percent volunteered their contact information. The other subjects were asked initially, "Do you consider yourself to be somebody who is adventurous and likes to try new things?" Almost all said yes—following which, 75.7 percent gave their email addresses.[11]

Two features of these findings strike me as remarkable. First, of the subjects who were asked if they counted themselves adventurous, 97 percent (seventy out of seventy-two) responded affirmatively. The idea that nearly everybody qualifies as an adventurous type is ludicrous. Yet when asked the single-chute question of whether they fit this category, people nominate themselves almost invariably. Such is the power of positive test strategy and the blinkered perspective it creates. The evidence shows that this process can significantly increase the percentage of individuals who brand themselves as adventurous or helpful or even unhappy. Moreover, the narrowed perspective, though temporary, is anything but inconsequential. For a persuasively privileged moment, it renders these individuals highly vulnerable to aligned requests—as the data of research scientists and the practices of cult recruiters attest.

The other noteworthy feature of the soft-drink experiment is not that a simple question could shunt so many people into a particular choice but that it could shunt so many of them into a potentially *dangerous* choice. In recent years, if there is anything we have been repeatedly warned to safeguard against by all manner of experts, it's opening ourselves to some unscrupulous individual who might bombard our computers with spam, infect them with destructive viruses, or hack into them to sting us with the protracted misery of identity theft. (Of course, to be fair, it must be acknowledged that experienced and discerning users are unlikely to be fooled by the offers they receive electronically. I, for instance, have been flattered to learn through repeated internet messages that many Ukrainian virgin prostitutes want to meet me; if that can't be arranged, they can get me an outstanding deal on reconditioned printer cartridges. Notwithstanding this particular exception, we'd be well advised to regard the authenticity of such solicitations skeptically.)[12]

Indeed, given the mass of negative publicity regarding computer fraud, it makes great sense that two-thirds of Bolkan and Andersen's first group of subjects turned down the request for their email addresses. After all, this was a complete stranger who advanced on them unintroduced and unbidden. The circumstances clearly called for prudence.

What's significant is that these circumstances applied equally to all those individuals (75.6 percent in Bolkan and Andersen's second group) who, after being channeled to their adventurous sides by an initial single-chute question, ignored the cues for caution and piled rashly into a potentially foolish choice. Their behavior, bewildering as it is on the surface, confirms this book's contention that the guiding factor in a decision is often not the one that counsels most wisely; it's one that has recently been brought to mind. But why? The answer has to do with the ruthlessness of channeled attention, which not only promotes the now-focal aspect of the situation but also suppresses all competing aspects of it—even critically important ones.[13]

THE DUES (AND DON'TS) OF FOCUSED ATTENTION

In the English language, we are said to "pay" attention, which plainly implies that the process extracts a cost. Research on cognitive functioning shows us the form of the fee: when attention is paid to something, the price is attention lost to something else. Indeed, because the human mind appears able to hold only one thing in conscious awareness at a time, the toll is a momentary loss of focused attention to *everything* else. Have you ever noticed how difficult it is to experience—genuinely experience—two things at once? I know, for example, that if I start looking intently for a highway exit while listening to a CD in my car, I'll stop hearing the music; and, if I am listening intently to the music, I'll often miss my exit.[14]

In this regard, my car's CD player is structured to work like my brain, allowing me but a single track of music at a time. That's for good reason, as it would be folly to play more than one simultaneously. I'd just hear noise. So it is with human cognition. Even though there are always multiple "tracks" of information available, we consciously select only the one we want to register at that moment. Any other arrangement would leave us overloaded and unable to react to distinct aspects of the mongrelized input.

The best we can do to handle multiple channels of information is to switch back and forth among them, opening and closing the door of mindfulness to each in turn. This skill allows for multitasking, the ability to focus on several activities in the same time frame—perhaps talking on the phone while reading an email message. Although it might seem that we are concentrating on more than one thing simultaneously, that's an illusion. We are just rapidly alternating our focus.

However, just as there is a price for paying attention, there is a charge for switching it: For about a half second during a shift of focus, we experience a mental dead spot, called an *attentional blink*, when we can't register the newly highlighted information consciously. It's for this reason that I am so annoyed when I'm interacting with an individual who is trying to do something else at the same time. Have you ever had a phone conversation with someone you can tell is engaged in another task, maybe because you can hear newspaper pages turning or computer keys clicking? I hate that. It shows me that my conversation partner is willing to lose contact with the information I'm providing to make contact with some other information. It always feels like a form of demotion. It advises me that my input is considered relatively unimportant.[15]

"Are you multitasking me?"

Dismissed. A dissed miss is a pissed miss. *William Haefeli.*
The New Yorker Collection/The Cartoon Bank

But, I'm not the only one it advises. It notifies my conversation partner of the same thing, because people rightly believe that what they choose to attend to (or away from) reflects what they value at the time. Here's the point for the influence process: whatever we can do to focus people on something—an idea, a person, an object—makes that thing seem more important to them than before.

Consider, for instance, a device used by the renowned psychotherapist Milton Erickson when dealing with patients who, over the course of treatment, had been unwilling to consider a point that Erickson felt was crucial to their progress—perhaps that failure to choose is a form of personal choice. Rather than inviting more resistance by amplifying his voice the next time he made this point, he recognized the wisdom of doing the opposite. True to his reputation as a master moment maker, Dr. Erickson would wait for a heavy truck to begin climbing the hill outside his office window. Then, while timing his reintroduction of the crucial insight to coincide with the worst of the noise, he would *lower* his voice. To hear what Erickson was saying, patients had to lean forward, into the information—an embodied signal of focused attention and intense interest. When asked about the tactic, Erickson, who was famous for orchestrating the nonverbal elements of effective therapy, attributed its success to the leaning-in posture that patients assumed when trying to hear the information he wanted them to see as important.

Instructive though it might be, we don't have to rely on this particular anecdote for evidence that people assign more significance to the things they see themselves choosing to move toward, as plenty of research shows that reducing the distance to an object makes it seem more worthwhile. Nor do we have to look far to see how this automatic tendency can affect the influence process. In one study, potential shoppers who just *envisioned* themselves moving toward (rather than away from) a container of snack food came to like it better and were willing to pay over four times more to obtain it.[16]

Besides arranging for others to orient themselves toward messages and products, there are numerous other ways for communicators to get an audience to assign special attention and, consequently, special import to an idea or item. As we'll see next, the implications for the act of presuasion are sizable.

3

The Importance of Attention . . .
Is Importance

For an unrelated reason, I was fortunate to be in London to witness a set of extraordinary festivities commemorating the fiftieth anniversary of Elizabeth II's accession to the throne of England. Although the queen had been traveling the globe for months to Commonwealth nations hosting Golden Jubilee events in her name, the celebrations peaked on June 4, 2002, with a program on the Mall in London that drew over a million well-wishers from around Britain and the world. The marked adulation surprised many in the national press who'd predicted the Jubilee would be a fizzle, demonstrating the modern-day irrelevance of the British monarchy in general and of Her Royal Highness in particular.

The opposite proved to be the case. In the several weeks' run-up to June 4, throngs within the United Kingdom flocked to dedications, parades, concerts, and special proceedings honoring the queen, which she honored in turn with her presence. Especially coveted were invitations to small parties where it was sometimes possible to be addressed personally by the queen in a receiving line.

Of course, the opportunity to meet Elizabeth II under any circumstances would be considered exceptional; but the chance to meet her amid the pomp and pageantry of the Golden Jubilee added even more significance to such occasions, which were widely reported by the media. One report stood out from all the others for me. A young woman moving through a reception line at one of the small fêtes experienced the horror of hearing the cell phone in her purse begin to ring just as she met the queen. Flustered and frozen with embarrassment as her phone pealed insistently, she stared helplessly into the royal eyes that had become fixed on her bag. Finally, Elizabeth leaned forward and advised, "You should answer that, dear. It might be someone important."

WHAT'S SALIENT IS IMPORTANT

While the graciousness of Elizabeth's advice offers an insight into her beloved standing among her subjects, the content of that advice offers another type of insight: anything that draws focused attention to itself can lead observers to overestimate its importance. Who, on the other end of the line, could conceivably have been more important at that singular moment than Her Majesty, the Queen of the Realm, on the occasion of the fiftieth anniversary of her reign? I can't think of anyone. Yet the unknown caller was proclaimed worthy of it—by the queen, no less.

Now, a critic might argue that Elizabeth didn't overestimate the potential import of the caller one whit; that her response was born of a characteristic personal tendency toward kindness and not at all of a characteristic human tendency toward misassessment in that sort of situation. The critic would be wrong, I believe, because although royals are often said to be of a different breed than the rest of us, they are not of a different species. Numerous researchers have documented the basic human inclination to assign undue weight to whatever happens to be salient at the time.

One of those researchers is Daniel Kahneman, who, for personal and professional reasons, is an excellent informant on the character and causes of human behavior. On the personal side, he's been able to observe from within a multitude of cultures and roles—having grown up in France, earned degrees in Jerusalem, Israel, and Berkeley, California, served as a soldier and personnel assessor in Israel, and taught in Canada and the United States. More impressive, though, are Kahneman's credentials as a renowned authority on matters of human psychology. His teaching positions have always been prestigious, culminating with an appointment at Princeton University that included simultaneous professorships in psychology and public affairs. His numerous awards have also been prestigious, but none as noteworthy as the 2002 Nobel Prize in Economic Sciences, the only Nobel in history given to an individual trained as a psychologist.

It's no wonder, then, that when Daniel Kahneman speaks on issues of human psychology, he gets hushed attention. I am reminded of a famous television commercial of many years ago for the financial services firm E. F. Hutton that depicts a pair of businessmen in a busy restaurant trying to talk over the din of clanking silverware, loud waiters, and neighboring table conversations. One of the men says to his colleague, "Well, my broker is E. F. Hutton, and E. F. Hutton says . . . " The place goes silent—waiters stop taking orders, busboys stop clearing tables, diners stop speaking—while everyone in the room turns to take in the advice, and an announcer's voice intones: "When E. F. Hutton talks, people listen."[17]

I've been to several scientific conferences at which Professor Kahneman has spoken; and, when Daniel Kahneman talks, people listen. I am invariably among them. So I took special notice of his answer to a fascinating challenge put to him not long ago by an online discussion site. He was asked to specify the one scientific concept that, if appreciated properly, would most improve everyone's understanding of the world. Although in response he provided a full five-hundred-word essay describing what he called "the focusing illusion," his answer is neatly summarized in the essay's title: "Nothing in life is as important as you think it is *while* you are thinking about it."[18]

– —— –

The implications of Kahneman's assertion apply to much more than the momentary status of the caller to a ringing phone. They apply tellingly well to the practice of pre-suasion, because a communicator who gets an audience to focus on a key element of a message *pre-loads* it with importance. This form of pre-suasion accounts for what many see as the principle role (labeled *agenda setting*) that the news media play in influencing public opinion. The central tenet of *agenda-setting theory* is that the media rarely produce change directly, by presenting compelling evidence that sweeps an audience to new positions; they are much more likely to persuade indirectly, by giving selected issues and facts better coverage than other issues and facts. It's this coverage that leads audience members—by virtue of the greater attention they devote to certain topics—to decide that these are the most important to be taken into consideration when adopting a position. As the political scientist Bernard Cohen wrote, "The press may not be successful most of the time in telling people what to think, but it is stunningly successful in telling them what to think about." According to this view, in an election, whichever political party is seen by voters to have the superior stance on the issue highest on the *media's* agenda at the moment will likely win.

That outcome shouldn't seem troubling provided the media have highlighted the issue (or set of issues) most critical to the society at the time of the vote. Regrettably, other factors often contribute to coverage choices, such as whether a matter is simple or complicated, gripping or boring, familiar or unfamiliar to newsroom staffers, inexpensive or expensive to examine, and even friendly or not to the news director's political leanings.

In the summer of 2000, a pipe bomb exploded at the main train station in Düsseldorf, Germany, injuring several Eastern European immigrants. Although no proof was ever found, officials suspected from the start that a fringe right-wing group with an anti-immigrant agenda was responsible. A sensational aspect of the story—one of the victims not only lost a leg in the blast but also the baby in her womb—stimulated a rash of news stories in the following month regarding right-wing extremism in Germany. Polls taken at the same time showed that the percentage of Germans who rated right-wing extremism as *the* most important issue facing their country spiked from near zero to 35 percent—a percentage that sank back to near zero again as related news reports disappeared in subsequent months.

A similar effect appeared more recently in the United States. As the tenth anniversary of the terrorist attacks of September 11, 2001, approached, 9/11-related media stories peaked in the days immediately surrounding the anniversary date and then dropped off rapidly in the weeks thereafter. Surveys conducted during those times asked citizens to nominate two "especially important" events from the past seventy years. Two weeks prior to the anniversary, before the media blitz began in earnest, about 30 percent of respondents named 9/11. But as the anniversary drew closer, and the media treatment intensified, survey respondents started identifying 9/11 in increasing numbers—to a high of 65 percent. Two weeks later, though, after reportage had died down to earlier levels, once again only about 30 percent of the participants placed it among their two especially important events of the past seventy years. Clearly, the amount of news coverage can make a big difference in the *perceived* significance of an issue among observers as they are exposed to the coverage.[19]

— — —

Why do we typically assume that whatever we are focusing on in the moment is especially important? One reason is that whatever we are focusing on typically *is* especially important in the moment. It's only reasonable to give heightened attention to those factors that have the most significance and utility for us in a particular situation: a strange noise in the dark, the smell of smoke in a theater, a CEO standing to speak. Nonhuman species have worked this out, too, and have evolved similar priorities. Rhesus monkeys, for example, will pay in the form of sacrificed food rewards just for the opportunity to view important (high-status) members of their colony; but they will require a reward to divert their attention to unimportant members. In all kinds of species and for all kinds of reasons, it makes great sense to direct attention to those options that scale largest in rank.

This sensible system of focusing our limited attentional resources on what does indeed possess special import has an imperfection, though: we can be brought to the mistaken belief that something is important merely because we have been led by some irrelevant factor to give it our narrowed attention. All too often, people believe that if they have paid attention to an idea or event or group, it must be important enough to warrant the consideration. That's not true, as the German and US agenda-setting examples revealed. In those instances, news coverage driven by a sensationalistic or timely story element grabbed audience attention and changed where it was concentrated. In turn, that changed focus influenced viewers' importance judgments of national issues.

After recognizing the extent of our vulnerability to the focusing illusion, I've come at last to appreciate a standard saying of Hollywood press agents: "There's no such thing as bad publicity." I'd always thought the statement nonsense, as there are memorable instances of bad publicity deflating the reputation and earnings of one or another high-profile figure. Golfer Tiger Woods's losing an estimated $22 million per year in endorsement revenues shortly after his sex scandal became public in 2009 is one example. But now I see how the idea, while false in one respect, can be true in another. It's often said that the fate celebrities fear most is to be ignored, forgotten, or otherwise dropped from the cultural consciousness. Powerful publicity of any sort spares them that worst of all fates because it brings them attention; and raw attention anoints them with presumed importance. Especially in the arts, where one's worth is almost entirely subjective, an elevated public presence contributes to that worth. Accordingly, people will pay to see high-profile celebrities (within their performances, productions, and appearances) because they, as individuals, seem to matter. Monkey colonies aren't the only environments where residents will pay to watch seemingly important figures.[20]

Thus, the persuader who artfully draws outsize attention to the most favorable feature of an offer becomes a successful pre-suader. That is, he or she becomes effective not just in a straightforward attention-based way—by arranging for audiences to consider that feature fully—but also by arranging for them to lend the feature exaggerated significance even before they have examined it. When audience members do then consider it fully, they experience a double-barreled effect. They are likely to be convinced that the attribute is especially desirable by the one-sidedness of the evidence they've been directed toward and to view that attribute as especially important besides.

Stars in their "I"s and our eyes. Focused attention leads celebrities and audiences to overestimate the celebrities' importance. *Calvin and Hobbes © Watterson. Reprinted with permission of Universal Uclick. All rights reserved.*

BACK ROADS TO ATTENTION

It is rousing and worrisome (depending on whether you are playing offense or defense) to recognize that these persuasive outcomes can flow from attention-shifting techniques so slight as to go unrecognized as agents of change. Let's consider three ways communicators have used such subtle tactics to great effect.

Managing the Background

Suppose you've started an online furniture store that specializes in various types of sofas. Some are attractive to customers because of their comfort and others because of their price. Is there anything you can think to do that would incline visitors to your website to focus on the feature of comfort and, consequently, to prefer to make a sofa purchase that prioritized it over cost?

You've no need to labor long for an answer, because two marketing professors, Naomi Mandel and Eric Johnson, have provided one in a set of studies using just such an online furniture site. When I interviewed Mandel regarding why she decided on this particular set of issues to explore, she said her choice had to do with two big, unresolved matters within the field of marketing—one relatively recent and one long-standing. The new topic at the time was e-commerce. When she began the research project in the late 1990s, the impact of virtual stores such as

Amazon and eBay was only beginning to be seen. But how to optimize success within this form of exchange had not been addressed systematically. So she and Johnson opted for a virtual store site as the context for their study.

The other matter that had piqued Mandel's interest is one that has vexed merchandisers forever: how to avoid losing business to a poorer-quality rival whose only competitive advantage is lower cost. That is why Mandel chose to pit higher-quality furniture lines against less expensive, inferior ones in her study. "It's a traditional problem that the business-savvy students in our marketing courses raise all the time," she said. "We always instruct them not to get caught up in a price war against an inferior product, because they'll lose. We tell them to make quality the battleground instead, because that's a fight they'll most likely win.

"Fortunately for me," she continued, "the best of the students in those classes have never been satisfied with that general advice. They'd say, 'Yeah, but how?' and I never really had a good answer for them, which gave me a great question to pursue for my research project."

Fortunately for *us*, after analyzing their results, Mandel and Johnson were in a position to deliver a stunningly simple answer to the "Yeah, but how?" question. In an article largely overlooked since it was published in 2002, they described how they were able to draw website visitors' attention to the goal of comfort merely by placing *fluffy clouds* on the background wallpaper of the site's landing page. That maneuver led those visitors to assign elevated levels of importance to comfort when asked what they were looking for in a sofa. Those same visitors also became more likely to search the site for information about the comfort features of the sofas in stock and, most notably, to choose a more comfortable (and more costly) sofa as their preferred purchase.

To make sure their results were due to the landing page wallpaper and not to some general human preference for comfort, Mandel and Johnson reversed their procedure for other visitors, who saw wallpaper that pulled their attention to the goal of economy by depicting pennies instead of clouds. These visitors assigned greater levels of importance to price, searched the site primarily for cost information, and preferred an inexpensive sofa. Remarkably, despite having their importance ratings, search behavior, and buying preferences all altered pre-suasively by the landing page wallpaper, when questioned afterward, most participants refused to believe that the depicted clouds or pennies had affected them in any way.

Soft sell. Visitors to an online furniture website who saw this landing page wallpaper decorated with clouds became more inclined toward soft, comfortable furniture. Those who saw wallpaper decorated with pennies became more inclined toward inexpensive furniture. *Courtesy of Naomi Mandel and Oxford University Press*

Additional research has found similarly sly effects for online banner ads—the sort we all assume we can ignore without impact while we read. Well-executed research has shown us mistaken in this regard. While reading an online article about education, repeated exposure to a banner ad for a new brand of camera made the readers significantly more favorable to the ad when they were shown it again later. Tellingly, this effect emerged even though they couldn't recall having ever seen the ad, which had been presented to them in five-second flashes near the story material.

Further, the more often the ad had appeared while they were reading the article, the more they came to like it. This last finding deserves elaboration because it runs counter to abundant evidence that most ads experience a wear-out effect after they have been encountered repeatedly, with observers tiring of them or losing trust in advertisers who seem to think that their message is so weak that they need to send it over and over. Why didn't these banner ads, which were presented as many as twenty times within just five pages of text, suffer any wear-out? The readers never processed the ads consciously, so there was no recognized information to be identified as tedious or untrustworthy.

These results pose a fascinating possibility for online advertisers: Recognition/recall, a widely used index of success for all other forms of ads, might greatly underestimate the effectiveness of banner ads. In the new studies, frequently interjected banners were positively rated and were uncommonly resistant to standard wear-out effects, yet they were neither recognized nor recalled. Indeed, it looks to be this third result (lack of direct notice) that makes banner ads so effective in the first two strong and stubborn ways. After many decades of using recognition/recall as a prime indicator of an ad's value, who in the advertising community would have thought that the *absence* of memory for a commercial message could be a plus?

Within the outcomes of the wallpaper and the banner ad studies is a larger lesson regarding the communication process: seemingly dismissible information presented in the background captures a valuable kind of attention that allows for potent, almost entirely uncounted instances of influence.

The influence isn't always desirable, however. In this regard, there's a body of data on consequential background factors that parents, especially, should take into account. Environmental noise such as that coming from heavy traffic or airplane flight paths is something we think we get used to and even block out after awhile. But the evidence is clear that the disruptive noise still gets in, reducing the ability to learn and perform cognitive tasks.

One study found that the reading scores of students in a New York City elementary school were significantly lower if their classrooms were situated close to elevated subway tracks on which trains rattled past every four to five minutes. When the researchers, armed with their findings, pressed NYC transit system officials and Board of Education members to install noise-dampening materials on the tracks and in the classrooms, students' scores jumped back up. Similar results have been found for children near airplane flight paths. When the city of Munich, Germany, moved its airport, the memory and reading scores of children near the new location plummeted, while those near the old location rose significantly.

Thus, parents whose children's schools or homes are subjected to intermittent automotive, train, or aircraft noise should insist on the implementation of sound-baffling remedies. Employers, for the sake of their workers—and their own bottom lines—should do the same. Teachers need to consider the potentially negative effects of another kind of distracting background stimuli (this one of their own making) on young students' learning and performance. Classrooms with heavily decorated walls displaying lots of posters, maps, and artwork reduce the test scores of young children learning science material there. It is clear that background information can both guide and distract focus of attention; anyone seeking to influence optimally must manage that information thoughtfully.[21]

Inviting Favorable Evaluation

Although communicators can use attention-drawing techniques to amplify the judged importance of a feature or issue, that's not always wise. Relevant here is Bernard Cohen's observation about press coverage—that it doesn't so much tell people what to think as what to think *about*. Any practice that pulls attention to an idea will be successful only when the idea has merit. If the arguments and evidence supporting it are seen as meritless by an audience, directed attention to the bad idea won't make it any more persuasive. If anything, the tactic might well backfire. After all, if audience members have come to see an idea as more important to them than before, they should then be even more likely to oppose it when it is a plainly poor one. Indeed, a lot of research has demonstrated that the more consideration people give to something, the more extreme (polarized) their opinions of it become. So attention-capturing tactics provide no panacea to would-be persuaders.[22]

Still, if you have a good case to make, there are certain places where those tactics will give your persuasive appeals special traction. One such place is in a field of strong competitors. In modern business, it is becoming increasingly difficult to outpace one's rivals. Easily copied advances in development technologies, production techniques, and business methods make it hard for a company to distinguish the essence of what it offers—bottled water, gasoline, insurance, air travel, banking services, industrial machinery—from what other contestants for the same market can deliver. To deal with the problem, alternative ways of creating separation have to be tried. Retailers can establish multiple, convenient locations; wholesalers can put big sales staffs into the field; manufacturers can grant broad guarantees; service providers can assemble extensive customer care units; and they all can engage in large-scale advertising and promotional efforts to create and maintain brand prominence. But there's a downside to such fixes. Because these means of differentiation are so costly, their expense might be too burdensome for many organizations to bear.

Could resolving the dilemma lie in finding an inexpensive way to shift attention to a particular product, service, or idea? Well, yes, as long as the spotlighted item is a good one—a high scorer in customer reviews, perhaps. Critical here would be to arrange for observers to focus their attention on *that* good thing rather than on rivals' equally good options. Then its favorable features should gain both verification and importance from the scrutiny.

Already some data show that these twin benefits can produce a substantial advantage for a brand when consumers focus on it in isolation from its competitors. Although the data have come from different settings (shopping malls, college campuses, and websites) and different types of products (cameras, big-screen TVs, VCRs, and laundry detergents), the results all point to the same conclusion: if you agreed to participate in a consumer survey regarding some product, perhaps 35-millimeter cameras, the survey taker could enhance your ratings of any strong brand—let's say Canon—simply by asking you to consider the qualities of Canon cameras but not asking you to consider the qualities of any of its major rivals, such as Nikon, Olympus, Pentax, or Minolta.

More than that, without realizing why, your intention to purchase a Canon 35mm camera would likely also jump, as would your desire to make the purchase straightaway, with no need to search for information about comparable brands. However, all of these advantages for Canon would drop away if you'd been asked to consider the qualities of its cameras but, *before rating those qualities*, to think about the options that Nikon, Olympus, Pentax, and Minolta could provide.

Thus, to receive the benefits of focused attention, the key is to keep the focus unitary. Some impressive research demonstrates that merely engaging in a single-chute evaluation of one of several established hotel and restaurant chains, consumer products, and even charity organizations can automatically cause people to value the focused-upon entity more and become more willing to support it financially.

One applicable tactic being employed with increasing frequency by various organizations is to request evaluation of their products and services—*only* their products and services. As a consumer, I am routinely asked by providers to consider and rate business performances of one sort or another. Occasionally I am petitioned through a phone call or direct mail, but typically it is via email. Sometimes I am to evaluate a single experience such as a recent hotel stay, online purchase, or customer service interaction. Periodically, the "How are we doing?" question asks me to assess features of an ongoing partnership with my travel agency, financial services firm, or phone provider. The requests seem innocent enough and acceptable because they appear intended (as I am sure they are) to gather information that will improve the quality of my commercial exchanges. But I'd be surprised if my compliance didn't also give the petitioners, especially the highly ranked ones, a hidden bonus: my focused attention to their mostly favorable facets with no comparable attention to the mostly favorable facets of their ablest rivals.

Other research has extended these findings to the way that leaders and managers make strategic choices inside their organizations.

Individuals assigned the responsibility for reversing a sales slump within a paint manufacturing company took part in a study. Each was asked to evaluate the wisdom of *only* one of four worthy possible solutions: (1) increasing the advertising budget, which would raise brand awareness among do-it-yourself painters; (2) lowering prices, which would attract more price-sensitive buyers; (3) hiring additional sales representatives, who could press for more shelf space in retail stores; or (4) investing in product development, to boost quality so that the brand could be promoted to professional painters as the best in the market. It didn't matter which of the four ideas the decision makers evaluated: the process of targeting and evaluating one, by itself, pushed them to recommend *it* among the options as the best remedy for the company to adopt.

But surely the typical highly placed decision maker wouldn't settle on an important course of action without evaluating all viable alternatives fully, and he or she certainly wouldn't make that choice after evaluating just one strong option, right? Wrong and wrong, for a pair of reasons. First, a thorough analysis of all legitimate roads to success is time consuming, requiring potentially lengthy delays for identifying, vetting, and then mapping out each of the promising routes; and highly placed decision makers didn't get to their lofty positions by being known as bottlenecks inside their organizations.

Second, for any decision maker, a painstaking comparative assessment of multiple options is difficult and stressful, akin to the juggler's task of trying to keep several objects in the air all at once. The resultant (and understandable) tendency is to avoid or abbreviate such an arduous process by selecting the first practicable candidate that presents itself. This tendency has a quirky name, "satisficing"—a term coined by economist and Nobel laureate Herbert Simon—to serve as a blend of the words *satisfy* and *suffice*. The combination reflects two simultaneous goals of a chooser when facing a decision—to make it good and to make it gone—which, according to Simon, usually means making it *good enough*. Although in an ideal world one would work and wait until the optimal solution emerged, in the real world of mental overload, limited resources, and deadlines, satisficing is the norm.

But even courses of action selected in this manner should not be allowed the unfair advantages of a different sort of unitary assessment—one focused only on upsides. In the excitement of a looming opportunity, decision makers are infamous for concentrating on what a strategy could do *for* them if it succeeded and not enough, or at all, on what it could do *to* them if it failed. To combat this potentially ruinous overoptimism, time needs to be devoted, systematically, to addressing a pair of questions that often don't arise by themselves: "What future events could make this plan go wrong?" and "What would happen to us if it did go wrong?" Decision scientists who have studied this consider-the-opposite tactic have found it both easy to implement and remarkably effective at debiasing judgments. The benefits to the organization that strives to rid itself of this and other decision-making biases can be considerable. One study of over a thousand companies determined that those employing sound judgment-debiasing processes enjoyed a 5 percent to 7 percent advantage in return on investment over those failing to use such approaches.[23]

Shifting the Task at Hand

On March 20, 2003, President George W. Bush ordered an invasion of Iraq by US-led forces. After a series of rapid military strikes that crushed the government of Saddam Hussein, it eventuated in an extended, agonizing, and brutal slog that cost the United States dearly in blood, money, prestige, and global influence. The Bush administration's initial justification for the war—to rid the region of Saddam's cache of "weapons of mass destruction"—was debunked (the weapons never materialized) and was revised regularly to incorporate such new purposes as eliminating Saddam's humanitarian abuses, terminating Iraq's support of Al Qaeda, safeguarding the world's oil supply, and establishing a bulwark for democracy in the Middle East. Nonetheless, the administration deflected attention from these questionable and shifting reasons through an ingenious media program—one that had the effect of directing the public's gaze away from the larger rationale for the war and onto its daily execution. That outcome was neatly accomplished by changing the task that representatives of the world's most important news agencies set for themselves in covering the conflict.

The "embedded reporter program" of the war in Iraq was the product of a joint decision by US officials and major media bureau chiefs to place reporters directly within combat units—to eat, sleep, and travel with them—during the course of military operations. Although the exact numbers vary depending on the source, at the program's height, between six hundred and seven hundred media representatives had the kind of access to the hostilities that had been denied them by US decision makers in the 1991 Gulf War and prior military operations in Afghanistan. Partly as a way to better ensure the safety of all concerned and partly as a public relations move, the US military developed the idea for the program with direction from Bush administration public affairs officials in the Department of Defense.

To media heads, the advantages of the program were obvious and exciting. With their personnel functioning alongside the troops in almost every sense, they would be able to convey to their audiences the experience of combat with levels of detail and currency rarely available to them before. The prospect of viscerally engaging video, graphic photographs, and riveting first-person accounts offered a dream come true to news organizations that had chaffed under the information restrictions of earlier military campaigns.

Besides a window into the reality of soldiering, their live-in status would allow embedded reporters special access to the soldiers themselves and, thus, to the personal circumstances of these men and women. Those human interest stories are also highly coveted by news media for their audience-drawing powers. One study found that embedded reporters were able to include such human interest elements in over a third of their stories, whereas unembedded reporters could do so in only 1 percent of theirs.

To US officials, the advantages of the program were different but no less compelling. First, under the wings of armed protectors, risks to the various media personnel in Iraq could be reduced significantly. The possibility of hundreds of news people trying to find headline-grabbing stories in a war zone and instead finding themselves hostages, casualties, or in need of rescue was a headache the military wanted to avoid. Also, the personal observations of journalists from around the world (nearly 40 percent of embedded slots went to non-US news agencies) provided an invaluable kind of risk protection to the military—from possible untruths about the war coming from Saddam's government. As Deputy Assistant Secretary of Defense for Public Affairs Bryan Whitman put it, embedded reporters would be in a direct position to undercut the credibility of "what the Iraqi Defense Ministry might be putting out."

There was a third, much larger benefit to the armed forces as well. Because the media chiefs were so attracted to the idea of an embedded reporter program, they made concessions that slanted the coverage more favorably to the military, which was allowed to play a role in the training, selection, and dismissal of reporters as well as to review their reports prior to publication. At an academic conference one year after the invasion, Colonel Rick Long, who was head of media relations for the US Marine Corps, was asked why the military advocated for the program. His answer could not have been more straightforward: "Frankly, our job is to win the war. Part of that is information warfare. So we are going to attempt to dominate the information environment . . . Overall, we were very happy with the outcome." Colonel Long and his colleagues had every right to be happy. Research analyzing the stories coming out of Iraq at the time detected a more positive tilt toward the military in those written by embedded reporters.

But this disparity in tone was modest compared with another difference between the reports of embedded and unembedded journalists. It was a difference that served the purposes of the Bush administration more than those of the military personnel on the ground. Embedded reporters' accounts were focused almost entirely on the troops: their daily activities, food, clothing, and supplies, how they prepared for battles, the tactics they employed, and the bravery they showed in battle. Indeed, 93 percent of all stories filed by embedded journalists came from the soldiers' perspectives, compared with less than half of that from their unembedded counterparts. And because, for the most part, the armed services had done a good job of feeding, clothing, supplying, and training the soldiers, who, for the most part, performed effectively and courageously, the military had a strong case to exhibit to those who could report on it firsthand.

Something crucial was lost, though, in this deepened but narrowed coverage: the embedded journalists—whose reports received an astonishing 71 percent of front-page war coverage during the conflict—were not reporting in any meaningful way on the broader political issues involved, such as the justifications for the war (as an example, the absence of weapons of mass destruction was mentioned in just 2 percent of all stories) or the operation's impact on US standing and power abroad. How could we expect anything else of them? Their eager superiors assigned them to cover what one analysis termed "the minutiae of the conflict," which absorbed all of their time, energy, and consideration.

Home again after leaving their combat units, many of the "embeds" were able to reflect on the constrained point of view that their assignment had created for them. But while they were in the field, their incessant focus on soldiers and soldiering set the media agenda for the conflict. After an extensive review of published articles at the time, news analyst and sociologist Andrew Lindner described the upshot starkly: "Not only did embedded reporting represent a majority of the total available press, it dominated public attention." Thus, with the vast majority of front-page war stories never addressing the whys of the fight but instead its whos and hows, the predominant media message to the public was evident: the thing you *should* be paying attention to here is the conduct of the war, not the wisdom of it.

One conclusion from research we've covered in this chapter is that issues that gain attention also gain presumed importance. Some of that same research demonstrates that if people fail to direct their attention to a topic, they presume that it must be of relatively little importance. With those basic human tendencies in mind, think of the implications of the embedded reporter program for US public opinion toward the invasion of Iraq. The dispatches of journalists in the program carried the kinds of content—vivid firsthand accounts of combat and emotionally charged human interest stories of combatants—that the media love to pitch and the public loves to catch. That content dominated public attention and thereby defined for the public which factors to consider more and less important about the invasion, such as those related to individual actions and battlefield outcomes versus those related to initial justifications and geopolitical ends. Because frontline combat factors represented a prime strength of the war, whereas larger strategic ones represented a prime weakness, the effect of the embedded reporter program was to award center stage import to the main success, not the main failure, of the Bush administration's Iraq campaign. The focusing illusion ensured it.

There is nothing to suggest that this topically imbalanced coverage was part of the grand design for the program on the part of administration and military officials, who seem to have been interested in it mostly for traditional information warfare purposes, such as gaining more control over the screening, training, and review of reporters, as well as putting them in an eyewitness position to counter enemy propaganda. Similarly, there is no evidence that the media chiefs who helped forge the program anticipated the full span of its public relations benefits to the Bush administration. Instead, it was only in retrospect, after the results of news story analyses started surfacing in academic journals, that this realization began to form. Ironically, then, the major public relations effect of the embedded reporter program appears to have been a side effect—a hidden one. It was an unexpected by-product of a decision to make the *task* of the most visible journalists covering the war molecular rather than molar in scope.[24]

— — —

The stealthy impact of bringing selective attention to a favorable type of information is not limited to the beneficial shaping of an assigned task. As we've seen, the persuasive consequences of managing background information and inviting singular evaluation went unrecognized by individuals subjected to those procedures, too. Through this cloaked influence, techniques designed merely to channel temporary attention can be particularly effective as pre-suasive devices. But there's another driving reason.

4

What's Focal Is Causal

It's no wonder that we assign elevated import to factors that have our attention. We also assign them causality. Therefore, directed attention gives focal elements a specific kind of initial weight in any deliberation. It gives them standing as causes, which in turn gives them standing as answers to that most essential of human questions: Why?

Because we typically allot special attention to the true causes around us, if we see ourselves giving such attention to some factor, we become more likely to think of it as a cause. Take monetary payments. Because the amount of money is so salient in the exchanges—"I'll pay you x when you do y"—we tend to infer that the payment spurred the act, when, in fact, it was often some other, less visible factor. Economists, in particular, are prone to this bias because the monetary aspects of a situation dominate their attentions and analyses.

Thus, when Harvard Business School economist Felix Oberholzer-Gee approached people waiting in line at several different venues and offered them money to let him cut in, he recognized that a purely economics-based model would predict that the more cash he offered, the more people would agree to the exchange. And that's what he found: half of everyone offered $1 let him cut in line; 65 percent did so if offered them $3, and acceptance rates jumped to 75 percent and 76 percent when he proposed the larger sums of $5 and $10.

According to classical economic theory, which enshrines financial self-interest as the primary cause of human behavior, those greater incentives convinced people to take the deal for their own fiscal betterment. How could any observer to the transaction doubt it? The highly visible incentives *caused* the obtained effects due to their direct links to personal monetary gain, right? Nothing surprising occurred here, right? Well, right, except for an additional finding that challenges all this thinking: almost no one took the money.

"Gee," Oberholzer-Gee must have said to himself, "that's odd." Indeed, a number of oddities appeared in his data, at least for adherents to the idea that the ultimate cause of human action is one's own financial interest. For instance, although bigger cash incentives upped compliance with the line cutter's wish, they didn't increase acceptance of the payment; richer deals increasingly caused people to sacrifice their places in line but without taking the greater compensation. To explain his findings, Oberholzer-Gee stepped away from a consideration of salient economic factors and toward a hidden factor: an obligation people feel to help those in need.

The obligation comes from the helping norm, which behavioral scientists sometimes call the *norm of social responsibility*. It states that we should aid those who need assistance in proportion to their need. Several decades' worth of research shows that, in general, the more someone needs our help, the more obligated we feel to provide it, the more guilty we feel if we don't provide it, and the more likely we are to provide it. When viewed through this lens, the puzzling findings make perfect sense. The payment offers stimulated compliance because they alerted recipients to the amount of need present in the situation. This account explains why larger financial inducements increased consent even though most people weren't willing to pocket them: more money signaled a stronger need on the part of the requester. ("If this guy is willing to pay a lot to jump ahead of me, he must really *need* to get to the front fast.")[25]

It would be naïve to assert that fiscal factors are less than potent determinants of human action. Still, I'd argue that merely because they are so visible (and, therefore, prominent in attention), they are often less determining than they seem. Conversely, there are many other factors—social obligations, personal values, moral standards—that, merely because they are not readily observable, are often *more* determining than they seem. Elements such as money that attract notice within human exchanges don't just appear more important, they also appear more causal. And presumed causality, especially when acquired through channeled attention, is a big deal for creating influence—big enough to account for patterns of human conduct that can range from perplexing to alarming.

Taking a Chance

In the first of these categories, consider the most famous case of product tampering of all time. In the autumn of 1982, someone went into supermarkets and drug stores in the Chicago area, injected packaged capsules of Tylenol with cyanide, and then returned the containers to the store shelves, where they were later purchased. Several reasons exist for the incident's long-standing notoriety. First, seven Chicago residents died from ingesting the poison—four of them family members who had swallowed capsules from the same Tylenol container. Second, their killer has never been found, giving the crime an uncomfortably memorable lack of closure.

But, for the most part, the case lives on today not so much for these regrettable reasons as for a pair of favorable ones: it led to the passage of important product safety legislation and to pharmaceutical industry shifts to tamperproof seals and packaging that have reduced risks to consumers. In addition—owing to the rapid, customer-centered steps taken by Tylenol's maker, Johnson & Johnson, which recalled thirty-one million of the capsules from all stores—it produced a textbook approach to proper corporate crisis management that is still considered the gold standard. (The recommended approach urges companies to act without hesitation to fully inform and protect the public, even at substantial expense to its own immediate economic interests.)

Aside from these high-profile features, another element of the case has gone almost entirely unnoticed but strikes me as remarkable. Early on, after it had been determined that the deaths were linked to bottles of Tylenol but before the extent of the tampering had been established, Johnson & Johnson issued nationwide warnings intended to prevent further harm. One widely communicated sort of warning alerted consumers to the production lot numbers on the affected bottles—numbers that identified where and when a particular batch of capsules had been manufactured. Because they were the first to be identified, two of the numbers received the most such publicity: lots 2,880 and 1,910.

Immediately, and bewilderingly, US residents of states that ran lotteries began playing those two numbers at unprecedented rates. In three states, Rhode Island, New Hampshire, and Pennsylvania, officials announced that they had to halt wagers on the numbers because betting on them shot above "maximum liability levels."

To know how best to account for this set of events, let's review the characteristics of the numbers. First, they were ordinary; not inherently memorable in any way. Second, they were associated with grievous misfortune. Moreover, they were intensely connected in American minds to imagery of poison-fed death. Yet many thousands of those minds responded to something about the numbers that lifted expectations of lottery success. What? Our previous analysis offers one answer: Because of all the publicity surrounding them, they had become focal in attention; and what is focal is seen to have causal properties—to have the ability to make events occur.

It turned out that every one of the minds that thought those numbers would provide an advantage over chance was proved wrong by the subsequent lottery results. But I doubt that the losses taught those minds to avoid, in any general way, similar future errors. The tendency to presume that what is focal is causal holds sway too deeply, too automatically, and over too many types of human judgment.

Taking a Life

Imagine that you are in a café enjoying a cup of coffee. At the table directly in front of you, a man and a woman are deciding which movie to see that evening. After a few minutes, they settle on one of the options and set off to the theater. As they leave, you notice that one of your friends had been sitting at the table behind them. Your friend sees you, joins you, and remarks on the couple's movie conversation, saying, "It's always just *one* person who drives the decision in those kinds of debates, isn't it?" You laugh and nod because you noticed that too: although the man was trying to be diplomatic about it, he clearly was the one who determined the couple's movie choice. Your amusement disappears, though, when your friend observes, "She sounded sweet, but she just pushed until she got her way."

Dr. Shelley Taylor, a social psychologist at the University of California at Los Angeles (UCLA), knows why you and your friend could have heard the same conversation but come to opposite judgments about who determined the end result. It was a small accident of seating arrangements: you were positioned to observe the exchange over the shoulder of the woman, making the man more visible and salient, while your friend had the reverse point of view. Taylor and her colleagues conducted a series of experiments in which observers watched and listened to conversations that had been scripted carefully so that neither discussion partner contributed more than the other. Some observers watched from a perspective that allowed them to see the face of one the parties over the shoulder of the other, while other observers saw both faces from the side, equally. All the observers were then asked to judge who had more influence in the discussion, based on tone, content, and direction. The outcomes were always the same: whomever's face was more visible was judged to be more causal.

Taylor told me a funny but nonetheless enlightening story about how she first became convinced of the power of the *what's-focal-is-presumed-causal* phenomenon. In setting up the initial study, she arranged for a pair of research assistants to rehearse a conversation in which it was critical for each discussion partner to contribute about equally. Standing alternately behind first one and then the other person, she found herself criticizing whomever she was facing for "dominating the exchange." Finally, after several such critiques, two of Taylor's colleagues, who were watching the conversation partners from the side, stopped her in exasperation, asserting that, to them, neither partner seemed to be dominating the conversation. Taylor reports that she knew then, without a single piece of data yet collected, that her experiment would be a success because the rehearsal had already produced the predicted effect—in her.

No matter what they tried, the researchers couldn't stop observers from presuming that the causal agent in the interaction they'd witnessed was the one whose face was most visible to them. They were astonished to see it appear in "practically unmovable" and "automatic" form, even when the conversation topic was personally important to the observers; even when the observers were distracted by the researchers; even when the observers experienced a long delay before judging the discussants; and even when the observers expected to have to communicate their judgments to other people. What's more, not only did this pattern emerge whether the judges were male or female, but also it appeared whether the conversations were viewed in person or on videotape.[26]

When I asked Taylor about this last variation, she recalled that the taping was done for reasons of experimental control. By recording the same discussion from different camera angles, she could ensure that everything about the conversation itself would be identical every time she showed it. When her results were first published, that videotaped interactions could produce the what's-focal-is-presumed-causal effect was not viewed as an important facet of Taylor's findings. But circumstances have now changed, because certain kinds of videotaped interactions are used frequently to help determine the guilt or innocence of suspects in major crimes. To register how and why this is so, it is necessary to take an instructive detour and consider a frightening component of all highly developed criminal justice systems: the ability of police interrogators to generate confessions from individuals who did not commit the crime.

Extracted false confessions are unsettling for a pair of reasons. The first is societal and concerns the miscarriages of justice and the affronts to fairness that such manufactured confessions create within any culture. The second is more personal, involving the possibility that we ourselves might be induced to confess by the tactics of interrogators convinced, mistakenly, of our guilt. Although for most of us such a possibility is remote, it is likely to be more real than we think. The idea that no innocent person could be persuaded to confess to a crime, especially a serious one, is wrong. It happens with disquieting frequency. Even though the confessions obtained in the great majority of police interrogations are in fact true and are corroborated by other evidence, legal scholars have uncovered a distressingly large number of elicited false confessions. Indeed, the confessions have often been shown later to be demonstrably false by evidence such as physical traces (DNA or fingerprint samples), newly obtained information (documentation of the suspect's presence hundreds of miles away from the crime), and even proof that no crime occurred (when a presumed murder victim is discovered alive and well).[27]

The same legal scholars have proposed a long list of factors that can help explain persuaded false confessions. Two strike me as particularly potent. I can relate to the first as an ordinary citizen. If I were asked by authorities to come to the police station to help them resolve the suspicious death of one of my neighbors—perhaps one I'd argued with in the past—I'd be glad to oblige. It would be the civically responsible thing to do. And if during the consequent questioning I began to feel that I was a suspect in police eyes, I might continue on anyway without demanding to be represented by a lawyer because, as an innocent man, I'd be confident that my interrogators would recognize the truth in what I told them. Plus, I wouldn't want to confirm any doubts they harbored about my innocence by seeming to hide behind a lawyer; instead, I'd want to walk away from the session with all those doubts dismissed.[28]

As a person of interest, my understandable inclinations—to help the police and then to convince them against my involvement—could lead me to ruin, though, for the other potent reason induced false confessions occur. In this instance, it's a reason I can relate to as a student of social influence: by deciding to persist through the interview on my own, I might subject myself to a set of techniques perfected by interrogators over centuries to get confessions from suspects. Some of the techniques are devious and have been shown by research to increase the likelihood of false confessions: lying about the existence of incriminating fingerprints or eyewitness testimony; pressing suspects to repeatedly imagine committing the crime; and putting them into a brain-clouded psychological state through sleep deprivation and relentless, exhaustive questioning. Defenders of such tactics insist that they are designed to extract the truth. An accompanying, complicating truth, however, is that sometimes they just extract confessions that are verifiably untrue.[29]

— —— —

Eighteen-year-old Peter Reilly's life changed forever one night in 1973 when he returned home from a youth meeting at a local church to find his mother on the floor, dying in a pool of blood. Though shaken and reeling from the sight, he had the presence of mind to phone for help immediately. By the time aid arrived, however, Barbara Gibbons had died. An examination of the body revealed that she had been murdered savagely: her throat had been cut, three ribs had been broken, and the thigh bones of both legs had been fractured.

At five foot seven and 121 pounds, and with not a speck of blood on his body, clothes, or shoes, Peter Reilly seemed an unlikely killer. Yet from the start, when they found him staring blankly outside the room where his mother lay dead, the police suspected that Peter had murdered her. Some people in their Connecticut town laughed at her unconventional ways, but many others were not amused, describing her as unpredictable, volatile, belligerent, and unbalanced. She appeared to take delight in irritating the people she met—men especially—belittling, confronting, and challenging them. By any measure, Barbara Gibbons was a difficult woman to get along with. So it didn't seem unreasonable to police officials that Peter, fed up with his mother's constant antagonisms, would "fly off the handle" and murder her in a spasm of rage.

At the scene and even later when taken in for questioning, Peter waived his right to an attorney, thinking that if he told the truth, he would be believed and released in short order. That was a serious miscalculation, as he was not prepared, legally or psychologically, for the persuasive assault he would face. Over a period of sixteen hours, he was interrogated by a rotating team of four police officers, including a polygraph operator who informed Peter that, according to the lie detector, he had killed his mother. That exchange, as recorded in the interrogation's transcript, left little question of the operator's certainty in the matter:

Peter: Does that actually read my brain?
Polygraph operator: Definitely. Definitely.

Peter: Would it definitely be me? Could it have been someone else?
Polygraph operator: No way. Not from these reactions.

Actually, the results of polygraph examinations are far from infallible, even in the hands of experts. In fact, because of their unreliability, they are banned as evidence in the courts of many states and countries.

The chief interrogator then told Peter, falsely, that physical evidence had been obtained proving his guilt. He also suggested to the boy how he could have done it without remembering the event: he had become furious with his mother and erupted into a murderous fit during which he slaughtered her, and now he had repressed the horrible memory. It was their job, Peter's and his, to "dig, dig, dig" at the boy's subconscious until the memory surfaced.

Dig, dig, dig they did, exploring every way to bring back that memory, until Peter began to recall—dimly at first but then more vividly—slashing his mother's throat and stomping on her body. By the time the interrogation was over, these imaginations had become reality for both the interrogators and Peter:

Interrogator: But you recall cutting her throat with a straight razor.
Peter: It's hard to say. I think I recall doing it. I mean, I imagine myself doing it. It's coming out of the back of my head.
Interrogator: How about her legs? What kind of vision do we get there? Can you remember stomping her legs?
Peter: You say it, then I imagine I'm doing it.
Interrogator: You're not imagining anything. I think the truth is starting to come out. You want it out.
Peter: I know . . .

Analyzing and reanalyzing these images convinced Peter that they betrayed his guilt. Along with his interrogators, who pressured him to break through his "mental block," the teenager pieced together from the scenes in his head an account of his actions that fit the details he'd been given of the murder. Finally, a little more than twenty-four hours after the grizzly crime, though still uncertain of many specifics, Peter Reilly confessed to it in a written, signed statement. That statement conformed closely to the explanation that had been proposed by his interrogators and that he had come to accept as accurate, even though he believed none of it at the outset of his questioning and even though, as events demonstrated later, none of it was true.

When Peter awoke in a jail cell the next day, with the awful fatigue and the persuasive onslaught of the interrogation room gone, he no longer believed his confession. But it was too late to retract it convincingly. To virtually every official in the criminal justice system, it remained compelling evidence of his guilt: a judge rejected a motion to suppress it at Peter's trial, ruling that it had been made voluntarily; the police were so satisfied that it incriminated Peter that they stopped considering other suspects; the prosecuting attorneys made it the centerpiece of their case; and the jury that ultimately convicted Peter of murder relied on it heavily in its deliberations.

To a one, these individuals did not believe that a normal person could be made to confess falsely to a crime without the use of threats, violence, or torture. And to a one, they were mistaken: Two years later, when the chief prosecutor died, evidence was found hidden in his files that placed Peter at a time and in a location on the night of the crime that established his innocence and that led to the repeal of his conviction, the dismissal of all charges, and his release from prison.

If you admit, we don't acquit. Peter Reilly surrounded by deputy sheriffs taking him to prison after his conviction. *Courtesy of Roger Cohn*

- —— -

There is an old saying that confession is good for the soul. But for criminal suspects, it is bad for just about everything else. Those who confess are much more likely to be charged, tried, convicted, and sentenced to harsh punishment. As the great American jurist Daniel Webster recognized in 1830, "There is no refuge from confession but suicide; and suicide is a confession." A century and a half later, renowned US Supreme Court Justice William Brennan expanded upon Webster's assertion with a stunning observation about the criminal justice system: "the introduction of a confession makes other aspects of a trial in court superfluous; and the real trial, for all purposes, occurs as the confession is obtained."

There is chilling evidence that Brennan was right. An analysis of 125 cases involving fabricated confessions found that suspects who first confessed but then renounced their statements and pled not guilty were still convicted at trial 81 percent of the time—yet these, recall, were all false confessions! Peter Reilly suffered the same fate as the great majority of individuals persuaded to confess to crimes they didn't commit, which raises a legitimate question: Why should we spotlight his confession over other more publicized and harrowing cases with the same outcome—for example, those in which multiple suspects were convinced to claim that, as a group, they had perpetrated a crime none of them had committed?

Notably, it wasn't anything that had occurred during his interrogation, trial, conviction, or subsequent legal battles. It surfaced at an event twenty years later where Peter, who had been employed on and off in various low-level sales jobs, was a speaker on a panel considering the causes and consequences of wrongfully obtained confessions and where it was described, not by Peter, but by a man sitting next to him with the ordinary name of Arthur Miller. This, though, was no ordinary Arthur Miller. It was *the* Arthur Miller, who some view as the greatest-ever American playwright, who wrote what some view as the greatest-ever American drama, *Death of a Salesman*, and who—if that isn't enough to draw our notice— was married for five years to the woman some view as the greatest-ever American sex symbol, Marilyn Monroe.

Gary Tucker/Donald S. Connery

After being introduced to the audience by Peter as one of his key supporters, Miller explained his presence on the panel as due to a long-standing concern with "the business of confessions, in my life as well as in my plays." During the period of anti-Communist fervor in the United States, in the 1950s, several of Miller's friends and acquaintances were summoned to appear at hearings before congressional committees. There they were pushed in calculated questioning to confess to Communist Party affiliations as well as to knowing (and then revealing) the names of members of the party prominent in the entertainment world. Miller himself was subpoenaed by the US House Un-American Activities Committee (HUAC) and was blacklisted, fined, and denied a passport for failing to answer all the chairman's questions.

The role of confessions in Miller's plays can be seen in *The Crucible*, the most frequently produced of all his works. Although set in 1692 during the Salem witchcraft trials, Miller wrote it allegorically to reflect the form of loaded questioning he witnessed in congressional hearings and that he later recognized in the Peter Reilly case.

Miller's comments on the panel with Reilly were relatively brief. But they included an account of a meeting he had in New York with a Chinese woman named Nien Cheng. During Communist China's Cultural Revolution of the 1960s and 1970s, which was intended to purge the country of all captialistic elements, she was subjected to harsh interrogations designed to get her to confess to being an anti-Communist and a spy. With tear-rimmed eyes, Nien related to the playwright her deep feelings upon seeing, after her eventual release from prison, a production of *The Crucible* in her native country. At the time, she was sure that parts of the dialogue had been rewritten by its Chinese director to connect with national audiences, because the questions asked of the accused in the play "were exactly the same as the questions I had been asked by the Cultural Revolutionaries." No American, she thought, could have known these precise wordings, phrasings, and sequencings.

She was shocked to hear Miller reply that he had taken the questions from the record of the 1692 Salem witchcraft trials—and that they were the same as were deployed within the House Un-American Activities Committee hearings. Later, it was the uncanny match to those in the Reilly interrogation that prompted Miller to get involved in Peter's defense.[30]

A scary implication arises from Miller's story. Certain remarkably similar and effective practices have been developed over many years that enable investigators, in all manner of places and for all manner of purposes, to wring statements of guilt from suspects—sometimes innocent ones. This recognition led Miller and legal commentators to recommend that all interrogations involving major crimes be videotaped. That way, these commentators have argued, people who see the recordings—prosecutors, jury members, judges—can assess for themselves whether the confession was gained improperly. And, indeed, video recording of interrogation sessions in serious criminal cases has been increasingly adopted around the globe for this reason. It's a good idea in theory, but there's a problem with it in practice: the point of view of the video camera is almost always behind the interrogator and onto the face of the suspect.

The legal issue of whether a confession had been made freely by the suspect or extracted improperly by an interrogator involves a judgment of causality—of who was responsible for the incriminating statement. As we know from the experiments of Professor Taylor, a camera angle arranged to record the face of one discussant over the shoulder of another biases that critical judgment toward the more visually salient of the two. We also know now—from the more recent experiments of social psychologist Daniel Lassiter—that such a camera angle aimed at a suspect during an interrogation leads observers of the recording to assign the suspect greater responsibility for a confession (and greater guilt). Moreover, as was the case when Taylor and her coworkers tried it, Lassiter and his coworkers found this outcome to be stubbornly persistent. In their studies, it surfaced regardless of whether the observers were men or women, college students or jury-eligible adults in their forties and fifties, exposed to the recording once or twice, intellectually deep or shallow, and previously informed or not about the potentially biasing impact of the camera angle. Perhaps most disturbingly, the identical pattern appeared whether the watchers were ordinary citizens, law enforcement personnel, or criminal court judges.

Nothing could change the camera angle's prejudicial impact—except changing the camera angle itself. The bias disappeared when the recording showed the interrogation and confession from the side, so that the suspect and questioner were equally focal. In fact, it was possible to reverse the bias by showing observers a recording of the identical interaction with the camera trained over the suspect's shoulder onto the interrogator's face; then, compared with the side-view judgments, the interrogator was perceived to have coerced the confession. Manifestly here, what's focal seems causal.

Thus, a potential dilemma exists for an innocent person—perhaps you—invited to a police station to help investigators solve a major crime. There is certainly nothing wrong with complying and providing that assistance; it's what good citizens do. But matters would get more complicated if you began to sense that the session was designed not so much to obtain information from you as to obtain a possible confession from you. The standard recommendation of defense attorneys at this point would be to stop the proceedings and request a lawyer. That choice, though, has its risks. By terminating the session, you might not be able to give your questioners the facts they need to solve the crime quickly and to discount your involvement fully, which would allow you to dispel the specter of suspicion then and there.

Being suspected of a serious crime can be a terrifying, nasty, lingering experience that might well be prolonged by the appearance of having something to conceal. But choosing to go on with the increasingly interrogation-like session includes perils of its own. You might be laying yourself open to tactics that have evolved in disparate places over centuries to extract incriminating statements from suspects, including blameless ones. There are ample grounds for caution here because, wherever employed, *these* are the techniques that have proven themselves to interrogators most able to achieve that end.

Suppose, after considering your options, you decide to soldier on through the interview in an earnest attempt to clear your name. Is there anything you could do to increase the odds that, should you be somehow tricked or pressured into making falsely incriminating comments, external observers would be able to identify the tricks and pressure as the causes?

There is. It comes in two steps, straight from the research of Professors Taylor and Lassiter.

First, find the camera in the room, which will usually be above and behind the police officer. Second, *move your chair*. Position yourself so that the recording of the session will depict your face and your questioner's face equally. Don't allow the what's-focal-is-presumed-causal effect to disadvantage you at trial. Otherwise, as Justice Brennan believed, your trial might already be over.[31]

By the way, if you ever found yourself in the interview situation I described, and you chose to end the session and demand a lawyer, is there anything you might do to reduce police suspicions that you therefore have something to hide? I have a suggestion: blame me. Say that, although you'd like to cooperate fully on your own, you once read a book that urged you to consider extensive police questioning unsafe, even for *innocent* individuals. Go ahead, blame me. You can even use my name. What are the police going to do, arrest me on a trumped-up charge, bring me down to the stationhouse, and employ Machiavellian tactics to gain a false confession? They'll never win a conviction, because I'll just find the camera and move my chair.

Evidence that people automatically view what's focal as causal helps me to understand other phenomena that are difficult to explain. Leaders, for example, are accorded a much larger causal position than they typically deserve in the success or failure of the teams, groups, and organizations they head. Business performance analysts have termed this tendency "the romance of leadership" and have demonstrated that other factors (such as workforce quality, existing internal business systems, and market conditions) have a greater impact on corporate profits than CEO actions do; yet the leader is assigned outsize responsibility for company results. Thus even in the United States, where worker wages are relatively high, an analysis showed that the average employee in a large corporation is paid one half of 1 percent of what the CEO is paid. If that discrepancy seems hard to account for on grounds of economic or social fairness, perhaps we can account for it on other grounds: the person at the top is visually prominent, psychologically salient, and, hence, assigned an unduly causal role in the course of events.[32]

—   —   —

In sum, because what's salient is deemed important and what's focal is deemed causal, a communicator who ushers audience members' attention to selected facets of a message reaps a significant persuasive advantage: recipients' *receptivity* to considering those facets prior to actually considering them. In a real sense, then, channeled attention can make recipients more open to a message pre-suasively, before they process it. It's a persuader's dream, because very often the biggest challenge for a communicator is not in providing a meritorious case but in convincing recipients to devote their limited time and energy to considering its merits. Perceptions of issue importance and causality meet this challenge exquisitely.

If captured attention does indeed provide pre-suasive leverage to a communicator, a related issue arises: Are there any features of information that don't even require a communicator's special efforts to draw attention to them because, by their nature, they draw attention to themselves?

5

Commanders of Attention 1:
The Attractors

When I was first sending around the manuscript of my book *Influence* to possible publishers, its working title was *Weapons of Influence*. An acquisitions editor phoned to say that his house would be interested in publishing the book but with an important modification. To ensure that bookstore aisle browsers would notice and reach for it, he recommended changing the title to *Weapons of Social Seduction*. "Then," he pointed out, "they'd register both sex *and* violence in the same glance."

Although I didn't accept his suggestion, I can see some of its logic. Certain cues seize our attention vigorously. Those that do so most powerfully are linked to our survival. Sexual and violent stimuli are prime examples because of their connections to our fundamental motivations to reproduce on the one hand and to avoid harm on the other—life and death, literally.

THE SEXUAL

There's no secret that prominent sexual stimuli can commandeer human attention from other (sometimes all other) matters. Novelists, playwrights, and movie screenwriters know it and use it in their plotlines—think of Vladimir Nabokov's *Lolita*, Tennessee Williams's *A Streetcar Named Desire*, and Steven Soderbergh's *Magic Mike*. Advertisers and marketers know it and use it in their commercial appeals. Behavioral scientists know it, too. What's more, they've shown how easy it can be to sneak a sexual association into things and have it direct conduct.

Consider a small study done in France. The researchers arranged for an attractive nineteen-year-old woman to approach two random samples of middle-aged men walking alone and ask them for a hazardous type of help. Pointing to a pack of four young toughs, she claimed they had stolen her mobile phone. "Could you get it back for me?" she asked. It's understandable that a lone man would be reluctant to intervene under the circumstances. He didn't know the mademoiselle; and he would be outnumbered four to one in any altercation. Indeed, in one sample, only 20 percent of the men took up the young woman's cause. But in the other sample, almost twice as many launched themselves into the dispute just as requested.

What accounted for the difference? All the men had been approached a few minutes before by a different young woman who asked for street directions, but some had been asked for the whereabouts of Martin Street; the others, for Valentine Street. Those asked about the latter location made up the far braver sample of men. According to the researchers (who had collected evidence from an earlier study), being asked about Valentine Street led the men to thoughts of a sexually linked lovers' holiday: Valentine's Day. It was the sexual connections to the word *Valentine* that triggered their bravado, propelling them to win the favor of a pretty ingénue no matter the risks.

Although the results are striking regarding the ease with which sexual stimuli provoked middle-aged male foolishness, the same results point to an instructive complication. The attractiveness of the young woman requesting assistance with her phone was not enough, by itself, to accomplish it. Something crucial to the process had to be put into place first. The men had to be exposed to a sexually linked concept, Valentine's Day, before she could prompt them to act. An *opener* was needed that rendered them receptive to her plea prior to ever encountering it. In short, an act of pre-suasion was required.

Complexities involving matters of the groin don't stop there. Take a statistic that belies the notion that infusing sex into advertising is a surefire way to increase sales: in *Advertising Age* magazine's list of the top hundred ad campaigns of the twentieth century, only eight employed sexuality in the copy or imagery. Why so few? Although responses to sexual content can be strong, they are not unconditional. Using sex to sell a product works only for items that people frequently buy for sexually related purposes. Cosmetics (lipstick, hair color), body scents (perfume, cologne), and form-fitting clothing (jeans, swimwear) fall into this category. Soft drinks, laundry detergents, and kitchen appliances do not, despite the occasionally misguided efforts of advertisers who don't appreciate the point.

Sex sells selectively. Although both ads are sexy, only the first is likely to spur sales of the product. *Courtesy of the Advertising Archives*

There's a wider lesson here, as well, that goes beyond the domain of advertising. In any situation, people are dramatically more likely to pay attention to and be influenced by stimuli that fit the goal they have for that situation. Just within the realm of sexual stimuli, studies have found that straight, sexually aroused males and females spent more time gazing at photos of members of the opposite sex who were especially attractive. This inclination seems natural and hardly newsworthy. The surprise was that the tendency appeared only if the gazers were in the market for a romantic/sexual relationship. Individuals who weren't looking for a new partner didn't spend any more time locked on to the photos of good-looking possibilities than average-looking ones. Once again, physical attractiveness alone wasn't enough to sweep people up and along. Something else—in this case, the goal of finding a new partner—had to be in place first to make that happen. There is a strong connection, then, between a person's current romantic/ sexual goals and that person's tendency to pay concentrated attention to even highly attractive others.

As an aside, that connection might give us a little-recognized way of gauging the chance that an existing relationship will survive. In a survey, college students in a romantic partnership were asked a series of standard questions that normally predict the stability of relationships: questions about how much in love they were with their partner, how satisfied they were with the relationship, how long they wanted to be in the relationship, and so on. In addition, the survey included some new questions for the participants that inquired into *attentional* factors such as how much they noticed and were distracted by good-looking members of the opposite sex. Two months after the survey, the participants were recontacted and asked if their relationships had remained intact or had ended. Remarkably, the best indicator of a breakup was not how much love they felt for their partner two months earlier or how satisfied they were with their relationship at that time or even how long they had wanted it to last. It was how much they were regularly aware of and attentive to the hotties around them back then.

These findings cast doubt on the time-worn defense of spouses accused of developing a roving eye—"Hey, I know I'm on a diet, but there's no harm in reading the menu"—as there might well be harm ahead. In our relationships, then, we might want to be sensitive to any sustained upswing in our partner's (or our own) attentiveness to attractive alternatives, as it might well offer an early signal of a partnership in peril.[33]

THE THREATENING

Violence, with its associated threat to safety, has always been able to draw human attention. Proof is available in everything from our can't-not-look fascination with automobile accidents, to the chart-topping sales of gruesome video games, to the box office power of violent films that used to be called "shoot-'em-ups" but have been transformed into more gory "blow-'em-ups" and "slash-'em-ups." This tendency to lend special attention to potentially threatening stimuli appears to be with us from infancy and often pushes us into silly (indeed, scared silly) actions.

There are, for instance, *dread risks*, which involve risky steps that people take to avoid harm from something that is actually less risky but that they happen to be focused on at the time and have thereby come to dread. After the terrorizing events of September 11, 2001, when four commercial airliners were simultaneously flown to their destruction by Al Qaeda hijackers, media coverage of 9/11-related stories was heaviest. As a result, many thousands of Americans with long-distance travel plans abandoned the dreaded skies for the roads. But the fatality rate for highway travel is considerably higher than for air travel, making that choice the more deadly one. It's estimated that about 1,600 Americans lost their lives in additional auto accidents as a direct result, six times more than the number of passengers killed in the only US commercial plane crash that next year.

Of course, it's possible that this switch from air to road travel was not due to dread risk effects but to the increased inconvenience of enhanced security procedures in US airports. The likelihood of such an account is reduced by a study showing a similar drop in London Underground system travel after the July 2005 subway train bombings in that city, even though no more inconvenient security procedures were put into place. Instead of taking the trains, Londoners began buying and riding bicycles. Because bicycle trips in London are generally more hazardous than Underground trips, travel-related injuries there spiked during the next several months due to hundreds of additional bicycle casualties. Dread risks turn out to be risky—and dreadful—indeed.[34]

– —— –

It's obvious that marketers of certain items—from home fire alarms, to computer backup programs, to deodorants—fill their ads with menacing information designed to capture our attention. However, most of the data on the *effectiveness* of such information come from the messages of communicators trying to steer us away from unhealthy lifestyle choices. As a rule, communications that present the most frightening consequences of poor health habits work better than milder messages or messages that present the positive consequences of good habits. Plus, the more prominent and attention grabbing the fearsome appeals are, the better they work. In over a dozen countries, placing large, scary images and warnings on cigarette packages has had the double-barreled effect of convincing more nonsmokers to resist and more smokers to stop the practice.

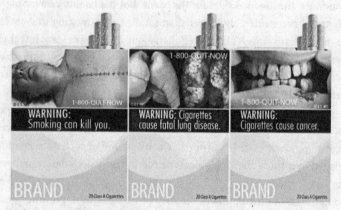

Lighting up will bring you down. Frightening cigarette pack images like these have reduced smoking around the world. *HHS.gov. US Department of Health & Human Services*

But there's a particular type of fear-stoking message that appears most capable of changing behavior. It does so, ironically enough, by reducing the fear it produces. That's no small advantage, because high levels of fear about the ominous consequences of lung cancer (or diabetes or hypertension) might cause certain likely victims to deny that they will encounter those consequences personally. "Hell," a heavy smoker might say, "my grandfather on my mother's side smoked all his life and lived to eighty. So I've probably got good cancer-fighting genes." Others might entertain different but similarly misleading nonsense to dampen the inflamed anxiety. A favorite among young people just starting to smoke is to suppose that by the time they suffer the ills of their actions, medical cures will be both available and easily obtained.

What's the persuasive alchemy that allows a communicator to trouble recipients deeply about the negative outcomes of their bad habits without pushing them to deny the problem in an attempt to control their now-heightened fears? The communicator has only to add to the chilling message clear information about legitimate, available steps the recipients can take to change their health-threatening habits. In this way, the fright can be dealt with not through self-delusional baloney that deters positive action but through genuine change opportunities that mobilize such action.

Consider how a Dutch team redirected the behaviors of individuals who, after undergoing tests, were informed of their especially high vulnerability to hypoglycemia (a blood glucose disorder also known as chronic low blood sugar) and of its sometimes severe consequences such as organ failure, convulsions, and depression. Paired with this alarming news, the recipients got information about a workshop they could attend to improve their diets and, hence, their chances of avoiding the disease. Most of them sought out further information about the diet workshop and, compared with similar health status individuals who received a less fear-inducing message, were four times more likely to sign up for the workshop then and there. That was because they believed the workshop would have a favorable impact on their health, and they used *that* new belief, rather than denial, to manage their anxieties. This approach, then, is how public health communicators can best deploy truthful yet frightening facts: by waiting to convey those facts until information about accessible assistance systems—programs, workshops, websites, and help lines—can be incorporated into their communications.[35]

– —– –

Overall, sexual and threatening stimuli, though often compelling, are not simple or unitary in their effects. With their complexities in mind, it becomes possible to understand how employing those stimuli can lead to great successes in some influence situations but to reversals in others. When several research teammates and I thought about the matter, we recognized that advertisers often ignore these complexities and, consequently, can produce expensive campaigns that actually undermine product sales. After one member of our research team, Vlad Griskevicius, urged us to take an evolutionary perspective, we realized that humans encountering threatening circumstances would have developed early on a strong tendency to be part of a group (where there is safety and strength in numbers) and to avoid being separate (where there is vulnerability to a predator or enemy). The opposite would be true, however, in a situation with sexual possibilities. There a person would want distance from the pack in order to be the prime recipient of romantic consideration.

We also realized that these two contrary motivations, to fit in and to stand out, map perfectly onto a pair of longtime favorite commercial appeals. One, of the "Don't be left out" variety, urges us to join the many. The other, of the "Be one of the few" sort, urges us to step away from the many. So, which would an advertiser be better advised to launch into the minds of prospects? Our analysis made us think that the popularity-based message would be the right one in any situation where audience members had been exposed to frightening stimuli—perhaps in the middle of watching a violent film on TV—because threat-focused people want to join the crowd. But sending that message in an ad to an audience watching a romantic film on TV would be a mistake, because amorously focused people want to step away from the crowd.

When we tested this idea in an experiment, the results stunned me. An advertisement we created stressing the popularity of San Francisco's Museum of Modern Art ("Visited by over a million people each year") supercharged favorability toward the museum among people who had been watching a violent movie at the time; yet among those who'd been watching a romantic movie, the identical ad deflated attraction to the museum.

But a slightly altered ad—formulated to emphasize the distinctiveness rather than the popularity of museum attendance ("Stand out from the crowd")—had the opposite effect. The distinctiveness ad was exceedingly successful among individuals who'd been watching the romantic film, and it was particularly unsuccessful among those who'd been viewing the violent one.

Although the data pattern seems complex, it becomes simplified when viewed through the prism of a core claim of this book: the effectiveness of persuasive messages—in this case, carrying two influence themes that have been commonly used for centuries—will be drastically affected by the type of opener experienced immediately in advance. Put people in a wary state of mind via that opener, and, driven by a desire for safety, a popularity-based appeal will soar, whereas a distinctiveness-based appeal will sink. But use it to put people in an amorous state of mind, and, driven by a consequent desire to stand out, the reverse will occur.

— —— —

Nearly all television and radio stations have a person who handles "traffic" information. Their responsibilities are not what you might think: to coordinate on-air reports of local road conditions, automobile crashes, and street closures. Instead, most often in the role of log editor, this individual positions advertising spots so that any given ad is spaced appropriately at various times throughout the day and is not aired too closely to an ad for a direct competitor. As advertising practitioners know, it would be a grievous "traffic management" sin if, for example, the log editor scheduled an ad for Ford pickup trucks back-to-back with an ad for Toyota pickups. Such errors prompt bitter complaints from advertisers, who recognize that mistakes of this sort blur their message and waste their money. I am confident, though, that no advertiser has recognized the potentially much larger monetary consequences of a different approach to ad placement that recognizes the content of media programming—a popular TV show, for instance—as doing more than exposing audiences to accompanying commercial messages but as also opening those audiences, pre-suasively, to certain *types* of commercial messages.

I'd bet, for instance, that if Ford media buyers plan to purchase TV slots for ads trumpeting the Ford F-150 pickup as "America's largest-selling truck for thirty-nine years" (as some ads do), they never consider favoring placements during crime dramas, scary movies, and news programming, while shunning romantic comedies and love stories. Conversely, I'd bet that if they plan to purchase slots for F-150 ads touting the distinctive FX Appearance Package to prod buyers to "Get ready to stand out!" (as some ads do), they never consider prioritizing those placements in the opposite fashion. Too bad for Ford.[36]

AND NOW FOR SOMETHING DIFFERENT: CHANGE-O, PRESTO

Whenever we first register a change around us, our attention flies to it. We are not alone in this regard. The reaction appears widely across the animal kingdom. It is so basic that it was able to overpower the most renowned behavior patterns of perhaps the most renowned group of animals in the history of psychological science: Pavlov's dogs.

Anyone who has taken a psychology class knows the headlines of their story. In a ground-breaking series of experiments, the great Russian scientist Ivan Pavlov got the dogs to salivate to the presence of something—the sound of a bell, for instance—that had no business extracting that reaction. To accomplish the trick, he just rang the bell immediately prior to introducing food to them on repeated occasions. Before long, the dogs were drooling at the sound of the bell, even in the absence of any food. But almost no one who's taken a psychology class knows the full story, because few psychology professors know it.

After many tests had convinced Pavlov of the reliability and strength of his momentous discovery of "classical conditioning," he wanted to show it to others. Yet when visitors were invited to his institute to observe a demonstration, it usually failed. The same happened when one of his assistants would condition a dog in one of the institute's experimental rooms and would then ask Pavlov to view the results. All too frequently,

Conditioning interruptus. One of Pavlov's dogs is pictured with the saliva collection tube used to show how its salivation response to food could be conditioned (shifted) to the sound of a bell. When some new stimulus in the lab drew the dog's attention, the conditioned response vanished. *Courtesy of Rk-lawton*

the dog wouldn't respond, leaving the assistant crestfallen and his boss mystified.

It finally dawned on Pavlov that he could account for both breakdowns in the same way: upon entering a new space, both he and the visitors became novel (new) stimuli that hijacked the dog's attention, diverting it from the bell and food while directing it to the changed circumstances of the lab. Although he was not the first scientist to notice this type of occurrence, Pavlov recognized its purpose in the label he gave it: the *investigatory reflex*. He understood that in order to survive, any animal needs to be acutely aware of immediate changes to its environment, investigating and evaluating these differences for the dangers or opportunities they might present. So forceful is this reflex that it supersedes all other operations.

The potent effect of a rapid change in environmental circumstances on human concentration can be seen in a mundane occurrence that afflicts us all. You walk from one room to another to do something specific, but, once there, you forget why you made the trip. Before cursing your faulty powers of recollection, consider the possibility of a different (and scientifically documented) reason for the lapse: walking through doorways causes you to forget because the abrupt change in your physical surroundings redirects your attention to the new setting—and consequently from your purpose, which disrupts your memory of it. I like this finding because it offers a less personally worrisome account of my own forgetfulness. I get to say to myself, "Don't worry, Cialdini, it wasn't you; it was the damned *doorway*."

More than a century after Pavlov's characterization, our bodily reaction to change is no longer called a reflex. It's termed the *orienting response*, and scores of studies have enlightened us about it. It isn't limited to the senses, as Pavlov had thought, but extends to all manner of bodily adjustments, including respiration, blood flow, skin moisture, and heart rate. The indication that has attracted recent scientific scrutiny takes place in the brain, where a pattern of electrical activity known as the "O-wave" (for orienting wave) flows across sectors associated with evaluation. By charting the rise and fall of O-waves in people hooked up to brain-imaging devices, neuroscientists have identified the kinds of stimuli that most powerfully produce shifts in attention. One such category of cues—associated with change—deserves our consideration, as it possesses intriguing implications for the psychology of influence.[37]

I once spent a year as a visiting scholar at the Annenberg School for Communication and Journalism at the University of Southern California, where I wanted to learn about mass media approaches to persuasion. A big reason I chose the Annenberg School, besides the quality of its faculty, was the background of its students. Many pursuing advanced degrees had prior experience in the broadcasting or motion picture industries, and I thought they'd be valuable sources of information about how to communicate with impact in a mass medium. One woman, who had produced successful television advertising spots as well as documentary films, was particularly instructive on the topic.

She claimed that, in both those arenas, a persuasion-oriented producer, writer, or director needs to be concerned principally with shots and cuts. All else, she said, is just variations and refinements of those foundational elements. I remember thinking, "Well, of course you'd want to manage your shots carefully because they provide the content of your message;

that's obvious. But to give equal standing to *cuts*—the mere shifts to and from aspects of your content—that's new to me; that's different." And, true to the larger point here, it was that difference that grabbed my interest.

When I asked about it, she offered a justification that fits with a pre-suasive dynamic: "You use your cuts to get people to swing attention to the parts of your message you really want them to focus on." In other words, cuts are crucial to persuasive success because they can be manipulated to bring into focus the feature of a message the persuader believes to be most convincing—by shifting the scene to that feature. That cut will instigate an orienting response to the winning feature in audience members' brains *before* they even experience it.

I'm aware of no evidence that other advertisers or film producers have learned to employ this insight, systematically, as moment makers. But I do know that television advertisers, at least, seem to have misunderstood its essence. Research confirms that rather than using cuts judiciously to direct attention solely to the most important facets of their material, TV advertisers have chosen instead to increase indiscriminately and dramatically the overall frequency of scene shifts within their ads by more than 50 percent over the years. Predictably, viewers end up confused as to the point of the ad and irritated by having their focus whipped around so often and so haphazardly. As a result, even though cut-heavy TV commercials draw more total attention, they produce significantly less memory for the ad's persuasive claims and significantly less persuasion. It's easy to understand why: viewers' attention isn't fixated on the ads' best points but is scattered all over the material's relevant *and* irrelevant attributes. For everyone concerned, it's a case of death by a thousand cuts.[38]

— — —

Of course, there are many communication channels that, unlike the broadcast media, present a piece of persuasive information in finalized, unchanging form—newspapers, magazines, books, handbills, window signs, billboards, emails, and so on—and, consequently, can't use cuts to capture and direct audience attention strategically. To leverage the power of difference when employing these vehicles, persuaders typically resort to a more traditional tactic. They insert novelty into the appeal,—that is, something designed to appear distinctive (original or unfamiliar or surprising) which also works well to attract attention. Indeed, almost anything a persuader can do to set an item apart from competitors has this effect. And as long as the spotlighted item has worth, its allure can leapfrog over that of equally worthy or even more worthy rivals. Some new research charts a previously undiscovered route to differentiation of that enviable sort.

In chapter 3, we covered one way that marketers get us to pay selective attention to the value of their products: they ask us in some type of questionnaire to evaluate the quality of their offerings without asking us to evaluate their rivals' comparable offerings. But there are subtler ways to accomplish the same goal. Consider the results of a study conducted at Northwestern University. Researchers gave online participants information about a pair of sofas we'll call the Dream and the Titan. The two, manufactured by different furniture companies, were comparable in all respects except for their cushions. The Dream's cushions were softer and more comfortable than the Titan's but less durable.

In this one-on-one comparison, the potential customers preferred the Titan's sturdier cushions to the Dream's softer cushions, 58 percent to 42 percent. But that changed when the researchers sent the same information to another sample of online participants along with information about the features of three other sofa models. The added sofas were not strong competitors, being weak on a variety of dimensions, but they all had durable cushions like the Titan. Within that set of comparisons, the Dream vaulted over all the other models—this time winning 77 percent of the preferred choices.

That's an astonishing finding. One would think that adding competitors to the mix of options would reduce rather than increase the number of times the Dream would be selected, if for no other reason than the raw probabilities involved. Besides, the Titan was still among the available alternatives and still possessed all its strengths. Why would the additional sofas bring about a drastic shift in favor of the Dream? After performing multiple studies on the topic, the researchers are confident they know: adding three models with durable cushions made the Dream stand out as distinct from the other four possibilities on the feature of cushion softness and comfort—and distinctiveness, as we've seen, swings attention to the distinguishing factor, which in this instance led to cushion comfort's greater perceived importance.

Unfortunately, the great majority of scientific data on persuasion goes unused by practitioners—even valuable findings such as this.[39, 40]

6

Commanders of Attention 2: The Magnetizers

Besides the persuasive advantages of drawing attention to a particular stimulus, there is considerable benefit to holding it there. The communicator who can fasten an audience's focus onto the favorable elements of an argument raises the chance that the argument will go unchallenged by opposing points of view, which get locked out of attention as a consequence.

Certain kinds of information do, in fact, combine initial pulling power with staying power. Information about oneself, for example, packs that potent one-two punch. If you doubt it, try a small experiment with some friends. Take a group shot with a digital camera and then pass the camera and resultant photo from hand to hand. Watch how each individual scans the picture before passing it on. If your friends are anything like mine—or like me, for that matter—they will look first, longest, and last at themselves.

THE SELF-RELEVANT

There is no question that information about the self is an exceedingly powerful magnet of attention. The ramifications for pre-suasive social influence are significant. In the province of personal health, when recipients get a message that is self-relevant because it has been tailored specifically for them (for example, by referencing the recipient's age, sex, or health history), they are more likely to lend it attention, find it interesting, take it seriously, remember it, and save it for future reference—all of which leads to greater communication effectiveness, as reflected in arenas as diverse as weight loss, exercise initiation, smoking cessation, and cancer screening. The continuing emergence of large-scale electronic databases, digitized medical records, and personal contact devices such as mobile phones makes individualized message customization and delivery increasingly possible and economical. Purely from an effectiveness standpoint, any health communicator who has not fully investigated the potential use of such tools should be embarrassed.

The focus-fixing impact of self-relevance applies to commercial appeals, too. Suppose you are a persuasion consultant approached to help market a new underarm antiperspirant to NASCAR dads. Let's call it Pit Stop. Suppose further that the product has concrete, convincing scientific evidence of its superior effectiveness, which the manufacturer's advertising agency plans to feature in its launch ads. But the agency is unsure about what to say *first* to draw audience attention to the rest of the ad and its compelling case. That's why it has come to you, to get your opinion on the lead-in lines of ad copy, which read:

"After all these years, people might accept that antiperspirants just aren't gonna get any better. They might even accept the ugly stains on clothes from hot days and hard work. They won't have to anymore."

What seemingly minor wording change could you suggest to improve the odds that the Pit Stop campaign will be a big success, the ad agency will be delighted, and your reputation as a wizard of influence will be burnished? It would be to replace the externalizing words *people* and *they* in the opener with the personalizing pronoun *you*. According to the results of an analogous study done at Ohio State University, your small modification will enhance audience attitude toward the product. Of course, because self-relevant cues only bring attention—not automatic approval—to a message, a strong subsequent case for Pit Stop was necessary within your ad to make the switch to "*you*'s" outperform the original ad. As the Ohio State study also demonstrated, if the rest of your ad had provided feeble evidence for Pit Stop's effectiveness, the switch to a personalized introduction would have made the now-more-attentive audience less fa-vorable to the product as a result.

Here, then, is another lesson in pre-suasion available for your use: when you have a good case to make, you can employ—as openers—sim-ple *self*-relevant cues (such as the word *you*) to predispose your audience toward a full consideration of that strong case before they see or hear it.[41]

There's another type of setting in which the attention-gripping quality of self-relevant cues can affect persuasive success: meetings or gatherings where individuals are expected to deliver their views in a public forum along with others doing the same. I got a memorable lesson in this regard when early in my career I was asked to speak about my research at a global conference sponsored by a large corporation. I was nervous. I'd rarely spo-ken to a business audience before and never to an international one. My anxiety spiked further when I learned that my talk was scheduled to fol-low an "arts break" in which the celebrated dancer Edward Villella would perform a scene from George Balanchine and Igor Stravinsky's ballet mas-terpiece *Apollo*. This sequencing is responsible for the two major disap-pointments I had with the conference. The first was to be expected: the audience was enthralled by the dance performance—it was Balanchine, it was Stravinsky, it was Villella, it was *Apollo* after all—and my ensuing presentation seemed pallid by comparison.

But there was a second misfortune I didn't anticipate. Even though I was sitting in the front row as the dance unfolded, I never saw it. I missed it completely, and I know why: I was focused on myself and my upcom-ing speech, with all of its associated phrasings and transitions and pauses and points of emphasis. The missed experience is one of my enduring regrets—it was Balanchine, Stravinsky, etc., after all. I'd been the victim of what behavior scientists call the *next-in-line effect*, and, as a consequence, I have since figured out how to avoid it and even use it on my behalf. You might be able to do the same.

Let's say that because you have a terrific plan in mind, you are looking forward to attending a meeting at work designed to attack a recurring staffing problem. Let's also say that the group meets often enough that everyone is familiar with the other participants and the basic format of the meeting: each member around the table is supposed to take a turn providing an initial position-and-recommendation statement. Finally, let's say you've noticed that one of those turn takers is Alex, a manager who reliably wields the most influence at the meetings. He usually determines the problem-solving path the group eventually takes. Deciding on your strategy for the upcoming meeting is easy: you'll secure a seat next to Alex, so that he'll be able to take in everything you say in your carefully wrought initial statement.

That would be a mistake. Whether you offer your statement just before or after his, according to the next-in-line effect, Alex will have a hard time processing your solution, no matter how good it is. If your statement comes immediately prior to Alex's, he'll likely miss the specifics because he'll be mentally rehearsing what he plans to say. If it comes immediately following Alex's, he'll likely miss those specifics because he'll be internally rehashing what he just said. It's what happened to me at that international conference. The pulling and holding power of my heightened self-focus within those *underprivileged* moments prevented me from appreciating the event's merits.[42]

How might you sail the waters of your meeting more expertly than your first inclination suggested? I'd propose charting a course that takes into account both the next-in-line effect and the what's-focal-is-presumed-causal effect. Take a spot at the table across from Alex where (1) he'll be sufficiently distant from his own presentation to hear yours fully, and (2), because of your visual prominence, he'll see you as fully responsible for the insights within your fine recommendation for resolving the problem. Of course, if you haven't come up with a creditably reasoned solution to the problem, you might want to grab a chair right next to his so that in his self-focus-induced bubble, he won't likely register the fact.

Although self-relevance might justly be considered the superglue of attention, another kind of information also has this binding effect, but to a less recognized degree. To explain it properly requires a food-related side trip into the history of psychology—one that takes us to a beer garden in mid-1920s Germany.

THE UNFINISHED

The widely acknowledged father of modern social psychology is Kurt Lewin, who before emigrating to the United States taught for a decade at the University of Berlin and who, as an early champion of women's role in higher education, gave the field several noteworthy academic daughters. One, a gifted young Lithuanian woman named Bluma Zeigarnik, was in a collection of students and research assistants who met regularly with Lewin at a local beer garden restaurant to discuss ideas when, one evening, the talk turned to a remarkable talent of a veteran waiter there. Without keeping any written record, he could remember and distribute perfectly the food and drink selections of large tables of diners. As the university group's conversation progressed, Lewin and Zeigarnik developed a plan to explore the limits of the man's impressive memory. After he had served all of the group members (once again flawlessly), they covered their plates and glasses and asked him to return to the table and recall what each had ordered. This time, though, he couldn't do it; he couldn't even come close.

What accounted for the difference? A length of time had passed, of course; but that seemed an unlikely cause, as it was only long enough for the diners to hide their plates and glasses under napkins. Lewin and Zeigarnik suspected a different reason: As soon as the waiter correctly placed the last dish in front of the last diner at the table, his task of serving the group changed from unfinished to finished. And unfinished tasks are the more memorable, hoarding attention so they can be performed and dispatched successfully. Once completed, attentional resources are diverted from the undertaking to other pursuits; but while the initial activity is under way, a heightened level of cognitive focus must be reserved for it.

To test this logic, Zeigarnik performed an initial set of experiments that she, Lewin, and numerous others have used as the starting point for investigating what has come to be known as the *Zeigarnik effect*. For me, two important conclusions emerge from the findings of now over six hundred studies on the topic. First (and altogether consistent with the beer garden series of events), on a task that we feel committed to performing, we will remember all sorts of elements of it better if we have not yet had the chance to finish, because our attention will remain drawn to it. Second, if we are engaged in such a task and are interrupted or pulled away, we'll feel a discomforting, gnawing desire to get back to it. That desire—which also pushes us to return to incomplete narratives, unresolved problems, unanswered questions, and unachieved goals—reflects a craving for cognitive closure.

Girl, uninterrupted. Bluma Zeigarnik, in Berlin, shortly before the start of her work on the Zeigarnik effect and fifty years later, in Moscow, shortly before the end of a continuously productive life. *Courtesy of Dr. Ardrey V. Zeigarnik*

The first of these conclusions—that not completing an activity can make everything about it more memorable—helps explain certain research results I never would have understood otherwise. In one set of studies, people either watched or listened to television programming that included commercials for soft drinks, mouthwash, and pain relievers. Later, their memory for the commercials was tested. The greatest recall occurred for details of ads that the researchers stopped five to six seconds before their natural endings. What's more, better memory for specifics of the unfinished ads was evident immediately, two days later, and (especially) two weeks later, demonstrating the holding power that a lack of closure possesses.

Perhaps even more bewildering at first glance are findings regarding college women's attraction to certain good-looking young men. The women participated in an experiment in which they knew that attractive male students (whose photographs and biographies they could see) had been asked to evaluate them on the basis of their Facebook information. The researchers wanted to know which of these male raters the women, in turn, would prefer at a later time. Surprisingly, it wasn't the guys who had rated them highest. Instead, it was the men whose ratings remained yet unknown to the women.

An additional piece of information allows us to understand this puzzling result. During the experiment, the men who kept popping up in the women's minds were those whose ratings hadn't been revealed, confirming the researchers' view that when an important outcome is unknown to people, "they can hardly think of anything else." And because, as we know, regular attention to something makes it seem more worthy of attention, the women's repeated refocusing on *those* guys made them appear the most attractive.[43]

－ —— -

What of the implication that a lack of closure can instigate a nagging, uncomfortable feeling that people will take action to avoid or escape? Are there lessons we can take from that insight?

A problem that afflicts most writers is procrastination. Writing is hard; at least, writing well (texting doesn't count) is hard. On this point, consider an exchange between the great British novelist Somerset Maugham and a young interviewer.

"So, Mr. Maugham, do you enjoy writing?"

"I enjoy having written."[44]

And that's the dilemma. Writers all want to get to the place of having written, but getting there is no straightforward, trouble-free task. That reality applies to nonprofessionals as well: authors of extended reports and documents designed for coworkers or superiors, for example. So it becomes easy to submit to the impulse to turn our attention to some other activity such as organizing our desk, checking the news, making a call, or getting a coffee shop latte. I have not been immune. However, one of my colleagues seemed to be.

She'd always impressed me with the quantity of her written output in a consistent stream of commentaries, articles, chapters, and books. When I asked how she managed it, she said she didn't have any one secret. Instead, she showed me a magazine article she'd saved from years prior advising authors on how to increase their productivity. Indeed, there were no secrets in the list of recommendations, which included tactics such as setting up a specific time to write every day, limiting distractions during that time, and rewarding oneself for a good day's yield. (This, apparently, is the right time for that latte.) The ideas on the list appeared reasonable but not particularly helpful in my case, as I'd already tried several without noticeable effect. Then, offhandedly, she mentioned a strategy of her own that I have used profitably ever since.

She never lets herself finish a writing session at the end of a paragraph or even a thought. She assured me she knows precisely what she wants to say at the end of that last paragraph or thought; she just doesn't allow herself to say it until the next time. Brilliant! By keeping the final feature of every writing session near-finished, she uses the motivating force of the drive for closure to get her back to her chair quickly, impatient to write again. So my colleague did have a writing secret after all. It was one that hadn't occurred to me, although it should have because it was present— if I'd just thought about it—in the body of work on the Zeigarnik effect that I knew well. That was a type of lapse I've tried not to let recur, either in my writing or in another of my professional roles at the time: university teaching. I learned that I could increase my classroom effectiveness, pre-suasively, by beginning each lecture with a special kind of unfinished story: a mystery.

THE MYSTERIOUS

Teaching at a university is a *really* great job for all kinds of reasons. Yet there are inherent difficulties. They surface not only in the ongoing challenges of proper topic coverage within one's courses, consistently updated lectures, and reliably fair examination/grading procedures, but also in a more basic way: in getting students to devote their full attention to the lecture material so that they comprehend the concepts involved. It's a traditional problem because, first of all, the average class period lasts upward (sometimes far upward) of forty-five minutes, which is a long time to count on concentrated focus. Besides, these are college students at or near their peaks of sexual attractiveness and sexual inclination. How could we expect them to deny systematic attention to the eye-catchingly outfitted, viscerally stimulating romantic possibilities all around them in favor of the physically fading academic at the front of the room whose unfashionable "look" is relentlessly similar from session to session?[45]

A number of years ago, while looking elsewhere, I came across an effective way to reduce the problem. It involves employing a combination of the Zeigarnik effect and what Albert Einstein proclaimed as "the most beautiful thing we can experience" and simultaneously "the source of all true science and art."

I was preparing to write my first book for a general audience. Before beginning, I decided to go to the library to get all the books I could find that had been written by academics for nonacademics. My strategy was to read the books, identify what I felt were the most and least successful sections, photocopy those sections, and arrange them in separate piles. I then reread the entries, looking for particular qualities that differentiated the piles.

In the unsuccessful segments, I found the usual suspects: lack of clarity, stilted prose, use of jargon, and so on. In the successful group, I found pretty much what I expected, too: the polar-opposite traits of the weak sections plus logical structure, vivid examples, and humor. But I also found something I had not anticipated: the most successful of the pieces each began with a *mystery story*. The authors described a state of affairs that seemed perplexing and then invited the reader into the subsequent material as a way of dispatching the enigma.

In addition, there was something about this discovery that struck me as more than a little curious—something I'll tee up, unashamedly, as a mystery: Why hadn't I noticed the use of this technique before, much less its remarkably effective functioning in popularized scholarship? After all, I was at the time an avid consumer of such material. I had been buying and reading it for years. How could the recognition of this mechanism have eluded me the whole while?

The answer, I think, has to do with one reason the technique is so effective: it grabs readers by the collar and pulls them in to the material. When presented properly, mysteries are so compelling that the reader can't remain an aloof outside observer of story structure and elements. In the throes of this particular literary device, one is not thinking of literary devices; one's attention is magnetized to the mystery story because of its inherent, unresolved nature.

I saw evidence of the force of the craving for closure born within mystery stories after I began using them in my classroom lectures. I was still inexperienced enough that on one particular day I got the timing wrong, and the bell rang, ending the lecture before I'd revealed the solution to a puzzle I'd posed earlier. In every college course I'd ever taught, about five minutes before the scheduled end of a class period, some students start preparing to leave. The signs are visible, audible, and, consequently, contagious: pencils and notebooks are put away, laptops closed, backpacks zipped. But in this instance, not only were there no such preparations but also after the bell rang, no one moved. In fact, when I tried to end the lecture there, students pelted me with protests. They would not let me stop until I had given them closure on the mystery. I remember thinking, "Cialdini, you've stumbled onto dynamite here!"

Besides mystery stories being excellent communication devices for engaging and holding any audience's interest, I encountered another reason to use them: they were instructionally superior to the other, more common forms of teaching I had been using, such as providing thoroughgoing descriptions of course material or asking questions about the material. Whereas descriptions require notice and questions require answers, mysteries require *explanations*. When I challenged students to engage in the process of providing explanations to account for states of affairs that otherwise wouldn't make sense, their test scores went up. Why? Because that process also provided them the best chance to understand the lecture material in a meaningful and enduring way.[46]

An example is in order. A little-recognized truth I often try to convey to various audiences is that, in contests of persuasion, counterarguments are typically more powerful than arguments. This superiority emerges especially when a counterclaim does more than refute a rival's claim by showing it to be mistaken or misdirected in the particular instance, but does so instead by showing the rival communicator to be an untrustworthy source of information, generally. Issuing a counterargument demonstrating that an opponent's argument is not to be believed because its maker is misinformed on the topic will usually succeed on that singular issue. But a counterargument that undermines an opponent's argument by showing him or her to be dishonest in the matter will normally win that battle *plus* future battles with the opponent. In keeping with the holding power of puzzles, I've learned that I can arrange for an audience to comprehend those teaching points more profoundly if I present them in mystery-story format.

Of course, there are various ways to structure a mystery-story-based case for the potency of counterarguments. One that has worked well in my experience involves supplying the following information in the following sequence:

1. *Pose the Mystery.* Most people are familiar with legendary cigarette advertising campaign successes featuring Joe Camel, the Marlboro Man, and Virginia Slims's "You've come a long way, baby." But perhaps the most effective marketing decision ever made by the tobacco companies lies buried and almost unknown in the industry's history: after a three-year slide of 10 percent in tobacco consumption in the United States during the late 1960s, Big Tobacco did something that had the

extraordinary effect of ending the decline and boosting consumption while slashing advertising expenditures by a third. What was it?

2. *Deepen the Mystery.* The answer also seems extraordinary. On July 22, 1969, during US congressional hearings, representatives of the major American tobacco companies strongly advocated a proposal to ban all of their *own* ads from television and radio, even though industry studies showed that the broadcast media provided the most effective routes to new sales. As a consequence of that unprecedented move, tobacco advertising has been absent from the airwaves in the United States since 1971.

3. *Home In on the Proper Explanation by Considering (and Offering Evidence Against) Alternative Explanations.* Could it be that American business interests, sobered by the 1964 Surgeon General's report that detailed the deadly denouement of tobacco use, decided to forgo some of their profits to improve the well-being of fellow citizens? That appears unlikely, because representatives of the other major US business affected by the ban—the broadcast industry—filed suit in US Supreme Court to overturn the law one month after it was enacted. Thus, it was only the tobacco industry that supported the restriction on its ads. Could it have been the tobacco company executives, then, who became suddenly concerned with the health of the nation? Hardly. They didn't reduce their concentrated efforts to increase tobacco sales one whit. They merely shifted their routes for marketing their products away from the broadcast media to print ads, sports sponsorships, promotional giveaways, and movie products. For instance, one tobacco company, Brown & Williamson, paid for product placements in twenty-two films in just a four-year period.

4. *Provide a Clue to the Proper Explanation.* So, by tobacco executives' logic, magazines, newspapers, billboards, and films were

fair game; only the airwaves should be off-limits to their marketing efforts. What was special about the broadcast media? In 1967, the US Federal Communications Commission (FCC) had ruled that its "fairness doctrine" applied to the issue of tobacco advertising. The fairness doctrine required that equal advertising time be granted on radio and television—*solely* on radio and television—to all sides of important and controversial topics. If one side purchased broadcast time on these media, the opposing side must be given free time to counterargue.

5. *Resolve the Mystery.* That decision had an immediate impact on the landscape of broadcast advertising. For the first time, anti-tobacco forces such as the American Cancer Society could afford to air counterarguments to the tobacco company messages. They did so via counter-ads that disputed the truthfulness of the images displayed in tobacco company commercials. If a tobacco ad featured healthy, attractive, independent characters, the opposing ads would counterargue that, in fact, tobacco use led to diseased health, damaged attractiveness, and slavish dependence.

During the three years that they ran, those anti-tobacco spots slashed tobacco consumption in the United States by nearly 10 percent. At first the tobacco companies responded predictably, increasing their advertising budgets to try to meet the challenge. But, by the rules of the fairness doctrine, for each tobacco ad, equal time had to be provided for a counter-ad that would take another bite out of industry profits. When the logic of the situation hit them, the tobacco companies worked politically to ban their own ads, but solely on the air where the fairness doctrine applied—thereby ensuring that the anti-tobacco forces would no longer get free airtime to make their counterargument. As a consequence, in the year following the elimination of tobacco commercials on air, the tobacco companies witnessed a significant jump in sales coupled with a significant reduction in advertising expenditures.

6. *Draw the Implication for the Phenomenon Under Study.* Tobacco opponents found that they could use counterarguments to undercut tobacco ad effectiveness. But the tobacco executives learned (and profited from) a related lesson: one of the best ways to enhance audience acceptance of one's message is to reduce the availability of strong counterarguments to it— because counterarguments are typically more powerful than arguments.

At this stage in the sequence, the teaching point about the superior impact and necessary availability of counterarguments is an explanation. As such, it produces more than recognition of basic facts (for example, "US tobacco companies argued successfully for a ban of *their* ads from TV and radio") or answers to related questions ("What was the result? The companies witnessed a jump in sales *and* a reduction in advertising costs"). It produces an understanding of how certain psychological processes associated with the prepotency of counterarguments brought about both of those otherwise baffling events.[47,48]

Notice that this type of explanation offers not just any satisfying conceptual account. Owing to its intrigue-fueled form, it carries a bonus. It's part of a presentational approach constituted to attract audiences to the *fine points* of the information— because to resolve any mystery or detective story properly, observers have to be aware of all the relevant details. Think of it: we have something available to us here that not only keeps audience members focused generally on the issues at hand but also makes them want to pay attention to the details—the necessary but often boring and attention-deflecting particulars— of our material. What more could a communicator with a strong but intricate case want?

Oh, by the way, there's a telling answer to the question of

what Albert Einstein claimed was so remarkable it could be
labeled as both "the most beautiful thing we can experience"
and "the source of all true science and art." His contention: the
mysterious.

Mysterious attraction. Considered the most famous painting of all time, da Vin-
ci's *Mona Lisa* has raised unanswered questions from the start. Is she smiling? If
so, what does the smile signify? And how did the artist produce so enigmatic an
expression? Despite continuing debate, one thing is clear: the unresolved mysteries account for a significant portion of the attention. *© Andrei Iancu/Dreamstime.com*

PROCESSES: THE ROLE OF ASSOCIATION

7

The Primacy of Associations: I Link, Therefore I Think

In the family of ideas, there are no orphans. Each notion exists within a network of relatives linked through a shared system of associations. The physiology and biochemistry of the links—involving the brain's neurons, axons, dendrites, synapses, neurotransmitters and the like—have been a source of fascination to many scientists. Alas, not to me. I've been less interested in the internal workings of these neuronal processes than in their external consequences—especially their consequences for the ways in which a precisely worded communication can alter human assessment and action.

THINKING IS LINKING

Still, for those like me intrigued by the persuasive properties of a communication, there is a crucial insight to be gained from the underlying structure of mental activity: the brain's operations arise fundamentally and inescapably from raw associations. Just as amino acids can be called the building blocks of life, associations can be called the building blocks of thought.[49]

In various influence training programs, it's common to hear instructors advise participants that to convince others to accept a message, it is necessary to use language that manages the recipients' thoughts, perceptions, or emotional reactions. That strikes me as partially right. We convince others by using language that manages their mental *associations* to our message. Their thoughts, perceptions, and emotional reactions merely proceed from those associations.

Nowhere are the implications for effective messaging so stark than in a relatively recent research program designed to answer the question "What is language principally for?" The leader among the group of researchers pursuing this line of inquiry is the renowned psycholinguist Gün Semin, whose conclusion, in my view, comes down to this: the main purpose of speech is to direct listeners' attention to a selected sector of reality. Once that is accomplished, the listeners' existing associations to the now-spotlighted sector will take over to determine the reaction.

For issues of persuasion, this assertion seems to me groundbreaking. No longer should we think of language as primarily a mechanism of conveyance; as a means for delivering a communicator's conception of reality. Instead, we should think of language as primarily a mechanism of influence; as a means for inducing recipients to share that conception or, at least, to act in accord with it. When describing our evaluation of a film, for instance, the intent is not so much to explain our position to others as to persuade them to it. We achieve the goal by employing language that orients recipients to those regions of reality stocked with associations favorable to our view.

Especially interesting are the linguistic devices that researchers have identified for driving attention to one or another aspect of reality. They include verbs that draw attention to concrete features of a situation, adjectives that pull one's focus onto the traits (versus behaviors) of others, personal pronouns that highlight existing relationships, metaphors that frame a state of affairs so that it is interpreted in a singular way, or just particular wordings that link to targeted thoughts. We'll benefit by considering the last, and simplest, of these devices first.

Speak No Evil, Leak No Evil

Not long ago, I came across an organization that, more self-consciously than any other I've encountered, has sought to shape the elements of its internal language to ensure that the mental associations to those language elements align with its corporate values. The company, SSM Health—a not-for-profit system of hospitals, nursing homes, and related entities— had asked me to speak at its annual leadership conference. I agreed, in part because of SSM's stellar reputation. I knew it as the first health care provider to be designated a Malcolm Baldrige National Quality Award winner. The Baldrige Awards, traditionally presented each year by the president of the United States and determined by the nation's Commerce Department, honor organizations that demonstrate stratospheric levels of performance and leadership in their fields. I wondered how SSM operated to attain such excellence and was glad to accept the invitation as a way to find out.

At the conference, I learned, for example, that the company's web-site claim that "Employees drive success" was much more than a claim. Despite being subjected to a rigorous vetting process and imported from a thousand miles away, I was not a conference keynote speaker. On the day I spoke, the keynote presentation, labeled "Our People Keynote," was delivered by seven employees who, one after another, described how they had participated in something exceptional on the job during the previous year. I also learned that on two additional days of the conference, four-teen other employees delivered similar "Our People Keynote" speeches. Of course, I realized that the practice of elevating twenty-one employ-ees to keynote speaker status is unusual; and installing the practice as a follow-through on a stated belief in employee-driven exceptionalism is even more unusual. But by then, I wasn't surprised to see it, as I'd already experienced how relentlessly SSM people walk their talk—literally, their talk.

A month earlier, on a call with organizers of the leadership conference intended to help me prepare my remarks, I spoke not to the usual one or two informants that organizations normally assign to the task but to six SSM employees. Although each contributed valuably, the spokesper-son for the team was the conference chairperson, Steve Barney. Steve was amiable and warm throughout the process until the end when his tone turned stern, and he issued an admonition: "Your presentation is not to include bullet points, and you are not to tell us how to attack our influence problems." When I protested that removing these elements would weaken my talk, Steve responded, "Oh, you can keep them in; you just have to call them something else." My cleverly phrased comeback—I believe it was, "Uh . . . *what*?"—got Steve to elaborate: "As a health care organization, we're devoted to acts of healing, so we never use language associated with violence. We don't have *bullet* points; we have information points. We don't *attack* a problem, we approach it."

At the conference, I asked one of the participants, a physician, about the nonviolent-language policy. He responded with even more examples: "We've replaced business *targets* with business goals. And one of those goals is no longer to *beat* our competition; it's to outdistance or outpace them." He even offered an impassioned rationale: "Can't you see how much better it is for us to associate ourselves with concepts like 'goal' and 'outdistance' than 'target' and 'beat'?" In truth, I couldn't. I was skeptical that such small wording shifts would affect the thinking and conduct of individuals within the SSM system in any meaningful fashion.[50]

But that was then. I'm a convert now. My response to SSM's strict language policy transformed from "Geez, this is silly" to "Geez, this is smart." The conversion occurred after I undertook a concentrated review of an astounding body of research findings.

Incidental (but Not Accidental) Exposure to Words

> He who wants to persuade should put his trust not in the right argument, but in the right word.
>
> **—Joseph Conrad**

Staying within the realm of violent language for the moment, consider the results of an experiment that exposed people to hostile words and then measured their subsequent aggressiveness. In the study, subjects completed a task requiring them to arrange thirty sets of scrambled words to make coherent sentences. For half of the subjects, when the words they were given were arranged correctly, they resulted mostly in sentences associated with aggression; for example, "hit he them" became "he hit them." For the other half of the subjects, when the words they were given were arranged correctly, they resulted mostly in sentences with no connections to aggression; for example, "door the fix" became "fix the door." Later, all the subjects participated in another task in which they had to deliver twenty electric shocks to a fellow subject and got to decide how painful the required shocks would be. The results are alarming: prior exposure to the violence-linked words led to a 48 percent jump in selected shock intensity.

In light of such findings, nonviolent language requirements make perfect sense for SSM. As a health care organization, it should operate within the bounds of the fundamental principle of medical ethics, "Above all, do no harm." But note that, as a *high-performance* health care organization, SSM did not prohibit the use of achievement-related words. Instead, it replaced such words possessing menacing associations (*target, beat*) with comparable words that did not (*goal, outdistance*). Perhaps this practice reveals the belief of SSM's leadership that, just as violence-laden language could lead to elevated harm doing and therefore should be eliminated, achievement-laden language could lead to elevated performance and therefore should be retained.

If SSM leaders do hold that belief, they'd be right. Multiple studies have shown that subtly exposing individuals to words that connote achievement (*win, attain, succeed, master*) increases their performance on an assigned task and more than doubles their willingness to keep working at it. Evidence like this has changed my mind about the worth of certain kinds of posters that I've occasionally seen adorning the walls of business offices. Call centers appear to be a favored location. The signs usually carry a single word in capital letters (*OVERCOME, SUCCEED, PERSEVERE, ACHIEVE*) designed to spur employees toward greater accomplishments. Sometimes the word is presented alone; sometimes it's accompanied by a related image such as a runner winning a race; sometimes just the image is presented.

In any of their forms, I'd always thought it only laughably likely that signs of this sort would work. But once again—this time thanks to some Canadian researchers—that was then. I've since become aware of a project those researchers undertook to influence the productivity of fund-raisers who operated out of a call center. At the start of callers' work shifts, all were given information designed to help them communicate the value of contributing to the cause for which they were soliciting (a local university). Some of the callers got the information printed on plain paper. Other callers got the identical information printed on paper carrying a photo of a runner winning a race. It was a photo that had previously been shown to stir achievement-related thinking. Remarkably, by the end of their three-hour shifts, the second sample of callers had raised 60 percent more money than their otherwise comparable coworkers. It appears, then, that initial incidental exposure either to simple words or simple images can have a pre-suasive impact on later actions that are merely associated with the words or images. Let's explore some influence-related implications, beginning with words of a special kind.[51]

Winners incite winning. This photo increased both the achievement-related thoughts and the productivity of individuals exposed to it. *John Gichigi/Getty Images*

Metaphor Is a Meta-Door (to Change)

> If you want to change the world, change the metaphor.
>
> —Joseph Campbell

Since Aristotle's *Poetics* (circa 350 BCE), communicators have been advised to use metaphor to get their points across. They've been told that an effective way to convey a somewhat elusive concept to an audience is to describe it in terms of another concept that the audience can recognize readily. Long-distance runners, for instance, recount the experience of being unable to continue a race as "hitting the wall." Of course, there is no real wall involved. But certain characteristics of a physical barrier—it blocks further passage, it can't be dispatched easily, it can't be denied—have enough in common with the runners' bodily sensations that the label delivers useful meaning.

Yet, the use of metaphor has its critics, complaining that it is often misleading. They point out that when one thing (such as the inability to take another step in a race) is understood in terms of another (like a wall), some genuine overlap between the two might be revealed, but the correspondence is usually far from perfect. For instance, a physical wall normally owes its presence to the actions of someone other than the person who hits it, whereas a runner's wall normally owes its presence to the actions of the runner—whose training (or lack thereof) and race pacing led to the problem. So runners employing the wall metaphor might be doing more than choosing a frame designed to communicate the feeling of motoric collapse. For strategic purposes, they might be choosing a frame designed to depict the failing as external to them, as not of their doing, and, thus, not their fault.

Recall that new psycholinguistic analysis suggests that the main function of language is not to express or describe but to influence—something it does by channeling recipients to sectors of reality pre-loaded with a set of mental associations favorable to the communicator's view. If so, we can see why metaphor, which directs people to think of one thing in terms of their associations to a *selected* other thing, possesses great potential as a linguistic device. Indeed, for well over a half century, researchers have been documenting the superior impact of metaphor, applied properly. More recently, though, emphasis on the transfer of associations inherent in metaphor has generated an eye-opening array of persuasive effects.

Suppose, for instance, that you are a political consultant who has been hired by a candidate for mayor of a nearby city to help her win an election in which a recent surge in crime is an important issue. In addition, suppose that this candidate and her party are known for their tough stance on crime that favors policies designed to capture and incarcerate lawbreakers. The candidate wants your counsel on what she could do to make voters believe that her approach to the problem is correct. With an understanding of the workings of metaphoric persuasion, your advice could be swift and confident: in any public pronouncements on the topic, she should portray the crime surge as a wild beast rampaging through the city that must be stopped. Why? Because to bring a wild beast under control, it's necessary to catch and cage it. In the minds of her audiences, these natural associations to the proper handling of rampaging animals will transfer to the proper handling of crime and criminals.

Now imagine instead that the candidate and her party are known for a different approach to the problem: one that seeks to halt the growth of crime by treating its societal causes such as joblessness, lack of education, and poverty. In this instance—still on the basis of an understanding of metaphoric persuasion—your advice could also be swift and confident: in all her public pronouncements on the topic, the candidate should portray the crime surge as a spreading virus infecting the city that must be stopped. Why? Because to bring a virus under control, it's necessary to remove the unhealthy conditions that allow it to breed and spread. These disease-related associations should now frame the way citizens think about how best to deal with their crime problem.

If other advisers within the candidate's campaign scoff at the metaphor-based rationale for your plan, calling it simplistic, you might ask them to consider some relevant data: Stanford University researchers exposed a randomly chosen set of online readers to a news account of a three-year rise in city crime rates that depicted crime as a ravaging *beast*. Other randomly chosen readers saw the same news account and statistics except for one word: the criminality was depicted as a ravaging *virus*. Later the survey asked them all to indicate their preferred solutions. In the most precise analysis of the results, readers who initially saw crime portrayed as a beast recommended catch-and-cage solutions rather than remove-unhealthy-conditions solutions. But the opposite pattern emerged among readers who initially saw crime portrayed as a virus.

Remarkably, the size of the difference due to the change of a single word (22 percent) was more than double the size of preferred solution differences that were naturally due to the readers' gender (9 percent) or political party affiliation (8 percent). When predicting voter preferences, political campaigns include the role of demographic factors such as gender and party affiliation. Rarely, though, do they consider the potentially greater predictive power of a pre-suasively deployed metaphor.

If the mayor's other advisers are of the sort that dismisses findings from controlled scientific research as irrelevant to real-world settings, you could offer them a form of evidence from the real world. Maximally effective salespeople understand the power of metaphor. You might ask the advisers to consider the case of high school dropout Ben Feldman, who, despite never doing business outside a sixty-mile radius of his little hometown of East Liverpool, Ohio, became the greatest life insurance salesman of his time (and perhaps of all time). Indeed, at his peak, in the 1970s and 1980s, he sold more life insurance by himself than 1,500 of the 1,800 insurance *agencies* in the United States. In 1992, after he had been admitted to a hospital because of a cerebral hemorrhage, his employer, New York Life, decided to honor the great salesman's fifty years with the company by declaring "Feldman February"—a month in which all its agents would compete to get the largest total in new sales. Who won? Ben Feldman. How? By calling prospects from his hospital bed, where the eighty-year-old closed $15 million in new contracts in twenty-eight days.

That kind of relentless drive and commitment to the job accounts for some, but not all, of the man's phenomenal success. According to chroniclers of that success, he never pressured reluctant prospects into a sale. Instead, he employed a light (and enlightened) touch that led them smoothly toward a purchase. Mr. Feldman was a master of metaphor. In his portrayal of life's end, for instance, people didn't die, they "walked out" of life—a characterization that benefitted from associations to a breach in one's family responsibilities that would need to be filled. He was then quick to depict life insurance as the (metaphorically aligned) solution: "When you *walk out*," he would say, "your insurance money *walks in*." When exposed to this metaphoric lesson in the moral responsibility of buying life insurance, many a customer straightened up and *walked right*.

Although metaphors require a language-based link between two things to work, once that link is in place, metaphoric persuasion can be triggered nonverbally. For instance, in English and many other languages, the concept of weight—heaviness—is linked metaphorically to the concepts of seriousness, importance, and effort. For that reason, (1) raters reading a job candidate's qualifications attached to a heavy (versus light) clipboard come to see the applicant as a more serious contender for the job; (2) raters reading a report attached to a heavy clipboard come to see the topic as more important; and (3) raters holding a heavy object (requiring more effort of them) put more effort into considering the pros and cons of an improvement project for their city. This set of findings raises the specter that manufacturers' drive to make e-readers as light as possible will lessen the seeming value of the presented material, the perceived intellectual depth of its author, and the amount of energy readers will be willing to devote to its comprehension.

Comparable findings have appeared in studies of another arena of human judgment: personal warmth, where individuals who have held a warm object briefly—for example, a cup of hot (versus iced) coffee—immediately feel warmer toward, closer to, and more trusting of those around them. Hence, they become more giving and cooperative in the social interactions that follow shortly afterward. It's evident, then, that powerful metaphoric associations can be pre-suasively activated without a word; touch is enough.[52]

More Hot Stuff

Because negative associations can be transferred as easily as positive ones, spontaneously shared meaning can be as much a nightmare as a dream for communicators. A few years ago, a white government official received so much criticism that he resigned his position after using the word *niggardly* to describe how he planned to handle his office's tight budget. The word means "miserly" or "reluctant to spend," but, plainly, another family of associations provoked the negative reaction. For a fundamentally related reason, used-car salespeople are taught not to describe their cars as "used"—which links to notions of wear and tear—but to say "preowned," which bridges to thoughts of possession and ownership. Similarly, information technology providers are counseled against telling customers the "cost" or "price" of their offerings, which are terms associated with the loss of resources; rather, they are to speak of the "purchase" or "investment" amount involved—terms that make contact with the concept of gain. The pilot and flight attendant training programs of some commercial airlines now include hints on how to avoid death-related language when communicating to passengers before or during a flight: The scary-sounding "your final destination" is to be trimmed to "your destination," and "terminal" is to be replaced with "gate" whenever possible.

It goes without saying that savvy marketers not only want to avoid coupling their products and services to elements with negative associations; they want to play both defense and offense by eliminating connections to factors that carry the most unfavorable connotations while maximizing connections to those with the most favorable ones. What are those most intensely evaluated elements? There is much to say in chapter 13 about the concept that people respond to with the greatest passion on the negative side of the ledger, so its coverage will be deferred until then. But to reduce any resulting Zeigarnik-effect tensions, a brief advance notice is in order: The concept pre-loaded with associations most damaging to immediate assessments and future dealings is *untrustworthiness*, along with its concomitants, such as lying and cheating.

Our hotties, ourselves. On the upside of things, though, the factor with most favorable impact in the realm of human evaluation is one we have encountered before: the self, which gains its power from a pair of sources. Not only does it draw and hold our attention with nearly electromagnetic strength, thereby enhancing perceived importance; it also brings that attention to an entity that the great majority of us shower with positive associations. Therefore, anything that is self-connected (or can be made to seem self-connected) gets an immediate lift in our eyes. Sometimes the connections can be trivial but can still serve as springboards to persuasive success.

People who learn that they have a birthday, birthplace, or first name in common come to like each other more, which leads to heightened cooperativeness and helpfulness toward each other. Potential customers are more willing to enroll in an exercise program if told they have the same date of birth as the personal trainer who'll be providing the service. Learning of such connections online offers no immunity: young women are twice as likely to "friend" a man who contacts them on Facebook if he claims to have the same birthday. The small-business loans to citizens of developing nations brokered through a microfinance website are significantly more likely to be offered by loan providers to recipients whose names share their initials. Finally, researchers studying this general tendency to value entities linked to the self (called implicit egoism) have found that individuals prefer not just people but also commercial products—crackers, chocolates, and teas—with names that share letters of the alphabet with their own names. To take advantage of this affinity, in the summer of 2013 the British division of Coca-Cola replaced its own package branding with one or another of 150 of the most common first names in the United Kingdom—doing so on 100 million packs of their product! What could justify the expense? Similar programs in Australia and New Zealand had boosted sales significantly in those regions the year before.

When finally tried in the United States, it produced the first increase in Coke sales in a decade.

Even organizations can be susceptible to the tendency to overvalue things that include elements of their names. In 2004, to celebrate the fiftieth anniversary of rock and roll, *Rolling Stone* magazine issued a list of the five hundred greatest songs of the rock era. The two highest-ranked songs, as compiled and weighted by *Rolling Stone* editors, were "Like a Rolling Stone" by Bob Dylan and "(I Can't Get No) Satisfaction" by the Rolling Stones. At the time of this writing, I checked ten comparable lists of the greatest rock-and-roll songs, and none listed either of *Rolling Stone*'s picks as its number one or number two choice.[53]

I Am We, and We Are Number One. When considering the persuasive implications of implicit egoism, there's an important qualification to be taken into account. The overvalued self isn't always the personal self. It can also be the social self—the one framed not by the characteristics of the individual but by the characteristics of that individual's group. The conception of self as residing outside the individual and within a related social unit is particularly strong in some non-Western societies whose citizens have a special affinity for things that appear connected to a collectively constructed self. An analysis of two years of magazine ads in the United States and South Korea found that (1) in South Korea, the ads attempted to link products and services mostly to the reader's family or group, whereas in America it was mostly to the individual reader; and (2) in terms of measured impact, group-linked ads were more effective in South Korea, while ads linked to the individual were more effective in the United States.

The recognition of what Eastern-world audiences value furnished South Korea's government with a wise negotiating tactic to use in dealing with Afghan militants. It was a tactic that, although simple, had been almost absent from the approach of Western negotiators in Afghanistan up to that point and is still underused there by Western powers.

In July 2007 the Afghan Taliban kidnapped twenty-one South Korean church-sponsored aid workers, holding them hostage and killing two as a savage initial show of will. Talks designed to free the remaining nineteen went so badly that the kidnappers named the next two hostages they planned to murder, prompting the head of the South Korean National Intelligence Service, Kim Man-bok, to fly in to try to salvage the negotiations. He brought a plan. It was to connect the South Korean bargaining team to something central to the group identity of the militants: their language. Upon his arrival, Kim replaced his head negotiator, whose appeals had been transmitted through an Afghan translator, with a South Korean representative who spoke fluent Pashtun.

According to Kim, who won the hostages' swift release, "The key in the negotiations was language." However, it was not because of any greater precision or lucidity of the verbal exchanges involved but because of something more primitive and pre-suasive. "When our counterparts saw that our negotiator was speaking their language, Pashtun, they developed a kind of strong intimacy with us, and so the talks went well."[54]

"Easy" Does It. Besides the self, there is another concept possessed of decidedly positive associations worth examining because of how communicators can fumble the opportunity to harness those associations effectively. It is "easy."

There is much positivity associated with getting something with ease, but in a particular way. When we grasp something *fluently*—that is, we can picture or process it quickly and effortlessly—we not only like that thing more but also think it is more valid and worthwhile. For this reason, poetry possessing rhyme and regular meter evokes something more than greater favor from readers; it is also evokes perceptions of higher aesthetic value—the opposite of what the proponents of free verse and the gatekeepers of modern poetry journals appear to believe. Researchers in the field of *cognitive poetics* have even found that the fluency-producing properties of rhyme lead to enhanced persuasion. The statement "Caution and measure will win you riches" is seen as more true when changed to "Caution and measure win you treasure." There's a mini-lesson here for persuasive success: to make it climb, make it rhyme.

Within the domain of general attraction, observers have a greater liking for those whose facial features are easy to recognize and whose names are easy to pronounce. Tellingly, when people can process something with cognitive ease, they experience increased neuronal activity in the muscles of their face that produce a smile. On the flip side, if it's difficult to process something, observers tend to dislike that experience and, accordingly, that thing. The consequences can be striking. An analysis of the names of five hundred attorneys at ten US law firms found that the harder an attorney's name was to pronounce, the lower he or she stayed in the firm's hierarchy. This effect held, by the way, independent of the foreignness of the names: a person with a difficult-to-pronounce foreign name would likely be in an inferior position to one with an easy-to-pronounce foreign name. A similar effect occurs when observers encounter hard-to-pronounce drugs or food additives; they become less favorable toward the products and their potential risks. So why do nutritional supplement and pharmaceutical companies give their products names that are difficult to pronounce and spell, such as Xeljanz and Farxiga? Maybe they are trying to communicate the family of plants or chemicals the product comes from. If so, it seems a poor trade-off.

A lack of fluency in business communication can be problematic in additional ways. I can't count the number of times I've sat at restaurant tables struggling to read extended descriptions of menu items presented in almost illegible, flourish-filled fonts or in inadequate light—or both. You would think that restaurateurs, hoping to tempt us, would know better, as research has revealed that the food detailed in difficult-to-process descriptions is seen as less tempting and that difficult-to-read claims are, in general, seen as less true.

But perhaps the most damaging failure of business professionals to heed these effects occurs within stock exchanges. One analysis of eighty-nine randomly selected companies that began trading shares on the New York Stock Exchange between 1990 and 2004 found that although the effect dwindled over time, those companies with easier-to-pronounce names outperformed those with difficult-to-pronounce names. A comparable analysis of easy-to-pronounce three-letter stock ticker codes (such as KAR) versus difficult-to-pronounce codes (such as RDO) on the American Stock Exchange produced comparable results.[55]

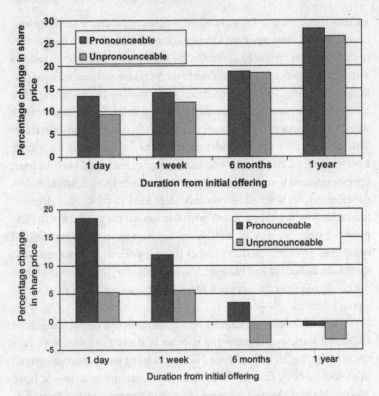

When names are easy to pronounce, early profits are easy to announce. On US stock exchanges, the initial value of a company's shares was greater if the company's name (top graph) or stock ticker code (bottom graph) was easy to pronounce. *Courtesy of Adam Oppenheimer and the National Academy of Sciences, U.S.A.*

If it seems from this evidence that we are relegated to a discomforting pawnlike status in many ordinary situations, much of the research covered so far in this book indicates that there is good reason for the concern. Must we resign ourselves, then, to being moved around haphazardly on the chessboard of life by the associations to whatever words, symbols, or images we happen to encounter? Fortunately, no. Provided that we understand how associative processes work, we can exert strategic, pre-suasive control over them. First, we can choose to enter situations that possess the set of associations we want to experience. When we don't have such available choices, we can frontload impending situations with cues carrying associations that will send us in personally gainful directions. We consider how next.

8

Persuasive Geographies: All the Right Places, All the Right Traces

There is a geography of influence.

When I began writing my first book for a general audience, I was on a leave of absence at a university other than my own. Because my campus office was located on an upper floor, it was possible to arrange my desk so that as I wrote, I could look out the window at an array of imposing buildings housing various academic institutes, centers, and departments. On either border of this outside window to the academic world, I'd lined shelves with materials that provided an inside window to that world: my professional books, journals, articles, and files.

In town, I'd leased an apartment and would try to write at a desk there, which I'd also positioned in front of a window. Although I didn't intend it, that home location offered a view unlike the one outside my university office. Instead of rigid strongholds of scholarly industry, I'd see the flow of passersby—mostly pedestrians on their way to work or to shop or to do any of a thousand ordinary things that people ordinarily do. The environment around my desk was importantly different too, especially the information environment. Newspapers, magazines, tabletops, and television shows took the place of scientific publications, textbooks, filing cabinets, and conversations with colleagues.

Writing in those separate places produced an effect I didn't anticipate and didn't even notice until about a month into the process, when I gathered all of the book project's preliminary pages and read them as a piece: the work I'd done at home was miles better than what I'd done at the university, because it was decidedly more appropriate for the general audience I'd envisioned. Indeed, in style and structure, the output from my campus desk was poorly suited to anyone but professional colleagues.

Surprised, I wondered how it could be that despite a clear grasp of my desired market, I couldn't write for it properly while in my university office. Only in retrospect was the answer obvious. Anytime I lifted or turned my head, the sight lines from my on-campus desk brought me into contact with cues linked to an academic approach and its specialized vocabulary, grammar, and style of communication.

It didn't matter what I knew (somewhere in my head) about the traits and preferences of my intended readers. There were few cues in that environment to spur me to think routinely and automatically of those individuals as I wrote. From my desk at home, though, the cues were matched to the task. There, surrounded by prompted associations to the people I wanted to write for all along, I could harmonize with them much more successfully.

With this guiding realization, I took all the pages I'd written at the university and, making a persuasive-geography-based decision, revised them at home. It was a worthwhile undertaking. Take as proof that the book's initial opening line, "My academic subdiscipline, experimental social psychology, has as a principal domain the study of the social influence process," changed (mercifully) to "I can admit it freely now: all my life I've been a patsy." Knowing what to do next wasn't difficult. Toil on the book was routed home, while I consigned colleague-targeted work to my university office.[56]

Certain lessons from this experience extend beyond crafting popular scholarship. They apply to the much broader question of how any of us might arrange our physical environments pre-suasively to send us down selected associative pathways (chutes) toward desired ends.

Several consultancy firms develop for corporate clients systems designed to stimulate employees to work more effectively, mostly through incentive programs that reward them for reaching performance goals. While talking to a project manager from one of these firms at a marketing conference, I raised a question I regularly pose to experienced practitioners regarding what makes them successful in their fields. In her case, I asked what she had found that allowed her to forge the most successful incentive programs. After listing several factors whose positive impact she could easily understand—extent of experience of her team in the client's industry, level of information the client's team provided to hers, amount of preparation on the part of both teams—she mentioned one she didn't understand at all. There was a type of *working space* at client headquarters that lent itself to crafting programs that had later turned out particularly well: centrally located rooms with glass walls.

She told me she'd noticed this odd outcome because she'd expected the opposite, thinking that the sight of all manner of employees swirling around and by would pull the attention of the room's program planners away from relevant task considerations and toward irrelevant ones. "Wouldn't you have thought the same thing?" she asked. I related my two-writing-desks story, explaining that my answer once would have been yes, but not since that important learning experience. In its aftermath, I now thought she was treating as irrelevant certain aspects of the work environment that had been highly related to task success. To do the best job of developing employee incentive programs, I suspected that she and her team needed ongoing visual exposure to employees who would be covered by the programs. It had been true for me: I needed present reminders of my prospective audience members to keep my writing aligned with their interests and communication styles. That was why I'd decided to write my book exclusively in the space that provided those reminders.

Although persuaded by my account, the lady was not pleased by it. She claimed, rightly, that the ability to choose an ideal production environment didn't apply to her as it had to me. Her team had never been in a position to control which working space it would get at client headquarters. That was always the client's prerogative. "Besides," she complained, "most of these buildings don't even *have* a glass-walled conference room; so just knowing why those rooms work out well doesn't really help me." I could understand her frustration. For most people, recognizing how the influence process functions in a particular situation isn't sufficient; they also want to know how to harness the recognition. She left our conversation disappointed—but not defeated, it turned out.

Months later, she called in an upbeat mood to tell me about the "great success" of a new quality-enhancement tactic she had been trying. It emerged during a discussion with her staffers when she'd mentioned my claim that getting visual access to a client's employees while developing programs for them could improve the process. Her team's challenge then became finding a way to give themselves continuous low-level exposure to those employees, even when operating in a closed-up conference room. The youngest of her staff hit on a solution that was easy to implement and has since proven effective. Before traveling to any working meeting, the team now downloads photos of program-eligible employees from the client's website and internal publications. They then enlarge the pictures, put them on big poster boards, and lean them against the walls in whichever conference room they work. The clients reportedly love the idea because they appreciate "the personalized touch" the consultants bring to the job.

Notice that because the manager and her team structure the cues of their production environments *before* they begin working in them, they are engaging in what is as much an act of pre-suasion as any we've treated in this book. The only difference is that they've chosen themselves, rather than others, as their targets.

During the rest of her phone report, I recognized that the manager and her team were treating the undertaking as a learning process, perfecting the tactic as they go. They believe they've found that action shots of employees at work produce better results for the program design team than simple headshots. Even more impressive is the clever way in which they've taken a piece of psychological information—that background cues in one's physical environment can guide how one thinks there—and employed it to generate a desired effect. Most impressively, they haven't allowed themselves to be disadvantaged by an existing reality that relegates them to task environments with suboptimal cues and associations. Instead, they've changed that reality by infusing their task environments with more helpful varieties that automatically activate a preferred way of responding.[57]

We can do the same. Why not? The rewards stand to be great, and there are two attractive options for accomplishing this kind of synchronizing cues with goals. We can follow the lead of the design team and alter key components of our external self-persuasive geography. Or we can alter key components of our internal self-persuasive geography. We've already covered the former; so let's turn to the latter.

WHAT'S ALREADY IN US

It's easy for some feature of the outside world to redirect our attention to an inner feature—to a particular attitude, belief, trait, memory, or sensation. As I've reported, there are certain consequential effects of such a shift in focus: within that moment, we are more likely to grant the focal factor importance, assign it causal status, and undertake action associated with it.

Have you ever attended an arts performance disturbed by another audience member's loud coughs? In addition to the distracting noise, there's another reason that performers of all sorts—stage actors, singers, musicians, dancers—hate the sound of even one cough: it can become contagious. Although there is solid scientific proof of this point, the most dramatic testament comes from the ranks of the artists. The author and playwright Robert Ardrey described how the offensive sequence operates in a theater: "One cougher begins his horrid work in an audience, and the cough spreads until the house is in bedlam, the actors in a rage, and the playwright in retreat to the nearest saloon."

This kind of contagion isn't confined to gatherings of playgoers. In one case, two hundred attendees at a newspaper editorial writers' dinner were overcome by coughing fits after the problem began in one corner of the room and spread so pervasively that officials had to evacuate everyone, including the attorney general of the United States at the time, Janet Reno. Despite rigorous testing of the room, no physical cause for the coughing spasms could be found. Every year, thousands of similar incidents, involving sundry symptoms besides coughing, take place around the world. Consider a few representative examples:

- In Austria, the news media reported several sightings of a poisonous variety of spider whose bite produced a combination of headache and nausea. Residents flooded hospitals certain that they had been bitten. Those who were wrong outnumbered those who were right by 4,000 percent.

- When a Tennessee high school teacher reported that she smelled gas in her classroom and felt dizzy and nauseous, an array of individuals—including students, other teachers, and staff—started experiencing the same symptoms. A hundred people from the school went to hospital emergency rooms that day with symptoms associated with the gas leak, as did seventy-one more when the school reopened five days later. No gas leak was found on either day—or ever.

- Citizens of two small Canadian towns located near oil refineries learned from an epidemiological study that cancer rates in their communities were 25 percent higher than normal, which led residents to begin perceiving escalations in a variety of health problems associated with exposure to toxic chemicals. However, the validity of these perceptions was undercut when the study's authors issued a retraction months later. The elevated incidence of cancer in the communities had initially been reported in error due to a statistical miscalculation.

- In Germany, audience members listening to a lecture on dermatological conditions typically associated with itchy skin immediately felt skin irritations of their own and began scratching themselves at an increased rate.

This last example offers the best indication of what's going on, as it seems akin to the well-known occurrence of "medical student syndrome." Research shows that 70 percent to 80 percent of all medical students are afflicted by this disorder, in which they experience the symptoms of whatever disease they happen to be learning about at the time and become convinced that they have contracted it. Warnings by their professors to anticipate the phenomenon don't seem to make a difference; students nonetheless perceive their symptoms as alarmingly real, even when experienced serially with each new "disease of the week." An explanation that has long been known to medical professionals tells us why. As the physician George Lincoln Walton wrote in 1908:

"Medical instructors are continually consulted by students who fear that they have the diseases they are studying. The knowledge that pneumonia produces pain in a certain spot leads to a *concentration of attention upon that region* [italics added], which causes any sensation there to give alarm. The mere knowledge of the location of the appendix transforms the most harmless sensations in that region into symptoms of serious menace."[58]

What are the implications for achieving effective influence—in this case effective self-influence? Lying in low-level wait within each of us are units of experience that can be given sudden standing and force if we just divert our attention to them. There are the constituents of a cough in all of us, and we can activate them by concentrating on the upper half of the lungs, where coughs start. Try it; you'll see. The same applies to the constituents of dizziness, nausea, or headache, which we can activate by focusing on a spot in the middle of the brain or at the top of the stomach or just above the eyes, respectively. But those units of experience waiting within us also include advantageous attitudes, productive traits, and useful capacities that we can energize by merely channeling attention to *them* instead.

Let's explore how that might work for our most coveted unit of experience: felt happiness. Although cherished for its own sake, happiness provides an additional benefit. It doesn't just flow from favorable life circumstances, it also creates them—including higher levels of physical health, psychological well-being, and even general success. There's good justification, then, for determining how to increase our joyfulness through self-influence. But to do so, first we have to unravel a mystery from the arena of happiness studies.[59]

The Positivity Paradox

Suppose that following an extensive physical checkup, your doctor returned to the examination room conveying undeniable news of a medical condition that will impair your health in multiple ways. Its relentless advance will erode your ability to see, hear, and think clearly. Your enjoyment of food will be undercut by the combination of a dulled sense of taste and a compromised digestive system that will limit your dietary choices to mostly bland options. You'll lose access to many of your favorite activities as the condition saps your energy and strength, eventually making you unable to drive or even to walk on your own. You'll become increasingly vulnerable to an array of other afflictions, such as coronary heart disease, stroke, atherosclerosis, pneumonia, arthritis, and diabetes.

You don't have to be a health professional to identify this progressive medical condition. It's the process of growing old. The undesirable outcomes of aging vary from person to person, but, on average, elderly individuals experience significant losses in both physical and mental functioning. Yet they don't let the declines undermine their happiness. In fact—and here's the paradox—old age produces the opposite result: the elderly feel happier than they did when younger, stronger, and healthier. The question of why this paradox exists has intrigued camps of lifespan researchers for decades. After considering several possibilities, one set of investigators, led by the psychologist Laura Carstensen, hit upon a surprising answer: when it comes to dealing with all the negativity in their lives, seniors have decided that they just don't have time for it, literally.

They've come to desire a time of emotional contentment for their remaining years, and they take deliberate steps to achieve it—something they accomplish by mastering the geography of self-influence. The elderly go more frequently and fully to the locations inside and outside themselves populated by mood-lifting personal experiences. To a greater extent than younger individuals, seniors recall *positive* memories, entertain *pleasant* thoughts, seek out and retain *favorable* information, search for and gaze at *happy* faces, and focus on the *upsides* of their consumer products.

Notice that they route their travels to these sunny locales through a highly effective mental maneuver we've encountered before: they focus their *attentions* on those spots. Indeed, the seniors with the best "attention management" skills (those good at orienting to and staying fixed on positive material) show the greatest mood enhancement. Those with poor such skills, however, can't use strong attentional control to extricate themselves from their tribulations. They are the ones who experience mood degeneration as they age. I'd bet that they are also the ones who account for the misguided stereotype of the elderly as irascible and sour—because the grumpy are just more conspicuous than the contented.

I once asked Professor Carstensen how she first got the idea that many elderly have decided to make the most of their remaining days by concentrating on the positive over the negative. She reported having interviewed a pair of sisters living in a senior home and asking them how they dealt with various negative events—for example, the sickness and death they witnessed regularly all around them. They replied in unison, "Oh, we don't have time for worrying about that." She recalled being puzzled by the answer because, as retirees with no jobs, housekeeping tasks, or family responsibilities, they had nothing *but* time in their days. Then, with an insight that launched her influential thinking on the topic of life span motivation, Carstensen recognized that the "time" the sisters referred to wasn't the amount available to them in any one day but in the rest of their lives. From that perspective, allocating much of their remaining time to unpleasant events didn't make sense to the ladies.[60]

What about the rest of us, though? Must we wait for advanced age to bring about a happy outlook on life? According to research in the field of positive psychology, no. But we do have to alter our tactics to be more like seniors'. Luckily for us, someone has already prepared a list of ways to go about it pre-suasively.

Dr. Sonja Lyubomirsky is not the first researcher to study happiness. Yet, in my view, she has made noteworthy contributions to the subject by choosing to investigate a key question more systematically than anyone else. It's not the conceptual one you might think: "What are the factors associated with happiness?" Instead, it's a procedural one: "Which specific activities can we perform to increase our happiness?" As a child, Lyubomirsky came to the United States as part of a family of Russian immigrants who, in the midst of meager economic circumstances, had to deal with the relentless additional problems of fitting into an unfamiliar and sometimes challenging culture. At the same time, this new life brought many favorable and gratifying features. Looking back on those days, she wondered what actions family members could have taken to disempower the dispiriting emotions in favor of the uplifting ones.

"It wasn't all bleak," she wrote in her 2013 book, *The Myths of Happiness*, "but if I knew then what I know now, my family would have been better positioned to make the best of it." That statement made me curious to know what she does *know now* on the matter. I phoned and asked what she could say with scientific confidence about the steps people can take to make their lives better, emotionally. Her answer offered good news and bad news to anyone interested in securing a gladness upgrade.

On the one hand, she specified a set of manageable activities that reliably increase personal happiness. Several of them—including the top three on her list—require nothing more than a pre-suasive refocusing of attention:

1. Count your blessings and gratitudes at the start of every day, and then give yourself concentrated time with them by writing them down.
2. Cultivate optimism by choosing beforehand to look on the bright side of situations, events, and future possibilities.
3. Negate the negative by deliberately limiting time spent dwelling on problems or on unhealthy comparisons with others.

There's even an iPhone app called Live Happy that helps users engage in certain of these activities, and their greater happiness correlates with frequent use.

On the other hand, the process requires consistent work. "You can make yourself happier just like you can make yourself lose weight," Dr. Lyubomirsky assured me. "But like eating differently and going to the gym faithfully, you have to put in the effort every day. You have to stay with it." That last comment seemed instructive about how the elderly have found happiness. They don't treat the most hospitable places of their inner geographies the way visitors or sightseers would. Instead, they've elected to *stay* in those vicinities mentally. They've relocated to them psychologically for the same reason they might move physically to Florida or Arizona: for the warming climates they encounter every morning.

When I asked Dr. Lyubomirsky why, before attaining senior status, most people have to work so hard at becoming happier, she said her team hadn't uncovered that answer yet. But I think it might be revealed already in the research of Professor Carstensen, who, you'll recall, found that the elderly have decided to prioritize emotional contentment as a main life goal and, therefore, to turn their attentions systematically toward the positive. She also found that younger individuals have different primary life goals that include learning, developing, and striving for achievement. Accomplishing those objectives requires a special openness to discomforting elements: demanding tasks, contrary points of view, unfamiliar people, and owning mistakes or failures. Any other approach would be maladaptive.

It makes sense, then, that in early and middle age, it can be so hard to turn our minds away from tribulations. To serve our principal aims at those times, we need to be receptive to the real presence of negatives in order to learn from and deal with them. The problem arises when we allow ourselves to become mired in the emotions they generate; when we let them lock us into an ever-cycling loop of negativity. There's where Dr. Lyubomirsky's activities list can be so helpful. Even if we're not ready to take up full-time residence in our most balmy psychological sites, we can use those attention-shifting activities to visit regularly and break the sieges of winter.[61]

The field of happiness studies has shown us that relatively simple attention-based tactics can help manage our emotional states. Can we use similar methods to manage other desirable states, such as those involving personal achievement and professional success?

When I first went to graduate school, I was among an incoming class of six students who had been recruited as part of an established social psychology doctoral program. A sweet guy named Alan Chaikin inspired early awe in the rest of us because word had spread of his remarkable achievement on the Graduate Record Examination (GRE)—the standardized test all students have to take before applying to most graduate programs. He scored in the top 1 percent of all test takers around the world in each of the three sections of the exam: verbal aptitude, mathematical proficiency, and analytical reasoning. Moreover, he scored in the top 1 percent of all psychology students in knowledge of *that* subject. Some of us had hit such scores on one or two of the sections, but rarely three and never all four. So we were ready to be consistently surprised by the level and range of Alan's intellect. And indeed we were, although not in the manner we'd expected.

Alan was a smart man. But it became apparent after a while that he wasn't any smarter than the rest of us, in a general sense. He wasn't any better at generating good ideas or spotting flawed arguments or making perceptive comments or offering clarifying insights. What he was better at was taking standardized tests—in particular the Graduate Record Exam. I shared an office with him during our first year and grew close enough to him to ask how he had done so stunningly well compared with the rest of our class. He laughed, but when I assured him it was a serious question, he told me without hesitation that he thought his relative success had to do with two main differentiators.

First, he was a speed reader. He had taken a course the year before that taught him how to move rapidly through written material without missing its important features. That gave him a sizable advantage on the GRE because, at the time, it was scored in terms of the raw number of items a student answered correctly. Alan realized that by harnessing his speed-reading skills, he could zip through all of the large set of items in any given section of the test and, on a first pass, immediately answer each whose solution was simple or already known to him. After piling up every easy point this way, he could then go back and address the tougher items. Other students would almost always advance from one item to the next, bogged down in the difficult ones likely to carry the twin penalties of producing incorrect answers and preventing contact with easier questions they would then never reach before time ran out. Most standardized tests, including the GRE, have since been redesigned in ways that no longer allow Alan's speed-reading technique to provide a competitive edge. Hence, it won't benefit current test takers.

But that's not the case for his other (pre-suasive) tactic. Alan told me that just prior to taking any standardized exam, he'd spend systematic time "getting psyched up" for it. He described a set of activities that could have come from a modified version of Dr. Lyubomirsky's list. He didn't take up the minutes before the exam room doors opened as I always had: notes in hand, trying to cram every piece of information I was unsteady about into my brain. He knew, he said, that focusing on material that was still vexing him would only elevate his anxieties. Instead, he spent that crucial time consciously calming his fears and simultaneously building his confidence by reviewing his past academic successes and enumerating his genuine strengths. Much of his test-taking prowess, he was convinced, stemmed from the resultant combination of diminished fear and bolstered confidence: "You can't think straight when you're scared," he reminded me, "plus, you're much more persistent when you're confident in your abilities."

I was struck that he could create an ideal state of mind for himself not just because he understood where, precisely, to focus his attention but also because as a savvy moment maker, he understood how to do it presuasively immediately before the test. So Alan *was* smarter than the rest of us in a meaningful way. His was a particular type of smart: a kind of tactical intelligence that allowed him to turn common general knowledge—for example, that fear worsens test takers' performance but earned confidence improves it—into specific applications with desirable outcomes. That's a useful sort of intelligence. Let's follow Alan's lead and see how we can do the same—this time to move others rather than ourselves toward desired outcomes.[62]

WHAT'S ALREADY IN THEM

Imagine yourself as a regional school superintendent in the following predicament: your district is applying for a large federal grant that would fund upgrading your outmoded science labs, equipment, and classrooms. But to have a chance of winning the award, you have to provide evidence that the high schools under your supervision have made recent progress in readying women students for STEM (science, technology, engineering, and mathematics) careers. A successful application would require a documented increase, compared with last year, in your female students' scores on the mathematics section of a standardized test that all high school seniors must take.

You are worried. Despite your best efforts in recent years—recruiting more women science and math teachers, making sure that information about STEM careers and scholarships are available to the girls as well as the boys—you've seen no increase in the female students' math scores on that standardized test. Hoping for the best, you prepare to give the crucial exam at your district's high schools in the same way you have in the past, which involves the following steps:

1. The entire senior class takes the exam simultaneously. Because all the test takers can't fit into a single room at their schools, they are assigned to one of two big rooms based on the first letter of their last names: *A* through *L* in one room; *M* through *Z* in the other.
2. In each room, the exam is monitored by several teachers chosen through a lottery drawing.
3. For ten minutes before the start of the exam, students are instructed to collect their thoughts and anticipate how they'll handle any difficult material they think might appear on the test.
4. At the test's outset, students are required to record their name, ID number, and gender.

Although each of these practices is commonly employed in mass testing programs, it would be a mistake for you to undertake any of them. Why? Because of a piece of common knowledge that you've heard your schools' guidance counselors repeat: there is a societal stereotype, which many girls believe, that women aren't as good at math as men are.

Research has demonstrated that almost anything you do that causes women to focus up front on this belief reduces their math performance in several ways. It increases their anxiety, which interferes with their ability to remember what they know; it diverts their attention from the test itself, making them more likely to miss vital information; and it leads them to attribute difficulty with an advanced problem to an inherent personal deficit rather than to the complexity of the solution, which makes them give up too soon.

All four of your pretest procedures will likely intensify the unsettling initial focus among your women students. Fortunately, there is an easy, research-based fix for each.

1. Assign test takers to a room on the basis of a relevant factor (their gender), not an irrelevant one (the first letter of their last names). Why? When girls are taking a math test in the same room as boys, they are more likely to be reminded of the mathematics-and-gender stereotype. Thus, college women solving math problems in a room along with college men score worse than in a room with only other women. Notably, this drop in performance doesn't occur on tests of verbal ability, because there is no societal stereotype suggesting that women's verbal capacities are inferior to men's.

2. Don't assign teachers randomly to monitor the tests. Assign them tactically, on the basis of gender and teaching specialty. Girls' monitors should be female science and mathematics teachers. Why? Evidence that other women have defied the stereotype deflates the stereotype's impact. Thus, women students solve significantly more mathematics test problems, even the most difficult ones, immediately after being exposed to instances of successful women in science- and math-related fields, including the women administering the test.

3. Eliminate the ten-minute period when students collect their thoughts about how to respond to the test items likely to give them trouble, because to focus on the daunting aspects of the task will undercut their success. Instead, ask the girls to pick a personal value of importance to them (such as maintaining relationships with friends or helping others) and to write down why they find that value important. Why? This sort of "self-affirmation" procedure directs initial attention to an interpersonal strength and reduces the effects of threatening stereotypes. In one university physics class, women students who engaged in such a self-affirmation exercise just twice—once at the outset and once in the middle of the semester—scored better on the course's math-intensive examinations by a full letter grade.

4. Do not instruct students to record their gender at the start of the math exam, as that will likely remind female test takers of the mathematics-and-gender stereotype. In its place, ask students to record their year in school, which in your sample would always be "graduating senior." Why? In keeping with the power of mere attention shifts, that change will supplant a pre-suasive focus on a perceived academic shortcoming with a pre-suasive focus on a perceived academic accomplishment. When such a procedure has been tried, it has eliminated women test takers' math performance deficits.

Of all the demonstrations of how steering attention from one feature of a person's inner geography to another can affect performance, I have a clear favorite: besides the belief that women don't do well in math, there is the belief that Asians do. Prior to a mathematics test, researchers asked some Asian American women students to record their gender; others were asked to record their ethnicity. Compared with a sample of Asian American women students who weren't asked to record either characteristic, those who were reminded of their gender scored worse, while those reminded of their ethnicity scored better.[63]

At one level, certain of the pre-suasive effects I've described in this chapter seem hard to believe: that just sitting at a particular desk before beginning to write made me write better; that adorning a conference room with selected photos prior to a meeting led to higher-quality work; that having women students first write about a seemingly unrelated personal value increased their physics grades; and that merely asking Asian American women to record their gender at the start of a mathematics test damaged their performance, but asking them to start by recording their ethnicity boosted their performance. The phenomena involved appear to emerge more than automatically. They seem to surface auto*magically*.

But, as with all magic, appearances don't reflect the actual mechanisms involved, the real causes at work beneath the surface. Next, we'll take a deeper look at what those mechanisms and causes are and at how they fit within the framework of pre-suasion.

The Mechanics of Pre-Suasion: Causes, Constraints, and Correctives

The basic idea of pre-suasion is that by guiding preliminary attention strategically, it's possible for a communicator to move recipients into agreement with a message before they experience it. The key is to focus them initially on concepts that are aligned associatively with the yet-to-be-encountered information. But how does this work? By what mental mechanism could a wine store manager lead shoppers to purchase more German vintages by playing German music on the store's sound system or could a job candidate cause evaluators to view her credentials as more substantial by presenting them in a weighty binder?

READIED AND WAITING

> The readiness is all.
>
> —William Shakespeare, *Hamlet*, act 5, scene 2

The answer has to do with a rather underappreciated characteristic of mental activity: its elements don't just fire when ready; they fire when *readied*. After we attend to a specific concept, those concepts closely linked to it enjoy a privileged moment within our minds, acquiring influence that nonlinked concepts simply can't match. That is so for a pair of reasons. First, once an opener concept (German music, weight) receives our attention, closely associated secondary concepts (German wine, substance) become more accessible in consciousness, which greatly improves the chance that we will attend and respond to the linked concepts. This newly enhanced standing in consciousness elevates their capacity to color our perceptions, orient our thinking, affect our motivations, and thereby change our relevant behavior. Second, at the same time, concepts not linked to the opener are suppressed in consciousness, making them less likely than before to receive our attention and gain influence. Rather than being readied for action, they get decommissioned temporarily.

This mechanism, in which an opened secondary concept becomes more cognitively accessible, appears to account for the consequences of a controversial relatively recent phenomenon: video game participation. We know from considerable research that playing violent video games incites immediate forms of antisocial behavior. For instance, such games make players more likely to deliver loud blasts of noise into the ears of someone who has annoyed them. The reason? The games plant aggression-related thoughts in players' heads, and the resulting easy contact with those thoughts provokes aggressiveness.

A tellingly similar but mirror-image effect occurs after participating in *prosocial* video games—those that call for protecting, rescuing, or assisting characters in the game. Studies have found that after playing such games, players became more willing to help clean up a spill, volunteer their time, and even intervene in a harassment situation involving a young woman and her ex-boyfriend. Moreover, this helpfulness is the direct result of participants' easy access to a range of prosocial thoughts that the games install in consciousness. In an interesting twist, newer research shows that sometimes violent video game play can decrease later aggressive behavior, provided that the participants have to cooperate with one another in the game to destroy an enemy. Additional details of the new research fit the accessibility account: playing a game cooperatively, even one with violent content, suppresses aggressive thoughts.[64]

Remaining Questions. Surprising Answers

Useful implications of this basic mechanism of pre-suasion come from research answering three additional questions about the reach of the process.

How soon? The first concerns its primitiveness. We've seen that closely linked associations can produce impressive pre-suasive effects. We learned, for example, that visitors steered to a furniture store website with fluffy clouds in the background of its landing page preferred *comfortable* sofas—because fluffiness and comfort were related in their previous experience. How early in life can we expect an opener to create such a privileged moment? Consider the results of a study designed to stimulate helpfulness in subjects who were shown a series of photographs that included a pair of individuals standing close together. The experimenters predicted correctly that because togetherness and helpfulness are linked in people's minds, observers of these photos would then become especially helpful. Indeed, compared with other subjects who'd seen photographs of two individuals standing apart or of one person alone, those shown the togetherness images were three times more likely to assist the researcher in picking up some items she "accidently" dropped.

Although the behavior in question—helpfulness—was different, this demonstration of pre-suasion seems consistent with data we've already reviewed showing that routing initial attention to a depiction of fluffy clouds leads to a preference for comfortable furniture, and that routing it to a depiction of a runner winning a race leads to more workplace achievement, and so on. Two elements of the togetherness experiment strike me as newly instructive, though.

The first got me to whistle under my breath when I read it: the study's subjects, whose helpfulness tripled, were eighteen months old—hardly able to talk, barely able to review or reflect or reason. Yet the mechanism involved is so fundamental to human functioning that even these infants were powerfully mobilized by it.

Second, its effect on them was spontaneous. Prior exposure to the idea of togetherness sent them rapidly to the researcher's aid with no prodding or request required. (Foreshadowing alert: we'll see in chapters 11 and 12 that notions of togetherness have a large and automatic impact on important forms of *adult* responding as well. In one set of studies, giving people "cues of togetherness" increased their enjoyment of working simultaneously on a task, which led to greater persistence and better performance. Thus, when unity is made focal, all kinds of desirable concepts besides helpfulness are readied for action.)

How far? There's a second question that, if answered confidently, would help us gauge the scope of pre-suasive processes. It concerns the strength of the connections involved: Can any link between two concepts, no matter how distant or tenuous, trigger a privileged moment for the second after the first has been brought to mind? No. There's an important limit to pre-suasive effects. Attention to the first concept readies the second for influence in proportion to the degree of association between the two.

I experienced this personally several years ago when I embarked on a program of research designed to discourage littering in public places. Even though littering is not the worst of environmental sins, it's not trivial, either. Besides the aesthetic damage it does to the environment and the health threats it creates through water pollution, fire hazards, and insect infestations, its worldwide cleanup operations cost billions of dollars annually. My research team and I were convinced that one good way to get people to refrain from littering would be to focus their attention on the social norm against littering. But we wondered what the effect on littering would be if we used, as openers, other social norms distant by varying amounts from the anti-littering norm.

Discovering the answer wasn't hard to arrange. A preliminary survey revealed three social norms that people rated as *close to*, *moderately far from*, and *far from* the norm against littering. They were, respectively, the norms for recycling, for turning off lights to conserve energy at home, and for voting. The next step was much more interesting. We went to a public library parking lot and put a handbill on the windshield of each car. At random, the vehicles got a handbill with one of four messages: (1) against littering, (2) for recycling, (3) for turning off lights, and (4) for voting. As a control-group communication, we included a fifth handbill that contained a message that didn't refer to any social norm; it promoted the local arts museum. When the owners returned to their cars and read a handbill, we watched to see if they dropped them on the ground.

The behavior pattern we observed could not have been clearer. A message focusing people specifically on the anti-littering norm best equipped them to resist the tendency to litter. But directing their attention to opener concepts progressively distant from the anti-littering norm made them less able, at each remove, to resist that impulse. Just as these results are straightforward, so are their implications for optimal pre-suasion: the strength of the association between an opener concept and a related concept will determine the strength of the pre-suasive effect. Therefore, an aspiring pre-suader wishing to prompt an action (helping, let's say) should find a concept already associated strongly and positively with the action (togetherness would be a good choice) and bring that concept to mind in potential helpers just before requesting their aid.[65]

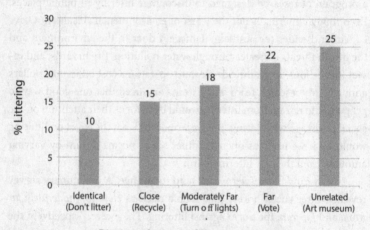

Distance of message from the anti-littering norm

Closer association, cleaner location. The stronger the link between a handbill message and the norm against littering, the less littering there was. *Courtesy of Robert Cialdini and the American Psychological Association*

How manufacturable? But there is another approach that doesn't require finding a strong existing connection. In fact, it doesn't require an existing connection at all. Rather, it involves *creating* a connection from scratch. Advertisers have been using the tactic for more than a century: they present something that attracts their target audience—a beautiful vista, a good-looking model, a popular celebrity—and then link it to the product through nothing more than a simultaneous presence inside the ad. There, observers of advertisers' handiwork might experience—and, indeed, have experienced—a connection between Tiger Woods and Buick; Beyoncé and Pepsi; Brad Pitt and Chanel No. 5; or (unsettlingly to me) Bob Dylan and Victoria's Secret. The hope, of course, is that viewers' attraction to the celebrity will transfer to the product by virtue of the now-extant connection.

Transfer of attraction. Advertisers know that linking their products to popular celebrities makes the products more popular. *Splash News/Newscom; Francis Dean/ Deanpictures/Newscom*

There is little need to belabor the advertising industry's use of this approach. Almost everybody is aware of what its practitioners are attempting. But besides the fact that the device works nonetheless, the take-away here is that an effective linkage between concepts doesn't have to be located in prevailing reality. It can be *constructed*. The concepts only have to be experienced as linked directly in some way for the subsequent presentation of one to prepare the other for pertinent action. Recall that for Pavlov's dogs, there was no natural connection between the sound of a bell and food; indeed, there was no link of any sort until the two were experienced as occurring together. After enough of these pairings had strengthened the connection, ringing the bell spontaneously readied the animals (via salivation) for the act of eating.

The evidence is overwhelming that, like Pavlov's dogs, we can be susceptible to such strategically fashioned pairings and just as clueless about our susceptibility. For instance, to the delight of advertisers, simply superimposing a brand of Belgian beer five times on pictures of pleasant activities such as sailing, waterskiing, and cuddling increased viewers' positive feelings toward the beer. Similarly, superimposing a brand of mouthwash on pictures of beautiful nature scenes six times led observers to feel more favorable toward the brand right away and *still* more favorable three weeks afterward. Subliminally exposing thirsty people eight times to pictures of happy (versus angry) faces just before having them taste a new soft drink caused them to consume more of the beverage and to be willing to pay three times more for it in the store. In none of these studies were the participants aware that they'd been influenced by the pairings.[66]

If/When-Then Plans

The recognition that pre-suasive associations are manufacturable can lead us to much personal profit, even if we are not savvy advertising copywriters or renowned Russian scientists. From time to time we all set objectives for ourselves, targets to hit, standards to meet and exceed. But too often, our hopes go unrealized as we fail to reach the goals. There's a well-studied reason for the difficulty: although generating an intention is important, that process alone isn't enough to get us to take all the steps necessary to achieve a goal. Within health, for instance, we translate our good intentions into *any* type of active step only about half the time. The disappointing success rates have been traced to a pair of failings. First, besides sometimes forgetting about an intention—let's say, to exercise more—we frequently don't recognize opportune moments or circumstances for healthy behaviors, such as taking the stairs rather than the elevator. Second, we are often derailed from goal strivings by factors—such as especially busy days—that distract us from our purpose.

Fortunately, there is a category of strategic self-statements that can overcome these problems pre-suasively. The statements have various names in scholarly usage, but I'm going to call them *if/when-then plans*. They are designed to help us achieve a goal by readying us (1) to register certain cues in settings where we can further our goal, and (2) to take an appropriate action spurred by the cues and consistent with the goal. Let's say that we aim to lose weight. An if/when-then plan might be "*If/when,* after my business lunches, the server asks if I'd like to have dessert, *then* I will order mint tea." Other goals can also be effectively achieved by using these plans. When epilepsy sufferers who were having trouble staying on their medication schedules were asked to formulate an if/when-then plan—for example, "*When* it is eight in the morning, and I finish brushing my teeth, *then* I will take my prescribed pill dose"—adherence rose from 55 percent to 79 percent.

In one particularly impressive demonstration, hospitalized opiate drug addicts undergoing withdrawal were urged to prepare an employment history by the end of the day to help them get a job after their release. Some were asked to form an if/when-then plan for compiling the history, whereas those in the control group were not asked to do so. A relevant if/when-then plan might be, "*If/when* lunch is over and space has become available at the lunchroom table, *then* I will start writing my employment history there." By day's end, not one person in the control group had performed the task, which might not seem surprising—after all, these were drug addicts in the process of opiate withdrawal! Yet at the end of the same day, 80 percent of those in the relevant if/when-then treatment group had turned in a completed job résumé.

Additionally impressive is the extent to which if/when-then plans are superior to simple intention statements or action plans such as "I intend to lose five pounds this month" or "I plan to lose weight by cutting down on sweets." Merely stating an intention to reach a goal or even forming an ordinary action plan is considerably less likely to succeed. There are good reasons for the superiority of if/when-then plans: the specific sequencing of elements within the plans can help us defeat the traditional enemies of goal achievement. The "if/when-then" wording is designed to put us on high alert for a particular time or circumstance when a productive action could be performed. We become prepared, first, to *notice* the favorable time or circumstance and, second, to *associate* it automatically and directly with desired conduct. Noteworthy is the self-tailored nature of this pre-suasive process. We get to install in ourselves heightened vigilance for certain cues that we have targeted previously, and we get to employ a strong association that we have constructed previously between those cues and a beneficial step toward our goal.[67]

There are certain strongly motivating concepts that communicators *don't* initially need to make ready to influence an audience through pre-suasion. These concepts have been previously primed for influence. By analogy, think of almost any computer program you use. It is likely to contain transfer links (to desired sources of information) that you need to click twice: once to ready the link and once to launch it. But the program also likely contains links that launch with just one click, because they have already been readied—that is, hyperlinked to the desired information. The effect of hyperlinking to a location has been labeled by Web browser engineers as "prefetching it." Just as the designers of our information technology software have installed rapid access to particular sources of information within our computers' programming, the designers of our lives—parents, teachers, leaders, and, eventually, we ourselves— have done the same within our mental programming. These prefetched sources of information have already been put on continuing "standby" in consciousness so that only a single reminder cue (click) will launch them into action.

This recognition highlights the potential usefulness of if/when-then plans for accomplishing our main goals. These goals exist as prefetched sources of information and direction that have been placed on standby, waiting to be launched into operation by cues that remind us of them. Notice again that the form of if/when-then plans puts the specification of those reminders in our own hands so that we are likely to encounter them at a time and under a set of circumstances that work well for us ("when it is eight in the morning, and I finish brushing my teeth . . ."). Even seemingly

intractable bad habits can be improved as a result. Chronically unsuccessful dieters eat fewer high-calorie foods and lose more weight after
forming if/when-then plans such as "*If/when* I see chocolate displayed in
the supermarket, *then* I will think of my diet." Especially for goals we are
highly committed to reaching, we'd be foolish not to take advantage of the
pre-suasive leverage that if/when-then plans can provide.[68]

CORRECTION: MINDING THE GAP

To this point, we've covered a lot of data showing that (1) what is more
accessible in mind becomes more probable in action, and (2) this accessibility is influenced by the informational cues around us and by our raw
associations to them. The section on if/when-then plans and the chapter
on the geography of influence provided welcome evidence that we can
derive higher-order benefits from these elementary processes. We can do
so by engineering into our everyday settings cues to actions associated
strongly with our greater goals.

But is this sort of tactical alignment with primitive mental mechanisms our only protection against their potential downsides? After all, it's
not possible to frontload every situation we face with cues likely to take
us in desirable directions. We frequently enter physical environments and
social interactions for the first time. We often get carefully crafted persuasion appeals whose components we can't anticipate. In those cases, will we
be leaves in the wind, blown here and there by powerful associations to
the cues we happen to encounter? The answer depends on whether we've
noticed the breeze.

It stands to reason that if our preferences and choices can be swayed
unduly—at times by cues as immaterial as whether a business has a slogan
that rhymes, or a name that's similar to ours, or an ad featuring a beautiful
vista, or a stock market symbol that's easy to pronounce—we'd want to
be able to correct for those biases in our transactions with that business.
Doubtless, we'd want to correct for such influences generally, whenever
they stood to bias our judgments and dealings. There *is* some encouraging
news in this regard. Often, simply recognizing these undesired influences

will be enough to block their effects. That recognition can come to us in more than one way.

Mere Reminders

We all know that when we are in a good mood, the people and items around us seem better somehow. After passersby on the street received a mood-enhancing free gift of high-quality writing paper, they rated their cars and TVs as working better. We also know that fine weather lifts our spirits and thus can produce unwarranted judgments of this type. One study showed that a man who complimented young women and then asked for their phone numbers to arrange a date was considerably more successful when he asked on a sunny morning versus a cloudy morning (22.4 percent and 13.9 percent success rates, respectively).

Sunny days don't just inflate how we feel about what we own and the people we meet; they do the same for how we feel about our lives. Individuals surveyed by phone reported themselves 20 percent more satisfied with their existence—as a whole—when asked on sunny days compared with rainy days. Hence, the unappealing leaf-in-the-wind (and, it appears, rain) label looks to fit our species lamentably well. Fortunately, there's an optimistic side to the findings: the label's fit differed dramatically when respondents were reminded of the weather before the survey began. If the interviewer asked first, "By the way, how's the weather over there?" the sunny-versus-rainy-day effect didn't materialize at all. Simply being focused on the weather for a moment, reminded the survey participants of its potentially biasing influence and allowed them to correct their thinking accordingly. Besides the comforting evidence that we are not so slavishly subject to the pulls of primal processes, there is another implication of this particular result that's worth consideration: it took only a simple, short *question* to eliminate the bias.

In their book *The 776 Stupidest Things Ever Said*, Ross and Katherine Petras include some statements that clearly belong on that list. For example: "And, what is more, I agree with everything I have just said."— Piet Koornhoff, former South African ambassador to the United States. Another: "I've been traveling so much, I haven't had time to grow a beard."—Bob Horner, former Major League baseball player (and former student at my home university). But the authors also place in their collection a quote from Hollywood director Gregory Ratoff, who said, "Let me ask you a question, for your information."

Although the book's authors consider Ratoff's quote nonsensical, I disagree. Posing a question can provide invaluable information to its recipient. It can spur him or her to bring to mind a piece of possessed knowledge not high in consciousness at the time but that, when made focal, changes everything: for instance, the awareness that on sunny days we don't just wear dark-colored glasses but rose-colored ones as well. In the realm of self-correction mechanisms, then, we can find another source of validation for a core tenet of pre-suasion: immediate, large-scale adjustments begin frequently with practices that do little more than redirect attention.[69]

Signs of Stealthy Persuasive Intent: A Nudge Too Far

Standard product placements—the sneaky insertions of consumer products into the plotlines of movies and TV shows—have been with us for a long time. Hollywood studios have had official offices negotiating such placements, and extracting a charge, for close to a century. Likewise, television producers have been getting paid for decades by merchandisers who want to see characters depicted using their goods and services. The pay in this pay-for-play arrangement is especially high for well-liked actors or admired fictional figures. In those cases, considerable amounts of money are contracted for the right association: a popular character reaching for a Coke or driving a Lexus or eating a Snickers. The market for such fabricated linkages has burgeoned into the billions in recent years, with the majority of broadcast advertisers currently using the practice, and multiple product-placement agencies emerging to handle the business that now flows into the production of music, stage plays, and video games. So it's clear that advertisers believe that product placements, and the associations they create, work. They're right, but perhaps not always in the way they suspect.

A belief among many product-placement practitioners is that the more perceptible the constructed connection, the more effective it will be. This view stems from the seemingly inescapable logic that the prominence of a piece of information increases the chance that audience members will notice it and thereby be influenced by it. The opinion is bolstered by evidence that more prominent product placements are, in fact, more effective, as judged by the standby advertising industry measures of success: recognition and recall, which gauge memory for what was encountered. Take, for instance, the results of a study that examined the prominence of product placements in episodes of the popular TV sitcom *Seinfeld*. Just as expected, the most noticeable placements (in which the brand was both shown on camera and mentioned aloud) produced the most recognition and recall compared with less obvious placements (in which the brand name was either only heard or only seen).

But besides assessing recognition and recall, the study's authors did something that prior researchers had not done: they obtained a third measure of placement success that undercut conventional wisdom. From a list of brands, audience members indicated which ones they would be likely to choose when shopping. Guess what? It turned out that the survey respondents were *least* likely to select the products that had been inserted most prominently. It seems that the conspicuousness of the placements cued viewers to the advertisers' sly attempts to sway their preferences and caused a correction against the potential distortion. Whereas the most subtly placed brands were chosen by 47 percent of the audience, only 27 percent picked the most prominently placed ones.

People recognize that advertisers' practices can influence their judgments unduly, but it's not until they are reminded of the source of the possible bias that they act to rebalance the system. In this instance, the reminder took the form of a nudge too far—an overly exposed version of the trick (of fictionally established linkages) at play inside product placements. Noteworthy is the operative reason that the only thing necessary to trigger the correction was a reminder: it becomes evident when we deconstruct the word *remind* into its constituent parts. All that's required to arrange for people to act in accord with a piece of already-held knowledge is to get them to put their minds on it again immediately before the act—literally, to *re*mind it.[70, 71]

Sometimes the adjustments we make to counteract unwarranted influences take place without much forethought or delay. The recalibrations that occur when we are reminded of current weather conditions are a good example. Other times, the correction mechanism works much more planfully and slowly. This second kind of mechanism operates through deliberative reasoning, which can be used to overcome biases that flow from rudimentary psychological tendencies. If we go to the supermarket with the idea of purchasing healthy, nutritious, and inexpensive foods, we can neutralize the draw of heavily advertised, attractively packaged, or easy-to-reach items on the shelves by weighing our choices on the basis of caloric, nutritional, and unit-pricing information on the labels.

GAPPING THE MIND

On the other hand, compared with those natural psychological responses (to select familiar, attractively presented, easily accessed options), extensive analysis requires more time, energy, and motivation. As a consequence, its impact on our decisions is limited by the rigor it requires. If we don't have the wherewithal (time, capacity, will) to think hard about a choice, we're unlikely to deliberate deeply. When any of these requirements isn't met, we typically resort to decision-making shortcuts. This approach doesn't necessarily lead to poor outcomes, because in many situations the shortcuts allow us to choose rapidly and effectively. But in many other situations, they can send us to places we didn't want to go—at least not if we'd thought about it.

When we don't have the ability to think properly—perhaps because we are tired—we can't rely on a balanced assessment of all the pros and cons to correct for an emotionally based choice we might regret later. I once attended a conference of infomercial producers. I'd assumed that the sole reason they commonly place ads in late-hour slots was the lower broadcast fees charged at those times. I quickly learned differently. Although that started out as the main reason most such programming begins far into the night, there is a more important reason: the ads perform better then. At the tail of a long day, viewers don't have the mental energy to resist the ads' emotional triggers (likable hosts, enthusiastic studio audiences, dwindling supplies, and so on).

Infomercials aren't the only context in which mental fatigue undermines considered analysis and its accompanying potential for resistance. Sleep researchers have noted that in field tests of combat artillery units, teams that are fully rested often challenge orders to fire on hospitals or other civilian targets. But after twenty-four to thirty-six sleepless hours, they often obey superiors' directives without question and become more likely to shell anything. Similarly, in criminal interrogations, even innocent suspects often can't resist interrogators' pressure for them to confess after hours of mentally exhausting questioning. That's why, although the typical interrogation lasts for less than an hour, interviews generating *false* confessions average sixteen hours.

Besides fatigue, numerous other conditions can keep people from recognizing and correcting potentially foolish tendencies. Indeed, such foolish tendencies are likely to predominate when a person is rushed, overloaded, preoccupied, indifferent, stressed, distracted, or, it seems, a conspiracy theorist.

The list is too long to explore in its entirety, so, let's just examine the first condition. When we are rushed, we don't have the time to take into account all of the factors at play within a decision. Instead, we are likely to rely on a lone shortcut factor to steer us. It might be the belief that, when selecting among options for a purchase, we should buy the item with the largest *number* of superior features. Even though we might know that relying on this single factor could lead to mistakes, when time is short we don't have the luxury of painstakingly breaking down and assessing all the pluses and minuses.

One study showed that time limitations drastically affected how viewers of camera product reports made their preferred choices. The reports compared two brands on an array of twelve features. One brand was superior on the three most important features to consider when buying a camera: quality of the lens, mechanism, and pictures. The other brand was rated superior on eight features, but they were relatively unimportant (for example, the purchase price included a shoulder strap). When some viewers were exposed to information about the twelve features for only two seconds per feature, just 17 percent preferred the higher-quality camera. The majority opted for the brand with the greater number of unimportant advantages. When other viewers were given five seconds per feature, the pattern changed somewhat, but still only 38 percent favored the more sensible choice. It wasn't until a final set of observers was allowed *unlimited* time to consider the feature information that the pattern reversed itself, and the majority (67 percent) favored the camera with fewer but more significant advantages.

Does the idea of having insufficient time to analyze all the points of a communication remind you of how you have to respond to the rapid-fire presentation of many messages these days? Think about it for a second. Better yet, think about it for an *unlimited* time: Isn't this the way the broadcast media operate, transmitting a swift stream of information that can't be easily slowed or reversed to give us the chance to process it thoroughly? We're not able to focus on the real quality of the advertiser's case in a radio or television spot. Nor are we able to respond mindfully to a news clip of a speech by a politician. Instead, we're left to a focus on secondary features of the presentations, such as the attractiveness of the advertising spokesperson or the politician's charisma.[72]

In addition to its time-challenged character, other aspects of modern life undermine our ability (and motivation) to think in a fully reasoned way about even important decisions. The sheer amount of information today can be overwhelming—its complexity befuddling, its relentlessness depleting, its range distracting, and its prospects agitating. Couple those culprits with the concentration-disrupting alerts of devices nearly everyone now carries to deliver that input, and careful assessment's role as a ready decision-making corrective becomes sorely diminished. Thus, a communicator who channels attention to a particular concept in order to heighten audience receptivity to a forthcoming message—via the focus-based, automatic, crudely associative mechanisms of pre-suasion—won't have to worry much about the tactic being defeated by deliberation. The cavalry of deep analysis will rarely arrive to reverse the outcome because it will rarely be summoned.

A highly related question naturally arises: on which concepts, then, should an audience's attention be focused for the broadest pre-suasive effect? Our next chapters identify a set of seven.

PART 3

BEST PRACTICES: THE OPTIMIZATION OF PRE-SUASION

10

Six Main Roads to Change: Broad Boulevards as Smart Shortcuts

We've seen how it's possible to move others in our direction by saying or doing just the right thing immediately before we want them to respond:

> If we want them to buy a box of expensive chocolates, we can first arrange for them to write down a number that's much larger than the price of the chocolates.
>
> If we want them to choose a bottle of French wine, we can expose them to French background music before they decide.
>
> If we want them to agree to try an untested product, we can first inquire whether they consider themselves adventurous.
>
> If we want to convince them to select a highly popular item, we can begin by showing them a scary movie.
>
> If we want them to feel warmly toward us, we can hand them a hot drink.
>
> If we want them to be more helpful to us, we can have them look at photos of individuals standing close together.
>
> If we want them to be more achievement oriented, we can provide them with an image of a runner winning a race.
>
> If we want them to make careful assessments, we can show them a picture of Auguste Rodin's *The Thinker*.

Notice that whatever is just the right thing to say or do in a situation changes depending on what we want of others there. Arranging for them to hear a French song might get them to purchase French wine, but it isn't going to get them to become more achievement oriented or helpful. And asking if they are adventurous might get them to try an untested product, but it isn't going to make them more willing to select a highly popular item or make careful assessments. This specificity fits with the way that *successful* openers operate for a communicator. They pre-suasively channel recipients' attention only to those concepts that are associated favorably with the communicator's particular goal.

But isn't there an overarching goal common to all would-be persuaders: the goal of assent? After all, any persuasive communicator wants to spur audiences toward "Yes." Are there concepts that are aligned especially well with the broad goal of obtaining agreement? I believe so. In my book *Influence*, I argued that there are six such concepts that empower the major principles of human social influence. They are reciprocation, liking, social proof, authority, scarcity, and consistency. These principles are highly effective *general* generators of acceptance because they typically counsel people correctly regarding when to say yes to influence attempts.

To take the principle of authority as an example, people recognize that in the great majority of circumstances, they are likely to be steered to a good choice if that choice fits with the views of experts on the topic. This recognition allows them a valuable decision-making shortcut: when they encounter the presence of solid authoritative data, they can cease further deliberation and follow the lead of authorities in the matter. Therefore if a message points to authority-based evidence, the odds of persuasive success will jump.

In recognition of the mounting behavioral science evidence for pre-suasion, though, I'd like to extend my earlier contention. Let's stay with the principle of authority to illustrate the expanded point: communicators stand to be more effective by highlighting the idea of authority not just inside their message but inside the moment before their message. In this pre-suasive way, audiences will become sensitized to (and thus readied for) the coming authoritative evidence in the message, making them more likely to pay attention to it, assign it importance, and, consequently, be influenced by it.[73]

THE ROADS OFT TAKEN

If it is indeed the case that directing attention (both before and during a message) to the concepts of reciprocation, liking, social proof, authority, scarcity, and consistency can influence recipients toward assent, it makes sense for us to review and update the information on how each concept operates. Accordingly, this chapter is not designed to focus primarily on the *process* of pre-suasion. Instead, we take a step back and explore the specifics of why these six concepts possess such sweeping psychological force.

Reciprocation

People say yes to those they owe. Not always, of course—nothing in human social interaction works like that—but often enough that behavioral scientists have labeled this tendency the *rule for reciprocation*. It states that those who have given benefits to us are entitled to benefits from us in return. So valuable is it to the functional health of societies that all human cultures teach the rule from childhood and assign socially punishing names—*freeloader, user, taker, parasite*—to those who don't give back after receiving.

As a result, children respond to the rule before they are two years old. By the time they are adults, its pre-suasive power influences all aspects of their lives, including their buying patterns. In one study, shoppers at a candy store became 42 percent more likely to make a purchase if they'd received a gift piece of chocolate upon entry. According to sales figures from the retail giant Costco, other types of products—beer, cheese, frozen pizza, lipstick—get big lifts from free samples, almost all accounted for by the shoppers who accept the free offer.

Much more worrisome is the impact of the rule on the voting actions of legislators. In the United States, companies making sizable campaign contributions to lawmakers who sit on tax policy–making committees see significant reductions in their tax rates. The legislators will deny any quid pro quo. But the companies know better. And so should we.[74]

Requesters who hope to commission the pre-suasive force of the rule for reciprocation have to do something that appears daring: they have to take a chance and give first. They must begin an interaction by providing initial gifts, favors, advantages, or concessions without a formal guarantee of compensation. But because the tendency to reciprocate is so embedded in most people, the strategy frequently works better than the traditional approach to commercial exchange, in which a requester offers benefits only *after* an action has been taken: a contract signed, a purchase made, a task performed. Dutch residents who received an advance letter asking if they would take part in a long survey were much more likely to agree if the proposed payment was sent to them before they decided to participate (the money accompanied the letter) than if it was to be paid, as is normally the case, after they had participated. Similarly, hotel guests in the United States encountered a card in their rooms asking them to reuse their towels. They read in addition either that the hotel had already made a financial contribution to an environmental protection organization in the name of its guests or that it would make such a contribution after guests did reuse their towels. The before-the-act donation proved 47 percent more effective than the after-the-act one.[75]

Still, supplying resources up front without the traditional guarantee of agreed-upon compensation can be risky. Returns might not be forthcoming at adequate levels—or at all—because certain recipients might resent being given something they didn't invite, while others might not judge what they got as beneficial to them. Others (the "freeloaders" among us) might not feel compelled by the rule. It makes sense to inquire, then, if there are specific features of an initial gift or favor that increase significantly the chance that it will be returned at high levels of recompense.

There are three main features of this sort: in order to optimize the return, what we give first should be experienced as meaningful, unexpected, and customized.

Meaningful and Unexpected. The first two of these optimizing features have been shown to affect the size of tips that food servers receive. Some diners in a New Jersey restaurant were offered a piece of chocolate at the end of their meals, one per person, from a basket carried to the table by the waitress. Her tips went up 3.3 percent compared with those from guests who weren't offered chocolate. However, when other diners were invited to take two chocolates from the basket, the waitress's tips rose by 14.1 percent. What could account for the dramatic difference? For one, the second chocolate represented a meaningful increase in the size of the gift—a doubling. Plainly, *meaningful* is not the same as *expensive*, as the second chocolate cost only pennies. Providing a costly gift can often be meaningful, but costliness isn't necessary.

Of course, the receipt of two chocolates was not only twice that of one chocolate but also more unexpected. The clear-cut impact of a gift's unexpectedness became evident when the waitress tried yet a third technique. After offering guests one chocolate from her basket and turning to walk away, she unexpectedly returned to the table and offered a second chocolate to each diner. As a result, her average tip improved by 21.3 percent. There's a lesson in these multiple findings that goes well beyond informing restaurant servers of how to enrich their gratuities: requesters of various sorts can elevate the likelihood that they will receive high levels of benefit from others if they first deliver benefits viewed by the others as meaningful and unexpected. But besides these features, there's a third element in the reciprocity-optimizing triumvirate that, in my opinion, is more influential than the other two combined.

Customized. When a first favor is customized to the needs, preferences, or current circumstances of the recipient, it gains leverage. Consider as evidence what happened in a fast-food restaurant where visitors were greeted as they entered and given one of two equally priced gifts.

If the gift was not food related (a key chain), the amount they then spent increased by 12 percent compared with visitors who were greeted without being given a gift. But if the gift was food related (a cup of yogurt), their increased outlay climbed to 24 percent. From a purely economic perspective, this finding is puzzling. Giving restaurant visitors free food before they order should make them likely to purchase *less*, because they won't need to spend as much on a meal. Although the obtained (reverse) outcome doesn't make good logical sense, it makes good psycho-logical sense: Visitors went to the restaurant because they were hungry. An upfront gift of food activated not only the rule for reciprocation but a more muscular version, which states that people should feel especially obligated to reciprocate a gift designed to meet their particular needs.

If a gift, favor, or service incorporates all three features of meaningfulness, unexpectedness, and customization, it can become a formidable source of change. But might we be asking too much to expect it to make a difference in the struggle against hard-core terrorists? Perhaps not, for a pair of reasons. First, the rule for reciprocation is a cultural universal taught in all societies, including those from which terrorists spring. Second, accounts from within that struggle shed light on the singular power of favors that combine the three optimizing features.

Take the case of Abu Jandal, Osama bin Laden's former chief bodyguard, who, following his capture, was questioned in a Yemeni prison in the days after 9/11. Attempts to get him to reveal information about Al Qaeda's leadership structure appeared hopeless, as his responses consisted only of screeds against the ways of the West. But when interrogators noticed that he never ate the cookies he was served with food and learned that the man was diabetic, they did something for him that was meaningful, unexpected, and customized: At the next interrogation session, they brought him sugar-free cookies to eat with tea. According to one of those interrogators, *that* was a key turning point: "We had shown him respect, and we had done this nice thing for him. So he started talking to us instead of giving us lectures." In subsequent sessions, Jandal provided extensive data on Al Qaeda operations, as well as the names of seven of the 9/11 hijackers.

But as any veteran of the battles with terrorism knows, sometimes the way to win those battles requires winning allies to the cause. US intelligence officers in Afghanistan frequently visited rural territories to gain the assistance of tribal chiefs against the Taliban. These interactions were challenging because the leaders were often unwilling to help, owing to a dislike of Westerners, a fear of Taliban retribution, or both. On one such visit, a Central Intelligence Agency (CIA) operative noted a patriarch's exhaustion from the duties of heading his tribe and his immediate family, which included four younger wives. On the following visit, the CIA man came prepared with a fully optimized gift: four Viagra tablets, one per wife. The "potency" of this meaningful, unexpected, customized favor became manifest during the CIA agent's next trip, when the beaming leader responded with a wealth of information about Taliban movements and supply routes.[76]

Cookies as kindness. Abu Jandal's refusal to disclose information to his interrogators changed after they did him an unexpected and meaningful favor customized to his diabetic condition.
Brent Stirton/Getty Images

Liking

Back when I was infiltrating the training programs of various sales organizations, I heard an assertion made repeatedly with great confidence: "The number one rule for salespeople is to get your customer to like you." That was the case, we trainees were assured, because people say yes to those they like—something that was so undeniable that it never seemed interesting to me. What did interest me, though, was what we were told to do to arrange for customers to like us. Being friendly, attractive, and humorous were mentioned frequently in this regard. Accordingly, we were often given smiling lessons, grooming tips, and jokes to tell. But by far, two specific ways to create positive feelings got the most attention. We were instructed to highlight similarities and provide compliments. There's good reason why these two practices would be emphasized: each increases liking and assent.

Similarities. We like those who are like us. It's a tendency that's part of the human experience almost from the start: infants smile more at adults whose facial expressions match their own. And the affinity can be activated by seemingly trivial similarities that might nonetheless generate big effects. Parallels in language style (the types of words and verbal expressions conversation partners use) increase romantic attraction, relationship stability, and, somewhat amazingly, the likelihood that a hostage negotiation will end peacefully. What's more, this influence occurs even though the overlap of styles typically goes unnoticed by the conversation partners.

In addition, the consequences of the basic tendency are visible within helping decisions. People are massively more willing to help an emergency victim if they share a nationality or even a favorite sports team. The tendency also operates in educational settings. The factor that plays the largest role in the success of youth mentoring programs is the initial similarity of interests between student and mentor. But it is in the business arena where the impact on assent seems most direct. Waitresses coached to mimic the verbal style of customers doubled their tips. Negotiators coached to do the same with their opponents got significantly better final outcomes. Salespeople who mimicked the language styles and nonverbal behaviors (gestures, postures) of customers sold more of the electronic equipment they recommended.[77]

Thanks, Doctor. I feel like you really understand me.

Uncovered similarities. Even seemingly unimportant matches can lead to greater rapport. © 2012 Bizarro Comics. Distributed by King Features Syndicate, Inc.

Compliments. "I can live for two months," confessed Mark Twain, "on a good compliment." It's an apt metaphor, as compliments nourish and sustain us emotionally. They also cause us to like and benefit those who provide them; and this is true whether the praise is for our appearance, taste, personality, work habits, or intelligence. In the first of these categories, consider what happened in one hair salon when stylists complimented customers by saying, "Any hairstyle would look good on you." Their tips rose by 37 percent. Indeed, we seem so charmed by flattery that it can work on us even when it appears to have an ulterior motive. Chinese college students who received a *preprinted* flier from a clothing store saying "We're contacting you because you're fashionable and stylish" developed positive attitudes toward the store and were more likely to want to shop there. Other researchers found that individuals who worked on a computer task and received flattering task-related feedback from the computer developed more favorable feelings toward the machine, even though they were told that the feedback had been *preprogrammed* and did not reflect their actual task performance at all. Nonetheless, they became prouder of their performances after receiving this hollow form of praise.[78]

The Real Number One Rule for Salespeople. I am hesitant to disagree with knowledgeable professionals that the number one rule for salespeople is to get your customer to like you and that similarities and compliments are the best routes to that end. But I've seen research that makes me want to rethink their claims for why these statements are true. The account I heard in traditional sales training sessions always went as follows: similarities and compliments cause people to like you, and once they come to recognize that they like you, they'll want to do business with you.

Although this kind of pre-suasive process no doubt operates to some degree, I am convinced that a more influential pre-suasive mechanism is at work. Similarities and compliments cause people to feel that you like *them*, and once they come to recognize that you like them, they'll want to do business with you. That's because people trust that those who like them will try to steer them correctly. So by my lights, the number one rule for salespeople is to show customers that you genuinely like them. There's a wise adage that fits this logic well: people don't care how much you know until they know how much you care.[79]

Social Proof

In John Lennon's song "Imagine," he proposes a world without hunger, greed, possessions, or countries—one characterized by universal brotherhood, peace, and unity. It's a world different from today's and, indeed, any other day's in the long track of human history. While conceding that his vision seems that of a dreamer, he tries to convince listeners to accept it with a single follow-on fact: "But I'm not the only one."

Lennon's trust in this lone argument is a testament to the projected power of the principle of social proof. The principle asserts that people think it is *appropriate* for them to believe, feel, or do something to the extent that others, especially comparable others, are believing, feeling, or doing it. Two components of that perceived appropriateness—validity and feasibility—can drive change.

Validity. After receiving information that multiple, comparable others have responded in a particular way, that response seems more valid, more right to us, both morally and practically. As regards the first of these dimensions, when we see evidence of the increased frequency of an action, it elevates our judgments of the act's moral correctness. In one study, after learning that the majority of their peers supported the military's use of torture to gain information, 80 percent of group members found the practice more acceptable and demonstrated greater support for it in their public pronouncements and, more revealingly, their private opinions. Fortunately, besides increasing the acceptability of what might be undesirable, the responses of others can do the same for desirable behavior. Working professionals who were told that the great majority of people try to overcome their stereotypes became more resistant to stereotypes of women in their own work-related conduct.

In addition to clarifying what's right morally, social proof reduces uncertainty about what's right pragmatically. Not every time, but the crowd is usually correct about the wisdom of actions, making the popularity of an activity a stand-in for its soundness. As a result, we typically follow the lead of those around us who are like us. The upshots can be remarkable, creating simple, almost costless solutions to traditional influence challenges. Restaurant managers can increase the demand for particular dishes on their menus without the expense of upgrading the recipes with more costly ingredients, the kitchen staff with new personnel, or the menu with flowery descriptions of the selected items. They have only to label the items as "most popular" dishes. When this entirely honest yet rarely employed tactic was tried in a set of restaurants in Beijing, China, each dish became 13 percent to 20 percent more popular.

Restaurateurs aren't the only ones who can use social proof to affect food choices. Instead of bearing the cost of assembling and communicating extensive nutritional information regarding the health benefits of eating fruit, a school can lift its students' fruit intake by stating, contrary to what students think, that the majority of their schoolmates *do* try to eat fruit to be healthy. This kind of information increased the fruit consumption of Dutch high schoolers by 35 percent—even though, in classic adolescent fashion, they claimed no intention to change.

Social proof signage. Internet merchandisers aren't alone in telling us what to buy because others have done so. *Rina Piccolo Panel Cartoon used with permission of Rina Piccolo and the Cartoonist Group. All rights reserved.*

Many governments expend significant resources regulating, monitoring, and sanctioning companies that pollute our air and water; these expenditures often appear wasted on some of the offenders, who either flout the regulations altogether or are willing to pay fines that are smaller than the costs of compliance. But certain nations have developed cost-effective programs that work by firing up the (nonpolluting) engine of social proof. They initially rate the environmental performance of polluting firms within an industry and then publicize the ratings, so that all companies in that industry can see where they stand relative to their peers. The overall improvements have been dramatic—upward of 30 percent—almost all of which have come from changes made by the relatively heavy polluters, who recognized how poorly they'd been doing compared with their contemporaries.[80]

Feasibility. With a set of estimable colleagues leading the way, I once did a study to see what we could best say to get people to conserve household energy. We delivered one of four messages to their homes, once a week for a month, asking them to reduce their energy consumption. Three of the messages contained a frequently employed reason for conserving energy: the environment will benefit; or it's the socially responsible thing to do; or it will save you significant money on your next power bill. The fourth message played the social-proof card, stating (honestly) that most of your fellow community residents do try to conserve energy at home. At the end of the month, we recorded how much energy was used and learned that the social-proof-based message had generated 3.5 times as much energy savings as any of the other messages. The size of the difference surprised almost everyone associated with the study—me, for one, but also my fellow researchers, and even a sample of other home owners. The home owners, in fact, expected that the social-proof message would be least effective.

When I report on this research to utility company officials, they frequently don't trust it because of an entrenched belief that the strongest motivator of human action is economic self-interest. They say something like, "C'mon, how are we supposed to believe that telling people their neighbors are conserving is three times more effective than telling them they can cut their power bills significantly?" Although there are various possible responses to this legitimate question, there's one that's nearly always proven persuasive for me. It involves the second reason, besides validity, that social-proof information works so well: feasibility. If I inform home owners that by saving energy, they *could* also save a lot of money, it doesn't mean they would be able to make it happen. After all, I *could* reduce my next power bill to zero if I turned off all the electricity in my house and curled up on the floor in the dark for a month; but that's not something I'd reasonably do. A great strength of social-proof information is that it destroys the problem of uncertain achievability. If people learn that many others like them are conserving energy, there is little doubt as to its feasibility. It comes to seem realistic and, therefore, implementable.[81]

Authority

For most people, the way to make a message persuasive is to get its content right: to ensure that the communication possesses strong evidence, sound reasoning, good examples, and clear relevance. Although this view ("The *merit* is the message") is certainly correct to an extent, some scholars have argued that other parts of the process can be just as important. The most famous of these contentions is embodied in the assertion of the communication theorist Marshall McLuhan that "The *medium* is the message"— the idea that the channel through which information is sent is a form of consequential messaging itself, which affects how recipients experience content. In addition, persuasion scientists have pointed to compelling support for yet a third claim: "The *messenger* is the message."

Of the many types of messengers—positive, serious, humorous, emphatic, modest, critical—there is one that deserves special attention because of its deep and broad impact on audiences: the authoritative communicator. When a legitimate expert on a topic speaks, people are usually persuaded. Indeed, sometimes information becomes persuasive only because an authority is its source. This is especially true when the recipient is uncertain of what to do.

Take as evidence the results of a study in which individuals had to make a series of difficult economic decisions while hooked up to brain-scanning equipment. When they made choices on their own, related activity jumped in the areas of the brain associated with evaluating options. But when they received expert advice on any of these decisions (from a distinguished university economist), they not only followed that advice, they did so without thinking about the inherent merits of the options. Related activity in the evaluating sectors of their brains flatlined. Tellingly, not all brain regions were affected in this way; the sectors associated with understanding another's intentions were activated by the expert's advice. The messenger had become the focal message.

As should be plain from this illustration, the kind of authority we are concerned with here is not necessarily someone who is *in* authority—someone who has hierarchical status and can thereby command assent by way of recognized power—but someone who is *an* authority and can thereby induce assent by way of recognized expertise. Moreover, within this latter category, there is a type—the credible authority—who is particularly productive. A credible authority possesses the combination of two highly persuasive qualities: expertise and trustworthiness. We've already considered the effects of the first. Let's concentrate on the second.[82]

Trustworthiness. If there is one quality we most want to see in those we interact with, it is trustworthiness. And this is the case compared with other highly rated traits such as attractiveness, intelligence, cooperativeness, compassion, and emotional stability. In a persuasion-focused interaction, we want to trust that a communicator is presenting information in an honest and impartial fashion—that is, attempting to depict reality accurately rather than to serve self-interest.

Over the years, I've attended a lot of programs designed to teach influence skills. Almost to a one, they've stressed that being perceived as trustworthy is an effective way to increase one's influence and that it takes time for that perception to develop. Although the first of these points remains confirmed, a growing body of research indicates that there is a noteworthy exception to the second. It turns out to be possible to acquire instant trustworthiness by employing a clever strategy. Rather than succumbing to the tendency to describe all of the most favorable features of an offer or idea up front and reserving mention of any drawbacks until the end of the presentation (or never), a communicator who references a weakness early on is immediately seen as more honest. The advantage of this sequence is that, with perceived truthfulness already in place, when the major strengths of the case are advanced, the audience is more likely to believe them. After all, they've been conveyed by a trustworthy source, one whose honesty has been established (pre-suasively) by a willingness to point not just to positive aspects but also to negative ones.

The effectiveness of this approach has been documented (1) in legal settings, where a trial attorney who admits to a weakness before the rival attorney points it out is viewed as more credible and wins more often; (2) in political campaigns, where a candidate who begins with something positive to say about an opponent gains trustworthiness and voting intentions; and (3) in advertising messages, where merchandisers who acknowledge a drawback before highlighting strengths often see large increases in sales. The tactic can be particularly successful when the audience is already aware of the weakness; thus, when a communicator mentions it, little additional damage is done, as no new information is added—except, crucially, that the communicator is an honest individual. Another enhancement occurs when the speaker uses a transitional word—such as *however*, or *but*, or *yet*—that channels the listeners' attention away from the weakness and onto a countervailing strength. A job candidate might say, "I am not experienced in this field, *but* I am a very fast learner." An information systems salesperson might state, "Our set-up costs are not the lowest; *however*, you'll recoup them quickly due to our superior efficiencies.

Elizabeth I of England employed both of these enhancements to optimize the impact of the two most celebrated speeches of her reign. The first occurred at Tilbury in 1588, when, while addressing her troops massed against an expected sea invasion from Spain, she dispelled the soldiers' concern that, as a woman, she was not up to the rigors of battle: "I know I have the body of a weak and feeble woman; *but* I have the heart of a king, and a king of England, too!" It is reported that so long and loud were the cheers after this pronouncement that officers had to ride among the men ordering them to restrain themselves so that the queen could continue.

Thirteen years later, perhaps recalling the success of this rhetorical device, she used it again in her final formal remarks to Parliament members, many of whom mistrusted her. Near the completion of those remarks, she proclaimed, "And though you have had, and may have, many mightier and wiser princes sitting in this seat, *yet* you have never had, nor shall have, any that will love you better." According to British historian Richard Cavendish, audience members left the hall "transfigured, many of them in tears" and, on that very day, labeled her oration the queen's "Golden Speech"—a label that has endured ever since.

Notice that Elizabeth's bridging terms, *but* and *yet*, took listeners from perceived weaknesses to *counteracting* strengths. That their leader possessed the heart of a king, once accepted, filled the troops with the confidence they lacked—and needed—before battle; similarly, that she loved her subjects transcendently, once accepted, disarmed even her wary opponents in Parliament. This feature of the queen's pre-suasive assertions fits with scientific research showing that the weakness-before-strength tactic works best when the strength doesn't just add something positive to the list of pros and cons but, instead, challenges the relevance of the weakness. For instance, Elizabeth didn't seek to embolden the troops at Tilbury by saying there is no one "that will love you better," as her fighters had to be assured of a stout-hearted commander, not a soft-hearted one. She understood that to maximize its effect, an initially deployed weakness should not only be selected to preestablish the trustworthiness of one's later claims, but also it should also be selected to be undercut by those claims. Her "weak and feeble" woman's body became inconsequential for battlefield leadership if, in the minds of her men, it carried "the heart of a king, and a king of England, too."[83]

Scarcity

We want more of what we can have less of. For instance, when access to a desired item is restricted in some way, people have been known to go a little crazy for it. After the chain of pastry shops Crumbs announced in 2014 that it would be closing all of its locations, its signature cupcakes, which had been priced at around $4, began commanding up to $250 apiece online. The effect isn't limited to cupcakes. On the morning of the retail release of the latest iPhone, my local TV news channel sent a reporter to interview individuals who had been waiting all night to secure one. A woman who was twenty-third in line disclosed something that fits this well-established point, but it still astounded me. She had started her wait as twenty-fifth in line but had struck up a conversation during the night with number twenty-three—a woman who admired her $2,800 Louis Vuitton shoulder bag. Seizing her opportunity, the first woman proposed and concluded a trade: "My bag for your spot in line." At the end of the woman's self-satisfied account, the understandably surprised interviewer stammered, "But . . . why?" and got a telling answer. "Because," the new number twenty-three replied, "I heard that this store didn't have a big supply, and I didn't want to risk *losing* the chance to get one."

Although there are several reasons that scarcity drives desire, our aversion to losing something of value is a key factor. After all, loss is the ultimate form of scarcity, rendering the valued item or opportunity unavailable. At a financial services conference, I heard the CEO of a large brokerage firm make the point about the motivating power of loss by describing a lesson his mentor once taught him: "If you wake a multimillionaire client at five in the morning and say, 'If you act now, you will gain twenty thousand dollars,' he'll scream at you and slam down the phone. But if you say, 'If you don't act now, you will lose twenty thousand dollars,' he'll thank you."

But the scarcity of an item does more than raise the possibility of loss; it also raises the judged value of that item. When automobile manufacturers limit production of a new model, its value goes up among potential buyers. Other restrictions in other settings generate similar results. At one large grocery chain, brand promotions that included a purchase limit ("Only x per customer") more than doubled sales for seven different types of products compared with promotions for the same products that didn't include a purchase limit. Follow-up studies showed why. In the consumer's mind, any constraint on access increased the worth of what was being offered.[84]

Consistency

Normally, we want to be (and to be seen) as consistent with our existing commitments—such as the previous statements we've made, stands we've taken, and actions we've performed. Therefore communicators who can get us to take a pre-suasive step, even a small one, in the direction of a particular idea or entity will increase our willingness to take a much larger, congruent step when asked. The desire for consistency will prompt it. This powerful pull toward personal alignment is used in a wide range of influence settings.

Psychologists warn us that sexual infidelity within romantic relationships is a source of great conflict, often leading to anger, pain, and termination of the relationship. Fortunately, they've also located a pre-suasive activity that can help prevent the occurrence of this toxic sequence: prayer—not prayer in general, though, but a particular kind. If one romantic partner agrees to pray *for the other's well-being* every day for an extended period of time, he or she becomes less likely to be unfaithful while doing so. After all, such behavior would be inconsistent with the daily, actively made commitment to the partner's welfare.

Influence practitioners have frequently found the human tendency for consistency with one's prior (pre-suasive) words and deeds to be of service. Automobile insurance companies can reduce policyholders' misreporting of odometer readings by putting an honesty pledge at the beginning of the reporting form rather than at the end. Political parties can increase the chance that supporters will vote in the next election by having arranged for them (through various get-out-the-vote activities) to vote in the previous one. Brands can deepen the loyalty of customers by getting them to recommend the brand to a friend. Organizations can raise the probability that an individual will appear at a meeting or event by switching from saying at the end of a reminder phone call, "We'll mark you on the list as coming then. Thank you!" to "We'll mark you on the list as coming then, okay? [*Pause for confirmation.*] Thank you." One blood services organization that made this tiny, commitment-inducing wording change increased the participation of likely donors in a blood drive from 70 percent to 82.4 percent.[85]

Sometimes practitioners can leverage the force of the consistency principle without installing a new commitment at all. Sometimes all that's necessary is to remind others of a commitment they've made that fits with the practitioners' goals. Consider how the legal team arguing to the US Supreme Court for marriage equality in 2013 structured a months-long national PR campaign with *one man* as its primary target, Supreme Court Justice Anthony Kennedy. (Public opinion had already moved in favor of same-sex marriage.) Despite the operation's nationwide scope before the court hearings, the campaign most wanted to influence Kennedy for two reasons.

First, he was widely considered to be the one to cast the deciding vote in both of the companion cases the court was considering on the issue. Second, he was a frequent fence-sitter on ideological matters. On the one

hand, he was a traditionalist, holding that the law should not be interpreted in a way that drifted far from its original language. On the other
hand, he believed the law to be a living thing with meanings that evolved
over time. This foot-in-each-camp position made Kennedy a prime candidate for a communication approach designed not to change one of his
contrasting points of view but, rather, *to connect only one of them* to the
issue of marriage equality. The media campaign provided just such an approach by employing a set of concepts, and even wordings, that Kennedy
had used in prior court opinions: "human dignity," "individual liberty,"
and "personal freedoms/rights." As a consequence, wherever Kennedy
went in the weeks and months before oral arguments in the cases, he
would likely hear the relevant issues linked in the media campaign to
that selected set of three of his stated views. The intent was to get him to
perceive his prior pertinent legal stances as associated with the pro-mar-
riage-equality position.

The intent was enacted much more explicitly once the hearings began.
Legal team members repeatedly developed their in-court arguments from
the same Kennedy-tied language and themes. Did this tactic contribute
to the court's 5-to-4 rulings in favor of marriage equality? It is difficult to
know for certain. But members of the legal team think so, and they point
to an affirming piece of evidence: in his written opinions, Kennedy leaned
heavily on the concepts of dignity, liberty, and freedoms/rights—all of
which they had labored to prioritize within his marriage-equality-related
thinking both before and during the formal hearings. It is perhaps testament to the durability of properly evoked commitments that in another
marriage-equality case two years later, these same three concepts figured
prominently once again in Justice Kennedy's majority opinion.[86]

WHAT ELSE CAN BE SAID ABOUT THE UNIVERSAL PRINCIPLES OF INFLUENCE?

After presenting the six principles of social influence to a business-
focused audience, it is not unusual for me to hear two questions. The first

concerns the issue of optimal timing: "Are different stages of a commercial relationship suited better to certain of the principles?" Thanks to my colleague Dr. Gregory Neidert, I have an answer, which is yes. Moreover, I have an explanation, which comes from what Dr. Neidert has developed as the *core motives model of social influence*. Of course, any would-be influencer wants to effect change in others but, according to the model, the stage of one's relationship with them affects which influence principles to best employ.

At the first stage, the main goal involves *cultivating a positive association*, as people are more favorable to a communication if they are favorable to the communicator. Two principles of influence, reciprocity and liking, seem particularly appropriate to the task. Giving first (in a meaningful, unexpected, and customized fashion), highlighting genuine commonalities, and offering true compliments establish mutual rapport that facilitates all future dealings.

At the second stage, *reducing uncertainty* becomes a priority. A positive relationship with a communicator doesn't ensure persuasive success. Before people are likely to change, they want to see any decision as wise. Under these circumstances, the principles of social proof and authority offer the best match. Pointing to evidence that a choice is well regarded by peers or experts significantly increases confidence in its wisdom. But even with a positive association cultivated and uncertainty reduced, a remaining step needs to be taken.

At this third stage, *motivating action* is the main objective. That is, a well-liked friend might show me sufficient proof that experts recommend (and almost all my peers believe) that daily exercise is a good thing, but that might not be enough to get me to do it. The friend would do well to include in his appeal the principles of consistency and scarcity by reminding me of what I've said publicly in the past about the importance of my health and the unique enjoyments I would miss if I lost it. That's the message that would most likely get me up in the morning and off to the gym.

The second question I am frequently asked about the principles is whether I've identified any new ones. Until recently, I'd always had to answer in the negative. But now I believe that there is a seventh universal principle that I had missed—not because some new cultural phenomenon or technological shift brought it to my attention but because it was hiding beneath the surface of my data all along. I explain what it is and how I came to see it next.

11

Unity 1: Being Together

For years, as part of a university class lecture, I would describe a study showing that sending holiday greeting cards to complete strangers produced a surprisingly large number of greeting cards sent dutifully in return. In class, I'd attribute the finding to the operation of the principle of reciprocity, which obligates people to give back to those who've first given to them—even, apparently, under wholly puzzling circumstances. I liked lecturing about that study because it illustrated the point I wanted to make about the power of the principle and, in the interests of improving my teacher's ratings, the students got a laugh from it.

After one of those lectures, an older student (one who had returned to school after having raised a family) stopped and thanked me for solving a decade-long mystery in her home. She said that ten years prior, her family had received a Christmas card from the Harrisons of Santa Barbara, California. But neither she nor her husband remembered knowing any Harrisons in Santa Barbara. She was sure there must have been a mistake and that the Harrisons misaddressed the envelope. Yet her family *had* received a holiday card from them; so, true to the principle of reciprocity, she sent one in return. "We're in the tenth year of exchanging cards with these people," she confessed, "and I *still* don't know who they are. But now at least I know why I sent them that first card."

Several months later, she came to my office, declaring that she had to bring me up to date on the story. Her youngest son, Skip, was about to

Harrisons?/Chattertons? The family names may change, but the circumstances that initiate human relationships stay the same. *Pickles used with permission of Brian Crane, the Washington Post Writers Group, and the Cartoonist G.*

begin college at the University of California at Santa Barbara. But because of a repair problem, his dormitory room wasn't ready, and he needed a place to stay for a few days until the problem was fixed. Although the university offered him temporary housing in a motel, his mother didn't like that idea. Instead, she thought, "Who do we know in Santa Barbara? The Harrisons!" So she called and was relieved to learn that they'd be happy to have Skip as a houseguest. She left my office claiming to be more amazed than ever by the influence the principle of reciprocity had on human behavior—in this case, her own and the Harrisons'.

I was less convinced, though. Certainly I could see that my student's initial decision to send a card fit with the obligation to reciprocate. But the Harrisons' decision to let Skip stay with them didn't fit with that obligation at all. There was no outstanding debt to be repaid by the Harrisons when they'd agreed. Holiday cards (and accompanying year-end letters) had been exchanged equally; thus, in terms of obligations, the two families were even. It seemed upon reflection that, although the rule for reciprocation might have started the process, it was the ten-year resultant *relationship* between the families that compelled the Harrisons to open their home to an eighteen-year-old they'd never met. That realization made me appreciate the freestanding power of social connections to generate assent—separate from the other six principles of influence. Relationships not only intensify willingness to help but also cause it.

There's a lesson here. Our ability to create change in others is often and importantly grounded in shared personal relationships, which create a pre-suasive context for assent. It's a poor trade-off, then, for social influence when we allow present-day forces of separation—distancing societal changes, insulating modern technologies—to take a shared sense of human connection out of our exchanges. The *relation* gets removed, leaving just the *ships*, passing at sea.[87]

UNITY

What kind of existing or perceived relationships maximize the favorable treatment of fellow members? The answer requires a subtle but crucial distinction. The relationships that lead people to favor another most effectively are not those that allow them to say, "Oh, that person is like us." They are the ones that allow people to say, "Oh, that person is *of* us." For instance, I might have many more tastes and preferences in common with a colleague at work than with a sibling, but there is no question which of the two I would consider *of* me and which I would consider merely *like* me—and which, consequently, I would more likely help in a time of need. The experience of *unity* is not about simple similarities (although those can work too, but to a lesser degree, via the liking principle). It's about shared identities. It's about the categories that individuals use to define themselves and their groups, such as race, ethnicity, nationality, and family, as well as political and religious affiliations. A key characteristic of these categories is that their members tend to feel at one with, merged with, the others. They are the categories in which the conduct of one member influences the self-esteem of other members. Put simply, *we* is the shared *me*.

The evidence for overlapping self and other identities within we-based groups is varied and impressive. People often fail to distinguish correctly between themselves and in-group members: unduly assigning their own characteristics to those others, repeatedly failing to recall which personal traits they had rated previously for in-group members or for themselves, and taking significantly longer to identify traits that differentiated in-group members from themselves—all of which reflects a confusion of self and other. Neuroscientists have offered an explanation for the confusion: mental representations of the concepts of *self* and of *close others* emerge from the same brain circuitry. Activating either of those concepts can lead to neuronal *cross-excitation* of the other concept and the consequent blurring of identities.[88]

Long before the neuroscientific evidence was available, social scientists were measuring the feeling of self-other overlap and identifying what brought it about. In the process, they uncovered two categories of factors that lead to a sense of we-ness—those involving particular ways of being together and particular ways of acting together. Each deserves our examination, the first in the present chapter.

Please circle the picture below that best describes your relationship with your partner.

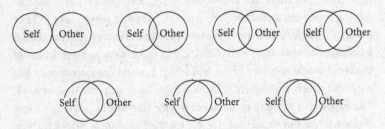

Overlapping circles, overlapping selves. Since its publication in 1992, scientists have been using the Inclusion of Other in the Self Scale to see which factors promote the feeling of being "at one" with another individual. *Courtesy of Arthur Aron and the American Psychological Association*

BEING TOGETHER

Kinship

From a genetic point of view, being in the same family—the same blood-line—is the ultimate form of self-other unity. Indeed, the widely accepted concept of "inclusive fitness" within evolutionary biology undermines specifically the distinction between self and related others, asserting that individuals do not so much attempt to ensure their own survival as the survival of copies of their genes. The crucial implication is that the *self* in self-interest can lie outside of one's body and inside the skin of another who shares a goodly amount of genetic material. For this reason, people are particularly willing to help genetically close relatives, especially in survival-related decisions such as whether to donate a kidney in the United States, rescue someone from a burning building in Japan, or intervene in an axe fight in the jungles of Venezuela. Brain-imaging research has identified one proximate cause: people experience unusually high stimulation in the self-reward centers of their brains after aiding a family member; it's almost as if by doing so, they are aiding themselves—and this is true even of teenagers!

From an evolutionary perspective, any advantages to one's kin should be promoted, including relatively small ones. Consider as confirmation the most effective influence technique I have ever employed in my professional career. I once wanted to compare the attitudes of college students with those of their parents on an array of topics, which meant arranging for both groups to fill out the same lengthy questionnaire. Getting a set of college students to perform the task wasn't difficult; I assigned the questionnaire as a course exercise in a large psychology class I was teaching. The harder problem was finding a way to get their parents to comply, since I had no money to offer, and I knew that adult participation rates in such surveys are dismal—often below 20 percent. A colleague suggested that I play the kinship card by offering an extra point on my next test (one of several in the class) to each student whose parent responded to the questionnaire.

The effect was astounding. All 163 of my students sent the questionnaire to a parent, 159 of whom (97 percent) mailed back a completed copy within a week. For one point, on one test, in one course, in one semester, for one of their children. As an influence researcher, I've never experienced anything like it. However, from subsequent personal experience, I now believe there is something I could have done to produce even better results: I could have asked my students to send a questionnaire to a grandparent. I figure that, of the 163 sent out, I would have gotten 162 back within a week.

The missing copy would probably be due to a grandfather's hospitalization from cardiac arrest while he was sprinting to the post office.

But is there any way that individuals with no special genetic connection to us could employ the power of kinship to gain our favor? One possibility is to use language and imagery pre-suasively to bring the concept of kin to our consciousness. For example, collectives that create a sense of we-ness among their members are characterized by the use of familial images and labels—*brothers*, *sisterhood*, *forefathers*, *motherland*, *heritage*—which lead to an increased willingness to sacrifice one's own interests for the welfare of the group. Because humans are symbolizing creatures, one international team of researchers found that these imagined "fictive families" produce levels of self-sacrifice associated typically with highly interrelated clans. In one pair of studies, reminding Spaniards of the family-like nature of their national ties led those feeling "fused" with their fellow citizens to become immediately and dramatically more willing to fight and die for Spain.[89]

Now let's ask a similar question about someone outside of our existing collectives. Could a lone genetically unrelated communicator harness the concept of kinship to obtain agreement? When I speak at conferences of financial services firms, I sometimes ask, "Who would you say is the most successful financial investor of our time?" The answer, voiced in unison, is always "Warren Buffett." Mr. Buffett, in exquisite collaboration with his partner, Charlie Munger, has led Berkshire Hathaway Inc.—a holding company that invests in other companies—to amazing levels of worth for its shareholders since taking over in 1965.

Several years ago, I received a gift of Berkshire Hathaway stock. It's been a gift that's kept on giving, and not just monetarily. It's provided me a vantage point from which to observe the approaches of Messrs. Buffett and Munger to strategic investing, about which I know little, and strategic communication, about which I do know something. Sticking to the process I know, I can say that I've been impressed by the amount of skill I've seen. Ironically, Berkshire Hathaway's financial attainments have been so remarkable that a communication problem has arisen: how to give current and prospective shareholders confidence that the company will maintain such success into the future. Absent that confidence, stockholders might be reasonably expected to sell their shares, while potential buyers could be expected to purchase elsewhere.

Make no mistake, based on an excellent business model and several unique advantages of scale, Berkshire Hathaway has a compelling case to make for its future valuation. But having a compelling case to make is not the same as making a case compellingly—something that Buffett does invariably in the company's annual reports. For instance, to establish his credibility early (usually in the first one or two pages of text), he describes a mistake he's made or a problem the company has encountered during the past year and examines the implications for future outcomes. Rather than burying, minimizing, or papering over difficulties, which seems to be the tack taken all too frequently in other annual reports, Buffett demonstrates that he is, first, fully aware of problems inside the company and, second, fully willing to reveal them. The emergent advantage is that when he then describes the formidable strengths of Berkshire Hathaway, readers have been pre-suaded to trust in them more deeply than before. After all, they are coming from a discernibly credible source.

This practice has not been the only arrow in Mr. Buffett's persuasion quiver. But in February 2015 something more influential than usual seemed necessary because it was time, in a special fiftieth-anniversary letter to shareholders, to summarize the company's results over the relevant span of years and to make the argument for the continuing vitality of Berkshire Hathaway in coming years. Implicit in the fifty-year character of the anniversary was a concern that had been around for a while but was reasserting itself in online commentary: a half century into the enterprise, Buffett and Munger were clearly no youngsters, and should either no longer be present to lead the company, its future prospects and share price could tumble. I remember reading the commentary and being troubled by it. Would the value of my stock, which had more than quadrupled under Buffett-Munger management, hold up if either departed due to advancing age? Was it time to sell and take my extraordinary profits before they might evaporate?

In his letter, Mr. Buffett addressed the issue head-on—specifically, in the section labeled "The Next 50 Years at Berkshire," in which he laid out the affirmative, forward-reaching consequences of Berkshire Hathaway's proven business model, its nearly unprecedented bulwark of financial assets, and the firm's already completed identification of the "right person" to take over as CEO when appropriate. But more telling for me as a persuasion scientist attuned to pre-suasive approaches was how Mr. Buffett began that all-important section. In characteristic fashion, he reestablished his trustworthiness by being up front about a potential weakness: "Now let's look at the road ahead. Bear in mind that if I had attempted 50 years ago to gauge what was coming, certain of my predictions would have been far off the mark." Then he did something I'd never seen or heard him do in any public forum. He added, "With that warning, I will tell you what I would say to my family today if they asked me about Berkshire's future."

What followed was careful construction of the case for Berkshire Hathaway's foreseeable economic health: the proven business model, the bulwark of financial assets, the scrupulously vetted future CEO. As convincing as these components of his argument were on their merits, Mr. Buffett had pre-suasively done something that made me judge them as even more convincing: he had claimed that he was going to advise me about them as he would a family member. Because of everything I knew about the man, I believed that claim. As a result, I have never since thought seriously about selling my Berkshire Hathaway stock. There's a memorable moment in the movie *Jerry Maguire* in which the title character, played by Tom Cruise, bursts into a room, greets the inhabitants (including his estranged wife, Dorothy), and launches into a long soliloquy in which he lists the reasons she should continue to be his life partner. Partway through the list, Dorothy looks up and cuts the monologue short with a now-famous line: "You had me at *hello*." In his letter, Mr. Buffett had me at *family*.

Even though his anniversary letter begins on page twenty-four of the report, it is perhaps a testament to Mr. Buffett's recognition of the value of pre-suasion that, at the top of the first page of the report's text, he recommends that shareholders jump ahead and read that *frame-setting* letter before anything else. Mr. Munger, too, wrote a fiftieth-anniversary letter published within the larger report. Although he didn't establish a familial context for his remarks, prior to predicting the continuation of abnormally good results for the firm, he did employ the trustworthiness-enhancing procedure of describing certain mistakes that management had made in the past. I'll have more to say on the topic of the ethics of persuasion in chapter 13. But for now, I can state that in no way do I view Mr. Munger's (or Mr. Buffett's) use of this approach as a form of trickery. Rather, I see it as illustrating how genuinely trustworthy communicators can also be smart enough (in the case of these guys, *way smart* enough) to recognize the benefits of gaining pivotal trust through pre-suasive, truthful disclosures.

— ——— —

It's instructive that in the flood of favorable reaction to his fiftieth-anniversary letter (with headlines like "Warren Buffett just wrote his best annual letter ever" and "You'd be a fool not to invest in Berkshire Hathaway"), no one remarked on the familial frame into which Buffett had so adeptly placed his arguments. I can't say I was surprised at this lack of recognition. In the world of hard-minded, fact-based financial investing, the default is to focus on the merit of the message. And, of course, it's true that the *merit* (of the arguments) can be the message. But at the same time, there are other dimensions of effective communication that can become the essential message. We learned via Marshall McLuhan that the *medium* can be the message; via the principle of social proof that the *multitude* can be the message; via the authority principle that the *messenger* can be the message; and now via the concept of unity that the *merger* (of self and other) can be the message. It's worth considering, then, which additional features of a situation, besides direct kinship, lend themselves to the perceived merging of identities.

Noteworthy is how many of these features are nonetheless traceable to cues of heightened kinship. Obviously, no one can look inside another and determine the percentage of genes the two share. That is why, to operate in an evolutionarily prudent fashion, people have to rely on certain aspects of another that are simultaneously detectible and associated with genetic overlap—the most evident being physical and personal similarities. Inside families, individuals are more helpful to kin they resemble. Outside of the family unit, people use facial similarity to judge (fairly accurately) their degree of genetic relatedness to strangers. However, they can be tricked into misplaced favoritism in this regard. Observers of a photograph of someone whose face has been modified digitally to look more like them come to trust that person to a greater extent. If the now-more-similar face is of a political candidate, they become more willing to vote for him or her.[90]

Place

There is another usually reliable cue of heightened genetic commonality. It has less to do with physical similarity than with physical proximity. It is the perception of being *of* the same place as another, and its impact on human behavior can be arresting. I know of no better way of documenting that impact than by resolving some puzzles of human conduct that surfaced during one of the most harrowing eras of our time: the years of the Holocaust. Let's begin with the physically smallest installation of one's place and then move to more expanded forms.

Home. Humans as well as animals react to those present in their homes while growing up as if they are relatives. Although this clue to relatedness can be misleading occasionally, it is normally accurate because people in the home typically are family members. In addition, the longer the length of residing together in the home, the greater its effect on individuals' sense of family and, accordingly, their willingness to sacrifice for one another. But there is a related factor that produces these same consequences without extensive time together. When people observe their parents caring for the needs of another in the home, they also experience a family-like feeling and become more willing to give to that other. An intriguing upshot of this process is that children who see their parents open their homes to a range of differing people should be more likely, as adults, to help strangers. For them, we-ness should reach beyond their immediate or extended family and apply to the human family as well.

– — –

How does this insight help solve a major mystery of the Holocaust? History records the names of the most famous and successful helpers of the era: Raoul Wallenberg, the courageous Swede whose relentless rescue efforts eventually cost him his life, and the German industrialist Oskar

Schindler, whose "list" saved 1,100 Jews. Yet what might have been the most effective concentrated helping action taken during the time of the Holocaust has gone relatively unrecognized in the years since.

It began near dawn on a summer day in 1940 when two hundred Polish Jews crowded together outside the Japanese consulate in Lithuania to plead for help in their attempts to escape the sweeping Nazi advance through Eastern Europe. That they would choose to seek the aid of Japanese officials represents a puzzle in itself. At the time, the governments of Nazi Germany and Imperial Japan had close ties and shared interests; indeed, it was only a few months later, in September 1940, that Japan, Germany, and Italy signed the Tripartite Pact formally declaring themselves allies. Why then would these Jews, the hated targets of the Third Reich, throw themselves on the mercy of one of Adolf Hitler's international partners? What possible aid could they expect from Japan?

Before its close strategic associations with Nazi Germany developed in the late 1930s, Japan had allowed displaced Jews easy access to Japanese territories as a way of gaining some of the financial resources and political goodwill that the international Jewish community could provide in return. Because support for the plan remained strong within some circles in Japan, the government never revoked completely its policies of granting travel visas to European Jews. The paradoxical result was that in the prewar years, as most of the countries of the world (the United States included) were turning away the desperate prey of Hitler's Final Solution, it was Japan—Hitler's ally—that provided them sanctuary in the Japanese-controlled Jewish settlement of Shanghai, China, and the city of Kobe, Japan.

By July 1940, then, when two hundred of the prey massed outside the door of the Japanese consulate in Lithuania, they knew that the man behind that door offered their best and perhaps last chance for safety. His name was Chiune Sugihara, and, by all appearances, he was an unlikely candidate to arrange for their salvation. A midcareer diplomat, Sugihara had become Japan's consul general in Lithuania by virtue of sixteen years of committed and obedient service in a variety of earlier posts. The right credentials facilitated his rise within the diplomatic corps: he was the son of a government official and a samurai family. He had set his professional

goals high, becoming proficient in the Russian language in hopes of some-
day being the Japanese ambassador to Moscow. Like his better-known
counterpart, Oskar Schindler, Mr. Sugihara was a great lover of games,
music, and parties. On the surface, therefore, there was little to suggest
that this comfortable, pleasure-seeking lifelong diplomat would risk his
career, reputation, and future to try to save the strangers who woke him
from a sound sleep early one morning. That, though, is what he did—with
full knowledge of the potential consequences for him and his family.

After speaking with members of the crowd waiting outside his gate,
Sugihara recognized their plight and wired Tokyo for permission to au-
thorize travel visas for them. Although aspects of Japan's lenient visa and
settlement policies were still in place for Jews, Sugihara's superiors at the
Foreign Ministry worried that to continue those policies would damage
Japan's diplomatic relations with Hitler. As a consequence, his request was
denied, as were his more urgent second and third petitions. It was at that
point in his life—age forty, with no hint of prior disloyalty or disobedi-
ence—that this personally indulgent, professionally ambitious career official did what no one could have suspected. He began writing the needed
travel documents in outright defiance of his clearly stated, and twice re-
stated, orders.

That choice shattered his career. Within a month, Sugihara was transferred from his consul general post to a much diminished position outside
of Lithuania, where he could no longer operate independently. Ultimately,
he was expelled from the Foreign Ministry for insubordination. In dis-
honor after the war, he sold lightbulbs for a living. But in the weeks before
he had to close the consulate in Lithuania, Sugihara stayed true to the
choice he had made, interviewing applicants from early morning to late
night and completing the papers required for their escape. Even after the
consulate had been shut and he had taken up residence in a hotel, he continued to write visas. Even after the strain of the task had left him thinned
and exhausted, even after the same strain had left his wife incapable of
nursing their infant child, he wrote without respite. Even on the platform
for the train set to take him from his petitioners, even on the train itself,
he wrote and thrust life-granting papers into life-grasping hands, saving
thousands of innocents in the process. And at last, when the train began

to draw him away, he bowed deeply and apologized to those he had to leave stranded—begging their forgiveness for his deficiencies as a helper.

Sugihara and family: Inside/Outside. After writing thousands of travel visas for Jews in his consulate office in Lithuania (top), Chiune Sugihara was transferred from his post to lesser roles in Nazi-held Europe. In Czechoslovakia (bottom), he positioned his family (wife, son, and sister-in-law) for a photo *outside* a park with a sign that read "No Jews allowed" in German. Was that sign an incidental feature of the shot or a consciously included piece of bitter irony? For suggestive evidence, see if you can locate the sister-in-law's right hand. *United States Holocaust Memorial Museum. Courtesy of Hiroki Sugihara [both photos]*

Sugihara's decision to help thousands of Jews escape to Japan is likely not attributable to a single factor. Normally, multiple forces act and interact to bring about this kind of extraordinary benevolence. But in Sugihara's case, one *home-based* factor stands out. His father, a tax official who had been sent to Korea for a time, moved the family there and opened an inn. Sugihara remembered being powerfully affected by his parents' willingness to take in a broad mix of guests, tending to their basic needs for food and shelter in the family's home, even providing baths and washing their clothes, despite the fact that some were too impoverished to pay. From this perspective, we can see one reason—an expanded sense of family flowing from exposure to diverse individuals in the home—for Sugihara's later efforts to help thousands of European Jews. As he stated in an interview forty-five years after the events, the nationality and religion of the Jews did not matter; it mattered only that they were members with him in the human family, and they needed his help. His experience suggests a piece of advice for prospective parents who want their children to develop a broadly charitable nature: give them contact *in the home* with individuals from a wide spectrum of backgrounds and treat those individuals there like family.[91]

Locality. Because humans evolved as a species from small but stable groupings of genetically related individuals, we have also evolved a tendency to favor the people who, outside the home, exist in close proximity to us. There is even a named "ism"—localism—to represent the tendency. Its sometimes enormous influence can be seen from the neighborhood to the community level. A look back to a pair of incidents from the Holocaust offers it gripping confirmation.

The first comes from the sociologist Ronald Cohen, who recounted a hideous form of localism perpetrated by a guard at a Nazi concentration camp. At such work camps, when just one prisoner violated a rule, it was not uncommon for all to be lined up and for a guard to walk along the line counting to ten, stopping only to shoot each tenth person dead. In Cohen's account, a veteran guard assigned this task was performing it as routinely as he always had when, inexplicably, he did something different: Coming upon one seemingly unfortunate tenth prisoner, he raised an eyebrow and executed the eleventh. It's possible to imagine several potential reasons for his action. Perhaps he had gotten good effort from the spared prisoner in the past or had noticed a high level of strength or intelligence or health that foretold of future productive work. But when asked to explain himself by another of the guards (Cohen's informant in the matter), it was clear that his choice sprang from none of these practical considerations. The simplicity of his stated justification speaks to its sufficiency: he had recognized the man as being from his home town.

After describing the incident in a scholarly article, Cohen commented on a deeply contradictory aspect of it: "[W]hile engaged dutifully in mass murder, the guard was merciful and sympathetic to one particular member of the victimized group." Although Cohen didn't pursue the related issue, it is important to identify the factor potent enough to turn a cold killer carrying out mass murder into a (specifically focused) "merciful and sympathetic" enactor. It was mutuality of place.

Now let's examine how that same unitizing factor, during the same period of history, produced a radically different outcome. Multiple historical accounts of rescuers of Holocaust-era Jews reveal a little-analyzed yet noteworthy phenomenon: in the great majority of instances, the rescuers who chose to house, feed, and hide these targets of Nazi persecution did not spontaneously seek out the targets to offer them needed help. Even more notably, they were typically not asked for that help by the victims themselves. Instead, the direct requester would most frequently be a relative or neighbor who'd petitioned them for assistance on behalf of a hunted individual or family. In a real sense, then, these rescuers didn't so much say yes to the needy strangers as to their own relatives and neighbors.

Of course, it wasn't the case that no rescuers acted primarily out of compassion for victimized others. Protestant pastor André Trocmé, after taking in an initial, lone refugee outside his door, persuaded other residents of his small French town of Le Chambon-sur-Lignon to sustain, harbor, conceal, and smuggle away thousands of Jews during the Nazi occupation. The instructive feature of Trocmé's extraordinary story is not how he arranged for the care of that first refugee but how he arranged for the care of the many that followed: He began by requesting the help of individuals who would have a difficult time saying no to him—his relatives and neighbors—and then pressed them to do the same among their relatives and neighbors. It was this strategic leveraging of existing *unities* that made him more than a compassionate hero. It made him an inordinately successful one as well.[92]

– —— –

Region. Even being from the same general geographical region can lead to we-ness. Around the globe, sports team championships stimulate feelings of personal pride in residents of the team's surrounding zones— as if the *residents* had won. In the United States alone, research evidence reinforces the general point in additional and varied ways: citizens agreed to participate in a survey to a greater extent if it emanated from a home-state university; readers of a news story about a military fatality in Afghanistan became more opposed to the war there upon learning that the fallen soldier was from their own state; and, going back two centuries to the Civil War, if infantrymen came from the same region as one another, they were less likely to desert, remaining loyal to comrades in their "more unitized" units. From fans to fighters, we can see the considerable impact of regional identities on we-like responding. But it's another seemingly bewildering event of the Holocaust that yields the most telling instance.

Although Chiune Sugihara's visas saved thousands of Jews, when they arrived in Japanese-held territory, they became part of an even larger contingent of Jewish refugees concentrated in Kobe, Japan, and the Japanese-controlled city of Shanghai. After the 1941 Japanese attack on Pearl Harbor, which catapulted the United States into World War II, all refugee passage in and out of Japan ended, and the safety of its Jewish community became precarious. Japan, after all, was by then a full-fledged wartime conspirator with Adolf Hitler and had to protect the solidarity of its alliance with this virulent anti-Semite. What's more, in January 1942 Hitler's plan to annihilate Jewry was formalized at the Wannsee Conference in Berlin. With the Final Solution installed as Axis policy, Nazi officials began to press Tokyo to extend that "solution" to Japan's Jews. Proposals involving death camps, medical experiments, and mass drownings at sea were forwarded to Tokyo following the conference. Yet despite the potentially damaging impact on its relations with Hitler, the Japanese government resisted these pressures in early 1942 and maintained that resistance through the end of the war. Why?

The answer might well have to do with a set of events that had taken place several months earlier. The Nazis had sent Josef Meisinger, a colonel in the Gestapo known as the "Butcher of Warsaw" for ordering the execution of sixteen thousand Poles, to Tokyo. Upon his arrival in April 1941, Meisinger began pressing for a policy of brutality toward the Jews under Japan's rule—a policy he stated he would gladly help design and enact. Uncertain at first of how to respond and wanting to hear all sides, high-ranking members of Japan's military government called upon the Jewish refugee community to send two leaders to a meeting that would influence their future significantly. The chosen representatives were both respected religious leaders, but respected in different ways. One, Rabbi Moses Shatzkes, was renowned as a studious man, one of the most brilliant Talmudic scholars in Europe before the war. The other, Rabbi Shimon Kalisch, was much older and was known for his remarkable ability to understand basic human workings—a social psychologist of sorts.

After the two entered the meeting room, they and their translators stood before a tribunal of powerful members of the Japanese High Command, who would determine their community's survival and who wasted little time in asking a pair of fateful questions: Why do our allies the Nazis hate you so much? And why should we take your side against them? Rabbi Shatzkes, the scholar, comprehending the tangled complexity of the historical, religious, and economic issues involved, had no ready response. But Rabbi Kalisch's knowledge of human nature had equipped him to deliver the most impressive persuasive communication I have encountered in over thirty years of studying the process: "Because," he said calmly, "we are Asian, *like you*."

Rabbis in Japan. Throughout WWII, the Japanese did not succumb to Nazi pressure to treat Jews harshly. One reason might have been the assertion of one of two rabbis (pictured with escorts on the day of a crucial meeting) that included his people in Japanese officials' sense of "we" and excluded the Nazis. *Courtesy of Marvin Tokayer*

Although brief, the assertion was inspired. It shifted the Japanese officers' reigning in-group identity from one based in a temporary wartime alliance to one based in a regional, genetically related mutuality. It did so by implicating the Nazis' own racial claim that the "superior" Aryan master race was innately different from the peoples of Asia. Within a single, penetrating observation, it was the Jews who were aligned with the Japanese and the Nazis who (self-proclaimedly) were not. The older rabbi's response had a powerful effect on the Japanese officers. After a silence, they conferred among themselves and announced a recess. When they returned, the most senior military official rose and granted the reassurance the rabbis had hoped to bring home to their community: "Go back to your people. Tell them we will provide for their safety and peace. You have nothing to fear while in Japanese territory." And so it was.[93]

— — —

There is no doubt that the unitizing powers of family and of place can be harnessed by a skilled communicator—witness the effectiveness of Warren Buffett and Rabbi Kalisch. At the same time, there is another kind of unitizing effect available to those seeking elevated influence. It comes not from *being* together in the same genealogy or geography but from *acting* together synchronously or collaboratively. It comes next.

12

Unity 2: Acting Together

My colleague Professor Wilhelmina Wosinska remembers growing up in 1950s and 1960s Soviet-controlled Poland with mixed feelings. On the negative side, besides constant shortages of basic commodities, there were dispiriting limitations on all manner of personal freedoms, including speech, privacy, information, dissent, and travel. Yet she and her schoolmates were led to register the limitations positively—as necessary for establishing a fair and equal social order. These positive feelings were displayed regularly and fueled by celebratory events, in which participants sang and marched together while waving flags in unison. The effects, she says, were impressive: physically stirring, emotionally uplifting, and psychologically validating. Never has she felt more impelled to the concept of "All for one, and one for all" than in the midst of those scrupulously choreographed and powerfully coordinating involvements. Whenever I have heard Professor Wosinska speak of these activities, it has been in a sober academic presentation on group psychology. Despite the scholarly context, the description of her participation invariably brings volume to her voice, blood to her face, and a light to her eyes. There is something indelibly visceral about such *synchronized* experiences that marks them as primitive and central to the human condition.

Indeed, the archeological and anthropological records are clear on the point: all human societies have developed ways to respond together, in unison or synchrony, inside songs, marches, rituals, chants, prayers, and dances. What's more, they've been doing so since prehistoric times; collective dance, for instance, is depicted extraordinarily often in the drawings, rock art, and cave paintings of the Neolithic and Chalcolithic periods. The behavioral science record is equally clear as to why. When people act in unitary ways, they become unit*ized*. The resultant feeling of group solidarity serves societies' interests well, producing degrees of loyalty and self-sacrifice associated usually with much smaller family units. Thus, human societies, even ancient ones, seem to have discovered group bonding "technologies" involving coordinated responding. The effects are similar to those of kinship: feelings of we-ness, merger, and the confusion of self and other.

Neolithic Line Dancing? According to archaeologist Yosef Garfinkel, depictions of social interaction in prehistoric art were nearly always of dance. A cave painting from Bhimbetka, India, provides an example. © *Arindam Banerjee/Dreamstime.com*

The feeling of being merged with others sounds rare, but it's not. It can be produced easily and in multiple ways. In one set of studies, participants played a game in which, to win money, they had to make either the same choice as their partner or a different choice. Compared with the participants who had to win by mismatching choices, those who had to win by matching choices came to see their partners as more comparable to them; there was something about performing in the same way as another person that led to greater perceived likeness.

Another study showed that synchronous responding between two people doesn't have to be movement based to produce this perception; it can involve sensory responding as well. Participants watched a video of a stranger whose face was being stroked with a soft brush while their own faces were being brushed either (for some participants) in an identical way or (for other participants) in a different way in terms of the direction and sequence of the strokes. The results were remarkable: those given the matched sensory experience rated themselves and the depicted stranger as more alike in both looks and personality. Even more remarkably, a blurred sense of self-other identity emerged, with matching participants reporting more intensely, "It felt as if my face was turning into the face in the video," "Sometimes I had the impression that if I had moved my eyes, the eyes of the person's in the video would have moved too," and "It seemed as if the touch I felt was caused by the brush touching the face in the movie."

If *acting* together—in motoric, vocal, or sensory ways—can serve as a surrogate for *being* together in a kinship unit, we ought to see similar consequences from both forms of togetherness. And we do. Two of these consequences are especially important for individuals seeking to become more influential: enhanced liking and greater support from others, both of which can be accomplished pre-suasively.[94]

LIKING

When people act in unison, they not only see themselves as more alike, they evaluate one another more positively afterward. Their elevated like-*ness* turns into elevated lik*ing*. The actions can involve finger tapping in a laboratory, smiling in a conversation, or body adjustments in a teacher-student interaction—all of which, if synchronized, cause people to rate one another more favorably. But one set of Canadian researchers wondered if they could ask something more socially significant of coordinated movement: could its ability to convert likeness into liking be employed to reduce racial prejudice? The researchers noted that although we normally try to "resonate" (harmonize) with members of our in-groups, we typically *don't* with out-group members. They speculated that the consequent differences in feelings of unity might be at least partially responsible for an automatic human tendency to favor the in-group. If so, then arranging for people to harmonize their actions with those of out-group members might reduce the bias.

To test the idea, they conducted an experiment in which white subjects watched seven video clips of black individuals taking a sip of water from a glass and then placing it down on a table. Some of the subjects merely observed the clips and actions. Others were asked to imitate the actions by sipping from a glass of water in front of them in exact coordination with the movements they witnessed on the clips. Later, in a procedure designed to measure their hidden racial preferences, the subjects who had merely observed the black actors showed the typical white favoritism for whites over blacks. But those who had synchronized their actions with those of the black actors exhibited none of this favoritism.

Before making too much of the results of the experiment, we should recognize that the positive change in evaluations was measured just a few minutes after the study's unitizing procedure. The researchers presented no evidence indicating that the shifts would persist beyond the time or place of the study. Still, even with that caveat in mind, there is room for optimism here, as a less biased approach to in-group/out-group preferences can be all that's necessary to make a difference within the boundaries of a specific situation such as a job interview, sales call, or first meeting.[95]

SUPPORT

Okay, fine, there's good evidence that acting together with others, even strangers, generates feelings of unity and increased liking. But are the forms of unity and liking that flow from coordinated responding strong enough to alter meaningfully the gold standard of social influence: consequential behavior? Two studies help answer the question. One examined aid given to a previously unitized, single individual, and the other examined cooperation with a group of previously unitized team members. In both instances, the requested behavior required self-sacrifice.

In the first study, participants listened to an array of recorded audio tones on headphones while tapping a table to the beats they heard. Some listened to the same tones as a partner and therefore saw themselves tapping in concert with that person; others listened to a different array of tones than their partner, and thus the two did not act in synchrony. Afterward, all participants learned that they were free to leave the study, but their partners had to remain to answer a lengthy series of math and logic problems. However, they could choose to stay to help their partners by taking on some of the task themselves. The results left no doubt about pre-suasive coordinated activity's capacity to escalate self-sacrificial, supportive conduct. While only 18 percent of the participants who did not initially tap the table in synchrony with their partners chose to stay and help, of those who did initially tap in synchrony, 49 percent gave up their free time to provide assistance to their partners.

A different set of researchers conducted the second study of interest, employing a time-honored military tactic to instill a sense of group cohesion. After assigning participants to teams, the researchers asked some of the teams to walk together, *in step*, for a time; they asked others to walk together for the same amount of time, but normally. Later, all team members played an economic game in which they could either maximize the chance of increasing their own financial gain or forgo that opportunity to ensure instead that their teammates would do well financially. Members of teams that had pre-suasively marched together were 50 percent more cooperative toward their teammates than were those who had just walked together normally. A follow-up study helped explain why: preliminary-response synchrony led to a feeling of unity, which led to a greater willingness to sacrifice personal gain for the group's greater good.[96]

- —— -

It appears, then, that groups can promote unity, liking, and subsequent supportive behavior in a variety of situations by first arranging for synchronous responding. But the tactics we've reviewed so far—simultaneous table tapping, water sipping, and face brushing—don't seem readily implementable, at least not in any large-scale fashion. Marching in unison might be better in this regard, but only marginally. Isn't there some *generally* applicable mechanism that social entities could deploy to bring about such synchrony to influence members toward group goals? There is. It's music. And fortunately for individual communicators, it also can be co-opted to move others toward the goals of a single agent of influence.

MUSIC IN THE STRUGGLE FOR INFLUENCE: IT'S A JINGLE OUT THERE

There is a good explanation for why the presence of music stretches both from the start of human recorded history and across the breadth of human societies. Because of a unique collection of detectible regularities (rhythm, meter, intensity, pulse, and time), music possesses rare synchronizing power. Listeners can easily become aligned with one another along motoric, sensory, vocal, and emotional dimensions—a state of affairs that leads to familiar markers of unity such as self-other merging, social cohesion, and supportive conduct.

In this last respect, consider the results of a study in Germany of four-year-old children. As part of a game, some of the kids walked around a circle with a partner while singing and keeping time in their movements with recorded music. Other kids did nearly the same but without the accompaniment of music. Later, when the children had an opportunity to show helpfulness, those who had sung and walked together in time with music were over three times more likely to help their partner than were those who did not have a pre-suasive joint musical experience.

The study's authors made a pair of instructive points about the helping they observed. First, they noted that it was self-sacrificial, requiring the helper to give up some personal play time to assist a partner. That jointly experienced music and movement increased later self-sacrifice so impressively has to be a revelation to any parent who has tried to alter the characteristically selfish choices of a four-year-old at play. ("Leia, it's time to give Hailey a turn with that toy. Leia? *Leia!* Leia, you come back here with that right now!") The authors' second noteworthy comment strikes me as at least as important as the first: the children's personal sacrifice didn't arise from any rational weighting of the reasons for and against providing assistance. The help wasn't rooted in rationality at all. It was spontaneous, intuitive, and based on an emotional sense of connection that naturally accompanies shared musical engagement. The implications of this point for managing the social influence process are significant.[97]

SYSTEMS ENGINEERING

Behavioral scientists have long asserted the existence of two ways of assessing and knowing. The most recent such assertion to gain widespread attention is Daniel Kahneman's treatment of the distinction between System 1 and System 2 thinking. The first is fast, associative, intuitive, and often emotional, whereas the second is slower, deliberative, analytical, and rational. Support for the separateness of the two approaches comes from evidence that activating one inhibits the other. Just as it is difficult to think hard about an occurrence while experiencing it emotionally, fully experiencing the occurrence is difficult while parsing it logically. There's an implication for influence: persuaders would be wise to match the System 1 versus 2 orientation of any appeal to the corresponding orientation of the recipient. Thus, if you are considering a car purchase primarily from the standpoint of its emotionally relevant features (attractive looks and exhilarating acceleration), a salesperson would be well advised to convince you by using feelings-related arguments. Research suggests that even merely saying "I *feel* this is the one for you" will be more successful. But if you are considering the purchase primarily on rational grounds (fuel economy and trade-in value), "I *think* this is the one for you" would be more likely to close the sale.[98]

Music's influence is of the System 1 variety. In their sensory and visceral responses, people sing, swing, snake, and sway in rhythmic alignment with it—and, if together, with each other. Rarely do they think analytically while music is prominent in consciousness. Under music's influence, the deliberative, rational route to knowing becomes difficult to access and, hence, largely unavailable. Two commentaries speak to a regrettable upshot. The first, a quote from Voltaire, is contemptuous: "Anything too stupid to be spoken," he asserted, "is sung." The second, an adage from the advertising profession, is tactical: "If you can't make your case to an audience with facts, sing it to them." Thus, communicators whose ideas have little rational firepower don't have to give up the fight; they can undertake a flanking maneuver. Equipping themselves with music and song, they can move their campaign to a battleground where rationality possesses little force, and where sensations of harmony, synchrony, and unity win.

This recognition has helped me resolve a long-standing personal mystery, one that was particularly vexing to me as a young man with no musical talent: Why are young women so attracted to musicians? There's no logic to it, right? Precisely. It doesn't matter that the probabilities of a successful relationship with most musicians are notoriously low; those are *rational* probabilities. And it doesn't matter that the current and future economic prospects of most musicians are equally low; those are *economic* reasons. Music isn't about such practicalities. It's about harmonies— melodic ones that lead to emotional and relational ones.

Besides, because of their common grounding in emotion and harmony, music and romance are strongly associated with one another in life. What would you say is the percentage of contemporary songs with romance as their subject? According to a recent systematic count, it's 80 percent, the vast majority. That's amazing. Romance isn't at issue the vast majority of the time when we speak or think or write, but it is when we sing.

So now I understand why young women, who are at a peak age for interest in both romance and music, have a weakness for musicians. Powerful links between the two types of experiences make musicians hard to resist. Want some scientific proof? If not, just pretend I'm singing you the results of a French study in which the (initially skeptical) researchers had a man approach young women and ask for their phone numbers while he was carrying a guitar case, a sports bag, or nothing:

Those scientists in France
Worried about raising the chance
A guitar would prompt "Oui"
To a stranger's startling plea
Need not have been so troubled,
Phone numbers more than doubled.

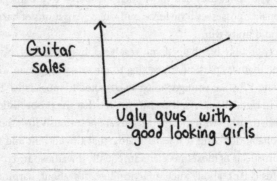

Turning zeros into (guitar) heros. *Via @jessicahagy and thisisindexed.com.*

For anyone interested in maximizing persuasive success, the critical take-away from this section should not be merely that music is allied with System 1 responding or that people act imprudently when channeled to that kind of responding. The far larger lesson involves the importance of matching the System 1 versus 2 character of a persuasive communication with the System 1 versus 2 mind-set of its intended audience. Recipients with nonrational, hedonistic goals should be matched with messages containing nonrational elements such as musical accompaniment, whereas those with rational, pragmatic goals should be matched with messages containing rational elements such as facts. In his outstanding book *Persuasive Advertising: Evidence-Based Principles*, marketing expert J. Scott Armstrong reported that in a 2008 analysis of thirty-second TV commercials, 87 percent incorporated music. But this routine addition of music to the message might well be flawed, as Armstrong also reviewed the relevant research and concluded that music should be used only to advertise familiar, feelings-based products (snack foods, body scents) in an emotional context—that is, where thinking is unlikely. For products that have high personal consequences and strong supportive arguments (safety equipment, software packages)—that is, for which hard thinking is likely and instructive—background music undercuts ad effectiveness.[99]

CONTINUING RECIPROCAL EXCHANGE

In early 2015 a *New York Times* article ignited an explosion of reader interest and commentary, going viral and becoming one of the most widely spread *Times* pieces ever. For a news outlet such as the *Times*, this occurrence might not seem extraordinary, given its elevated journalistic standing on topics of great national and international import. But this particular piece appeared not in its Politics, Business, Technology, Science, or Health pages but in the Fashion & Styles section. As is reflected in the essay's title, "To Fall in Love with Anyone, Do This," its author, Mandy Len Catron, claimed to have found a marvelously effective way to produce the intense emotional closeness and social bonds of love—in the space of forty-five minutes! She knew it worked, she said, because it had worked for her.

The technique came from a program of research initiated by a husband-and-wife team of psychologists, Arthur and Elaine Aron, who hit upon it in their investigations of close relationships. It involves a specific form of coordinated action, in which partners engage in a reciprocal, turn-taking exchange sequence. Other psychologists have demonstrated that a history of reciprocally exchanged favors leads individuals to give additional favors to their exchange partner, no matter who provided the last one. It's a tendency that fits with my account of the Harrisons' agreeing to house an eighteen-year-old student they had never met, not because they owed his family a favor but because they had a decade-long history of exchanging holiday cards with them. The process of reciprocal exchange had prompted the Harrisons' assent by creating a relationship rather than an unmet obligation.

The Arons and their coworkers helped explain this kind of willing assent by showing how extended reciprocal exchanges bind the transactors together. They did so by employing a particularly unifying type of reciprocal exchange strong enough to "unify" people into love with each other: personal self-disclosure. The procedure was not complicated: In pairs, participants took turns reading questions to their partner, who would answer, and who would then receive their partner's answer to the same item. Advancing through the thirty-six questions required participants to disclose progressively more personal information about themselves and, in turn, to learn more personal information about their partner. An early question would be, "What would constitute a perfect day for you?" whereas later in the sequence, a question would be, "What do you value most in a friendship?" And near the end of the list, a question would be, "Of all the people in your family, whose death would be the most disturbing?"

Relationships deepened beyond all expectations. The procedure generated feelings of emotional closeness and interpersonal unity that are unparalleled within a forty-five-minute span, especially among complete strangers in an emotionally sterile laboratory setting. Moreover, the outcome was no chance occurrence. According to an interview with Elaine Aron, hundreds of studies using the method have since confirmed the effect, and some participants have even gotten married as a result. In that same interview, Dr. Aron described two aspects of the procedure that she felt are key to its effectiveness. First, the items escalate in personal disclosure. Thus, when responding, participants increasingly open themselves up to one another in a trusting way representative of tightly bonded pairs. Second, and in keeping with the overarching theme of this chapter, participants do so by *acting* together—that is, in a coordinated, back-and-forth fashion, making the interaction inherently and continuously synchronous.[100]

CO-CREATION

Long before wilderness preservation became a value among many Americans, a man named Aldo Leopold was championing the cause. Principally during the 1930s and 1940s, when he held the first-ever professorship of wildlife management in the United States, at the University of Wisconsin, he developed a distinctive ethical approach to the topic. As detailed in his bestselling book *A Sand County Almanac*, it challenged the dominant model of environmental conservation, in which natural ecologies were to be managed for the purpose of human usage. It advocated instead for an alternative based on the right of all plant and animal species to existence in their natural state whenever possible. Possessed of such a clear and heartfelt position, he was more than surprised one day to find himself, ax in hand, behaving in contradiction of it—by cutting down a red birch tree on his property, so that one of his white pines would get more light and space to grow.

Why, he wondered, would he act to favor the pine over the birch that, according to his avowed ethic, had as much right to exist naturally as any tree on his land? Perplexed, Leopold searched his mind for the "logic" behind his bias and, in considering various differences between the two types of trees that might account for the preference, encountered only one he was convinced was a primary factor. It was one that had nothing to do with logic but was entirely founded on feelings: "Well, first of all, I planted the pine with my shovel, whereas the birch crawled in under the fence and planted itself. My bias is thus to some extent paternal. . . ."[101]

Leopold was not unique in feeling a special affinity for something he had a hand in creating. It's a common human occurrence. For example, in what researchers have termed the Ikea effect, people who have built items themselves come to see "their amateurish creations as similar in value to experts' creations." As suits our current focus on the effects of acting together, it is worth inquiring into an additional pair of possibilities. Would people who had a hand in creating something *hand in hand* with another come to feel a special affinity not only for their creation but also for their co-creator? What's more, might this exceptional affinity stem from a feeling of unity with the other that's detectible in the characteristic consequences of elevated liking and self-sacrificial support for the partner?

Let's seek the answer to those questions by resolving a prior one: Why would I begin this section on *co*-creation with Aldo Leopold's description of the effect of planting of a pine by himself? It's simply that, as I am certain he would agree, he was no lone actor in the process. He was a co-creator, with nature, of the mature pine he once put in the ground as a sapling. The intriguing possibility that arises is whether, as a result of acting together with Mother Nature, he came to feel more merged with her—and, as a consequence, even more enamored and respectful of his partner in the collaboration. If that were so, we'd have an indication that co-creation can be a route to unification. Regrettably, Mr. Leopold has not been available for questioning on the possibility since 1948. But I am confident of the answer.

A portion of that confidence comes from the results of a study I helped conduct to investigate the effects of managers' degree of personal involvement in the creation of a work product. I'd expected that the more involvement managers felt they'd had in generating the final product in concert with an employee, the higher they would rate its quality, which is what we found: managers led to believe that they'd had a large role in developing the end product (an ad for a new wristwatch) rated the ad 50 percent more favorably than did managers led to believe they'd had little developmental involvement—even though the final ad they saw was identical in all cases. In addition, we found that the managers with the greatest perceived involvement rated themselves more responsible for the ad's quality in terms of their much greater perceived managerial control over their employee, which I'd also expected.

But I didn't expect a third finding at all. The more the managers attributed the success of the project to themselves, the more they also attributed it to the ability of their employee. I recall, data table in hand, experiencing a moment of surprise—perhaps not as striking as Leopold's ax-in-hand moment, but a moment of surprise nonetheless. How could supervisors with greater perceived involvement in the development of a work product see themselves and a single coworker on the project as *each* more responsible for its successful final form? Only 100 percent of personal responsibility can be distributed, right? And if one party's perceived personal contribution goes up, by simple logic, the work partner's should go down, not up. I just didn't get it at the time, but now I think I do. If co-creation causes at least a temporary merging of identities, then what applies to one partner also applies to the other, distributional logic notwithstanding.

Avoiding stagnation via "bossification." Creative accounting is a recognized business trick—and so, apparently, is creative co-creation. *Dilbert* © *2014. Scott Adams. Used by permission of Universal Uclick. All rights reserved.*

Asking for Advice Is Good Advice

Co-creation doesn't only reduce the problem of getting supervisors to give more credit to employees who've worked productively on a project. It can lessen a host of other traditionally hard-to-diminish difficulties. Children below the age of six or seven are typically selfish when it comes to sharing rewards, rarely distributing them equally with playmates—unless they have obtained those rewards through a collaborative effort with a playmate, whereupon even three-year-olds share equally the majority of the time. In the standard classroom, students tend to coalesce along racial, ethnic, and socioeconomic lines, finding friends and helpmates mainly within their own groups. However, this pattern declines significantly after they've engaged co-creatively with students from the other groups within "cooperative learning" exercises, in which each student has to teach a portion of the information to the others so that they can all get a good score. Companies struggle to get consumers to feel bonded with and therefore loyal to their brands; it's a battle they've been winning by inviting current and prospective customers to co-create with them novel or updated products and services, most often by providing the company with information as to desirable features.

However, within such marketing partnerships, consumer input must be framed as *advice to* the company, not as opinions about or expectations for the company. The differential phrasing might seem minor, but it is critical to achieving the company's unitization goal. Providing advice puts a person in a merging state of mind, which stimulates a linking of one's own identity with another party's. Providing an opinion or expectation, on the other hand, puts a person in an introspective state of mind, which involves focusing on oneself. These only slightly different forms of consumer feedback—and the nonetheless vitally different merging-versus-separating mind-sets they produce—can have a significant impact on consumer engagement with a brand.

That's what happened to a group of online survey takers from around the United States shown a description of the business plan for a new fast-casual restaurant, Splash!, that hoped to distinguish itself from competitors through the healthfulness of its menu items. After reading the description, all the survey participants were asked for feedback. But some were asked for any "advice" they might have regarding the restaurant, whereas others were asked either for any "opinions" or "expectations" they might have. Finally, they indicated how likely they'd be to patronize a Splash! restaurant. Those participants who provided advice reported wanting to eat at a Splash! significantly more than participants who provided either of the other sorts of feedback. And just as we would expect if giving advice is indeed a mechanism of unitization, the increased desire to support the restaurant came from feeling more linked with the brand.

One more finding from the survey clinches the unitization case for me: the participants rated all three types of feedback as equally helpful to the restaurateurs. So it wasn't that those who gave advice felt connected with the brand because they thought they had aided it more. Instead, having to give advice put participants in a togetherness state of mind rather than a separateness state of mind just before they had to reflect on what they would say about the brand—a finding that, I have to admit, pleases me because it implicates the *pre-suasive* character of the psychological process acting on those advice-giving participants.

This set of results also clinches for me the wisdom (and the ethicality, if done in an authentic search for useful information) of asking for advice in face-to-face interactions with friends, colleagues, and customers. It should even prove effective in our interactions with superiors. Of course, it is reasonable and rational to worry about a potential downside—that by asking a boss for advice, you might come off as incompetent or dependent or insecure. While I see the logic of such a concern, I also see it as mistaken because, as the study of supervisors' estimation of collaborators' contributions indicated, the effects of co-creation are not well captured by reason, rationality, or logic. But they are exceedingly well captured by a particular socially promotive *feeling* in the situation: the (highly beneficial for you) state of togetherness. The novelist Saul Bellow once observed, "When we ask for advice, we are usually looking for an accomplice." I'd only add on the basis of scientific evidence that, if we get that advice, we usually get that accomplice. And what better abettor to have on a project than someone in charge?[102]

GETTING TOGETHER

It's time to look back at—and, more dauntingly—look past what we've seen as the mostly favorable consequences of *being* together and *acting* together. We learned, for instance, that by installing one or another of those two unitizing experiences in people pre-suasively, we can arrange to solidify support from a company's shareholders as well as its customers, and to help ensure that soldiers will stand and fight rather than flee in wartime. In addition, we found that we can use those same two unitizing experiences to arrange for playmates, classmates, and workmates to like, help, and cooperate with one another; for nearly any parent to fill out a long survey with no financial compensation; and even for love to emerge in a lab. But here's an unanswered question: Might it be possible to apply the lessons from these arenas to much larger stages, such as those involving age-old international enmities, violent religious clashes, and simmering racial antagonisms? Could those lessons from what we know about being together and acting together increase our chance of *getting* together, as a species?

That's a tough question to answer, in large part because of the many complications inherent in such matters. Still, even on these fraught fields, I believe that procedures that establish a pre-suasive feeling of unity establish a context for desirable change. Moreover, provided that both parties share the feeling, the desirable change is likely to be mutual, reducing the probability that either party will feel exploited, deepening a sense of togetherness, and raising the likelihood of continued positive interaction. Although this idea sounds hopeful in hand-waving theory, it would be naïve, owing to the attendant procedural and cultural complications, to presume that the theory would work out smoothly in practice. The specifics of the unitizing procedures would have to be optimally designed and enacted with those complexities in mind—something with which the experts on the issues would surely agree and which might be the worthy subject of an entire follow-up book. Needless to say, I'd certainly welcome those experts' opinions—make that *advice*—in that regard.[103]

13

Ethical Use: A Pre-Pre-Suasive Consideration

A central assertion of this book is that our choice of what to say or do immediately before making an appeal significantly affects its persuasive success. But there's a related choice that occurs even before that one. It is whether, on ethical grounds, to try to attain success in such a way. I am not alone in considering this an important part of the equation, as ethical questions surface regularly whenever I convey information on the topic of effective persuasion. However, there is one specific type of question, as stated by one specific type of recipient, that is especially relevant to this book and the topic of pre-suasion: In revealing the "secrets of social influence," am I doing more harm than good by giving certain unethical practitioners the means to trick consumers into buying even more of whatever they might be peddling? The individuals most likely to pose the question to me have been representatives of the media.

Although the overall experience was mostly a blur, I do recall a steady diet of such media questioning during the only book tour I've ever agreed to undertake. The circuit traversed a marathon course of ten cities in ten days, each of which included multiple media interviews led by print journalists or radio or TV hosts who had little information about me and, in the bulk of instances, had not read the book. The exchanges varied in a few ways: some took place numbingly early in the morning, others throughout the day; some lasted only a few minutes, others as long as an hour; some were one-on-one interviews, others were led by a pair of cohosts; and some included audience call-in questions, often of the uncomfortably personal and professionally unanswerable variety: "So, *doctor of influence*, how do I get my jackass brother-in-law to stop borrowing my tools and then 'forgetting' to return them; and, besides, I think he's running around on my sister—what do I do about that?" But one feature didn't vary much: at some point the interviewer would raise the more-harm-than-good idea, asking me to respond to the possibility that my book was doing society a disservice by showing devious merchandisers how to use psychology to bamboozle us.

It was usually possible to counter the concern by pointing to a pair of aspects of the book that the interviewers, not having read it, did not know. First, it was written *for* consumers, to give them the information necessary to recognize and reject unwanted or unfair influence attempts. Second, much of the information came from the practitioners. More often than not, primarily in their training programs, they were informing *me* of which procedures reliably got consumers to say yes. Although they might not have appreciated the psychological factors that caused their practices to work, the majority of influence professionals knew quite well what did work for them. Consequently, I argued, the material in my book wasn't offering any new techniques for practitioners to adopt; instead, it was balancing the equation by providing information to consumers about the tactics routinely employed on them.

With this current book, though, those two responses aren't available to me. The conclusions drawn have been principally about how to harness influence rather than deflect it, so the "consumer defense" defense doesn't apply. What's more, the practice of pre-suasion, as described here, isn't widely employed within the community of influence professionals. I can't make the claim this time that I'm just revealing tactics already known to the preponderance of practitioners; only a rarified few understand the processes of pre-suasion well enough to commission them systematically on their behalf. It's therefore a legitimate concern that publication of the information might enlighten certain unethical organizations about how to trick people into assent more effectively. This possibility becomes even more worrisome with the realization that many pre-suasive processes operate unconsciously and, hence, go unrecognized.

As a result, whenever addressing commercial organizations regarding pre-suasive practices, I've had to change direction and revert to a traditional argument against deceptive business tactics. It goes as follows: although such tactics might increase profit in the short run, once exposed, they will produce unacceptably high costs—mostly in the form of severe damage to the company's reputation and to subsequent trust and future earnings. For a while, I thought this argument quite good for two reasons. First, it makes its case on the dimension of economic vitality, which business leaders have to take into account to maintain growth and, indeed, survival. That strikes me as a more motivating rationale for recommended action in commercial environments than finger wagging about a lack of virtue.

Accordingly, I'm sure there will never be a law against shouting "Ethics!" in a crowded boardroom, because—unlike "Fire!" in a crowded theater—the term doesn't possess enough mobilizing force there to spur urgent movement. That's not to say that, as a group, businesspeople wouldn't prefer to be ethical. All else being equal, most would unhesitatingly choose the high road. But except in hypothetical situations, all else is never equal; and we often see that factors with more motivational punch—sales quotas, financial status reports, competitive concerns, career advancements—prevail over higher-minded choices in commercial decisions.

Besides, acting to promote corporate profitability through sometimes less than ethical means can be seen as honorable by leaders who feel a moral responsibility to enhance and ensure the economic well-being of their employees. When viewed through this (admittedly tilted) lens, a decision to stretch the truth to benefit corporate fiscal stability could be judged to be the ethically proper one. Therefore, I assured myself, any argument pointing out how deceptive practices actually *threaten* the bottom line would be compelling.

The second reason I thought the case for reputational damage would be telling to business decision makers is that the evidence supporting it is solid. The size of financial loss from reputational consequences can be substantial, as large economic injury has been shown to flow from the reputational impact of false advertising, deceptive bidding practices, and financial misrepresentations. For example, a 2005 study of 585 firms

subjected to US Securities and Exchange Commission (SEC) enforcement proceedings for financial misrepresentation found that, on average,
companies lost 41 percent of their market value after the misconduct was
made public and that nearly two-thirds of the loss stemmed from reputational harm. Indeed, 80 percent of Americans stated that their perception of the ethicality of a particular company's business practices has
a direct effect on their decisions to purchase its goods or services. Such
effects received more recent validation in 2015, when, shortly after Volkswagen's diesel emissions trickery became known, its sales dropped to
one-sixteenth of the industry average, it suffered the largest annual loss
in company history, and its reputation among vehicle owners went from
70 percent favorable to 80 percent not favorable. Plus, the damage is singularly difficult to undo. Research indicates that a disreputable company
attempting to recover lost trust would need to demonstrate its newfound
integrity consistently and on many occasions to convince the wary that
the firm's values had changed. Such a recovery process could take years,
by which time the company's former customers and clients are likely to
have established links to rivals' products and services.

Satisfied that this strong economic argument would convince business leaders to avoid devious practices, I was content to describe the workings of pre-suasive influence strategies to them, provided that I invariably
made the "reputational disaster" case as well. Then I read the results of
a pair of global surveys that forced me to change my thinking. They revealed that senior business leaders are very much aware of the evidence in
support of the reputation-based case I was making, but that uncomfortably large numbers of them are willing to undertake misconduct anyway.
Despite understanding the risks, close to half of high-ranking executives
reported they would act unethically to get or retain business. In addition,
sales and marketing staffers, who were most likely to endorse ethically
dubious conduct to secure a win, were least likely to be questioned about
it by the company. Finally, employees of these firms saw few actions taken
at the top either to prevent profit-enhancing ethical violations or to pun-
ish those involved after the fact. As a consequence, the amount of unethical activity on the part of commercial organizations remains distressingly
high.

Apparently, many senior leaders are cognizant of the potentially ruinous consequences of discovered ethical misconduct but are not deterred by them. That seems clear; what's not is why not. It's conceivable that these leaders are engaging in a form of psychological compartmentalization, mentally walling off their knowledge of the reputational risks of wrongdoing from their active participation in or tacit permission of it. But I don't think so. Those at the highest levels of an organization don't get to their prominent positions by systematically ignoring clear and present dangers. I'd favor a simpler explanation: they just don't expect to get caught. They wouldn't engage in misconduct if they thought it would become visible to penalty-wielding customers, clients, and regulators. This explanation fits with findings from studies of crime deterrence demonstrating that individuals who commit violations carrying significant negative consequences do not believe they will be caught; otherwise they would be unlikely to undertake the punishable activities in the first place.[104]

"We're supposed to attend a conference on business-casual ethics."

Relaxed fit. In most workplaces, business-casual rules for dress apply only on Fridays. But surveys show that, in many companies, business-casual rules for ethics apply daily.
Leo Cullum / The New Yorker Collection/The Cartoon Bank

The dilemma is easy to see. On the one hand, many business leaders would likely be dissuaded from unethical activity by alarming economic considerations. On the other hand, the cautionary economic argument against such activity has failed to reduce misconduct because it involves an expectation of discovery, which most perpetrators surely would not possess when deciding to act. How can we extricate ourselves from the horns of this dilemma? One possibility would be to acknowledge business leaders' understandable tendencies to weigh economic factors heavily in business decisions and then to document several onerous financial penalties that flow from unethical conduct *even if it goes undetected by the public*. Along with my colleagues Jessica Li and Adriana Samper, I've recently conducted research to provide evidence of such expenses that come from the responses of individuals inside, not outside, the organization. We've also tried to detail how these harmful costs can develop and how they can slip, undiagnosed, under the radar of most business systems.

THE TRIPLE-TUMOR STRUCTURE OF ORGANIZATIONAL DISHONESTY

Do not seek dishonest gains; dishonest gains are losses.

—Hesiod

Here's what we've attempted to show: An organization that regularly approves, encourages, or allows the use of deceitful tactics in its external dealings (with customers, clients, stockholders, suppliers, distributors, regulators, and so on) will experience a nasty set of internal consequences that are akin to tumors. Not only will they become malignant—growing, spreading, and eating progressively at the organization's health and vigor—they will be difficult to trace and identify via typical accounting methods as the true causes of inferior profitability. Thus, they might easily lead to expensive, misguided efforts that fail to target the genuine culprits of the dysfunction.

Three features of a commercial organization known to ravage its health are poor employee performance, high employee turnover, and prevalent employee fraud and malfeasance. The costs of each can be staggering. Our claim is that organizations possessing an unethical work culture—in which employees participate in or simply observe regular wrongdoing—will be beset by the three outcomes. We are not assigning these outcomes to localized or infrequent ethical infractions but rather to a dominant organizational culture that permits or promotes dishonest business practices. Inferior work performance is probably the biggest saboteur of profitability. Let's begin with it.

Poor Employee Performance

Places of work can be stressful; we all know it. What we might not appreciate, though, is how costly that stress can be. One recent analysis found the toll to be heavy on both personal and economic dimensions, as various kinds of occupational stress, when combined, led annually to about 120,000 deaths and $200 *billion* in additional health care expenses in the United States alone, where employers bear much of the financial burden. However, there is yet another type of cost-carrying workplace stress that went unexamined in this analysis but is related directly to the issue of organizational misconduct. We can call it moral stress; and it comes from a conflict between an employee's ethical values and the perceived ethical values of the organization. In the case of employee performance, this kind of stress can be even more harmful than other stressors known to be highly damaging.

For example, a study of customer service agents in a financial service call center compared moral stress with other forms of stress there—including problems with difficult customers, lack of support from supervisors and/or coworkers, conflicting task demands, and dead-end job descriptions. Only moral stress predicted both of two performance-degrading outcomes: employee fatigue (low emotional spirit and physical energy) and job burnout (loss of enthusiasm for and interest in one's work). These two outcomes weren't chosen for study offhandedly by the researchers. Each is a serious managerial problem by itself; combined, they're a managerial nightmare, robbing workers of the vigor, desire, and capacity to do their jobs well. Might it be that in creating an unethical work environment, an organization unknowingly creates that nightmare for itself? Might an unethical work environment produce lower performance in workers who didn't behave unethically themselves but merely observed such behavior among their fellow workers?

To find out, we arranged an experimental situation that allowed us to test the effects of dishonest workplace activity not only on task performance but on our other specified organizational tumors. We invited university business students to sit at a computer networked to those of team members at various other universities. Their team would compete, they were told, on problem-solving tasks against other teams from around the country. If their team did well on the first task, it would be given a competitive advantage over the other teams on the next group task. Finally, they were told that because of some technology issues with only their computer, they wouldn't be able to send information to their teammates, although they would be able to see their teammates' online interactions with one another.

After the team members performed the first problem-solving task, they learned from their team leader that the team had gotten only 67 percent of the answers correct. They also learned that, nonetheless, this leader intended to report 80 percent correct answers to the researcher to improve the group's perceived performance—because, as the team leader confided, there was no way that cheating could be discovered by the researcher. None of the other team members stated any objection.

Of course, this sequence of events was something we manufactured for our study's participants. The information they got from their team leader and team members was programmed by us to appear on their computer screens as we'd designed it. The same was true for a second set of our participants, who received identical information with one crucial difference: they saw their team leader report intending to submit the group's 67 percent score *honestly* to the researcher; and, here again, they witnessed none of the other team members stating any objection. At this point, then, half of our participants had been made to be part of a work unit that approved of and engaged in deceit to obtain a competitive advantage, whereas the other half of our participants had not. Thus, we were poised to learn how the two experiences affected the costly consequences we had predicted.

First came an examination of subsequent work-relevant performance. All participants were informed that the next task would be an individual one, in which each would read about a business situation and then answer critical-reasoning questions associated with it. We took the business situation and its related questions from a well-validated test of business intelligence to ensure that performance on it would involve the kinds of judgments that affect business success. The ensuing data showed dramatic differences. Those participants whose work team had previously been deceptive scored 20 percent lower on the test than our other participants. Another finding gave us an indication of why the first group performed so poorly: after working on the business problem for a while, the members just stopped—significantly sooner than the other participants—suggesting they didn't have the same energy or motivation to continue.

Although these results were encouraging for at least one aspect of our thinking, we could imagine hearing the "nays" of a frustrating collection of naysayers, declaring themselves unconvinced because evidence on workplace issues coming from (1) a laboratory experiment (2) on university students who (3) encountered an artificially constructed unethical environment is inadequate. In truth, the most frustrating feature to us of these imagined critics was that they had a point. We recognized that to confirm that our data patterns applied to real-life employment situations, we needed to find out from a sample of workers how ethics-relevant workplace factors operated on them. We set out to do so by conducting a national survey of adults who had been at their current or most recent job for an average of three years.

The survey contained a lot of questions about these individuals and the places they worked. But for our current focus, three types of items carried special weight: those asking them to rate the ethical climate of the organization as set by its managers and leaders, the amount of stress they felt there, and the quality of their work performance. When we analyzed their responses, we found results that fit with and even exceeded the findings of our university laboratory experiment. According to their reports, first, the more unethical the climate, the poorer the workers' job performance; second, the more unethical the climate, the more stress they felt at work; and third, that particular stress caused their poor performance. With this evidence in hand, when making an economically centered pitch to business leaders against unethical activities, we thought we had the makings of "Strike one."[105]

Employee Turnover

For business leaders, there's one good feature of employee turnover costs: they can be assessed fairly precisely. But that's where the good news ends. Depending on the type of employee lost in the process, charges to the bottom line range from large to eye-wateringly large. Estimates of direct expenses associated with turnover (severance pay, recruitment, hiring, and training of the replacement) can extend from 50 percent of the employee's annual compensation package for lower-level positions to over 200 percent of the total package for executive-level positions. These costs spiral even higher when indirect hits are taken into account (loss of institutional memory, sales and productivity disruptions, lowered morale among remaining team members). But to get a conservative estimate of voluntary turnover costs, let's assume that, on average, the combined direct and indirect expenses were equal to just one year's total remuneration. Voluntary turnover rates in the United States are now above 15 percent per year. But for the average midsize firm of a thousand employees, even if only 10 percent of workers (who averaged $40,000 in total salary and benefits annually) walked out, they would take with them $4 million every year in turnover costs.

How is this economic toll related to unethical work practices? We thought it would be through the moral stress experienced by employees whose personal values conflicted with regular wrongdoing. One reason an honest person would want to leave a work unit would be if staying meant having to be a party to presiding duplicity. To test the possibility, we constructed another experiment on university business students that was much like our first study, in that half of them were part of a team led by a leader who advanced its agenda through deception, and the other half were part of a team that did not act deceptively. Afterward, they were told that, prior to beginning a second group task, they could elect either to stay with their team or to move to a different one. When we counted the votes, we found that 51 percent of those who had been in an ethical group decided to leave their team, but 80 percent of those in an unethical group chose to leave theirs.

To gain confidence that these results applied beyond our laboratory setting, we turned to the data from our national survey of workers, which revealed clear turnover-related patterns. Not only were employees of unethically rated organizations more likely to feel stressed and more likely to want to quit, it was this stress that was pushing them to leave—and to leave their employers with financially draining turnover costs as a consequence. "Strike two," we thought.[106]

Employee Fraud and Malfeasance

Notice that, according to our thinking, the flight of personnel from an ethically compromised company isn't expected to include everyone. Rather, because the exodus is launched by the stress from *conflicting* moral values, it will be specific to employees with high ethical standards. Those comfortable with the use of trickery to achieve financial gains should be happy to stay. And therein lies the source of our third specified tumor of organizational dishonesty. Phrased in terms of a caution to any leader responsible for shaping the ethical climate of an organization, it is as follows: those who cheat for you will cheat against you. If you encourage the first form of deceit, you will get the second, which will cost you dearly in the bargain.

Owing to the tendency for personnel to exit organizations where the ethical fit is poor, a company with an enduring culture of misconduct will push away many honest employees, leaving an accumulating precipitate of individuals disposed toward wrongdoing, and who, when given the opportunity, will do their wrong to the firm. By our argument, then, such an enterprise will draw under its coat a viper—a snake whose bite will be fiscally venomous, as the costs of employee fraud and malfeasance are figured in trillions of dollars worldwide. What's more, these losses (stemming from embezzlement, theft of inventory or equipment, expense account inflation, falsified purchasing reports, and under-the-table deals with vendors or business partners) are rarely recouped.

This argument seems a good one, with its proclaimed logic, major fiscal implications, poison-linked metaphorical flourish and all, but where's the evidence? To find it, we turned again to our experimental setting and one final procedure. Recall that in our second study, subjects became part of a work unit that either did or did not embrace dishonesty, and when we gave them the chance to stay with the unit or leave it for another, many more chose to quit their team if it had acted unethically. At this point, we told everyone that because of unforeseen logistical difficulties, we weren't able to accommodate any team switching; therefore, they'd be working on the next task with their original teammates. Actually, the next task required them to work *against* those teammates to determine who could best solve an array of word problems quickly. Whoever did so within one minute would increase the probability of winning a $100 prize. Before participants provided their solutions, we arranged for them to "accidentally" see the answer key for the problems in an untraceable way. Through pretests, we had learned that, on average, the typical student at the university could solve 3.17 of the problems in a minute. So, by comparing participants' reported number of problems solved to the 3.17 standard, we could see which types of participants were likely to cheat to elevate their own economic interests over those of their colleagues.

The results were clear. Among the participants who had been part of an honest work unit *and* had elected to stay in it, cheating was nonexistent to negligible, which suggests a high five should be given to the many leaders who have had the integrity and organizational wisdom to establish an ethical culture. Participants choosing to leave either an honest or a dishonest work unit cheated somewhat but not to a statistically significant degree. The big news, though, came from the actions of those who, when previously given the chance, had opted to remain in a dishonest environment. They cheated 77 percent more than the average of everyone else. That cheating, remember, didn't merely enhance their own financial prospects but also undermined those of the people around them. It might be too harsh to label these actions venomous, but they did appear sufficiently toxic to justify a close look into our survey numbers to assess the related evidence from naturally occurring workplace experiences.

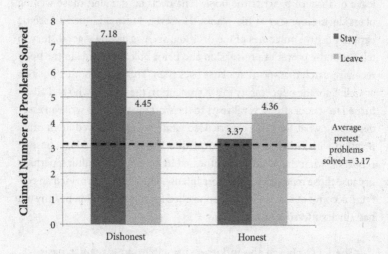

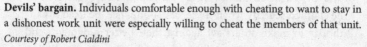

Devils' bargain. Individuals comfortable enough with cheating to want to stay in a dishonest work unit were especially willing to cheat the members of that unit. *Courtesy of Robert Cialdini*

We examined the relationships among items measuring employees' ratings of the ethicality of their workplace as set by its leaders, their desire to leave that workplace, and their admissions of malfeasance on the job (that is, economically harmful actions taken against their employers, such as altering expense reports, sabotaging equipment to avoid having to work, and using company resources for private purposes). The key finding was that employees in unethical organizations who preferred to remain in them were abnormally likely to engage in such deceitful, financially costly workplace activity. Just as in our laboratory experiment, individuals happy to reside in unethical workplace nests were revealed to be happy to foul those nests.

- —— -

Near the start of this book I admitted that its completion was several years late because a university administrator, using a pre-suasive tactic, got me to agree to teach an MBA course at his university while I was there on a leave of absence to write the book. The decision derailed those writing plans during my stay at his school. However, I also admitted to seeing certain positive outcomes of the decision, such as having a good story to tell about the power of pre-suasion and being able to include in the book recent research that wasn't available back then. There was another positive as well: I got the opportunity to ask students in the course, who had all returned to school after several years in the working world, to write an essay describing what they had experienced while being employed in an organization with either an ethical or unethical work climate. Most chose to report on what they'd felt and witnessed in an unethical culture, perhaps because those memories were more intense. One student provided an edifying account of a company he had worked for that started out healthy but had since suffered a $1 billion loss:

> The CEO abused the influence principles on a regular basis: he claimed scarcity when there was abundance, he used his authority to make others act against their better judgment, and created examples of social proof that didn't exist. People believed him in the short run, but as the truth leaked out, the company's reputation deteriorated. Few companies are willing to do business with him now—those that do will only do so on onerous terms.
>
> The culture of dishonesty trickled down throughout the organization. The marketing department was coerced to exaggerate the truth, the PR department wrote mostly false press releases, and salespeople coerced customers. Job dissatisfaction and turnover were incredibly high. People were attracted to the company by high salaries (which the CEO saw as justification for treating employees poorly) but left as soon as they could find work elsewhere. Taking a cue from the executives, employees would steal from the company whenever they could, usually via travel and expense reports. Some would cut side deals with suppliers. When I

visited a few months ago, nearly half the staff had left, and morale was lower than ever.

"Strike three"?

I am strongly inclined to hope so. Of course, whether that hope is ever realized depends on the extent to which leaders accept the financially based argument against duplicity and choose to act accordingly. The Tinker Bell scenario isn't going to apply here: unless those leaders set the proper organizational tone, this argument won't take wing and fly just because the rest of us *really, really* believe in it. The concurrence of those at the top is required. Fortunately, if they want, they can build and maintain an ethically commendable workplace culture as readily as an ethically objectionable one. What could be done to send senior leaders more eagerly down the virtuous path? For one large group of them, no shift in direction seems necessary. They've already decided on that route and should be admired for following it. But for the nearly half who feel that economic considerations do warrant dishonest conduct, it may be necessary to lay out certain countervailing costs (of employee underperformance, turnover, and malfeasance) that apply, even when the misconduct is not detected by outsiders.

As a set of general recommendations that all commercial organizations might want to adopt, three appear worth the effort. Honesty ratings by customers and clients of employees they interact with should be part of the employees' incentive structures. In addition, the ethical reputation of the company as a whole should be measured and included in assessments of yearly performance. Finally, ratings by employees of the firm's ethical orientation should be a component of senior management's (and especially the CEO's) compensation package. The effect of these steps would not only incentivize ethical conduct but also bring continuing, heightened attention to ethical standards. The consequent focused attention on these matters would (justifiably) elevate their perceived importance and causal role in organizational affairs.[107]

14

Post-Suasion: Aftereffects

Throughout this book, we've seen that successful pre-suasion can occur when audience members' attention is channeled temporarily to a psychological concept favorable to a follow-on message. However, if pre-suasion is indeed based on temporarily directed attention, there's an important question all pre-suaders must confront: When rival communicators or even everyday events divert that attention to some other concept, what can be done to prevent the favorability from evaporating? It's a worthwhile concern, as change agents are usually interested in generating more than short-term movement—although, as prior chapters attest, time-limited shifts can be extraordinarily productive when managed astutely. Nonetheless, for optimal impact, the hope is to have an enduring effect. Two effective strategies are available, each arising from a different approach to social influence—one old-school and one new-school.

CREATING LASTING CHANGE BY INSTALLING STRONG COMMITMENTS

Traditionally, behavioral scientists have offered a straightforward answer to the question of how to make a person's initially affirmative response persist: arrange for the individual to make a commitment to that response, usually in the form of an active step. Consider how this recommendation can reduce a costly social problem. Patients who fail to appear for medical and dental appointments are more than an inconvenience; they represent a sizable expense to the health care system. A standard practice designed to reduce these no-shows involves calling patients the day before to remind them of the appointment. In a study led by my colleague Steve J. Martin and conducted in British medical clinics, such efforts reduced failures to appear by 3.5 percent. But the reminder calls required time and money to deliver and didn't always reach their targets. Compare that to the wisdom of employing a commitment procedure. When making a future appointment after an office visit, we all know what happens. The receptionist writes down the time and date of the next appointment on a card and gives it to patients. If, instead, the *patients* are asked to fill in the card, that active step gets them more committed to keeping the appointment. When this costless procedure was tried in the British medical clinic study, the subsequent no-show rate dropped by 18 percent.

Although the effect of reducing missed medical appointments is no small thing (an 18 percent decline could net the equivalent of $180 million per year in the United Kingdom alone), it's possible that prompted behavioral commitments can have a much larger societal impact by influencing political elections. In 2008, shortly before the presidential election between Barack Obama and John McCain, Americans in several states were surveyed online regarding their political attitudes and beliefs. Half saw a small American flag at the top left corner of the survey questionnaire as they began to answer its questions; the other half saw no flag. Exposure to the American flag in this subtle way caused participants to become more favorable to McCain's Republican Party and its politically conservative ideology. Moreover, when participants were resurveyed after the election, the researchers learned that those who had encountered a US flag on the prior questionnaire had voted for McCain at a significantly greater rate than the other participants. Finally—and perhaps most remarkably—a full eight months after the election, participants who had made contact with their flag during the long-past survey were still embracing more Republican Party–oriented attitudes, beliefs, and judgments.

Could that single exposure really account for such lasting and consequential effects? Results such as these beg for explanation—explanations, actually, because there's more than one process involved. The first is pre-suasive in character. Background exposure to the American flag put participants in mind of Republican Party thinking; indeed, a pilot study done by the researchers showed that, in 2008 anyway, Americans reliably made that link between the flag and Republicanism. Just as we've seen previously that a background encounter with French music in a shop disposed people temporarily toward French things (such as French wine), and a background encounter with an image of fluffy clouds on a furniture store website made people more disposed temporarily toward soft things (such as comfortable sofas), such an encounter with the American flag made people temporarily more disposed toward Republican Party candidates and positions.

So much for the flag's immediate effects. But how can we explain their surprising persistence? The survey researchers think they know: after coming across the American flag and becoming temporarily more inclined toward Republicanism, participants were asked to *act* on that inclination by registering it in the survey, thereby committing to it behaviorally. Their commitment led to an even more committing form of activity when they subsequently voted in the election, which, in turn, led to a solidified Republican Party orientation when measured eight months later. This sequence is reminiscent of the outcomes of research examining the effect of a different pre-suasive experience (happy mood) on a different type of preference (for artwork). After people read a happy story, their temporarily elevated mood caused them to like a painting. But five days later, only those who had actively rated it while in that elated state still felt the same way about the painting. Those who had not rated it—and, therefore, had not "locked in" that evaluation behaviorally—showed no special preference for it at all after the happy mood had dissipated.[108]

The implication for effective pre-suasion is plain: pre-suasive openers can produce dramatic, immediate shifts in people, but to turn those shifts into durable changes, it's necessary to get commitments to them, usually in the form of related behavior. Not all commitments are equal in this respect, however. The most effective commitments reach into the future by incorporating behaviors that affect one's personal identity. They do so by ensuring that the commitment is undertaken in an *active, effortful, and voluntary* fashion, because each of these elements communicates deep personal preferences. For instance, if through someone's pre-suasive maneuver of showing me images of people standing together I become temporarily inclined toward an inclusive social policy—say, raising the minimum wage for all workers—and I see myself acting on that preference (by making a quickly requested financial contribution to the cause), I will become more committed to the idea on the spot. In addition, if the action was both made freely (it was entirely my choice) and difficult or costly to perform (the size of my donation was substantial), I'm even more likely to view it as indicating what I favor as a person. It's this behaviorally influenced self-perception that would anchor and align my later responding on the issue. And it would be so even if the sequence was instigated pre-suasively by a momentary shift of attention—in this case, to the concept of togetherness.[109]

CREATING LASTING CHANGE BY CUEING UP THE CUES

Back when I was trying to learn everything I could about influence professionals' persuasion practices, I received an invitation in the mail to experience "an amazing opportunity to achieve wealth, prosperity, and financial independence beyond your dreams." I was certain it involved some kind of pyramid scheme, which normally would ensure the end of my interest. But because I was curious at the time to learn how its promoters planned to sell the scheme, I called to reserve a place. The most intriguing aspect of the event for me was its location. Although I and about fifty other individuals—ranging from economically interested to desperate—came together on a Saturday morning at a Phoenix restaurant, we didn't stay for long. We were escorted onto an aging, distinctively colored yellow-and-blue bus for a two-hour highway drive to Tucson, where, we were told, the educational event would be take place. That was a lie. When we got to Tucson, there was no new enlightenment provided. At lunch, a speaker just briefly reviewed the points we'd heard on the bus ride.

Why would the program organizers spend good money on such a bewildering journey? By then, I knew: the program information was never envisioned for Tucson. It had always been designed for the *bus*. I was sure this was true because, halfway to Tucson, I'd looked out my window and observed another aging, distinctively colored yellow-and-blue bus carrying a load of riders from Tucson to Phoenix. That sight supplied an immediate, clarifying epiphany: from the start, the organizers had intended to expose us to the details of their wealth program (a pyramid scheme, as I'd suspected) on buses rattling along the road between the two cities. I believe that was the case for a pair of psychologically based reasons. First, *it was hard to think hard* in that rolling, noisy, bumpy, crowded, emotionally agitating environment, and hard thinking is the chief foe of pyramid sales systems.

Second, when people can't deliberate carefully, can't concentrate fully, they are much more likely to respond automatically to whatever decision-making cues are present in the situation. On our bus, the program organizers controlled those cues. They'd been able to fill the space with an array of features that, wherever we looked, set us up to be receptive to their message. Achievement-related posters adorned the walls and ceiling, wealth-linked slogans were taped to our seatbacks, and success-themed music preceded each new speaker's presentation. (Songs from the *Rocky* movies predominated; "Eye of the Tiger" was a favorite.) The speakers' basic message was always some version of "You can do it, you can do it, you can do it, you can do it—provided you use the system." This universal assertion was accompanied by a collection of supportive cues: an expensive, beautifully tailored suit worn by one speaker, an $11,000 commission check "from this month alone" waved by another, a glowing testimonial letter read by a third from an individual who before starting the program had "been just like you folks." By the time we'd returned to Phoenix, two-thirds of us had signed on.

Modern life is becoming more and more like that bus hurtling down the highway: speedy, turbulent, stimulus saturated, and mobile. As a result, we are all becoming less and less able to think hard and well about what best to do in many situations. Hence, even the most careful-minded of us are increasingly likely to react automatically to the cues for action that exist in those settings. So, given the quickening pace and concentration-disrupting character of today's world, are we all fated to be bozos on this bus? Not if, rather than raging against the invading automaticity, we invite it in but take systematic control of the way it operates on us. We have to become interior designers of our regular living spaces, furnishing them with features that will send us unthinkingly in the directions we most want to go in those spaces. This approach provides another way (besides making immediate, forceful commitments) to arrange for initially formed preferences to guide our future actions. By assuring that we regularly encounter cues that automatically link to and activate those preferences, we can commission the machinery in our behalf.

Previous chapters offered some examples of how we might go about it: if you want to write in a way that connects with a particular audience, perhaps as you are preparing a report or presentation, surround yourself with cues linked to the group: for instance, typical audience members' faces. If you want to approach a task while possessing a strong achievement orientation, perhaps at work, give yourself contact with images of success, striving, and accomplishment, such as a runner winning a race. If you want to approach a different task while possessing an analytical orientation, perhaps when figuring a budget, give yourself access to images of contemplation, thoughtfulness, and examination: for example, Rodin's *The Thinker*. And so on. You might even be able to optimize the performance of each of these types of tasks in the same place on the same computer by changing the desktop wallpaper to show a series of images appropriate to whichever orientation you want to apply to a specific task.

If/when-then plans provide yet another way to harness the power of associative connections for our long-term advantage. It's something they do by associating desirable goals and actions with cues that we will experience in regularly occurring future situations: "*If*, after my business lunches, the server asks for dessert choices, *then* I will order mint tea," or "*When* it's eight in the morning, and I've finished brushing my teeth, *then* I'll take my prescribed dose of medicine." Although each of these suggested tactics is consistent with research presented earlier in this book, there's another worthy tactic that gets its support from research we haven't yet seen on the role of mere reminders.[110]

PERSUASIVE GEOGRAPHIES 2: WHO WE ARE IS WHERE WE ARE

Whenever I speak to health care management groups about the influence process, I'll ask, "Which people in the system are most difficult to influence?" The answer is invariably and emphatically "Physicians!" On the one hand, this circumstance seems as it should be. To get to their elevated positions in the health care hierarchy, doctors endure years of training and practice, including medical school specializations, internships, and residencies that give them a great deal of information and experience on which to base their choices, making them understandably reluctant to be swayed from those choices. On the other hand, this kind of resistance can be problematic when physicians don't adopt recommendations for changes that would benefit their patients. All of which raises a larger issue: Why do most doctors enter the medical profession in the first place? Is it principally for other-serving or for self-serving reasons? Is it to benefit and relieve the suffering of their patients, or is it to obtain the considerable authority, respect, status, and income that normally accompany the role?

Showing doctors how to wash their hands of a serious problem. In 1847, at Vienna General Hospital, Ignaz Semmelweis showed that hand washing by medical practitioners reduced patient infections and deaths. But to this day, many physicians fail to follow proper procedures for hand hygiene. *Portrait of Ignaz Semmelweis (1818–1865). Engraving by Ernst Wenck, Musée d'Histoire de la Médecine, Paris.*

A study done in a US hospital gives us valuable insight into the issues. The researchers, Adam Grant and David Hofmann, noted that even though hand washing is strongly recommended before each patient examination, most physicians wash their hands less than half as often as the guidelines prescribe; what's more, various interventions aimed at reducing the problem have proved ineffective, leaving both doctors and patients at greater risk of infection. Grant and Hofmann thought they could do better just by bringing physicians' attention upon entering an examination room to one of two powerful motivations: concern for themselves or concern for their patients. To channel attention to the self-centered concern, the researchers placed signs above some examination room soap or gel dispensers that read "Hand hygiene protects you from catching diseases." To channel attention to the patient-centered concern, they placed signs over a different set of dispensers that read "Hand hygiene protects patients from catching diseases." Despite only a single word of difference, the effect of the two types of signs was dramatically one-sided. The sign that reminded the doctors to protect themselves had no effect on soap and gel use. But the one reminding them to protect their patients increased usage by 45 percent.

These results afford us important information about a pair of related issues. First, although many other kinds of interventions had failed to reduce the problem, simply drawing doctors' initial attention to the connection between hand washing and patient protection was a notable success. Of course, in the previous instances when the doctors *hadn't* washed their hands, a deep concern for patient welfare was no doubt present in them then, too, as was a recognized link between hand washing and patient welfare. What accounts for the difference? In those previous instances, there was nothing there to direct the doctors' attention to the link, to elevate it to top of mind, above the other relevant features of the situation: how the patient looks, what the attending nurse is saying, what the case notes are saying, and so on. All it took was one sign visible as the doctors entered, reminding them of the link, to change their behavior impressively.[111]

Plus, it appears from the study's data that we have an answer to the question of what most physicians are really like deep down. They appear to be (1) other-oriented individuals, strongly motivated to enhance the well-being of their patients and (2) not of the sort we'd have to worry would ever serve their own interests at their patients' expense.

Although the first of these conclusions seems correct, a study carried out at Carnegie Mellon University casts doubt on the second. It concerned another practice that physicians have been warned jeopardizes their patients' best interests. Doctors are frequently offered gifts from health industry companies—most notably pharmaceutical firms but also medical equipment manufacturers—in the form of pizza for their office staffs, lunches and dinners for themselves, all-expenses-paid trips to conferences, research and consulting contracts, and fees for teaching or speaking at meetings, and even for participating in product-related conference calls. The evidence is strong that these gifts and sponsorships influence physicians to return the favors by prescribing or endorsing products that further the welfare of the industry sponsors rather than of their patients. Despite such evidence and accompanying warnings, many continue to accept the patient-compromising bounty of their positions, even while recognizing its problematic implications.

What's going on here? How could it be that physicians would act more on behalf of their patients' interests than their own in the hand washing study, but the reverse seems to apply in the case of gift taking? Maybe it's that hand washing is a relatively small-cost act compared with rejecting industry-sponsored benefits, and, within such higher value choices, self-interest wins out, as it well might in any group of people. Maybe that's true; doctors are people, after all. But the rule for reciprocation, which states that those who give first are *entitled* to receive in return, and the findings of the Carnegie Mellon University study offer a less cynical, more textured view.

That study of 301 resident physicians in the United States began with a pertinent question: What might cause doctors to become more versus less accepting of industry-sponsored favors? One sample of the physicians was simply asked in an online survey whether and to what extent taking gifts and payments from industry representatives was acceptable to them. In the researchers' analysis, only about one-fifth (21.7 percent) found the practice acceptable. But when a second sample was asked the same question, preceded by items inquiring into how much they had sacrificed personally and financially to become MDs, nearly half (47.5 percent) thought gift taking acceptable. Finally, when a third sample was both reminded in the same way of their prior sacrifices and asked whether the resources they'd previously expended justified taking gifts, a clear majority (60.3 percent) came to see the practice as acceptable.

What should we make of these results? Speaking for myself, I've drawn multiple conclusions, including the heartening one that, despite a healthy (*unhealthy* is probably the better word here) minority who thought gift taking acceptable, most physicians found it an unworthy choice. However, focusing physicians pre-suasively on the large inputs they had supplied to the health care system made them much more willing to take large returns from it. That result—plus the fact that a reciprocity-based rationale caused the majority to embrace gift taking—implicates the temporarily surfaced rule for reciprocation as a major culprit here. Lastly, these findings tell me that the answer to the question of whether, as a group, MDs are primarily patient-serving or self-serving is . . . yes. They are each, depending on their attentional focus at the time. That's a conclusion that applies to far more than physicians, whose remarkably elastic preferences serve to illustrate how top-of-mind factors operate on all of us.

– —— –

It's also a conclusion that provides a fitting close to this book: In large measure, *who* we are with respect to any choice is *where* we are, attentionally, in the moment before the choice. We can be channeled to that privileged moment by (choice-relevant) cues we haphazardly bump into in our daily settings; or, of greater concern, by the cues a knowing communicator has tactically placed there; or, to much better and lasting effect, by the cues we have stored in those recurring sites to send us consistently in desired directions. In each case, the made moment is pre-suasive. Whether we are wary of the underlying process, attracted to its potential, or both, we'd be right to acknowledge its considerable power and wise to understand its inner workings.[112]

References

2011 National Business Ethics Survey: Workplace Ethics in Transition. Washington, DC: Ethics Resources Center.

Able, S., and G. Stasser. 2008. "Coordination Success and Interpersonal Perceptions: Matching Versus Mismatching." *Journal of Personality and Social Psychology* 95: 576–92.

Ackerman, J. M., C. C. Nocera, and J. A. Bargh. 2010. "Incidental Haptic Sensations Influence Social Judgments and Decisions." *Science* 328: 1712–15.

Acohido, B. 2013. "Fraudsters Swamp Web with Bogus IRS Emails." *Arizona Republic* (Phoenix) (April 17), A13.

Adamo, S. H., M. S. Cain, and S. R. Mitroff. 2013. "Self-Induced Attentional Blink: A Cause of Errors in Multiple-Target Search." *Psychological Science* 24: 2569–74.

Adarves-Yorno, I., S. A. Haslam, and T. Postmes. 2008. "And Now for Something Completely Different?' The Impact of Group Membership on Perceptions of Creativity." *Social Influence* 3: 248–66.

Aday, S., S. Livingston, and M. Hebert 2005. "Embedding the Truth: A

Cross-Cultural Analysis of Objectivity and Television Coverage of the Iraq War." *Press/Politics* 10: 3–21.

Ahktar, S., R. Faff, and B. Oliver. 2011. "The Asymmetric Impact of Consumer Sentiment Announcements on Australian Foreign Exchange Rates." *Australian Journal of Management* 36: 387–403.

Akerlof, G. A., and R. J. Shiller. 2015. *Phishing for Phools: The Economics of Manipulation and Deception*. Princeton, NJ: Princeton University Press.

Alba, J. W., and H. Marmorstein. 1987. "The Effects of Frequency Knowledge on Consumer Decision Making." *Journal of Consumer Research* 14: 14–25.

Algoe, S. B. 2012. "Find, Remind, and Bind: The Functions of Gratitude in Everyday Relationships." *Social and Personality Psychology Compass* 6: 455–69.

Algoe, S. B., S. L. Gable, and N. Maisel. 2010. "It's the Little Things: Everyday Gratitude as a Booster Shot for Romantic Relationships." *Personal Relationships* 17: 217–33.

Allen, M. P., S. K. Panian, and R. E. Lotz. 1979. "Managerial Succession and Organizational Performance: A Recalcitrant Problem Revisited." *Administrative Science Quarterly* 24: 167–80.

Alter, A. L. 2013. "The Benefits of Cognitive Disfluency." *Current Directions in Psychological Science* 22: 437–42.

Alter, A. L., and D. M. Oppenheimer. 2006. "Predicting Short-Term Stock Fluctuations by Using Processing Fluency." *Proceedings of the National Academy of Sciences of the USA* 103: 9369–72.

———. 2009. "Uniting the Tribes of Fluency to Form a Metacognitive Nation." *Personality and Social Psychology Review* 13: 219–35.

Alter, A. L., D. M. Oppenheimer, N. Epley, and R. N. Eyre. 2007. "Overcoming Intuition: Metacognitive Difficulty Activates Analytic Reasoning." *Journal of Experimental Psychology: General* 136: 569–76.

Ambrose, M. L., A. Arnaud, and M. Schminke. 2008. "Individual Moral Development and Ethical Climate." *Journal of Business Ethics* 77: 323–33.

Ames, D. L., A. C. Jenkins, M. R. Banaji, and J. P. Mitchell. 2008. "Taking Another Person's Perspective Increases Self-Referential Neural Processing." *Psychological Science* 19: 642–44.

Anderson, B. A., P. A. Laurent, and S. Yantis. 2013. "Reward Predictions Bias Attentional Selection." *Frontiers in Human Neuroscience* 7: 262. doi:10.3389/fnhum.2013.00262.

Anderson, C. A. 1982. "Inoculation and Counter-Explanation: Debiasing Techniques in the Perseverance of Social Theories." *Social Cognition* 7: 126–39.

Anderson, C. A., and K. E. Dill. 2000. "Video Games and Aggressive Thoughts, Feelings, and Behavior in the Laboratory and in Life." *Journal of Personality and Social Psychology* 78: 772–90.

Anderson, C. A., and E. S. Sechler. 1986. "Effects of Explanation and Counterexplanation on the Development and Use of Social Theories." *Journal of Personality and Social Psychology* 50: 24–34.

Anderson, C. A., N. L. Carnagey, M. Flannagan, A. J. Benjamin, J. Eubanks, and J. Valentine. 2004. "Violent Video Games: Specific Effects of Violent Content on Aggressive Thoughts and Behavior." *Advances in Experimental Social Psychology* 36: 199–249.

Anderson, J. C. 2013. "Experts Warn Against Giving Cybercriminals the Opening They Seek." *Arizona Republic* (Phoenix) (April 15), A1, A3.

Anderson, M. 2014. *After Phrenology: Neural Reuse and the Interactive Brain*. Cambridge, MA: MIT Press.

Aramovich, N. P., B. L. Lytle, and L. J. Skitka. 2012. "Opposing Torture: Moral Conviction and Resistance to Majority Influence." *Social Influence* 7: 21–34.

Ardrey, R. 1961. *African Genesis*. New York: Atheneum Publishers.

Ariely, D., G. Loewenstein, and D. Prelec. 2003. "Coherent Arbitrariness: Stable Demand Curves Without Stable Preferences." *Quarterly Journal of Economics* 118: 73–105.

Armel, K. C., A. Beaumel, and A. Rangel. 2008. "Biasing Simple Choices By Manipulating Relative Visual Attention." *Judgment and Decision Making*: 396–403.

Armitage, C. J., and M. Connor. 2001. "Efficacy of the Theory of Planned Behaviour: A Meta-Analytic Review." *British Journal of Social Psychology* 40: 471–99.

Armstrong, J. S. 2010. *Persuasive Advertising*. London: Palgrave Macmillan.

Aron, A., E. N. Aron, M. Tudor, and G. Nelson. 1991. "Self-Relationships as Including Other in the Self." *Journal of Personality and Social Psychology* 60: 241–53.

Aron, A., E. Melinat, E. N. Aron, R. D. Vallone, and R. J. Bator. 1997. "The Experimental Generation of Interpersonal Closeness: A Procedure and Some Preliminary Findings." *Personality and Social Psychology Bulletin* 23: 363–77.

Asp, E., K. Manzel, B. Koestner, C. A. Cole, N. Denburg, and D. Tranel. 2012. "A Neuropsychological Test of Belief and Doubt: Damage to Ventromedial Prefrontal Cortex Increases Credulity for Misleading Advertising." *Frontiers in Neuroscience* 6 (July). doi:10.3389/fnins.2012.00100.

Atalay, A. S., Bodur, H. O., and D. Rasolofoarison. 2012. "Shining in the Center: Central Gaze Cascade Effect on Product Choice." *Journal of Consumer Research* 39: 848–56.

Ayton, P., S. Murray, and J. A. Hampton. 2011. "Terrorism, Dread Risks, and Bicycle Accidents. International Conference on Behavioral Decision Making," The Interdisciplinary Center, Herzliya, Israel, May 30–June 1, 2011.

Bailenson, J. N., S. Iyengar, N. Yee, and N. A. Collins. 2008. "Facial Similarity Between Voters and Candidates Causes Influence." *Public Opinion Quarterly* 72: 935–61.

Baimel, A., R. L. Severson, A. S. Baron, and S. A. J. Birch. 2015. "Enhancing 'Theory of Mind' Through Behavioral Synchrony." *Frontiers in Psychology* 6: 870. doi:10.3389/fpsyg.2015.00870.

Balancher, S., Y. Liu, and A. Stock. 2009. "An Empirical Analysis of Scarcity Strategies in the Automobile Industry." *Management Science* 10: 1623–37.

Ball, P. 2010. *The Music Instinct: How Music Works and Why We Can't Do Without It*. New York: Oxford University Press.

Balliet, D., J. Wu, and C. K. W. De Dreu. 2014. "Ingroup Favoritism in Cooperation: A Meta-Analysis." *Psychological Bulletin* 140: 1556–81.

Banderet, L. E., J. W. Stokes, R. Francesconi, D. M. Kowal, and P. Naitoh. 1981. "Artillery Teams in Simulated Sustained Combat: Performance and Other Measures." In *The Twenty-Four Hour Workday: Proceedings of a Symposium on Variations in Work-Sleep Schedules*. Edited by L. C. Johnson, D. I. Tepas, W. P. Colquhon, and M. J. Colligan. DHHS publication no. 81–127) Washington, DC: US Government Printing Office, 81–127.

Bannan, N, ed. 2012. *Music, Language, and Human Evolution*. New York: Oxford University Press.

Bargh, J. A., M. Chen, and L. Burrows. 1998. "Automaticity of Social Behavior: Direct Effects of Trait Construct and Stereotype Activation on Action." *Journal of Personality and Social Psychology* 71: 230–44.

Bargh, J. A., P. M. Gollwitzer, A. Lee-Chai, K. Barndollar, and R. Trötschel. 2001. "The Automated Will: Nonconscious Activation and Pursuit of Behavioral Goals." *Journal of Personality and Social Psychology* 81: 1014–27.

Bargh, J. A., Lombardi, W. J., and E. T. Higgins. 1988. "Automaticity of Chronically Accessible Constructs in Person X Situation Effects on Person Perception: It's Just a Matter of Time." *Journal of Personality and Social Psychology* 55: 599–605.

Barlow, F. K., S. Paolini, A. Pedersen, M. J. Hornsey, H. R. M. Radke, J. Harwood, M. Rubin, and C. G. Sibley. 2012. "The Contact Caveat: Negative Contact Predicts Increased Prejudice More Than Positive Contact Predicts Reduced Prejudice." *Personality and Social Psychology Bulletin* 37: 1629–43.

Barnard, P. J., S. Scot, J. Taylor, J. May, and W, Knightley. 2004. "Paying Attention to Meaning." *Psychological Science* 15: 179–86.

Baron-Cohen, S. 1995. *Mindblindness: An Essay on Autism and Theory of Mind.* Cambridge, MA: MIT Press.

Barthel, J. 1976. *A Death in Canaan.* New York: Dutton.

Baumeister, R. F., E. Bratslavsky, C. Finkenauer, K. D. Vohs. 2001. "Bad Is Stronger Than Good." *Review of General Psychology* 5: 323–70.

Baumeister, R. J., E. J. Masicampo, K. D. Vohs. 2011. "Do Conscious Thoughts Cause Behavior?" *Annual Review of Psychology* 62: 331–61.

Bauml, K-H. 2002. "Semantic Generation Can Cause Episodic Forgetting." *Psychological Science* 13: 356–60.

Bayer, U. C, A. A. Achzinger, P. M. Gollwitzer, and G. B. Moskowitz. 2009. "Responding to Subliminal Cues: Do If-Then Plans Facilitate Action Preparation and Initiation Without Conscious Intent? *Social Cognition* 27: 183–201.

Bayer, U. C., and P. M. Gollwitzer. 2007. "Boosting Scholastic Test Scores by Willpower: The Role of Implementation Intentions." *Self and Identity* 6: 1–19.

Beck, R. 2011. "CEO Pay Tops Pre-Recession Levels." *Arizona Republic* (Phoenix) (May 7) D1, D4.

Becker, G. S. 1968. "Crime and Punishment: An Economic Approach." *Journal of Political Economy* 76: 169–217.

Becker, J. 2014. *Forcing the Spring: Inside the Fight for Marriage Equality*. New York: Penguin Press.

Belmi, P., and J. Pfeffer. 2015. "How 'Organization' Can Weaken the Norm of Reciprocity: The Effects of Attributions for Favors and a Calculative Mindset." *Academy of Management Discoveries* 1: 93–113.

Berkowitz, L. 1972. "Social Norms, Feelings and Other Factors Affecting Helping Behavior and Altruism." In *Advances in Experimental Social Psychology*. Vol. 6. Edited by L. Berkowitz. New York: Academic Press, 63–108.

Bernieri, F. J. 1988. "Coordinated Movement and Rapport in Teacher-Student Interactions." *Journal of Nonverbal Behavior* 12: 120–38.

Bhatia, S. 2013. "Associations and the Accumulation of Preference." *Psychological Review* 120: 522–43.

Bilalic, M., P. McLeod, and F. Gobet, 2010. "The Mechanism of the *Einstellung* (Set) Effect: A Pervasive Source of Cognitive Bias." *Current Directions in Psychological Science* 19: 111–15.

Birnbaum, R. 1989. "Presidential Succession and Institutional Functioning in Higher Education." *Journal of Higher Education* 60: 123–35.

Bischoff, S. J., K. B. DeTienne, and B. Quick. 1999. "Effects of Ethical Stress on Employee Burnout and Fatigue: An Empirical Investigation." *Journal of Health and Human Services Administration* 21: 512–32.

Blackmore, S. J. 1986. *The Adventures of a Parapsychologist*. Buffalo, NY: Prometheus Books.

———. 1997. "Probability Misjudgment and Belief in the Paranormal: A Newspaper Survey." *British Journal of Psychology* 88: 683–89.

Blagrove, M. 1996. "Effects of Length of Sleep Deprivation on Interrogative Suggestibility." *Journal of Experimental Psychology: Applied* 2: 48–59.

Blankenship, K. L., D. T. Wegener, and R. A. Murray. 2012. "Circumventing Resistance: Using Values to Indirectly Change Attitudes." *Journal of Personality and Social Psychology* 103: 606–21.

Blankenship, K. L., D. T. Wegener, and R. A. Murray. 2015. "Values, Inter-Attitudinal Structure, and Attitude Change: Value Accessibility Can Increase a Related Attitude's Resistance to Change." *Personality and Social Psychology Bulletin* 4: 1739–50.

Blanton, H., L. B. Snyder, E. Strauts, J. G. Larson. 2014. "Effect of Graphic Cigarette Warnings on Smoking Intentions in Young Adults." *PLoS ONE* 9, no. 5: e96315. doi:10.1371/journal.pone.0096315.

Bock, L. 2015. *Work Rules!* New York: Twelve. Hachette Book Group.

Boer, D., R. Fischer, M. R., Strack, M. H. Bond, E. Lo, and J. Lam. 2011. "How Shared Preferences in Music Create Bonds Between People: Values as the Missing Link." *Personality and Social Psychology Bulletin* 37: 1159–71.

Boland, W. A., M. Brucks, and J. H. Nielsen. 2012. "The Attribute Carryover Effect: What the 'Runner-Up' Option Tells Us about Consumer Choice Processes." *Journal of Consumer Research* 38: 872–85.

Bolkan, S. S., and P. A. Anderson. 2009. "Image Induction and Social Influence: Explication and Initial Tests. *Basic and Applied Social Psychology* 31: 317–24.

Bomey, N. 2015. "Volkswagen Sales Tepid as Scandal Affects Perception." *Arizona Republic* (Phoenix) (October 2), B3.

Bond, C. F., Jr. 1985. "The Next-In-Line Effect: Encoding or Retrieval Deficit?" *Journal of Personality and Social Psychology* 48: 853–62.

Bonneville-Roussy, A., P. J. Rentfrow, J. Potter, and M. K. Xu, 2013. Music through the Ages: Trends in Musical Engagement and Preferences from Adolescence through Middle Adulthood. *Journal of Personality and Social Psychology* 105: 703–17.

Boorstin, D. J. 1962. *The Image: A Guide to Pseudo-Events in America.* New York: Vintage Books.

Borgida, E., C. Conner, and L. Manteufal. 1992. "Understanding Living Kidney Donation: A Behavioral Decision-Making Perspective." In *Helping and Being Helped,* Edited by S. Spacapan and S. Oskamp. Newbury Park, CA: Sage, 183–212.

Borysenko, K. 2015. "What Was Management Thinking? The High Cost of Employee Turnover." TLNT (April 22). www.eremedia.com/tlnt/what-was-leadership-thinking-the-shockingly-high-cost-of-employee-turnover.

Bouchard, T. J., N. L. Segal, A. Tellegen, M. McGue, M. Keyes, and R. Krueger. 2003. "Evidence for the Construct Validity and Heritability of the Wilson-Paterson Conservatism Scale: A Reared-Apart Twins Study of Social Attitudes." *Personality and Individual Differences* 34: 959–69.

Bourgeois, M. J. 2002. "Heritability of Attitudes Constrains Dynamic Social Impact." *Personality and Social Psychology Bulletin* 28: 1063–72.

Boushey, H., and S. J. Glynn. 2012. *There Are Significant Business Costs to Replacing Employees.* Washington, DC: Center for American Progress (November 16). www.americanprogress.org/issues/labor/report/2012/11/16/44464/there-are-significant-business-costs-to-replacing-employees.

Boyce, C. J., A. M. Wood, J. Banks, A. E. Clark, and G. D. A. Brown. 2013. "Money, Well-Being, and Loss Aversion: Does an Income Loss Have a Greater Effect on Well-Being Than an Equivalent Income Gain?" *Psychological Science* 24: 2557–62.

Boydstun, A. E. 2013. *Making the News: Politics, The Media, and Agenda Setting.* Chicago: University of Chicago Press.

Boyle, J. 2008. *The Public Domain: Enclosing the Commons of the Mind.* New Haven, CT: Yale University Press.

Bradley, M. M. 2009. "Natural Selective Attention: Orienting and Emotion." *Psychophysiology* 46: 1–11.

Brandstätter, V., A. Lengfelder, and P. M. Gollwitzer. 2001. "Implementation Intentions and Efficient Action Initiation." *Journal of Personality and Social Psychology* 81: 946–60.

Brandt, M. J., and C. Reyna. 2011. "The Chain of Being: A Hierarchy of Morality." *Perspectives on Psychological Science* 6: 428–46.

Brendl, C. M., A. Chattopadhyay, B. W. Pelham, and M. R. Carvallo. 2005. "Name Letter Branding: Valence Transfers When Product Specific Needs Are Active." *Journal of Consumer Research* 32: 405–15.

Brenner, M. 1973. "The Next-In-Line Effect." *Journal of Verbal Learning and Verbal Behavior* 12: 320–23.

Bridwell, D. A., and R. Srinivasan. 2012. "Distinct Attention Networks for Feature Enhancement and Suppression in Vision." *Psychological Science* 23: 1151–58.

Brinol, P., M. Gasco, R. E. Petty, and J. Horcajo. 2013. "Treating Thoughts as Material Objects Can Increase or Decrease Their Impact on Evaluation. *Psychological Science* 24: 41–47.

Bronzaft, A. L. 1981. "The Effect of a Noise Abatement Program on Reading Ability." *Journal of Environmental Psychology* 1: 215–22.

Bronzaft, A. L., and McCarthy 1975. "The Effect of Elevated Train Noise on Reading Ability." *Environment and Behavior* 7: 517–28.

Brown, C. M., and A. R. McConnell. 2009. "When Chronic Isn't Chronic: The Moderating Role of Active Self-Aspects." *Personality and Social Psychology Bulletin* 35: 3–15.

Brown, I., P. Sheeran, and M. Reuber. 2009. "Enhancing Antiepileptic Drug Adherence: A Randomized Controlled Trial." *Epilepsy and Behavior* 16: 634–39.

Brown, J. L., K. D. Drake, and L. Wellman. 2015. "The Benefits of a Relational Approach to Corporate Political Activity: Evidence From Political Contributions to Tax Policymakers." *Journal of the American Taxation Association* 37: 69–102.

Bryan, C. J., G. M. Walton, T. Rogers, and C. S. Dweck. 2001. "Motivating Voter Turnout by Invoking the Self." *Proceedings of the National Academy of Sciences.* doi:10.1073/pnas.1103343108.

Buchan, N. R., M. B. Brewer, G. Grimalda, R. K. Wilson, E. Fatas, and M. Foddy. 2011. "Global Social Identity and Global Cooperation." *Psychological Science* 22: 821–28.

Bukowski, W. M., B. Hoza, and M. Boivin. 1994. "Measuring Friendship Quality During Pre- and Early Adolescence: The Development and Psychometric Properties of the Friendship Qualities Scale." *Journal of Social and Personal Relationships* 11: 471–84.

Buonomano, D. 2011. *Brain Bugs*. New York: W. W. Norton.

Burger, J. M., N. Messian, S. Patel, A. del Prado, and C. Anderson. 2004. "What a Coincidence! The Effects of Incidental Similarity on Compliance." *Personality and Social Psychology Bulletin* 30: 35–43.

Burgoon, M., E. Alvaro, J. Grandpre, and M. Voulodakis. 2002. "Revisiting the Theory of Psychological Reactance." In *The Persuasion Handbook: Theory and Practice*. Edited by J. P. Dillard and M. Pfau. Thousand Oaks, CA: Sage, 213–32.

Burks, S. V., and E. L. Krupka. 2012. "A Multimethod Approach to Identifying Norms and Normative Expectations Within a Corporate Hierarchy: Evidence from the Financial Services Industry." *Management Science* 58: 203–17.

Burnkrant, R. E., and H. R. Unnava. 1989. "Self-Referencing: A Strategy for Increasing Processing of Message Content." *Personality and Social Psychology Bulletin* 15: 628–38.

Burnstein, E., C. Crandall, and S. Kitayama. 1994. "Some Neo-Darwinian Decision Rules for Altruism: Weighing Cues for Inclusive Fitness as a Function of the Biological Importance of the Decision." *Journal of Personality and Social Psychology* 67: 773–89.

Burrus, J., and K. D. Mattern. 2010. "Equity, Egoism and Egocentrism: The Formation of Distributive Justice Judgments." *Basic and Applied Social Psychology* 32: 155–64.

Busemeyer, J. R., and Z. Wang. 2015. "What Is Quantum Cognition, and

How Is It Applied to Psychology?" *Current Directions in Psychological Science* 24: 163–69.

Busemeyer, J. R., E. M. Pothos, R. Franco, and J. S. Trueblood. 2001. "A Quantum Theoretical Explanation for Probability Judgment Errors." *Psychological Review* 118: 193–218.

Buttleman, D., and R. Bohm. 2014. "The Ontogeny of the Motivation That Underlies In-Group Bias." *Psychological Science* 25: 921–27.

Cacioppo, J. T., J. R. Priester, and G. G. Berntson. 1993. "Rudimentary Determinants of Attitudes: II. Arm Flexion and Extension Have Differential Effects on Attitudes." *Journal of Personality and Social Psychology* 65: 5–17.

Cadinu, M. R., and M. Rothbart. 1996. "Self-Anchoring and Differentiation Processes in the Minimal Group Setting." *Journal of Personality and Social Psychology* 70: 666–77.

Cai, H., Y. Chen, and H. Fang. 2009. "Observational Learning: Evidence from a Randomized Natural Field Experiment." *American Economic Review* 99: 864–82.

Cameron, C. D., J. L. Brown-Iannuzzi, and B. K. Payne. 2012. "Sequential Priming Measures of Implicit Social Cognition: A Meta-Analysis of Associations with Behavior and Explicit Attitudes." *Personality and Social Psychology Review* 16: 330–50.

Campbell, M. C. 1995. "When Attention-Getting Advertising Tactics Elicit Consumer Inferences of Manipulative Intent: The Importance of Balancing Benefits and Investments." *Journal of Consumer Psychology* 4: 225–54.

Campbell, M. C., and C. Warren. 2012. "A Risk of Meaning Transfer: Are Negative Associations More Likely to Transfer Than Positive Associations?" *Social Influence* 7: 172–92.

Cappella, J. N. 1997. "Behavioral and Judged Coordination in Adult Informal Social Interactions: Vocal and Kinesic Indicators." *Journal of Personality and Social Psychology* 72: 119–31.

Carnegie, D. 2009. *How to Win Friends and Influence People*. Reissue ed. New York: Simon & Schuster.

Carr, P. B., and G. M. Walton. 2014. "Cues of Working Together Fuel Intrinsic Motivation." *Journal of Experimental Social Psychology* 53: 169–84.

Carlson, K. A., M. G. Meloy, and E. G. Miller. 2013. "Goal Reversion in Consumer Choice." *Journal of Consumer Research* 39: 918–30.

Carstensen, L. L., B. Turan, S. Scheibe, N. Ram, H. Ersner-Hershfield, G. R. Samanez-Larkin, K. P. Brooks, and J. R. Nesselroade. 2011. "Emotional Experience Improves with Age: Evidence Based On over 10 Years of Experience Sampling." *Psychology and Aging* 26: 21–33.

Carter, T. J., M. J. Ferguson, and R. R. Hassin. 2011. "A Single Exposure to the American Flag Shifts Support Toward Republicanism Up to 8 Months Later." *Psychological Science* 22, no. 8: 1011–18.

Carver, C. S., R. J. Ganellen, W. J., Froming, and W. Chambers. 1983. "Modeling: An Analysis in Terms of Category Accessibility." *Journal of Experimental Social Psychology* 19: 403–21.

Cavicchio, F., D. Melcher, and M. Poesio. 2014. "The Effect of Linguistic and Visual Salience in Visual World Studies." *Frontiers in Psychology* 5: 176.

Ceci, S. J., D. K. Ginther, S. Kahn, and W. M. Williams, 2014. "Women in Academic Science: A Changing Landscape." *Psychological Science in the Public Interest* 15: 72–141.

Ceci, S. J., and W. M. Williams. 2010. "Sex Differences in Math-Intensive Fields." *Current Directions in Psychological Science* 19: 275–79.

Ceci, S. J., W. M. Williams, and S. M. Barnett. 2009. "Women's Under-representation in Science: Sociocultural and Biological Considerations." *Psychological Bulletin* 135: 218–61.

Cervone, D. 1989. "Effects of Envisioning Future Activities on Self-Efficacy Judgments and Motivation: An Availability Heuristic Interpretation." *Cognitive Therapy and Research* 13: 247–61.

Chagnon, N. A., and P. E. Bugos. 1979. "Kin Selection and Conflict: An Analysis of a Yanomamö Ax Fight." In *Evolutionary Biology and Human Social Behavior.* Edited by N. A. Chagnon and W. Irons. North Scituate, MA: Duxbury Press, 213–38

Chaiken, S., and A. H. Eagly. 1983. "Communication Modality as a Determinant of Persuasion: The Role of Communicator Salience." *Journal of Personality and Social Psychology* 45: 241–56.

Chambers, J. R. 2011. "Why the Parts Are Better (or Worse) Than the Whole: The Unique-Attributes Hypothesis." *Psychological Science* 21: 68–275.

Chambers, J. R., R. B. Schlenker, and B. Collisson. 2013. "Ideology and Prejudice: The Role of Value Conflicts." *Psychological Science* 24: 140–49.

Chan, E., and J. Sengupta. 2010. "Insincere Flattery Actually Works: A Dual Attitudes Perspective." *Journal of Marketing Research* 47: 122–33.

Charpak, G., and H. Broch. 2004. *Debunked!* Baltimore: Johns Hopkins University Press.

Chein, Y-W., D. T. Wegener, R. E. Petty, and C-C Hsiao. 2014. "The Flexible Correction Model: Bias Correction Guided by Naïve Theories of Bias." *Social and Personality Psychology Compass* 8/6: 275–86.

Chen, X., and Latham, G. P. 2014. "The Effect of Priming Learning vs. Performance Goals on a Complex Task." *Organizational Development and Human Decision Processes* 125: 88–97.

Chernev, A., and S. Blair. 2015. "Doing Well by Doing Good: The Benevolent Halo of Corporate Social Responsibility." *Journal of Consumer Research* 41, 1412–25.

Cheung, T. T. L., M. Gillebaart, F. Kroese, and D. De Ridder. 2014. "Why Are People with High Self-Control Happier? The Effect of Trait Self-Control on Happiness as Mediated by Regulatory Focus." *Frontiers in Psychology* 5. doi:10.3389/fpsyg.2014.00722.

Child, L. 2012. "A Simple Way to Create Suspense." *Opinionator* (blog). *New York Times* (December 8), http://opinionator.blogs.nytimes.com/2012/12/08/a-simple-way-to-create-suspense/?_r=0.

Chugani, S., J. E. Irwin, and J. P. Redden. In press. "Happily Ever After: The Effect of Identity-Consistency on Product Satiation." *Journal of Consumer Research*.

Cialdini, R. B. 2009. *Influence: Science and Practice*. 5th ed. Boston: Allyn and Bacon.

Cialdini, R. B., C. A. Kallgren, and R. R. Reno. 1991. "A Focus Theory of Normative Conduct: A Theoretical Refinement and Reevaluation of the Role of Norms in Human Behavior." In *Advances in Experimental Social Psychology*. Vol. 24. Edited by M. Zanna. New York: Academic Press, 201–34.

Cialdini, R. B., Y. J. Li, and A. Samper. In preparation. "The Varied Internal Costs of Unethical Leadership: Performance Decrements, Turnover Intentions, and the Selective Attrition Effect."

Cialdini, R.B., S. L. Brown, B. P. Lewis, C. Luce, S. L. Neuberg. 1997. "Reinterpreting the Empathy-Altruism Relationship: When One into One Equals Oneness." *Journal of Personality and Social Psychology* 73: 481–94.

Cialdini, R.B., W. Wosinska, D. W. Barrett, J. Butner, and M. Gornik-Durose. 1999. "Compliance with a Request in Two Cultures: The Differential Influence of Social Proof and Commitment/Consistency on Collectivists and Individualists." *Personality and Social Psychology Bulletin* 25: 1242–53.

Cirelli, L. K., K. M. Einarson, and L. J. Trainor. 2014, "Interpersonal Synchrony Increases Prosocial Behavior in Infants." *Developmental Science* 17: 1003–11.

Claessens, A., and C. Dowsett. 2014. "Growth and Changes in Attention Problems, Disruptive Behavior, and Achievement from Kindergarten to Fifth Grade." *Psychological Science* 25: 2241–51.

Clark, C., and P. Sörqvist. 2012. "A 3-Year Update on the Influence of Noise on Performance and Behavior." *Noise Health* 14: 292–96.

Clarkson, J. J., Z. L. Tormala, and D. D. Rucker. 2011. "Cognitive and Affective Matching Effects in Persuasion: An Amplification Perspective." *Personality and Social Psychology Bulletin*, 1415–27.

Coghlan, T. 2015. "Holocaust Survivor Lord Weidenfeld Rescues Syrian Christians." *Times* (London) (July 14). A30.

Cohen, B. 1963. *The Press and Foreign Policy*. Princeton, NJ: Princeton University Press.

Cohen, D., and A. Gunz. 2002. "As Seen by the Other . . . : Perceptions of the Self in the Memories and Emotional Perceptions of Easterners and Westerners." *Psychological Science* 13: 55–59.

Cohen, G. L., J. Garcia, N. Apfel, and A. Master. 2006. "Reducing the Racial Achievement Gap: A Social-Psychological Intervention." *Science* 313: 1307–10.

Cohen, R. 1972. "Altruism: Human, Cultural, or What?" *Journal of Social Issues* 28: 39–57.

Coleman, N. V., and P. Williams. 2015. "Looking for My Self: Identity-Driven Attention Allocation." *Journal of Consumer Psychology* 25: 504–11.

Coman, A., D. Manier, and W. Hirst. 2009. "Forgetting the Unforgettable through Conversation." *Psychological Science* 20: 627–33.

Combs, D. J. Y., and P. S. Keller. 2010. "Politicians and Trustworthiness: Acting Contrary to Self-Interest Enhances Trustworthiness." *Basic and Applied Social Psychology* 32: 328–39.

Condon, J. W., and W. D. Crano. 1988. "Inferred Evaluation and the Relation Between Attitude Similarity and Interpersonal Attraction." *Journal of Personality and Social Psychology* 54: 789–97.

Connell, P. M., M. Brucks, and J. H. Nielsen. 2014. "How Childhood Advertising Exposure Can Create Biased Product Evaluations That Persist into Adulthood." *Journal of Consumer Research* 41: 119–34.

Connery, D. S. 1977. *Guilty until Proven Innocent*. New York: Putnum.

Connery, D. S., ed. 1995. *Convicting the Innocent*. Cambridge, MA: Brookline Books.

Conway, P., and J. Peetz. 2012. "When Does Feeling Moral Actually Make You a Better Person? Conceptual Abstraction Moderates Whether Past Moral Deeds Motivate Consistency or Compensatory Behavior." *Personality and Social Psychology Bulletin* 38: 907–19.

Corning, A., and H. Schuman. 2013. "Commemoration Matters: The Anniversaries of 9/11 and Woodstock." *Public Opinion Quarterly* 77: 433–54.

Cortell, A. P., R. M. Eisinger, and S. L. Althaus. 2009. "Why Embed? Explaining the Bush Administration's Decision to Embed Reporters in the 2003 Invasion of Iraq." *American Behavioral Scientist* 52: 657–77.

Costa, D., and M. Kahn. 2008. *Heroes and Cowards: The Social Face of War*. Princeton, NJ: Princeton University Press.

Cottrell, C. A., S. L. Neuberg, and N. P. Li. 2007. "What Do People Desire in Others? A Sociofunctional Perspective on the Importance of Different Valued Characteristics." *Journal of Personality and Social Psychology* 92: 208–31.

"Coughing Fits Overcome 200 at Banquet." 1993. *San Francisco Examiner and Chronicle* (September 12). A16.

Craig, B. 1985. "A Story of Human Kindness." *Pacific Stars and Stripes* (July 30), 13–16.

Critcher, C. R., and T. Gilovich. 2007. "Incidental Environmental Anchors." *Journal of Behavioral Decision Making* 21: 241–51.

Cunningham, W. B., M. K. Johnson, C. L. Raye, J. C. Gatenby, J. C. Gore, and M. R. Banaji. 2004. "Separable Neural Components in the Processing of Black and White Faces." *Psychological Science* 15: 806–13.

Dai, H., K. L. Milkman, and J. Riis. 2014. "The Fresh Start Effect: Temporal Landmarks Motivate Aspirational Behavior." *Management Science* 10: 2563–82.

———. 2015. "Put Your Imperfections Behind You: Temporal Landmarks Spur Goal Initiation When They Signal New Beginnings." *Psychological Science* 26: 1927–36.

Dai, X., K. Wertenbroch, and C. M. Brendel. 2008. "The Value Heuristic in Judgments of Relative Frequency." *Psychological Science* 19: 18–19.

Dana, J., and G. Loewenstein. 2003. "A Social Science Perspective on Gifts to Physicians from Industry." *Journal of the American Medical Association* 290: 252–55.

Danziger, S., and R. Ward. 2010. "Language Changes Implicit Associations between Ethnic Groups and Evaluation in Bilinguals." *Psychological Science* 2: 799–800.

Darke, P. R., and R. B. Ritchie. 2007. "The Defensive Consumer: Advertising Deception, Defensive Processing, and Distrust." *Journal of Marketing Research* 44: 114–27.

Darke, P. R., L. T. A. Ashworth, and R. B. Ritchie. 2008. "Damage from Corrective Advertising: Causes and Cures." *Journal of Marketing* 72: 81–97.

Dasgupta, N. 2004. "Implicit Group Favoritism, Outgroup Favoritism, and Their Behavioral Manifestations." *Social Justice Research* 17: 143–69.

Davis, D. 2010. "Lies, Damned Lies, and the Path from Police Interrogation to Wrongful Conviction." In *The scientist and the Humanist: A Festschrift in Honor of Elliot Aronson*. Edited by M. H. Gonzales, C. Tavris, and J. Aronson. New York: Psychology Press, 211–47.

Davis, D. F., and P. M. Herr. 2014. "From Bye to Buy: Homophones as a Phonological Route to Priming." *Journal of Consumer Research* 40: 1063–77.

Davis, K. E., and M. J. Todd. 1985. "Assessing Friendship: Prototypes, Paradigm Cases and Relationship Description." In *Understanding Personal Relationships: An Interdisciplinary Approach*. Edited by S. Duck and D. Perlman. Beverly Hills, CA: Sage, 17–38.

De Dreu, C. K. W., D. B. Dussel, and F. S. Ten Velden. 2015. "In Intergroup Conflict, Self-Sacrifice Is Stronger among Pro-Social Individuals, and Parochial Altruism Emerges Especially among Cognitively Taxed Individuals." *Frontiers in Psychology* 6: 572.

De Hoog, N., W. Stroebe, and J. B. F. de Wit. 2008. "The Processing of Fear-Arousing Communications: How Biased Processing Leads to Persuasion." *Social Influence* 3: 84–113.

De la Rosa, M. D., D. Sanabria, M. Capizzi, and A. Correa. 2012. "Temporal Preparation Driven by Rhythms Is Resistant to Working Memory Interference." *Frontiers in Psychology* 3. doi:10.3389/psyg.2012.0308.

de Waal, F. B. M. 2008. "Putting the Altruism Back into Altruism: The Evolution of Empathy." *Annual Review of Psychology* 59: 279–300.

Deaner, R. O., A. V. Khera, and M. L. Platt. 2005. "Monkeys Pay Per View: Adaptive Valuation of Social Images by Rhesus Macaques." *Current Biology* 15: 543–48.

Deaux, K., and B. Major. 1987. "Putting Gender into Context: An Interactive Model of Gender-Related Behavior." *Psychological Review* 94: 369–89.

DeBruine, L. M. 2002. "Facial Resemblance Enhances Trust." *Proceedings of the Royal Society, Series B,* 269: 1307–12.

DeBruine, L. M. 2004. "Resemblance to Self Increases the Appeal of Child Faces to Both Men and Women." *Evolution and Human Behavior* 25: 142–54.

Dellande, S., and P. Nyer. 2007. "Using Public Commitments to Gain Customer Compliance." *Advances in Consumer Research* 34: 249–55.

DeSteno, D., R. E. Petty, D. T. Wegener, and D. D. Rucker. 2000. "Beyond Valence in the Perception of Likelihood: The Role of Emotion Specificity." *Journal of Personality and Social Psychology* 78: 397–416.

DeTienne, K. B., B. R. Agle, J. C. Phillips, M-C. Ingerson. 2012. "The Impact of Moral Stress Compared to Other Stressors on Employee Fatigue, Job Satisfaction, and Turnover: An Empirical Investigation." *Journal of Business Ethics* 110: 377–91.

Deval, H., S. P. Mantel, F. R. Kardes, and S. S. Posavac. 2013. "How Naïve Theories Drive Opposing Inferences from the Same Information." *Journal of Consumer Research* 39: 1185–1201.

DeWall, C. N., G. MacDonald, G. D. Webster, C. L. Masten, R. F. Baumeister, C. Powell, D. Combs, D. R. Schurtz, T. F. Stillman, D. M. Tice, N. I. Eisenberger. 2010. "Acetaminophen Reduces Social Pain: Behavioral and Neural Evidence." *Psychological Science* 21: 931–37.

Deyle, E. 2015. "The Global Retail Theft Barometer." http://lpportal.com /feature-articles/item/3495-the-global-retail-theft-barometer.html.

Dhar, R., and I. Simonson. 1992. "The Effect of the Focus of Comparison on Consumer Preferences." *Journal of Marketing Research* 29: 430–40.

Dhar, R., S. M. Nowlis, S. M., and S. J. Sherman. 1999. "Comparison Effects on Preference Construction." *Journal of Consumer Research* 26: 293–306.

DiDonato, T. E., J. Ulrich, and J. I. Krueger. 2011. "Social Perception as Induction and Inference: An Integrative Model of Intergroup Differentiation, Ingroup Favoritism, and Differential Accuracy." *Journal of Personality and Social Psychology* 100: 66–83.

Diekman, A. B., E. R. Brown, A. M. Johnston, and E. K. Clark. 2010. "Seeking Congruity Between Goals and Roles: A New Look at Why Women Opt Out of Science, Technology, Engineering, and Mathematics Careers." *Psychological Science* 21: 1051–57.

Diener, E., and R. Biswas-Diener. 2009. *Happiness: Unlocking the Secret of Psychological Wealth*. Malden, MA: Blackwell.

Dijker, A. M. J. 2010. "Perceived Vulnerability as a Common Basis of Moral Emotions." *British Journal of Social Psychology* 49: 415–23.

Dijksterhuis, A. 2004. "Think Different: The Merits of Unconscious Thought in Preference Development and Decision-Making." *Journal of Personality and Social Psychology* 87, 586–98.

Dijksterhuis, A., and H. Aarts. 2003. "On Wildebeests and Humans: The Preferential Detection of Negative Stimuli." *Psychological Science* 14: 14–18.

———. 2010. "Goals, Attention, and (Un)Consciousness." *Annual Review of Psychology* 61: 467–90.

Dijksterhuis, A., T. L. Chartrand, and H. Aarts. 2007. "Effects of Priming and Perception on Social Behavior and Goal Pursuit." In *Social Psychology and the Unconscious: The Automaticity of Higher Mental Processes*. Edited by J. A. Bargh. Philadelphia: Psychology Press, 51–132.

Dolinski D., M. Nawrat, and I. Rudak. 2001. "Dialogue Involvement as a Social Influence Technique." *Personality and Social Psychology Bulletin* 27: 1395–1406.

Dolnik, L., T. I. Case, and K. D. Williams. 2003. "Stealing Thunder as a Courtroom Tactic Revisited: Processes and Boundaries." *Law and Human Behavior* 27: 267–87.

Donahoe, J. W., and R. Vegas. 2004. "Pavlovian Conditioning: The CS-UR Relation." *Journal of Experimental Psychology: Animal Behavior Processes* 30: 17–33.

Drake, J. E., and E. Winner. 2013. "How Children Use Drawing to Regulate Their Emotions." *Cognition and Emotion* 27: 512–20.

Drizin, S., and R. A. Leo. 2004. "The Problem of False Confessions in the Post-DNA World." *North Carolina Law Review* 82: 891–1007.

Drolet, A., and J. Aaker. 2002. "Off-Target? Changing Cognitive-Based Attitudes." *Journal of Consumer Psychology* 12: 59–68.

Duckworth, A.L., and L. Steinberg. 2015. "Understanding and Cultivating Self-Control in Children and Adolescents." *Child Development Perspective*, 9: 32–37.

Duguid, M. M., and M. C. Thomas-Hunt. 2015. "Condoning Stereotyping? How Awareness of Stereotyping Prevalence Impacts Expression of Stereotypes." *Journal of Applied Psychology* 100: 343–59.

Dunbar, R. I. M. 2012. "On the Evolutionary Function of Song and Dance." In *Music, Language and Human Evolution*. Edited by N. Bannan. New York: Oxford University Press, 201–14.

Dunfield, K. A., and V. A. Kuhlmeier. 2010. "Intention-Mediated Selective Helping in Infancy." *Psychological Science* 21: 523–27.

Durrant, G. B., R. M. Groves, L. Staetsky, and F. Steele. 2010. "Effects of Interviewer Attitudes and Behaviors on Refusal in Household Surveys." *Public Opinion Quarterly* 74: 1–36.

Dux, P. E., and R. Marois. 2009. "The Attentional Blink: A Review of Data and Theory." *Attention, Perception, and Psychophysics*: 71: 1683–1700.

Eagly, A. H., P. Kulesa, L. A. Brannon, K. Shaw, and S. Hutson-Comeaux. 2000. "Why Counterattitudinal Messages Are as Memorable as Proattitudinal Messages: The Importance of Active Defense Against Attack." *Personality and Social Psychology Bulletin* 26: 1392–1408.

Eagly, A. H., W. Wood, and S. Chaiken. 1978. "Causal Inferences About Communicators and Their Effect on Opinion Change." *Journal of Personality and Social Psychology* 36: 424–35.

Edwards, M. L., D. A. Dillman, and J. D. Smyth. 2014. "An Experimental

Test of the Effects of Survey Sponsorship on Internet and Mail Survey Response." *Public Opinion Quarterly* 78: 734–50.

Associated Press. "Eight-Legged Invasion Has Austrians' Spider Sense Tingling." August 3, 2006. usatoday30.usatoday.com/news/offbeat/2006-08-03-spiders-austria_x.htm.

Ellen, P. S., L. A. Mohr, and D. J. Webb. 2000. "Charitable Programs and the Retailer: Do They Mix?" *Journal of Retailing* 76: 393–406.

Elliot, A. J., and T. M. Thrash. 2004. "The Intergenerational Transmission of Fear of Failure." *Personality and Social Psychology Bulletin* 30: 957–71.

Emery, N. J. 2000. "The Eyes Have It: The Neuroethology, Function, and Evolution of Social Gaze." *Neuroscience and Biobehavioral Reviews* 24: 581–604.

Engelberg, J., C. Sasseville, and J. Williams. 2012. "Market Madness? The Case of *Mad Money*." *Management Science* 58: 351–64.

Engelmann, J. B., C. M. Capra, C. Noussair, and G. S. Berns. 2009. "Expert Financial Advice Neurobiologically 'Offloads' Financial Decision-Making Under Risk." *PLoS One* 4, no. 3. e4957. doi:10.1371/journal.pone.0004957.

Enos, R. D., and E. D. Hersh. 2015. "Party Activists as Campaign Advertisers: The Ground Campaign as a Principal-Agent Problem." *American Political Science Review* 109: 252–78.

Enos, R. D., and A. Fowler. In press. "Aggregate Effects of Large-Scale Campaigns on Voter Turnout: Evidence from 400 Million Voter Contacts." *Political Science Research and Methods.*

Epstein, S., S. Donovan, and V. Denes-Raj. 1999. "The Missing Link in the Paradox of the Linda Conjunction Problem: Beyond Knowing and Thinking of the Conjunction Rule, The Intrinsic Appeal of Heuristic Processing." *Personality and Social Psychology Bulletin* 25: 204–14.

Epstein, S., A. Lipson, C. Holstein, and E. Huh. 1992. "Irrational Reactions to Negative Outcomes: Evidence for Two Conceptual Systems." *Journal of Personality and Social Psychology* 62: 328–39.

Eriksson, K, P. Strimling, and J. C. Coultas. 2015. "Bidirectional Associations Between Descriptive and Injunctive Norms." *Organizational Behavior and Human Decision Processes* 129: 59–69.

Ernst & Young. 2013. 12th Global Fraud Survey. *Growing Beyond: A Place for Integrity*. www.ey.com/Publication/vwLUAssets/Global-Fraud-Survey-a-place-for-integrity-12th-Global-Fraud-Survey/$FILE/EY-12th-global-fraud-survey.pdf.

———. 2014. 13th Global Fraud Survey. *Overcoming Compliance Fatigue: Reinforcing the Commitment to Ethical Growth*. www.ey.com/Publication/vwLUAssets/EY-13th-Global-Fraud-Survey/$FILE/EY-13th-Global-Fraud-Survey.pdf.

Fabrigar, L. R., and R. E. Petty. 1999. "The Role of the Affective and Cognitive Bases of Attitudes in Susceptibility to Affectively and Cognitively Based Persuasion." *Personality and Social Psychology Bulletin* 25, no. 3: 363–81.

Fang, X., S. Singh, and R. Ahluwala. 2007. "An Examination of Different Explanations for the Mere Exposure Effect." *Journal of Consumer Research* 34: 98–103.

Fein, S., A. L. McCloskey, and T. M. Tomlinson 1997. "Can the Jury Disregard That Information? The Use of Suspicion to Reduce the Prejudicial Effects of Pretrial Publicity and Inadmissible Testimony." *Personality and Social Psychology Bulletin* 23: 1215–26.

Feinberg, M., and R. Willer. 2011. "Apocalypse Soon? Dire Messages Reduce Belief in Global Warming by Contradicting Just-World Beliefs." *Psychological Science* 22: 34–38.

Fennis, B. M., and W. Stroebe. 2014. "Softening the Blow: Company Self-Disclosure of Negative Information Lessens Damaging Effects on Consumer Judgment and Decision Making." *Journal of Business Ethics* 120: 109–20.

Fennis, B. M., M. A. Adriaanse, W. Stroebe, and B. Pol. 2011. "Bridging the Intention-Behavior Gap: Inducing Implementation Intentions through Persuasive Appeals." *Journal of Consumer Research* 21: 302–11.

Fennis, B. M., E. Das, and M. L. Fransen. 2012. "Print Advertising: Vivid Content." *Journal of Business Research* 65: 861–64.

Fiedler, K., and M. Bluemke. 2009. "Exerting Control over Allegedly Automatic Associative Processes." In *The Psychology of Self-Regulation*. Edited by J. Forgas, R. Baumeister, and D. Tice. New York: Psychology Press, 249–69.

Finch, J. F., and R. B. Cialdini. 1989. "Another Indirect Tactic of (Self-) Image Management: Boosting." *Personality and Social Psychology Bulletin* 15: 222–32.

Fincham, F. D., N. M. Lambert, and S. R. H. Beach. 2010. "Faith and Unfaithfulness: Can Praying for Your Partner Reduce Infidelity?" *Journal of Personality and Social Psychology* 99: 649–59.

Finkel, E. J., and P. W. Eastwick. 2009. "Arbitrary Social Norms Influence Sex Differences in Romantic Selectivity." *Psychological Science* 20: 1290–95.

Fishbach, A., R. K. Ratner, and Y. Zhang 2011. "Inherently Loyal or Easily Bored? Nonconscious Activation of Consistency Versus Variety-Seeking Behavior." *Journal of Consumer Psychology* 21: 38–48.

Fisher, A. V., K. E. Godwin, and H. Seltman. 2014. "Visual Environment, Attention Allocation and Learning in Young Children: When Too Much of a Good Thing May Be Bad." *Psychological Science* 25: 1362–70.

Fiske, S. T. 2004. "Intent and Ordinary Bias: Unintended Thought and Social Motivation Create Casual Prejudice." *Social Justice Research* 17: 117–27.

Flynn, F. J., and B. M. Staw. 2004. "Lend Me Your Wallets: The Effect of Charismatic Leadership on External Support for an Organization." *Strategic Management Journal* 25: 309–33.

Foddy, M., M. J. Platow, and T. Yamagishi. 2009. "Group-Based Trust in Strangers." *Psychological Science* 20: 419–22.

Fogg, B. J., and C. Nass. 1997. "Silicon Sycophants: The Effects of Computers That Flatter." *International Journal of Human-Computer Studies* 46: 551–61.

Forster, J., N. Liberman, and E. T. Higgins. 2005. "Accessibility from Active and Fulfilled Goals." *Journal of Experimental Social Psychology* 41: 220–39.

Fredman, L. A., M. D. Buhrmester, A. Gomez, W. T. Fraser, S. Talaifar, S. M. Brannon, and W. B. Swann Jr. 2015, "Identity Fusion, Extreme Pro-Group Behavior, and the Path to Defusion." *Social and Personality Psychology Compass* 9: 468–80.

Friedman, H. H., and A. Rahman. 2011. "Gifts-Upon-Entry and Appreciative Comments: Reciprocity Effects in Retailing." *International Journal of Marketing Studies* 3: 161–64.

Fritschler, A. L. 1975. *Smoking and Politics.* Englewood Cliffs, NJ: Prentice-Hall.

Gaissmaier, W., and G. Gigerenzer. 2012. "9/11, Act II: A Fine-Grained Analysis of the Regional Variations in Traffic Fatalities in the Aftermath of the Terrorist Attacks." *Psychological Science* 23: 1449–54.

Galak, J., D. Small, and A. T. Stephen. 2011. "Microfinance Decision Making: A Field Study of Prosocial Lending," *Journal of Marketing Research* 48: 130–37.

Ganegoda, D. B., G. P. Latham, and R. Folger. "The Effect of a Consciously Set and a Primed Goal on Fair Behavior." *Human Resource Management*. Article first published online: 4 August 2015. doi: 10.1002/hrm.21743.

García, J. H., T. Sterner, and S. Afsah. 2007. "Public Disclosure of Industrial Pollution: The PROPER Approach in Indonesia." *Environment and Development Economics* 12: 739–56.

Garfinkel, Y. 2003. *Dancing at the Dawn of Agriculture*. Austin: University of Texas Press.

Gaspar, J. G., W. N. Street, M. B. Windsor, R. Carbonari, H. Kaczmarski, A. F. Kramer, and K. E. Mathewson. 2014. "Providing Views of the Driving Scene to Drivers' Conversation Partners Mitigates Cell Phone-Related Distraction." *Psychological Science* 25: 2136–46.

Gawronski, B., R. Balas, and L. A. Creighton. 2014. "Can the Formation of Conditioned Attitudes Be Intentionally Controlled?" *Personality and Social Psychology Bulletin* 40: 419–32.

Gayet, S., C. L. E. Paffen, and S. Van der Stigchel. 2013. "Information Matching the Content of Visual Working Memory Is Prioritized for Conscious Access." *Psychological Science* 24: 2472–80.

Geng, J. J. 2014. "Attentional Mechanisms of Distractor Suppression." *Current Directions in Psychological Science* 23: 147–53.

Gentile D. A., C. A. Anderson, S. Yukawa, N. Ihori, M. Saleem, L. K. Lim, A. Shibuya, A. Liau, A. Khoo, B. Bushman, L. R. Huesmann, and A. Sakamoto. 2009. "The Effects of Prosocial Video Games on Prosocial Behaviors: International Evidence from Correlational, Longitudinal, and Experimental Studies." *Personality and Social Psychology Bulletin* 35: 752–63.

Gerber, A. G., D. P. Green, and R. Shachar. 2003. "Voting May Be Habit-Forming: Evidence From a Randomized Field Experiment." *American Journal of Political Science* 47: 540–50.

Ghosh, B. June 8, 2009. "How to Make Terrorists Talk." *Time*, 40–43.

Gigerenzer, G. 2006. "Out of the Frying Pan into the Fire: Behavioral Reactions to Terrorist Attacks." *Risk Analysis* 26: 347–51.

Gilbert, D. T. 2006. *Stumbling on Happiness.* New York: Knopf.

Gino, F., and A. D. Galinsky. 2012. "Vicarious Dishonesty: When Psychological Closeness Creates Distance from One's Moral Compass." *Organizational Behavior and Human Decision Processes* 119: 15–26.

Gino, F., M. I. Norton, and D. Ariely. 2010. "The Counterfeit Self: The Deceptive Costs of Faking It." *Psychological Science* 21: 712–20.

Glaser, J., and M. R. Banaji. 1999. "When Fair Is Foul and Foul Is Fair: Reverse Priming in Automatic Evaluation." *Journal of Personality and Social Psychology* 77: 669–87.

Gluckman, M., and S. J. Johnson. 2013. "Attention Capture by Social Stimuli in Young Infants." *Frontiers in Psychology.* doi:10.3389/fpsyg.2013.00527.

Gneezy, A., A. Imas, A. Brown, L. D. Nelson, and M. I. Norton. 2012. "Paying to Be Nice: Consistency and Costly Prosocial Behavior." *Management Science* 58: 179–87.

Goh, J., J. Pfeffer, and S. A. Zenios. I2016. "The Relationship Between Workplace Stressors and Mortality and Health Costs in the United States." *Management Science, 62*, 608-628.

Gold, B. P., M. J. Frank, B. Bogert, and Ed Brattico. 2013. "Pleasurable

Music Affects Reinforcement Learning According to the Listener." *Frontiers in Psychology* 4. doi:10.3389/psyg.2013.00541.

Goldstein, N. J., V. Griskevicius, and R. B. Cialdini. 2011. "Reciprocity by Proxy: A New Influence Strategy for Motivating Cooperation and Prosocial Behavior." *Administrative Science Quarterly* 56: 441–73.

Gollwitzer, P. M., and P. Sheeran. 2006. "Implementation Intentions and Goal Achievement: A Meta-Analysis of Effects and Processes." *Advances of Experimental Social Psychology* 38: 69–119.

———. 2009. "Self-Regulation of Consumer Decision Making and Behavior: The Role of Implementation Intentions." *Journal of Consumer Research* 19: 593–607.

Goodman-Delahunty, J., N. Martschuk, and M. K. Dhami. 2014. "Interviewing High Value Detainees: Securing Cooperation and Disclosures." *Applied Cognitive Psychology* 28: 883–97.

Goodwin, G. P. 2015. "Moral Character in Person Perception." *Current Directions in Psychological Science* 24: 38–44.

Gordon, R. A. 1996. "Impact of Ingratiation on Judgments and Evaluations: A Meta-Analytic Investigation." *Journal of Personality and Social Psychology* 71: 54–70.

Granic, I., A. Lobel, and R. C. M. E. Engels. 2014. "The Benefits of Playing Video Games." *American Psychologist* 69, 66–78.

Grant, A. 2013. *Give and Take: A Revolutionary Approach to Success*. New York: Viking.

Grant, A. M., and D. A. Hofmann. 2011. "It's Not All About Me: Motivating Hand Hygiene among Health Care Professionals by Focusing on Patients." *Psychological Science* 22: 1494–99.

Grant, A., and J. Dutton. 2012. "Beneficiary or Benefactor: Are People More Prosocial When They Reflect on Receiving or Giving?" *Psychological Science* 23: 1033–39.

Grant, N. K., L. R. Fabrigar, and H. Lim. 2010. "Exploring the Efficacy of Compliments as a Tactic for Securing Compliance." *Basic and Applied Social Psychology* 32: 226–33.

Gray, K., D. G. Rand, E. Ert, K. Lewis, S. Hershman, and M. I. Norton. 2014. "The Emergence of 'Us' and 'Them' in 80 Lines of Code: Modeling Group Genesis in Homogeneous Populations." *Psychological Science* 25: 982–90.

Grecco, E., S. J. Robbins, E. Bartoli, and E. F. Wolff. 2013. "Use of Nonconscious Priming to Promote Self-Disclosure." *Clinical Psychological Science* 1: 311–15.

Greenwald, A. G., and T. F. Pettigrew. 2014. "With Malice Toward None and Charity for Some." *American Psychologist* 69: 669–84.

Greifeneder, R., A. Alt, K. Bottenberg, T. Seele, S. Zelt, and D. Wagener. 2010. "On Writing Legibly: Processing Fluency Systematically Biases Evaluations of Handwritten Material." *Social and Personality Science* 1: 230–37. 2010.

Greitemeyer, T., and D. O. Mügge. 2014. "Video Games Do Affect Social Outcomes: A Meta-Analytic Review of the Effects of Violent and Prosocial Video Game Play." *Personality and Social Psychology Bulletin* 40: 578–89.

Greitemeyer, T., and S. Osswald. 2010. "Effects of Prosocial Videogames on Prosocial Behavior." *Journal of Personality and Social Psychology* 98: 211–20.

Griskevicius, V., N. J. Goldstein, C. R. Mortensen, J. M. Sundie, R. B. Cialdini, and D. T. Kenrick. 2009. "Fear and Loving in Las Vegas: Evolution, Emotion, and Persuasion." *Journal of Marketing Research* 46: 384–95.

Gross, J. J., and R. A. Thompson, 2007. "Emotion Regulation: Conceptual Foundations." In *Handbook of Emotion Regulation.* Edited by J. J. Gross. New York: Guilford Press, 3–24.

Gruber, J., I. B. Mauss, and M. Tamir. 2011. "A Dark Side of Happiness? How, When, and Why Happiness Is Not Always Good." *Perspectives on Psychological Science* 6: 222–33.

Gu, Y., S. Botti, and D. Faro. 2013. "Turning the Page: The Impact of Choice Closure on Satisfaction." *Journal of Consumer Research* 40: 268–83.

Guadagno, R. E., and R. B. Cialdini. 2007. "Persuade Him by Email, but See Her in Person: Online Persuasion Revisited." *Computers in Human Behavior* 23: 999–1015.

Guadagno, R. E., K. V. Rhoads, and B. J. Sagarin. 2011. "Figural Vividness and Persuasion: Capturing the 'Elusive' Vividness Effect." *Personality and Social Psychology Bulletin* 37: 626–38.

Guéguen, N. 2012. " 'Say It . . . Near the Flower Shop': Further Evidence of the Effect of Flowers on Mating." *Journal of Social Psychology* 152, no. 5: 529–32.

———. 2013. "Weather and Courtship Behavior: A Quasi-Experiment with the Flirty Sunshine." *Social Influence* 8: 312–19.

Guéguen, N., S. Meineri, and J. Fischer-Lokou. 2014. "Men's Music Ability and Attractiveness to Women in a Real-Life Courtship Contest." *Psychology of Music* 42: 545–49.

Guéguen, N., N. Pichot, and G. Le Dreff. 2005. "Similarity and Helping Behavior on the Web: The Impact of the Convergence of Surnames between a Solicitor and a Subject in a Request Made by E-Mail." *Journal of Applied Social Psychology* 35: 423–29.

Guidotti, T. L., and P. Jacobs. 1993. "Implications of an Epidemiological Mistake: A Community's Response to a Perceived Excess of Cancer Risk." *American Journal of Public Health* 83: 233–39.

Guiteras, R., J. Levinsohn, and A. M. Mobarak. 2015. "Encouraging Sanitation Investment in the Developing World: A Cluster-Randomized Trial." *Science* 348 (May 22): 903–6.

Hagemann, N., B. Strauss, and J. Leissing. 2008. "When the Referee Sees Red." *Psychological Science* 19: 769–70.

Hagmann, C. E., and R. G. Cook. 2013. "Active Change Detection by Pigeons and Humans." *Journal of Experimental Psychology: Animal Behavior Processes* 39: 383–89.

Hall, C. C., J. Zhao, and E. Shafir. 2014. "Self-Affirmation Among the Poor: Cognitive and Behavioral Implications." *Psychological Science* 25: 619–25.

Halvorson, H. G., and E. T. Higgins. 2013. *Focus: Use Different Ways of Seeing the World for Success and Influence.* New York: Hudson Street Press.

Hamilton, R., J. Hong, and A. Chernev. 2007. "Perceptual Focus Effects in Choice." *Journal of Consumer Research* 34: 187–99.

Hamilton, W. D. 1964. "The Genetic Evolution of Social Behavior." *Journal of Theoretical Biology* 7: 1–52.

Hammond, D. 2010. "Health Warning Messages on Tobacco Products: A Review." *Tobacco Control* 20: 327–37.

Han, S-P., and S. Shavitt. 1994. "Persuasion and Culture: Advertising Appeals in Individualistic and Collectivistic Societies." *Journal of Experimental Social Psychology* 30: 326–50.

Hanson, J., and M. Wanke. 2010. "Truth from Language and Truth from Fit: The Impact of Linguistic Concreteness and Level of Construal on Subjective Truth. *Personality and Social Psychology Bulletin* 36: 1576–78.

Harman, W. S., T. W. Lee, T. R. Mitchell, W. Felps, and B. P. Owens. 2007. "The Psychology of Voluntary Employee Turnover." *Current Directions in Psychological Science* 16: 51–54.

Harter, J. K., F. L. Schmidt, J. W. Asplund, E. A. Killham, and S. Agrawal. 2010. "Causal Impact of Employee Work Perceptions on the Bottom Line of Organizations." *Perspectives on Psychological Science* 5: 378–89.

Hasan, Y., L. Bègue, M. Scharkow, and B. J. Bushman. 2013. "The More You Play, The More Aggressive You Become: A Long-Term Experimental Study of Cumulative Violent Video Game Effects on Hostile Expectations and Aggressive Behavior." *Journal of Experimental Social Psychology* 49: 224–27.

Haslam, N. 2006. "Dehumanization: An Integrative Review." *Personality and Social Psychology Review* 10: 252–64.

Hassan, S. 1990. *Combating Cult Mind Control.* Rochester, VT: Park Street Press.

———. 2000. *Releasing the Bonds: Breaking the Chains of Destructive Mind Control.* Boston: Freedom of Mind Press.

Hassin, R. R., M. J. Ferguson, D. Shidlovski, and L. Gross. 2007. "Subliminal Exposure to National Flags Affects Political Thought and Behavior." *Proceedings of the National Academy of Sciences* 104: 19757–61.

Hatemi, P. K., and R. McDermott. 2012. "The Genetics of Politics: Discovery, Challenges, and Progress." *Trends in Genetics* 28: 525–33.

Healy, A., J., N. Malhotra, and C. H. Mo. 2010. "Irrelevant Events Affect

Voters' Evaluations of Government Performance." *Proceedings of the National Academy of Sciences of the USA* 107: 12804–9.

Heath, C., and D. Heath. 2007. *Made to Stick: Why Some Ideas Survive and Others Die*. New York: Random House.

Heijkoop, M., J. S. Dubas, and M. A. G. van Aken. 2009. "Parent-Child Resemblance and Kin Investment: Physical Resemblance or Personality Similarity." *European Journal of Developmental Psychology* 6: 64–69.

Heilman, C. M., K. Nakamoto, and A. G. Rao. 2002. "Pleasant Surprises: Consumer Response to Unexpected In-Store Coupons." *Journal of Marketing Research* 39: 242–52.

Heilman, C., K. Lakishyk, and S. Radas. 2011. "An Empirical Investigation of In-Store Sampling Promotions." *British Food Journal* 113: 1252–66.

Heimbach, J. T., and J. Jacoby. 1972. "The Zeigarnik Effect in Advertising." In *Proceedings of the Third Annual Conference of the Association for Consumer Research*. Edited by M. Ventakesan. College Park, MD, 746–57.

Heintzelman, S., J., and L. A. King. 2014. "(The Feeling of) Meaning-as-Information." *Personality and Social Psychology Review* 18: 153–67.

Helie, S., and R. Sun. 2010. "Incubation, Insight, and Creative Problem Solving: A Unified Theory and a Connectionist Model." *Psychological Review* 17: 994–1024.

Herbig, P., J. Milewicz, and J. Golden. 1994. "A Model of Reputation Building and Destruction." *Journal of Business Research* 31: 23–31.

Herr, P. M., F. R. Kardes, and J. Kim. 1991. "Effects of Word-of-Mouth and Product Attribute Information on Persuasion: An Accessibility-Diagnosticity Perspective." *Journal of Consumer Research* 17: 454–62.

Herr, P. M., S. J. Sherman, and R. H. Fazio. 1983. "On the Consequences of Priming: Assimilation and Contrast Effects." *Journal of Experimental Social Psychology* 19: 323–40.

Hertel, G. and N. L. Kerr. 2001. "Priming In-Group Favoritism: The Impact of Normative Scripts in the Minimal Group Paradigm." *Journal of Experimental Social Psychology* 37: 316–24.

Herzog, S. M., and R. Hertwig. 2009. "The Wisdom of Many in One Mind: Improving Individual Judgments with Dialectical Bootstrapping." *Psychological Science* 20: 231–37.

Heyes, C. 2011. "Automatic Imitation." *Psychological Bulletin* 137: 463–83.

Higgins, E. T. 1996. "Knowledge Activation: Accessibility, Applicability, and Salience." In *Social Psychology: Handbook of Basic Principles*. Edited by E. T. Higgins and A. W. Kruglanski. New York: Guilford Press.

Higgins, E. T., and J. A. Bargh. 1987. "Social Cognition and Social Perception." *Annual Review of Psychology* 38: 369–425.

Higgins, G. E., A. L. Wilson, and B. D. Fell. 2005. "An Application of Deterrence Theory to Software Piracy." *Journal of Criminal Justice and Popular Culture* 12: 166–84.

Hirt, E. R., and K. D. Markman. 1995. "Multiple Explanation: A Consider-an-Alternative Strategy for Debiasing Judgments." *Journal of Personality and Social Psychology* 69: 1069–86.

Hoch, S. J. 1985. "Counterfactual Reasoning and Accuracy in Predicting Personal Events." *Journal of Experimental Psychology: Learning, Memory, and Cognition* 11: 719–31.

Hodges, B. 2004. "Medical Student Bodies and the Pedagogy of Self-Reflection, Self-Assessment, and Self-Regulation. *Journal of Curriculum Theorizing* 20: 41–51.

Hofmann, W., J. De Houwer, M. Perugini, F. Baeyens, and G. Crombez. 2010. "Evaluative Conditioning in Humans: A Meta-Analysis." *Psychological Bulletin* 136, no. 3: 390–421.

Holley, S. R., C. M. Haase, and R. W. Levenson. 2013, "Age-Related Changes in Demand-Withdraw Communication Behaviors." *Journal of Marriage and Family* 75: 822–36.

Homer, P. M. 2009. "Product Placements: The Impact of Placement Type and Repetition on Attitude." *Journal of Advertising* 58: 21–31.

Hoshino-Browne, E., A. S. Zanna, S. J. Spencer, M. P. Zanna, and S. Kitayama. 2005. "On the Cultural Guises of Cognitive Dissonance: The Case of Easterners and Westerners." *Journal of Personality and Social Psychology* 89: 294–310.

Houghton, D. C., and F. R. Kardes. 1998. "Market Share Overestimation and the Noncomplementarity Effect." *Marketing Letters* 9: 313–20.

Hove, M. J., and J. L. Risen. 2009. "It's All in the Timing: Interpersonal Synchrony Increases Affiliation." *Social Cognition* 27: 949–61.

Hovland, C. I., A. A. Lumsdaine, and F. D. Sheffield. 1949. "*Experiments on Mass Communication.*" Princeton, NJ: Princeton University Press.

Hsee, C. K., and F. LeClerc. 1998. "Will Products Look More Attractive When Presented Separately or Together?" *Journal of Consumer Research* 25: 175–86.

Huang, J., F. J. Chaloupka, and G. T. Fong. 2013. "Cigarette Graphic Warning Labels and Smoking Prevalence in Canada: A Critical Examination and Reformulation of the FDA Regulatory Impact Analysis." *Tobacco Control.* doi:10.1136/tobaccocontrol-2013-051170

Hudson, N. W., and C. Fraley. 2015. "Volitional Personality Trait Change: Can People Choose to Change Their Personality Traits?" *Journal of Personality and Social Psychology* 109: 490–507.

Hugenberg, K., and G. V. Bodenhausen. 2004. "Category Membership Moderates the Inhibition of Social Identities." *Journal of Experimental Social Psychology* 40: 233–38.

Hummel, J. E., and K. J. Holyoak. 2003. "A Symbolic-Connectionist Theory of Relational Inference and Generalization." *Psychological Review* 110: 220–64.

Humphreys, G. W., and Sui, J. 2016. Attentional control and the self: The Self-Attention Network (SAN). *Cognitive Neuroscience* 7: 5–17.

Huron, D. 2001. "Is Music an Evolutionary Adaptation?" *Annals of the New York Academy of Sciences.* 930: 43–61.

Hütter, M., F. Kutzner, and K. Fiedler. 2014. "What Is Learned from Repeated Pairings? On the Scope and Generalizability of Evaluative Conditioning." *Journal of Experimental Psychology: General* 143: 631–43.

Hütter, M., S. Sweldens, C. Stahl, C. Unkelbach, and K. C. Klauer. 2012. "Dissociating Contingency Awareness and Conditioned Attitudes: Evidence of Contingency-Unaware Evaluative Conditioning." *Journal of Experimental Psychology: General* 141, no. 3: 539–57.

Hygge, S., G. W. Evans, and M. Bullinger. 2002. "A Prospective Study of Some Effects of Aircraft Noise on Cognitive Performance in Schoolchildren." *Psychological Science* 13: 469–74.

Hyman, I. E., S. M. Boss, B. M. Wise, K. E. McKenzie, and J. M. Caggiano. 2009. "Did You See the Unicycling Clown? Inattentional Blindness While Walking and Talking on a Cell Phone." *Applied Cognitive Psychology* 24: 597–607.

Hyman, R. 1989. *The Elusive Quarry: A Scientific Appraisal of Psychical Research*. Buffalo: Prometheus Books.

———.1995. "Evaluation of Program on Anomalous Mental Phenomena." www.mceagle.com/remoteviewing/refs/science/air/hyman.html.

Ijzerman, H., and G. Semin. 2009. "The Thermometer of Social Relations." *Psychological Science* 20: 1214–20.

———. 2010. "Temperature Perceptions as a Ground for Social Proximity." *Journal of Experimental Social Psychology* 46: 867–73.

Inagaki, T. K., and N. I. Eisenberger. 2013. "Shared Neural Mechanisms Underlying Social Warmth and Physical Warmth." *Psychological Science* 24: 2272–80.

Inbau, F. E., J. E. Reid, J. P. Buckley, and B. C. Jayne. 2001. *Criminal Interrogation and Confessions*. 4th ed.. Gaithersburg, MD: Aspen.

Inglis, F. 2010. *A Short History of Celebrity*. Princeton, NJ: Princeton University Press.

Inman, J. J., A. C. Peter, and P. Raghubir. 1997. "Framing the Deal: The Role of Restrictions in Accentuating Deal Value." *Journal of Consumer Research* 24: 68–79.

Inzlicht, M., and T. Ben-Zeev. 2000. "A Threatening Intellectual Environment: Why Females Are Susceptible to Experiencing Problem-Solving Deficits in the Presence of Males." *Psychological Science* 11, no. 5 (September): 365–71.

Inzlicht, M., J. N. Gutsell, and L. Legault. 2012. "Mimicry Reduces Racial Prejudice." *Journal of Experimental Social Psychology* 48: 361–65.

Ireland, M. E., R. B. Slatcher, P. W. Eastwick, L. E. Scissors, E. J. Finkel, and J. W. Pennebaker. 2011. "Language Style Matching Predicts Relationship Initiation and Stability." *Psychological Science* 22: 39–44.

Isaacowitz, D. M., K. Toner, and S. D. Neupert. 2009. "Use of Gaze for Real-Time Mood Regulation: Effects of Age and Attentional Functioning." *Psychology and Aging* 24: 989–94.

Isen, A. M., T. E. Shalker, M. Clark, and L. Karp. 1978. "Affect, Accessibility of Material in Memory, and Behavior." *Journal of Personality and Social Psychology* 36: 1–12.

Issenberg, S. 2012. *The Victory Lab*. New York: Crown.

Ito, T. A., N. P. Friedman, B. D. Bartholow, J. Correll, C. Loersch, L. J. Altamirono, and A. Miyake. 2015. "Toward a Comprehensive Understanding of Executive Cognition and Cognitive Function in Implicit Racial Bias." *Journal of Personality and Social Psychology* 108: 187–218.

Iyengar, S., M. D. Peters, and D. R. Kinder. 1982. "Experimental Demonstrations of the 'Not-So-Minimal' Consequences of Television News Programs." *American Political Science Review* 76: 848–58.

Jabbi, M., J. Bastiaansen, and C. Keysers. 2008. "A Common Anterior Insula Representation of Disgust Observation, Experience and Imagination Shows Divergent Functional Connectivity Pathways." *PLoS ONE* 3, no. 8: e2939. doi:10.1371/journal.pone.0002939.

Jacob, C., N. Guéguen, A, Martin, and G. Boulbry. 2011. "Retail Salespeople's Mimicry of Customers: Effects on Consumer Behavior." *Journal of Retailing and Consumer Services* 18: 381–88.

James Jr., H. S. 2011. "Is the Just Man a Happy Man? An Empirical Study of the Relationship Between Ethics and Subjective Well-Being." *Kyklos* 64: 193–212.

James, W. 1950/1890. *The Principles of Psychology*. New York: Dover.

Janiszewski, C., A. Kuo, and N. T. Tavassoli. 2013. "The Influence of Selective Attention and Inattention to Products on Subsequent Choice." *Journal of Consumer Research* 39: 1258–74.

Jerabeck, J. M., and C. J. Ferguson. 2013. "The Influence of Solitary and Cooperative Violent Video Game Play on Aggressive and Prosocial Behavior." *Computers in Human Behavior* 29: 2573–78.

Jhang, J. H., and J. G. Lynch Jr. 2015. "Pardon the Interuption: Goal Proximity, Perceived Spare Time, and Impatience." *Journal of Consumer Research* 41: 1267–83.

Jiang, L., J. Hoegg, D. W. Dahl, and A. Chattopadhyay. 2009. "The Persuasive Role of Incidental Similarity on Attitudes and Purchase Intensions in a Sales Context." *Journal of Consumer Research* 36: 778–91.

Jo, H-G., M. Wittmann, T. Hinterberger, and S. Schmidt. 2014. "The Readiness Potential Reflects Intentional Binding." *Frontiers in Human Neuroscience* 8: 421.

Johnson, P. 2011. *Socrates*. New York: Viking Press.

Johnson, P. B., A. Mehrabian, and B. Weiner. 1968. "Achievement Motivation and the Recall of Incompleted and Completed Exam Questions." *Journal of Educational Psychology* 59: 181–85.

Johnson, S. K., and M. C. Anderson. 2004. "The Role of Inhibitory Control in Forgetting Semantic Knowledge." *Psychological Science* 15: 448–53.

Jones, J. T., B. W. Pelham, M. R. Carvallo, and M. C. Mirenberg. 2004. "How Do I Love Thee? Let Me Count the Js. Implicit Egoism and Interpersonal Attraction." *Journal of Personality and Social Psychology* 87: 665–83.

Jones, J. T., B. Pelham, M. C. Mirenberg, and J. J. Hetts. 2002. "Name Letter Preferences Are Not Merely Mere Exposure: Implicit Egoism as Self-Regulation." *Journal of Experimental Social Psychology* 38: 170–77.

Jones, T. F., A. S. Craig, D. Hoy, E. W. Gunter, D. L. Ashley, D. Bar, J. W. Brock, and W. Schaffner. 2000. "Mass Psychogenic Illness Attributed to Toxic Exposure at a High School." *New England Journal of Medicine* 342: 96–100.

Joorman, J., and W. M. Vanderlind. 2014. "Emotion Regulation in Depression: The Role of Biased Cognition and Reduced Cognitive Control." *Clinical Psychological Science, 2*, 402–21.

Jostmann, N. B., D. Lakens, and T. W. Schubert. 2009. "Weight as an Embodiment of Importance." *Psychological Science* 20: 1169–74.

Kahneman, D. 2011. *Thinking, Fast and Slow*. New York: Farrar, Straus and Giroux.

Kahneman, D., and A. Tversky. 1979. "Prospect Theory: An Analysis of Decision Under Risk." *Econometrica* 47: 263–91.

Kahneman, D., D. Lovallo, and O. Sibony. 2011. "The Big Idea: Before You Make That Big Decision." *Harvard Business Review* 89 (June): 50–61.

Kalisch, R., M. B. Müller, and O. Tüscher. 2015. "A Conceptual Framework for the Neurobiological Study of Resilience." *Behavioral and Brain Sciences* 38: 1–79.

Kalmoe, N., P., and K. Gross. In press. "Cuing Patriotism, Prejudice, and Partisanship in the Age of Obama." *Political Psychology*. Article first published online: 21 OCT 2015. doi: 10.1111/pops.12305.

Kaminski, G., F. Ravary, C. Graff, and E. Gentaz. 2010. "Firstborns' Disadvantage in Kinship Detection." *Psychological Science* 21: 1746–50.

Kandler, C., W. Bleidorn, and R. Riemann. 2012. "Left or Right? Sources of Political Orientation: The Roles of Genetic Factors, Cultural Transmission, Assortative Mating, and Personality." *Journal of Personality and Social Psychology* 102: 633–45.

Kang, S. K., J. B. Hirsh, and A. L. Chasteen. 2010. "Your Mistakes Are Mine: Self-Other Overlap Predicts Neural Response." *Journal of Experimental Social Psychology* 46: 229–32.

Kang, Y., L. E. Williams, M. S. Clark, J. R. Gray, and J. A. Bargh. 2010. "Physical Temperature Effects on Trust Behavior: The Role of the Insula." *SCAN* 6: 507–15.

Kardes, F. R. 2013. "Selective Versus Comparative Processing." *Journal of Consumer Psychology* 23: 150–53.

Kardes, F. R., D. M. Sanbonmatsu, M. L. Cronley, and D. C. Houghton. 2002. "Consideration Set Overvaluation: When Impossibly Favorable Ratings of a Set of Brands Are Observed." *Journal of Consumer Psychology* 12: 353–61.

Karpoff, J. M., D. S. Lee, and G. S. Martin. 2008. "The Cost to Firms of Cooking the Books." *Journal Financial Quantitative Analysis* 43: 581–612.

Karpoff, J. M., J. R. Lott, and E. W. Wehrly. 2005. "The Reputational Penalties for Environmental Violations: Empirical Evidence." *Journal of Law and Economics* 48: 653–75.

Karremans, J. C., and H. Aarts. 2007. "The Role of Automaticity in Determining the Inclination to Forgive Close Others." *Journal of Experimental Social Psychology* 43: 902–17.

Kassin, S. M. 2008. "False Confessions: Causes, Consequences and Implications for Reform." *Current Directions in Psychological Science* 17: 249–53.

———. 2012. "Why Confessions Trump Innocence." *American Psychologist* 67: 431–45.

Kassin, S. M., D. Bogart, and J. Kerner. 2012. "Confessions That Corrupt: Evidence from the DNA Exoneration Case Files." *Psychological Science* 23: 41–45.

Kassin, S. M., S. A. Drizin, T. Grisso, G. H. Gudjonsson, R. A. Leo, and A. D. Redlich. 2010. "Police-Induced Confessions: Risk Factors and Recommendations." *Law and Human Behavior* 34: 3–38.

Kelly, A. E., and L. Wang. 2012. "A Life Without Lies: Can Living More Honestly Improve Health?" Paper presented at the annual meeting of the American Psychological Association. Orlando, FL (August).

Kenrick, D. T., S. L. Neuberg, and R. B. Cialdini. 2015. *Social Psychology: Goals in Interaction*. Vol. 6. Boston: Pearson Education.

Kent, S. A., and D. Hall. 2000. "Brainwashing and Re-Indoctrination Programs in the Children of God/The Family." *Cultic Studies Journal* 17: 56–78.

Kesebir, S. 2012. "The Superorganism Account of Human Sociality: How and When Human Groups Are Like Beehives." *Personality and Social Psychology Review* 16: 233–61.

Kettle, K. I., and G. Haubl. 2011. "The Signature Effect: Signing Influences Consumption-Related Behavior by Priming Self-Identity." *Journal of Consumer Research* 38: 474–89.

Killeya, L. A., and B. T. Johnson. 1998. "Experimental Induction of Biased Systematic Processing: The Directed Thought Technique." *Personality and Social Psychology Bulletin* 24: 17–33.

Kim, B. K., G. Zauberman, and J. R. Bettman. 2012. "Space, Time and Intertemporal Preferences." *Journal of Consumer Research* 39: 867–80.

Kim, C. Y., and R. Blake. 2005. "Psychophysical Magic: Rendering the Visible 'Invisible.' *Trends in Cognitive Sciences* 9: 381–88.

Kim, J., N. Novemsky, and R. Dhar. 2013. "Adding Small Differences Can Increase Similarity and Choice." *Psychological Science* 24: 225–29.

Kimel, S. Y., R. Huesmann, J. R. Kunst, and E. Halprin, 2016. "Living in a Genetic World: How Learning about Interethnic Similarities and Differences affects Peace and Conflict. *Personality and Social Psychology Bulletin* 42: 688–700.

Kinneavy, J. L., and C. R. Eskin. 2000. "Kairos in Artistotle's Rhetoric." *Written Communication* 17: 432–44.

Kirchheimer, S. 2013. "12 Ways to Foil ID Thieves." *AARP Bulletin* (May), 26.

Kirschner, S., and M. Tomasello. 2010. "Joint Music Making Promotes Prosocial Behavior in 4-Year-Old Children." *Evolution and Human Behavior* 31: 354–64.

Klayman, J., and Y-M. Ha. 1987. "Confirmation, Disconfirmation, and Information in Hypothesis-Testing." *Psychological Review* 94: 211–28.

Klein, S. B., L. Cosmedes, J. Tooby, and S. Chance. 2002. "Decisions and the Evolution of Memory: Multiple Systems, Multiple Functions." *Psychological Review* 109: 306–29.

Klinger, E. 2013. "Goal Commitments and the Content of Thoughts and

Dreams: Basic Principles." *Frontiers in Psychology* 11 (July). doi:10.3389/fpsyg.2013.00415.

Klinger, M. R., P. C. Burton, and G. S. Pitts. 2000. "Mechanisms of Priming I: Response Completion, Not Spreading Activation." *Journal of Experimental Psychology: Learning, Memory, and Cognition* 26: 441–55.

Klucharev, V., M. A. M. Munneke, A. Smidts, and G. Fernandez. 2011. "Downregulation of the Posterior Medial Frontal Cortex Prevents Social Conformity." *Journal of Neuroscience* 31: 11934–40.

Koehler, D. J. 1991. "Explanation, Imagination and Confidence in Judgment." *Psychological Bulletin* 110: 499–519.

Koriat, A., S. Lichtenstein, and B. Fischhoff. 1980. "Reasons for Confidence." *Journal of Experimental Psychology: Human Learning and Memory* 6: 107–18.

Krajbich, I., C. Camerer, J. Ledyard, and A. Rangel. 2009. "Self-Control in Decision-Making Involves Modulation of the VmPFC Valuation System." *Science* 324: 12315–20.

Kranz, M. 2015. "CEO Pay on the Climb." *Arizona Republic* (Phoenix) (May 14), 4B.

Kranzler, D. 1976. *Japanese, Nazis, and Jews: The Jewish Refugee Community of Shanghai, 1938–1945*. New York: Yeshiva University Press.

Kriner, D. L., and F. X. Shen. 2012. "How Citizens Respond to Combat Casualties: The Differential Impact of Local Casualties on Support for the War in Afghanistan." *Public Opinion Quarterly* 76: 761–70.

Kristofferson, K., K. White, and J. Peloza. 2014. "The Nature of Slacktivism: How the Social Observability of an Initial Act of Token Support Affects Subsequent Prosocial Action." *Journal of Consumer Research* 40: 1149–66.

Krizan, Z., and J. Suls. 2008. "Losing Sight of Oneself in the Above-Average Effect: When Egocentrism, Focalism, and Group Diffusiveness Collide." *Journal of Experimental Social Psychology* 44: 929–42.

Kruger, J., and K. Savitsky. 2009. "On the Genesis of Inflated (and Deflated) Judgments of Responsibility: Egocentrism Revisited." *Organizational Behavior and Human Decision Processes* 108: 143–52.

Kruglanski, A. W., and D. M. Webster. 1996. "Motivated Closing of the Mind: Seizing and Freezing." *Psychological Review* 103: 263–83.

Ku, G., A. D. Galinsky, and J. K. Murnighan. 2006. "Starting Low but Ending High: A Reversal of the Anchoring Effect in Auctions." *Journal of Personality and Social Psychology* 90: 975–986.

Kuester, M., and M. Benkenstein. 2014. "Turning Dissatisfied into Satisfied Customers: How Referral Reward Programs Affect the Referrer's Attitude and Loyalty Toward the Recommended Service Provider." *Journal of Retailing and Consumer Services* 21: 897–904.

Kunda, Z., G. T. Fong, R. Sanitioso, and E. Reber. 1993. "Directional Questions Direct Self-Conceptions." *Journal of Experimental Social Psychology* 29: 63–86.

Kunz, J. 2000. Social Class Differences in Response to Christmas Cards. *Perceptual and Motor Skills* 90: 573–76.

Kunz, P. R., and M. Wolcott. 1976. "Season's Greetings: From My Status to Yours." *Social Science Research* 5: 269–78.

Kupor, D., T. Reich, and B. Shiv. 2015. "Can't Finish What You Started? The Effect of Climactic Interruption on Behavior." *Journal of Consumer Psychology* 25: 113–19.

Lab, S. P. 2013. *Crime Prevention: Approaches, Practices, and Evaluations.* 8th ed. Waltham, MA: Elsevier.

Labroo, A. A., and J. H. Nielsen. 2010. "Half the Thrill Is in the Chase: Twisted Inferences from Embodied Cognitions and Brand Evaluation." *Journal of Consumer Research* 37: 143–58.

Laham, S. M., P. Koval, and A. L. Alter. 2012. "The Name-Pronunciation Effect: Why People Like Mr. Smith More Than Mr. Colquhoun." *Journal of Experimental Social Psychology* 48: 752–56.

Lakens, D. 2010. "Movement Synchrony and Perceived Entitativity." *Journal of Experimental Social Psychology* 46: 701–8.

Lalich, J. 2004. *Bounded Choice.* Berkeley: University of California Press.

Lammers, H. B. 1991. "The Effect of Free Samples on Immediate Consumer Purchase." *Journal of Consumer Marketing* 8: 31–37.

Lamy, L., J. Fischer-Lokou, and N. Guéguen. 2010. "Valentine Street Promotes Chivalrous Helping." *Swiss Journal of Psychology,* 69: 169–72.

Landau, M. J., B. P. Meier, and L. A. Keefer. 2010. "A Metaphor-Enriched Cognition." *Psychological Bulletin* 136: 1045–67.

Landau, M. J., M. D. Robinson, and B. P. Meier. 2014. *The Power of Metaphor: Examining Its Influence on Social Life.* Washington, DC: American Psychological Association Press.

Langner, R., and S. B. Eickhoff. 2013. "Sustaining Attention to Simple Tasks: A Meta-Analytic Review of the Neural Mechanisms of Vigilant Attention." *Psychological Bulletin* 139: 870–900.

Laran, J., and K. Wilcox. 2011. "Choice, Rejection, and Elaboration on Preference Inconsistent Alternatives." *Journal of Consumer Research* 38: 229–41.

Lassiter, G. D. 2002. "Illusory Causation in the Courtroom." *Current Directions in Psychological Science* 11: 204–8.

———. 2010. "Psychological Science and Sound Public Policy: Video Recording of Custodial Interrogations." *American Psychologist* 65: 768–79.

Lassiter, G. D., and C. A. Meissner, eds. 2010. *Police Interrogations and False Confessions: Current Research, Practice, and Policy Recommendations*. Washington, DC: American Psychological Association.

Latham, G., and R. F. Piccolo. 2012. "The Effect of Content-Specific versus Nonspecific Subconscious Goals on Employee Performance." *Human Resource Management* 51: 535–48.

Latu, I. M., M. S. Mast, J. Lammers, and D. Bombari. 2013. "Successful Female Leaders Empower Women's Behavior in Leadership Tasks." *Journal of Experimental Social Psychology* 49: 444–48.

Law, S., and K. A. Braun. 2000. "I'll Have What She's Having: Gauging the Impact of Product Placements on Viewers." *Psychology and Marketing* 17: 1059–75.

Lawrence, Z., and D. Peterson. 2014. "Mentally Walking Through Doorways Causes Forgetting: The Location Updating Effect and Imagination." *Memory* 24, no. 1 (January): 12–20.

Lawson, M. (2013). "Visit Your Folks (or Else!)." *AARP Bulletin* (May), 10.

Leach, W. C., N. Ellemers, and M. Barreto. 2007. "Group Virtue: The Impact of Morality (vs. Competence and Sociability) in the Positive Evaluation of In-Groups." *Journal of Personality and Social Psychology* 93: 234–49.

Leding, J. K. 2012. "False Memories and Persuasive Strategies." *Review of General Psychology* 16: 256–68.

Lee, S. W. S., and N. Schwarz. 2012. "Bidirectionality, Mediation, and Moderation of Metaphorical Effects." *Journal of Personality and Social Psychology* 103: 737–49.

Leek, M., and P. K. Smith. 1989. "Phenotypic Matching, Human Altruism, and Mate Selection." *Behavioral and Brain Sciences* 12: 534–35.

———. 1991. "Cooperation and Conflict in Three-Generation Families." In *The Psychology of Grandparenthood: An International Perspective*. Edited by P. K. Smith, London: Routledge, 177–94.

Leo, R. A. 2008. *Police Interrogation and American Justice*. Cambridge, MA: Harvard University Press.

Leopold, A. 1989. *A Sand County Almanac*. New York: Oxford University Press.

Leppanen, J., and C. A. Nelson. 2012. "Early Development of Fear Processing." *Current Directions in Psychological Science* 13: 200–204.

Leroy, S. 2009. "Why Is It So Hard to Do My Work? The Challenge of Attention Residue When Switching between Work Tasks." *Organizational Behavior and Human Decision Processes* 109: 168–81.

Levine, H. 1997. *In Search of Sugihara*. New York: Free Press.

Levy, J., H. Pashler, and E. Boer. 2006. "Central Interference in Driving." *Psychological Science* 17: 228–35.

Lewin, K. 1935. *A Dynamic Theory of Personality*. New York: McGraw-Hill.

———. 1946. "Behavior and Development as a Function of the Total Situation." In *Manual of Child Psychology*. Edited by L. Carmichael, New York: John Wiley.

———. 1947. "Group Decision and Social Change," In *Readings in Social Psychology*. Edited by T. M. Newcomb and E. L. Hartley. New York: Henry Holt.

Lewis, D. E. 2003. "Corporate Trust a Matter of Opinion." *Boston Globe* (November 23), G2.

Lewis, G. J., and T. C. Bates. 2010. "Genetic Evidence for Multiple Biological Mechanisms Underlying In-Group Favoritism." *Psychological Science* 21: 1623–28.

Liberman, N., and Y. Trope. 1998. "The Role of Feasibility and Desirability Considerations in Near and Distant Future Decisions: A Test of Temporal Construal Theory." *Journal of Personality and Social Psychology* 75: 5–18.

Lick, D. J., and K. L. Johnson. 2015. "Interpersonal Consequences of Processing Ease: Fluency as a Metacognitive Foundation for Prejudice." *Current Directions in Psychological Science* 24: 143–48.

Lilienfeld, S. O., R. Ammirati, and K. Landfield. 2009. "Giving Debiasing Away: Can Psychological Research on Correcting Cognitive Errors Promote Human Welfare?" *Perspectives on Psychological Science* 4: 390–98.

Lim, S., J. P. O'Doherty, and A. Rangel. 2011. "The Decision Value Computations in the VmPFC and Striatum Use a Relative Value Code That Is Guided by Visual Attention." *Journal of Neuroscience* 31: 13214–23.

Lindberg, S. M., J. S. Hyde, M. C. Linn, and J. L. Petersen. 2010. "Trends in Gender and Mathematics Performance: A Meta-Analysis." *Psychological Bulletin* 136: 1123–35.

Lindner, A. M. 2008. "Controlling the Media in Iraq." *Contexts* 7: 32–39.

———. 2009. "Among the Troops: Seeing the Iraq War Through Three Journalistic Vantages Points." *Social Problems* 56: 21–48.

Lipsitz, A., K. Kallmeyer, M. Ferguson, and A. Abas. 1989. "Counting On Blood Donors: Increasing the Impact of Reminder Calls." *Journal of Applied Social Psychology* 19: 1057–67.

Liu, W., and D. Gal. 2011. "Bringing Us Together or Driving Us Apart: The Effect of Soliciting Consumer Input on Consumers' Propensity to Transact with an Organization." *Journal of Consumer Research* 38: 242–59.

Livingstone, K. M., and D. M. Isaacowitz. 2015. "Situation Selection and Modification for Emotion Regulation in Younger and Older Adults." *Social Psychological and Personality Science* 6, no. 8 (November): 904–10.

LoBue, V. 2009. "More Than Just a Face in the Crowd: Detection of Emotional Facial Expressions in Young Children and Adults." *Developmental Science* 12: 305–13.

———. 2010. "And Along Came a Spider: Superior Detection of Spiders in Children and Adults." *Journal of Experimental Child Psychology* 107: 59–66.

Lockwood, P., and Z. Kunda. 1997. "Superstars and Me: Predicting the Impact of Role Models on the Self." *Journal of Personality and Social Psychology* 73: 91–103.

Loersch, C., and N. L. Arbuckle. 2013. "Unraveling the Mystery of Music: Music as an Evolved Group Process." *Journal of Personality and Social Psychology* 105: 777–98.

Loersch, C., and B. K. Payne. 2011. "A Situated Inference Model: An Integrative Account of the Effects of Primes on Perception, Behavior, and Motivation." *Perspectives on Psychological Science* 6: 234–52.

Loftus, E. F. 2011. "Intelligence Gathering Post-9/11." *American Psychologist* 66: 532–41.

Lord, C. G., M. R. Lepper, and E. Preston. 1984. "Considering the Opposite: A Corrective Strategy for Social Judgment." *Journal of Personality and Social Psychology* 47: 1231–43.

Lovello, D., and O. Sibony. 2010. "The Case for Behavioral Strategy." *McKinsey Quarterly* (March): 1–16.

Lubinski, D., C. P. Benbow, and H. J. Kell. 2014. "Life Paths and Accomplishments of Mathematically Precocious Males and Females Four Decades Later." *Psychological Science* 25: 2217–32.

Lull, R. B., and B. J. Bushman. 2015. "Do Sex and Violence Sell? A Meta-Analytic Review of the Effects of Sexual and Violent Media and Ad Content on Memory, Attitudes and Buying Intentions." *Psychological Bulletin* 141: 1022–48.

Lyubomirsky, S. 2008. *The How of Happiness: A Scientific Approach to Getting the Life You Want.* New York: Penguin Press.

———. 2013. *The Myths of Happiness: What Should Make You Happy, but Doesn't. What Shouldn't Make You Happy, but Does.* New York: Penguin Press.

Lyubomirsky, S., and K. Layous. 2013. "How Do Simple Positive Activities Increase Well-Being?" *Current Directions in Psychological Science* 22: 57–62.

Lyubomirsky, S., S. A. King, and E. Diener. 2005. "Pursuing Happiness: Does Happiness Lead to Success?" *Psychological Bulletin* 131: 803–55.

Maaravi, Y., Y. Ganzach, and A. Pazy. 2011. "Negotiation as a Form of Persuasion: Arguments in First Offers." *Journal of Personality and Social Psychology* 101: 245–55.

MacKenzie, S. B., and R. J. Lutz. 1989. "An Empirical Examination of the Structural Antecedents of Attitude Toward the Ad in an Advertising Pretesting Context." *Journal of Marketing* 53: 48–65.

Macrae, C. N., and L. Johnston. 1998. "Help, I Need Somebody: Automatic Action and Inaction." *Social Cognition* 16: 400–17.

Macrae, N. C., G. V. Bodenhausen, and A. B. Milne. 1995. "The Dissection of Selection in Person Perception: Inhibitory Processes in Social Stereotyping." *Journal of Personality and Social Psychology* 69: 397–407.

Madanika, Y, and K. Bartholomew. 2014. "Themes of Lust and Love in Popular Music from 1971 to 2011." *SAGE Open* 4, no. 3 (August). doi:10.1177/2158244014547179.

Madden, M. 2014. "More Online Americans Say They've Experienced a Personal Data Breach." Pew Research Center Fact Tank (April 14). www.pewresearch.org/fact-tank/2014/04/14/more-online-americans-say-theyve-experienced-a-personal-data-breach.

Maddux, W. W., E. E. Mullen, and A. D. Galinsky. 2008. "Chameleons Bake Bigger Pies and Take Bigger Pieces: Strategic Behavioral Mimicry Facilitates Negotiation Outcomes." *Journal of Experimental Social Psychology* 44: 461–68.

Mahajan, N., M. A. Martinez, N. L. Gutierrez, G. Diesendruck, M. R. Banaji, and L. R. Santos. 2011. "The Evolution of Intergroup Bias: Perceptions and Attitudes in Rhesus Macaques." *Journal of Personality and Social Psychology* 100, no. 3 (March): 387–405.

Maio, G. R., A. Pakizeh, W-Y. Cheung, and K. J. Rees. 2009. "Changing, Priming, and Acting on Values: Effects via Motivational Relations in a Circular Model." *Journal of Personality and Social Psychology* 97: 699–715.

Mandel, N., and E. J. Johnson. 2002. "When Web Pages Influence Choice: Effects of Visual Primes on Experts and Novices." *Journal of Consumer Research* 29: 235–45.

Mandel, N., P. K. Petrova, and R. B. Cialdini. 2006. "Images of Success and the Preference for Luxury Brands." *Journal of Consumer Psychology* 16: 57–69.

Maner, J. K., M. T. Gailliot, and S. L. Miller. 2009. "The Implicit Cognition of Relationship Maintenance: Inattention to Attractive Alternatives." *Journal of Experimental Social Psychology* 45: 174–79.

Maner, J. K., M. T. Gailliot, D. A. Rouby, D. A., and S. L. Miller. 2007. "Can't Take My Eyes Off You: Attentional Adhesion to Mates and Rivals." *Journal of Personality and Social Psychology* 93: 389–401.

Maner, J. K., D. T. Kenrick, D. V. Becker, A. W. Delton, B. Hofer, C. Wilbur, and S. I. Neuberg. 2003. "Sexually Selective Cognition: Beauty Captures the Mind of the Beholder." *Journal of Personality and Social Psychology* 85: 1107–20.

Mann, T. C., and M. J. Ferguson. 2015. "Can We Undo Our First Impressions? The Role of Reinterpretation in Reversing Implicit Evaluations." *Journal of Personality and Social Psychology* 108: 823–49.

Marchetti, G. 2012. "Against the View That Consciousness and Attention Are Fully Dissociable." *Frontiers in Psychology* 3: 36.

Margolis, E. H. 2010. "When Program Notes Don't Help: Music Descriptions and Enjoyment." *Psychology of Music* 38: 285–302.

Markus, H., and S. Kitayama. 1991. "Culture and the Self: Implications for Cognition, Emotion, and Motivation." *Psychological Bulletin* 98: 224–53.

Marsh, J. E., R. Ljung, A. Nöstl, E. Threadgold, and T. A. Campbell. 2015. "Failing to Get the Gist of What's Being Said: Background Noise Impairs Higher-Order Cognitive Processing." *Frontiers in Psychology* 6: 548.

Marsh, R. L., J. L. Hicks, and M. L. Bink 1998. "Activation of Completed Uncompleted, and Partially Completed Intentions." *Journal of Experimental Psychology: Learning, Memory, and Cognition* 24: 350–61.

Marteau, T. M., G. J. Hollands, and P. C. Fletcher. 2012. "Changing Human Behavior to Prevent Disease: The Importance of Targeting Automatic Processes." *Science* 337: 1492–95.

Marti, S., M. Sigman, and S. Dehaene. 2012. "A Shared Cortical Bottleneck Underlying Attentional Blink and Psychological Refractory Period." *Neuroimage* 59: 2883–98.

Martin, A., C. Jacob, and N. Guéguen. 2013. "Similarity Facilitates Relationships on Social Networks: A Field Experiment on Facebook." *Psychological Reports* 113: 217–20.

Martin, L. R., K. B. Haskard-Zolnierek, and M. R. DiMatteo. 2010. "Health Behavior Change and Treatment Adherence." New York: Oxford University Press.

Martin, S. J., S. Bassi, and R. Dunbar-Rees. 2012. Commitments, Norms and Custard Creams—A Social Influence Approach to Reducing Did Not Attends (DNAs)." *Journal of the Royal Society of Medicine* 105: 101–4.

Marx, D. M., and J. S. Roman. 2002. "Female Role Models: Protecting Women's Math Test Performance." *Personality and Social Psychology Bulletin* 28: 1183–93.

Mashek, D. J., A. Aron, and M. Boncimino. 2003. "Confusions of Self with Close Others." *Personality and Social Psychology Bulletin* 29: 382–92.

Mason, M. F., E. P. Tatkow, and C. N. Macrae. 2005. "The Look of Love: Gaze Shifts and Person Perception." *Psychological Science* 16: 236–39.

Masuda, T., and R. Nisbett. 2001. "Attending Holistically versus Analytically: Comparing the Context Sensitivity of Japanese and Americans." *Journal of Personality and Social Psychology* 81: 922–34.

Masuda, T., R. Gonzalez, I. Kwan, and R. Nesbitt. 2008. "Culture and Aesthetic Preference: Comparing the Attention to Context of East Asians and Americans." *Personality and Social Psychology Bulletin* 34: 1260–75.

Mather, M., and M. Knight. 2005. "Goal-Directed Memory: The Role of Cognitive Control in Older Adults' Emotional Memory." *Psychology and Aging* 20: 554–70.

Mauboussin, M. J. 2009. *Think Twice: Harnessing the Power of Counterintuition.* Boston: Harvard Business Press.

Mauss, I. B., A. J. Shallcross, O. P. John, E. Ferrer, F. H. Wilhelm, and J. J. Gross. 2011. "Don't Hide Your Happiness!" *Journal of Personality and Social Psychology* 100: 738–48.

Mayer, D. M., M. Kuenzi, R. Greenbaum, M. Bardes, and R. Salvador. 2009. "How Does Ethical Leadership Flow? Test of a Trickle-Down Model." *Organization and Human Decision Processes* 108: 1–13.

Mazzoni, G., and A. Memon. 2003. "Imagination Can Create False Autobiographical Memories." *Psychological Science* 25: 266–81.

McAlister, A. L., A. G. Ramirez, C. Galavotti, and K. J. Gallion. 1989. "Anti-Smoking Campaigns: Progress in the Application of Social Learning Theory." *Public Communication Campaigns.* Edited by R. E. Rice and C. K. Atkin. Newbury Park, CA: Sage, 291–307.

McCaslin, M. J., R. E. Petty, and D. T. Wegener. 2010. "Self-Enhancement Processes and Theory-Based Correction Processes." *Journal of Experimental Social Psychology* 46: 830–35.

McClelland, J. L., M. M. Botvinick, D. C. Noelle, D. C. Plaut, T. T. Rogers, M. S. Seidenberg, and L. B. Smith. 2010. "Letting Structure Emerge: Connectionist and Dynamical Systems Approaches to Understanding Cognition." *Trends in Cognitive Sciences* 14: 348–56.

McCombs, M. E., and D. L. Shaw. 1972. "The Agenda-Setting Functions of Mass Media," *Public Opinion Quarterly* 36: 176–218.

McCormick, J., and W. L. Morris. 2015. "The Effects of Stereotype Threat and Power on Women's and Men's Outcomes in Face-to-Face and E-Mail Negotiations." *Psi Chi Journal of Psychological Research* 20: 114–24.

McCulloch, K. C., H. Arts, K. Fujita, and J. A. Bargh. 2008. "Inhibition in Goal Systems: A Retrieval-Induced Forgetting Account." *Journal of Experimental Social Psychology* 44: 857–65.

McFarland, S. In press. "Identification with All Humanity: The Antithesis of Prejudice, and More." In *The Cambridge Handbook of the Psychology of Prejudice*. Edited by C. G. Sibley and F. K. Barlow, Cambridge, UK: Cambridge University Press.

McFarland, S., M. Webb, and D. Brown. 2012. "All Humanity Is My In-Group. A Measure and Studies of Identification with All Humanity." *Journal of Personality and Social Psychology* 103: 830–53.

McGlone, M. S., and J. Tofighbakhsh. 2000. "Birds of a Feather Flock Conjointly (?): Rhyme as Reason in Aphorisms." *Psychological Science* 11: 424–28.

McGraw, K. O., and J. Fiala. 1982, "Undermining the Zeigarnik Effect: Another Hidden Cost of Reward." *Journal of Personality* 50: 58–66.

McGuire, W. J. 1961. "The Effectiveness of Supportive and Refutational Defenses in Immunizing and Restoring Beliefs against Persuasion." *Sociometry* 24: 184–97.

McIntyre, R. B., R. M. Paulson, and C. G. Lord. 2003. "Alleviating Women's Mathematics Stereotype Threat through Salience of Group Achievements." *Journal of Experimental Social Psychology* 39: 83–90.

McKenzie, C. R. M. 2005. "Judgement and Decision Making." In *Handbook of Cognition. Edited by* R. L. G. Koen Lamberts. Thousand Oaks, CA: Sage, 321–38.

McNeill, W. H. 1995. *Keeping Together in Time: Dance and Drill in Human History*. Cambridge, MA: Harvard University Press.

Meltzoff, A. 2007. "Like Me: A Foundation for Social Cognition." *Developmental Science* 10: 126–34.

Mendl, J. R., S. B. Ehrlich, and J. M. Dukerich. 1985. "The Romance of Leadership." *Adminstrative Science Quarterly* 30: 78–102.

Mercer, A., A. Caporaso, D. Cantor, and J. Townsend. 2015. "How Much Gets You How Much? Monetary Incentives and Response Rates in Household Surveys." *Public Opinion Quarterly* 79: 105–29.

Meyers-Levy, J., and B. Loken. 2015. "Revisiting Gender Differences: What We Know and What Lies Ahead." *Journal of Consumer Psychology* 25: 129–49.

Middleton, J. A., and D. P. Green. 2008. "Do Community-Based Voter Mobilization Campaigns Work Even in Battleground States? Evaluating the Effectiveness of MoveOn's 2004 Outreach Campaign." *Quarterly Journal of Political Science* 3: 63–82.

Midlarsky, E., and R. Nemeroff. 1995. "Heroes of the Holocaust: Predictors of Their Well-Being in Later Life." Paper presented at the American Psychological Society meetings. New York (July).

Millar, M. G., and A. Tesser. 1986. "Thought-Induced Attitude Change: The Effects of Schema Structure and Commitment." *Journal of Personality and Social Psychology* 51: 259–69.

Miller, D. T., and D. A. Effron. 2010. "Psychological License: When It Is

Needed and How It Functions." *Advances in Experimental Social Psychology* 43: 115–55.

Miller, D. T., J. S. Downs, and D. A. Prentice. 1998. "Minimal Conditions for the Creation of a Unit Relationship: The Social Bond Between Birthday Mates." *European Journal of Social Psychology* 28: 475–81.

Miller, R. S. 1997. "Inattentive and Contented: Relationship Commitment and Attention to Alternatives." *Journal of Personality and Social Psychology* 73: 758–56.

Mitchell, J. P., M. Banaji, and C. N. Macrae. 2005. "The Link Between Social Cognition and Self-Referential Thought." *Journal of Cognitive Neuroscience* 17: 1306–15.

Miyake, A., L. E. Kost-Smith, N. D. Finkelstein, S. J. Pollock, G. L. Cohen, and T. A. Ito. 2010. "Reducing the Gender Achievement Gap in College Science: A Classroom Study of Values Affirmation." *Science* 330: 1234–37.

Molnar-Szakacs, I., and K. Overy. 2006. "Music and Mirror Neurons: From Motion to 'E'motion." *Social Cognitive and Affective Neuroscience* 1: 235–41.

Monin, B., and D. T. Miller. 2001. "Moral Credentials and the Expression of Prejudice." *Journal of Personality and Social Psychology* 81: 33–43.

Monroe, B. M., and S. J. Read. 2008. "A General Connectionist Model of Attitude Structure and Change." *Psychological Review* 115: 773–59.

Monteith, M. J., L. Ashburn-Nardo, C. I. Voils, and A. M. Czopp. 2002. "Putting the Brakes on Prejudice: On the Development and Operation of Cues for Control." *Journal of Personality and Social Psychology* 83: 1029–50.

Moon, Y. 2010. *Different*. New York: Crown Business.

Moore, D. A., and D. Small. 2007. "Error and Bias in Comparative Social Judgment: On Being Both Better and Worse Than We Think We Are." *Journal of Personality and Social Psychology* 92: 972–89.

Moore, S. G. 2012. "Some Things Are Better Left Unsaid: How Word of Mouth Influences the Storyteller." *Journal of Consumer Research* 38: 1140–54.

Morling, D., and M. Lamoreaux. 2008. "Measuring Culture Outside the Head: A Meta-Analysis of Individualism-Collectivism in Cultural Products." *Personality and Social Psychology Review* 12, 199–221.

Morris, M. W., O. J. Sheldon, D. R. Ames, and M. J. Young. 2007. "Metaphors and the Market." *Organizational Behavior and Human Decision Processes* 102: 174–92.

Moyer, V. A. 2013. "Primary Care Interventions to Prevent Tobacco Use in Children and Adolescents: U.S. Preventive Service Task Force Recommendation Statement." *Pediatrics* 132: 560–65.

Murayama, K., T. Miyatsu, D. Buchli, and B. Storm. 2014. "Forgetting as a Consequence of Retrieval: A Meta-Analytic Review of Retrieval-Induced Forgetting." *Psychological Bulletin* 140: 1383–1409.

Muscanell, N. L., R. E. Guadagno, S. Murphy. 2014. "Weapons of Influence Misused: A Social Influence Analysis of Why People Fall Prey to Internet Scams." *Social and Personality Compass,* 8/7: 388–96.

Nagin, D., and G. Pogarsky. 2001. "Integrating Celerity, Impulsivity, and Extralegal Sanction Threats into a Model of General Deterrence Theory and Evidence." *Criminology* 39: 865–92.

Nelson, L. D., and M. I. Norton. 2005. "From Student to Superhero: Situational Primes Shape Future Helping." *Journal of Experimental Social Psychology* 41: 425–30.

Nestler, S., and B. Egloff. 2010. "When Scary Messages Backfire: Influence of Dispositional Cognitive Avoidance on the Effectiveness of Threat Communications." *Journal of Research in Personality* 44: 137–41.

Neumann, R., and F. Strack. 2000. "Approach and Avoidance: The Influence of Proprioceptive and Exteroceptive Cues on Encoding of Affective Information." *Journal of Personality and Social Psychology* 79: 39–48.

Neville, L. 2012. "Do Economic Equality and Generalized Trust Inhibit Academic Dishonesty? Search-Engine Queries." *Psychological Science* 23: 339–45.

Nguyen, H. D., and A. M. Ryan. 2008. "Does Stereotype Threat Affect Test Performance of Minorities and Women? A Meta-Analysis of Experimental Evidence." *Journal of Applied Psychology* 93: 1314–34.

Nguyen, N., and G. Lelanc. 2001. "Corporate Image and Corporate Reputation in Customers' Retention Decisions in Services." *Journal of Retailing and Consumer Services* 8: 227–36.

Nickerson, R. S. 1998. "Confirmation Bias: A Ubiquitous Phenomenon in Many Guises." *Review of General Psychology* 2: 175–220.

Niemeier, V., J. Kupfer, and U. Gieler. 2000. "Observations During an Itch-Inducing Lecture." *Dermatology and Psychosomatics* 1 (suppl. 1: 15–18.

Nisbett, R. 2003. *The Geography of Thought: How Asians and Westerners Think Differently . . . and Why.* New York: Free Press.

Noar, S. M., C. N. Benac, and M. S. Harris. 2007. "Does Tailoring Matter? Meta-Analytic Review of Tailored Print Health Behavior Change Interventions." *Psychological Bulletin* 133: 673–93.

Noh, S. R., M. Lohani, and D. M. Isaacowitz. 2011. "Deliberate Real-Time Mood Regulation in Adulthood: The Importance of Age, Fixation, and Attentional Functioning." *Cognition and Emotion* 25: 998–1013.

Nolan, J. M., P. W. Schultz, R. B. Cialdini, N. J. Goldstein, and V. Griskevicius. 2008. "Normative Social Influence Is Underdetected." *Personality and Social Psychology Bulletin* 34: 913–23.

Noor, M., R. Brown, R. Gonzalez, J. Manzi, and C. A. Lewis. 2008. "On Positive Psychological Outcomes: What Helps Groups with a History of Conflict to Forgive and Reconcile with Each Other?" *Personality and Social Psychology Bulletin* 34: 819–32.

Norman, L. J., C. A. Heywood, and R. W. Kentridge. 2013. "Object-Based Attention without Awareness." *Psychological Science* 24: 836–43.

North, A. C., D. J. Hargreaves, and J. McKendrick. 1997. "In-Store Music Affects Product Choice." *Nature* 390 (November 13): 132.

Norton, M. I., D. Mochon, and D. Ariely. 2012. "The IKEA Effect: When Labor Leads to Love." *Journal of Consumer Psychology* 22: 453–60. doi:10.1016/j.jcps.2011.08.002.

Oberholzer-Gee, F. 2006. "A Market for Time: Fairness and Efficiency in Waiting Lines." *Kyklos* 59: 427–40.

Obermeier, C., W. Menninghaus, M. von Koppenfels, T. Raettig, M. Schmidt-Kassow, S. Otterbein, and S. A. Kotz. 2013. "Aesthetic and Emotional Effects of Meter and Rhyme in Poetry." *Frontiers in Psychology* 4: 10.

Oettingen, G., G. Hönig, and P. M. Gollwitzer. 2000. "Effective Self-Regulation of Goal Attainment." *International Journal of Educational Research* 33: 705–32.

Oishi, S., S. Kesebir, and E. Diener. 2001. "Income Inequality and Happiness." *Psychological Science* 22: 1095–1100.

Oliner, S. P., and P. M. Oliner. 1988. *The Altruistic Personality: Rescuers of Jews in Nazi Europe*. New York: Free Press.

Olivers, C. N. L., and S. Niewenhuis. 2005. "The Beneficial Effect of Concurrent Task-Irrelevant Activity on Temporal Attention." *Psychological Science* 16: 265–69.

Olson, M. A., and R. H. Fazio. 2004. "Trait Inferences as a Function of Automatically Activated Racial Attitudes and Motivation to Control Prejudiced Reactions." *Basic and Applied Social Psychology* 26: 1–11.

Oosterhof, N. N., S. P. Tipper, and P. E. Downing. 2012. "Visuo-Motor Imagery of Specific Manual Actions: A Multi-Variate Pattern Analysis *f*MRI Study." *Neuroimage* 63: 262–71.

Oppenheimer, D. M., C. Diemand-Yauman, and E. B. Vaughan. 2011. "Fortune Favors the Bold (and the Italicized): Effects of Disfluency on Educational Outcomes." *Cognition* 118: 111–15.

Oppenheimer, D. M., R. E. LeBoeuf, and N. T. Brewer. 2008. "Anchors Aweigh: A Demonstration of Cross-Modality Anchoring and Magnitude Priming." *Cognition* 106: 13–26.

Ottati, V. C., and R. A. Renstrom. 2010. "Metaphor and Persuasive Communication: A Multifunctional Approach." *Social and Personality Psychology Compass* 49: 783–94.

Otten, S., and K. Epstude. 2006. "Overlapping Mental Representations of Self, Ingroup, and Outgroup: Unraveling Self-Stereotyping and Self-Anchoring." *Personality and Social Psychology Bulletin* 32: 957–69.

Over, H., and M. Carpenter. 2009. "Eighteen-Month-Old Infants Show Increased Helping Following Priming with Affiliation." *Psychological Science* 20: 1189–93.

Ovsiankina, M. 1928. "Die Wiederaufnahme von unterbrochener Handlungen." *Psychologische Forschung* 11: 302–79.

Oyserman, D. 2009. "Identity-Based Motivation: Implications for Action-Readiness, Procedural-Readiness, and Consumer Behavior." *Journal of Consumer Psychology* 19: 250–60.

Oyserman, D., and S. W. S. Lee. 2008. "Does Culture Influence What and How We Think? Effects of Priming Individualism and Collectivism." *Psychological Bulletin* 134: 311–42.

Packard, G., A. D. Gershoff, and D. B. Wooten, Impress. "When Boastful Word of Mouth Helps versus Hurts Social Perceptions and Persuasion." *Journal of Consumer Research.*

Paez, D., B. Rime, N. Basabe, A. Wlodarczyk, and L. Zumeta. 2015. "Psychosocial Effects of Perceived Emotional Synchrony in Collective Gatherings." *Journal of Personality and Social Psychology* 108: 711–29.

Page, L. A., C. Keshishian, G. Leonardi, V. Murray, G. J. Rubin, and S. Wessely. 2010. "Frequency and Predictors of Mass Psychogenic Illness." *Epidemiology* 21: 744–47.

Page-Gould, E., R. Mendoza-Denton, and L. R. Tropp. 2008. "With a Little Help from My Cross-Group Friend: Reducing Anxiety in Intergroup Contexts Through Cross-Group Friendship." *Journal of Personality and Social Psychology* 95: 1080–94.

Paladino, M-P., M. Mazzurega, F. Pavani, and T. W. Schubert. 2010. "Synchronous Multisensory Stimulation Blurs Self-Other Boundaries." *Psychological Science* 21: 1202–7.

Paluck, E. L., and D. P. Green. 2009. "Prejudice Reduction: What Works? A Review and Assessment of Research and Practice." *Annual Review of Psychology* 60: 339–67.

Park, J. H., and M. Schaller. 2005. "Does Attitude Similarity Serve as a

Heuristic Cue for Kinship? Evidence of an Implicit Cognitive Association." *Evolution and Human Behavior* 26: 158–70.

Park, J. H., M. Schaller, and M. Van Vugt. 2008. "Psychology of Human Kin Recognition: Heuristic Cues, Erroneous Inferences, and Their Implications." *Review of General Psychology* 12: 215–35.

Parker, J. R., and D. R. Lehmann. 2015. "How and When Grouping Low-Calorie Options Reduces the Benefits of Providing Dish-Specific Calorie Information." *Journal of Consumer Research* 41: 213–35.

Parks, A. C., M. D. Della Porta, R. S. Pierce, R. Zilca, and S. Lyubomirsky. 2012. "Pursuing Happiness in Everyday Life: The Characteristics and Behaviors of Online Happiness Seekers." *Emotion* 12: 1222–34.

Paternoster, R. 2010. "How Much Do We Really Know About Criminal Deterrence?" *Journal of Criminal Law and Criminology* 100: 765–24.

Pavlov, I. P. 1927. "Conditioned reflexes." Translated by G. V. Anrep. Oxford, UK: Oxford University Press.

Payne, L., and R. Sekuler. 2014. "The Importance of Ignoring: Alpha Oscillations Protect Selectivity." *Current Directions in Psychological Science* 23: 171–77.

Pelham, B. W., and M. R. Carvallo. 2011. "The Surprising Potency of Implicit Egoism: A Reply to Simonsohn." *Journal of Personality and Social Psychology* 101: 25–30.

Pennebaker, J. W. 1980. "Perceptual and Environmental Determinants of Coughing." *Basic and Applied Social Psychology* 1: 83–91.

Pennebaker, J. W., T. J. Mayne, and M. E. Francis. 1997. "Linguistic Predictors of Adaptive Bereavement." *Journal of Personality and Social Psychology* 72: 863–71.

Perillo, J. T., and S. M. Kassin. 2011. "Inside Interrogation: The Lie, the Bluff, and False Confessions." *Law and Human Behavior* 35: 327–37.

Perkins, A. W., and M. R. Forehand. 2012. "Implicit Self-Referencing: The Effect of Nonvolitional Self-Association on Brand and Product Attitude." *Journal of Consumer Research* 39: 142–56.

Peterson, D. K. 2002. The Relationship Between Unethical Behavior and the Dimensions of the Ethical Climate Questionnaire." *Journal of Business Ethics* 41: 313–26.

Petras, R., and K. Petras. 1993. *The 776 Stupidest Things Ever Said*. New York: Broadway Books.

Petrova, P. K., and R. B. Cialdini. 2005. "Fluency of Consumption Imagery and the Backfire Effects of Imagery Appeals." *Journal of Consumer Research* 32: 442–52.

———. 2011. "New Approaches Toward Resistance to Persuasion." In *The Sage Handbook of Social Marketing*. Edited by G. Hastings, C. Bryant., and K. Angus. London: Sage, 107–22.

Petrova, P. K., N. Schwarz, and H. Song. 2012. "Fluency and Social Influence." In *Six Degrees of Social Influence*. Edited by D. T. Kenrick, N. J. Goldstein, and S. L. Braver. New York: Oxford University Press.

Petty R. E., and P. Brinol. 2012. "The Elaboration Likelihood Model." In *Handbook of Theories of Social Psychology*. Edited by P. A. M. Van Lange, A. W. Kruglanski, and E. T. Higgins. Thousand Oaks, CA: Sage, 224–45.

Petty, R. E., and P. Brinol. 2010. "Attitude Change." In *Advanced Social Psychology: The State of the Science*. Edited by R. F. Baumeister and E. J. Finkel. New York: Oxford University Press, 217–59.

Petty, R. E., and J. T. Cacioppo. 1984. "Source Factors and the Elaboration Likelihood Model of Persuasion." *Advances in Consumer Research* 11: 668–72.

Pfaff, D. W. 2007. *The Neuroscience of Fair Play: Why We (Usually) Follow the Golden Rule.* Chicago: University of Chicago Press.

———. 2015. *The Altruistic Brain: How We Are Naturally Good.* Oxford, UK: Oxford University Press.

Pfau, M., and M. Burgoon. 1988. "Inoculation in Political Campaign Communication." *Human Communication Research* 15: 91–111.

Pfau, M., J. Danesi, R. Tallmon, T. Bunko, S. Nyberg, B. Thompson, C. Babin, S. Cardella, M. Mink, and B. Temple. 2006. "A Comparison of Embedded and Nonembedded Print Coverage of the U.S. Invasion and Occupation of Iraq." *International Journal of Press/Politics* 11: 139–53.

Pfau, M., M. M. Haigh, L. Logsdon, C. Perrine, J. P. Baldwin, R. E. Breitenfeldt, J. Cesar, D. Dearden, G. Kuntz, E. Montalvo, D. Roberts, and R. Romero." 2005. "Embedded Reporting During the Invasion and Occupation of Iraq: How the Embedding of Journalists Affects Television News Reports." *Journal of Broadcasting and Electronic Media* 49: 468–87.

Pfau, M., M. Haigh, M. Gettle, M. Donnelly, G. Scott, D. Warr, and E. Wittenberg. 2004. "Embedding Journalists in Military Combat Units: Impact on Newspaper Story Frames and Tone." *Journalism and Mass Communication Quarterly* 81: 74–88.

Pfeffer, J., and R. B. Cialdini. 1998. "Illusions of Influence." In *Power and Influence in Organizations.* Edited by R. M. Kramer and M. A. Neale. Thousand Oaks, CA: Sage, 1–20.

Pfeffer, J., and G. R. Salancik. 1978. *The External Control of Organizations. A Resource Dependence Perspective.* New York: Harper & Row.

Pillutia, M. M., D. Malhotra, and J. K. Murnighan. 2003. "Attributions of Trust and the Calculus of Reciprocity." *Journal of Experimental Social Psychology* 39: 448–55.

Pocheptsova, A., and N. Novemsky. 2010. "When Do Incidental Mood Effects Last? Lay Beliefs Versus Actual Effects." *Journal of Consumer Research* 36: 992–1001.

Posavac, S. S., F. R. Kardes, and J. Brakus. 2010. "Focus Induced Tunnel Vision in Managerial Judgment and Decision Making: The Peril and the Anecdote." *Organizational Behavior and Human Decision Processes* 113: 102–11.

Posavac, S. S., F. R. Kardes, D. M. Sanbonmatsu D. M., and Fitzsimons G. J. 2005. Blissful insularity: When brands are judged in isolation from competitors, *Marketing Letters* 16: 87–97.

Posavac, S. S., Sanbonmatsu, D. M., and E. A. Ho. 2002. "The Effects of Selective Consideration of Alternatives on Consumer Choice and Attitude-Decision Consistency." *Journal of Consumer Psychology* 12: 203–13.

Posavac, S. S., D. M. Sanbonmatsu, F. R. Kardes, and G. J. Fitzsimons. 2004. "The Brand Positivity Effect: When Evaluation Confers Preference." *Journal of Consumer Research* 31: 643–51.

Pothos, E. M., and J. R. Busemeyer. 2013. "Can Quantum Probability Provide a New Direction for Cognitive Modeling?" *Behavior and Brain Sciences* 36: 255–74.

Powers, N., A. Blackman, T. P. Lyon, and U. Narain. 2011. "Does Disclosure Reduce Pollution? Evidence from India's Green Rating Project." *Environmental and Resource Economics* 50: 131–55.

Preston, S. D. 2013. "The Origins of Altruism in Offspring Care." *Psychological Bulletin* 139: 1305–41.

Prestwich, A., M. Perugini, R. Hurling, and J. Richetin. 2010. "Using the Self to Change Implicit Attitudes." *European Journal of Social Psychology* 40: 61–71.

Priester, J. R., J. T. Cacioppo, and R. E. Petty. 1996. "The Influence of Motor Processes on Attitudes Toward Novel versus Familiar Semantic Stimuli." *Personality and Social Psychology Bulletin* 22: 442–47.

Prot, S., D. A. Gentile, C. A. Anderson, K. Suzuki, E. Swing, Y. Horiuchi, M. Jelic, B. Krahé, W. Liuqing, A. K. Liau, A. Khoo, P. D. Petrescu, A. Sakamoto, S. Tajima, R. A. Toma, W. Warburton, X. Zhang, and B. C. P. Lam. 2014. "Long-Term Relations Among Prosocial-Media Use, Empathy, and Prosocial Behavior." *Psychological Science* 25: 358–68.

Pulfrey, C. and F. Butera. 2013. "Why Neoliberal Values of Self-Enhancement Lead to Cheating in Higher Education: A Motivational Account." *Psychological Science* 24: 2153–62.

Global Economic Crime Survey 2014. Threat assessment and damage. www.pwc.com/gx/en/economic-crime-survey/damage.jhtml.

Quoidbach, J., M. Mikolajczak, and J. J. Gross. 2015. "Positive Interventions: An Emotion Perspective." *Psychological Bulletin* 141: 655–93.

Radvansky, G. A., and D. E. Copeland. 2006. "Walking Through Doorways Causes Forgetting: Situation Models and Experienced Space." *Memory and Cognition* 34: 1150–56.

Radvansky, G. A., S. A. Krawietz, and A. K. Tamplin. 2011. "Walking Through Doorways Causes Forgetting: Further Explorations." *Quarterly Journal of Experimental Psychology* 64: 1632–45.

Rajagopal, P., and N. V. Montgomery. 2011. "I Imagine, I Experience, I Like: The False Experience Effect." *Journal of Consumer Research* 38, no. 3 (October): 578–94.

Reber, R., and N. Schwarz. 1999. "Effects of Perceptual Fluency on Judgments of Truth." *Consciousness and Cognition* 8: 338–42.

Reed, A. E., and L. L. Carstensen. 2012. "The Theory Behind the Age-Related Positivity Effect." *Frontiers in Psychology* 27: 339.

Reed, C. 2009. "Journalists' Recent Work Examined Before Embeds" (electronic version). *Stars and Stripes* (August 24). www.stripes.com/article.asp?section=104andarticle=63348.

Reed, C., K. Baron, and L. Shane. 2009. "Files Prove Pentagon Is Profiling Reporters" (electronic version). *Stars and Stripes* (August 29). www.stripes.com/article.asp?section=104andarticle=64401.

Reichardt, C. S. 2010. "Testing Astrological Predictions About Sex, Marriage, and Selfishness." *Skeptic* 15: 40–45.

Reinhard, M-A., S. Schindler, V. Raabe, D. Stahlberg, and M. Messner. 2014. "Less Is Sometimes More: How Repetition of an Antismoking Advertisement Affects Attitudes Toward Smoking and Source Credibility." *Social Influence* 9: 116–32.

Rensink, R. A. 2002. "Change Detection." *Annual Review of Psychology* 53: 253–64.

Report to the Nations on Occupational Fraud and Abuse: 2014 Global Fraud Study. 2014. Austin, TX: Association of Certified Fraud Examiners. www.acfe.com/rttn.aspx.

Rimer, B. K., and Kreuter, M. W. 2006. "Advancing Tailored Health Communication: A Persuasion and Message Effects Perspective." *Journal of Communication* 56: S184–S201.

Risen, J. L., and T. Gilovich. 2008. "Why People Are Reluctant to Tempt Fate." *Journal of Personality and Social Psychology* 95: 293–307.

Robertson, K. F., S. Smeets, D. Lubinski, and C. P. Benbow. 2010. "Beyond the Threshold Hypothesis." *Current Directions in Psychological Science* 19: 346–51.

Robinson, J., and L. Zebrowitz-McArthur. 1982. "Impact of Salient Vocal Qualities on Causal Attribution for a Speaker's Behavior." *Journal of Personality and Social Psychology* 43: 236–47.

Rogers, T., C. R. Fox, and A. S. Gerber. 2012. *Rethinking Why People Vote: Voting as Dynamic Social Expression*. Princeton: Princeton University Press.

Romero, A. A., C. R. Agnew, and C. A. Insko. 1996. "The Cognitive Mediation Hypothesis Revisited." *Personality and Social Psychology Bulletin* 22: 651–65.

Roseth, C. J., D. W. Johnson, and R. T. Johnson. 2008. "Promoting Early Adolescent Achievement and Peer Relationships: The Effects of Cooperative, Competitive, and Individualistic Goal Structures." *Psychological Bulletin* 134: 223–46.

Ross, J. R. 1994. *Escape to Shanghai: A Jewish Community in China*. New York: Free Press.

Ross, M., and F. Sicoly. 1979. "Egocentric Biases in Availability and Attribution." *Journal of Personality and Social Psychology* 37: 322–36.

Rothbart, M. and B. Park. 1986. "On the Confirmability and Disconfirmability of Trait Concepts." *Personality and Social Psychology Bulletin* 50: 131–42.

Rowe C., J. M. Harris, and S. C. Roberts. 2005. "Sporting Contests: Seeing Red? Putting Sportswear in Context." *Nature* 437: E10.

Rozin, P., and E. B. Royzman. 2001. "Negativity Bias, Negativity Dominance, and Contagion." *Personality and Social Psychology Review* 5, 296–321.

Rydell, R. J., A. R. McConnell, and S. L. Beilock. 2009. "Multiple Social Identities and Stereotype Threat: Imbalance, Accessibility, and Working Memory." *Journal of Personality and Social Psychology* 96: 949–66.

Sagarin, B. J., R. B. Cialdini, W. E. Rice, and S. B. Serna. 2002. "Dispelling the Illusion of Invulnerability: The Motivations and Mechanisms of Resistance to Persuasion." *Journal of Personality and Social Psychology* 83: 526–41.

Sagarin, B., and K. D. Mitnick. 2011. "The Path of Least Resistance." In *Six Degrees of Social Influence*. Edited by D. T. Kenrick, N. J. Goldstein, and S. L. Braver. New York: Oxford University Press.

Sah, S., and G. Loewenstein. 2010. "Effect of Reminders of Personal Sacrifice and Suggested Rationalizations on Residents' Self-Reported Willingness to Accept Gifts." *Journal of the American Medical Association* 304: 1204–11.

Salancik, G. R., and J. R. Mendl. 1984. "Corporate Attributions as Strategic Illusions of Management Control." *Administrative Science Quarterly* 29: 238–54.

Salancik, G. R., and J. Pfeffer. 1977. "Constraints on Administrative Discretion: The Limited Influence of Mayors on City Budgets." *Urban Affairs Quarterly* 12: 475–98.

Sanbonmatsu, D. M., S. S. Posavac, F. R. Kardes, and S. P. Mantel. 1989. "Selective Hypothesis Testing." *Psychonomic Bulletin and Review* 5: 197–220.

Scherpenzeel, A., and V. Toepol. 2012. "Recruiting a Probability Sample for an Online Panel." *Public Opinion Quarterly* 76: 470–90.

Schkade, D, A., and D. Kahneman. 1998. "Does Living in California Make People Happy? A Focusing Illusion in Judgments of Life Satisfaction." *Psychological Science* 9: 340–46.

Schmader, T., M. Johns, and C. Forbes. 2008. "An Integrated Process Model of Stereotype Threat on Performance." *Psychological Review* 115: 336–56.

Schmidt, F. L. 2014. "A General Theoretical Integrative Model of Individual Differences in Interests, Abilities, Personality Traits, and Academic and Occupational Achievement: A Commentary on Four Recent Articles." *Perspectives on Psychological Science* 9: 211–18.

Schmiege, S. J., W. M. P. Klein, and A. D. Bryan. 2010. *European Journal of Social Psychology* 40: 746–59.

Schmierbach, M. 2010. "'Killing Spree': Exploring the Connection Between Competitive Game Play and Aggressive Cognition." *Communication Research* 37: 256–74.

Schneider, I. K., M. Parzuchowski, B. Wojciszke, N. Schwarz, and S. L. Koole. 2015. "Weighty Data: Importance Information Influences Estimated Weight of Digital Information Storage Devices." *Frontiers in Psychology* 5: 1536.

Schrift, R. Y., and J. R. Parker, 2014. "Staying the Course: The Option of Doing Nothing and Its Impact on Postchoice Persistence." *Psychological Science* 25: 772–80.

Schroder, T., and P. Thagard. 2013. "The Affective Meanings of Automatic Social Behaviors: Three Mechanisms That Explain Priming." *Psychological Review* 120: 255–80.

Schroeder, D. A., L. A. Penner, J. F. Dovidio, and J. A. Piliavin. 1995. *The Psychology of Helping and Altruism: Problems and Puzzles*. New York: McGraw-Hill.

Schulte, B. 1998. "Sleep Research Focusing on Mind's Effectiveness." *Arizona Republic* (Phoenix) (March 8), A33.

Schuman, H., and S. Presser. 1981. *Questions and Answers in Attitude Surveys: Experiments on Question Form, Wording, and Context*. New York: Academic Press.

Schwarz, N., and F. Strack. 1991. "Evaluating One's Life: A Judgmental Model of Subjective Well-Being." In *Subjective Well-Being: An Interdisciplinary Perspective*. Edited by F. Strack, M. Argyle, and N. Schwarz. Oxford, UK: Pergamon Press, 27–48.

Schyns, B., J. Felfe, and H. Blank. 2007. "Is Charisma Hyper-Romanticism? Empirical Evidence From New Data and a Meta-Analysis." *Applied Psychology: An International Review* 56: 505–27.

Scott, M. L., and S. M. Nowlis. 2013. "The Effect of Goal Specificity on Consumer Reengagement." *Journal of Consumer Research* 40: 444–59.

Sedikides, C., and J. J. Skoronski. 1990. "Toward Reconciling Personality and Social Psychology: A Construct Accessibility Approach. *Journal of Social Behavior and Personality* 5: 531–46.

Sedikides, C., L. Gaertner, and J. L. Vevea. 2005. "Pancultural Self-Enhancement Reloaded: A Meta-Analytic Reply." *Journal of Personality and Social Psychology* 89: 539–51.

Seidenberg, M. S. 2005. "Connectionist Models of Word Reading." *Current Directions in Psychological Science* 14: 238–42.

Seiter, J. S. 2007. "Ingratiation and Gratuity: The Effect of Complimenting Customers on Tipping Behavior in Restaurants." *Journal of Applied Social Psychology* 37: 478–85.

Seiter, J. S., and E. Dutson. 2007. "The Effect of Compliments on Tipping Behavior in Hairstyling Salons." *Journal of Applied Social Psychology* 37: 1999–2007.

Sekaquaptewa, D., and M. Thompson. 2003. "Solo Status, Stereotypes, and Performance Expectancies: Their Effects on Women's Public Performance." *Journal of Experimental Social Psychology* 39: 68–74.

Semin, G. R. 2012. "The Linguistic Category Model." In *Handbook of Theories of Social Psychology*. Vol. 1. Edited by P. A. M. Van Lange, A. Kruglanski, and E. T. Higgins. London: Sage, 309–26.

Semin, G. R., and K. Fiedler. 1988. "The Cognitive Functions of Linguistic Categories in Describing Persons: Social Cognition and Language." *Journal of Personality and Social Psychology* 54: 558–68.

Sergent, C., and S. Dehaene. 2004. "Is Consciousness a Gradual Phenomenon?" *Psychological Science* 15: 720–28.

Shah, J. Y., R. Friedman, and A. W. Kruglanski. 2002. "Forgetting All Else: On the Antecedents and Consequences of Goal Shielding." *Journal of Personality and Social Psychology* 83: 1261–80.

Shallcross, A. J., B. Q. Ford, V. A. Floerke, and I. B. Mauss. 2013. "Getting Better with Age: The Relationship between Age, Acceptance, and Negative Affect." *Journal of Personality and Social Psychology* 104: 695–715.

Shantz, A., and G. Latham. 2009. "An Exploratory Field Experiment of the Effect of Subconscious and Conscious Goals on Employee Performance." *Organizational Behavior and Human Decision Processes* 109: 9–17.

Shantz, A., and G. Latham. 2011. "Effect of Primed Goals on Employee Performance: Implications for Human Resource Management." *Human Resource Management* 50: 289–99.

Shapiro, J. R., and S. L. Neuberg. 2007. "From Stereotype Threat to Stereotype Threats: Implications of a Multi-Threat Framework for Causes, Moderators, Mediators, Consequences, and Interventions. *Personality and Social Psychology Review* 11: 107–30.

Shapiro, K. L. 1994. "The Attentional Blink: The Brain's 'Eyeblink.'" *Current Directions in Psychological Science* 3: 86–89.

Shapiro, S. A., and J. H. Nielson. 2013. "What the Blind Eye Sees: Incidental Change Detection as a Source of Perceptual Fluency." *Journal of Consumer Research* 39: 1202–18.

Sharot, T., S. M. Fleming, X. Yu, R. Koster, and R. J. Dolan. 2012. "Is Choice-Induced Preference Change Long Lasting?" *Psychological Science* 23: 1123–29.

Sharot, T., C. M. Velasquez, and R. J. Dolan. 2010. "Do Decisions Shape Preference? Evidence from Blind Choice." *Psychological Science* 21: 1231–35.

Shaw, J., and S. Porter. 2015. "Constructing Rich False Memories of Committing a Crime." *Psychological Science* 26: 291–301.

Sheppard, D. M., J. Duncan, K. L. Shapiro, and A. P. Hillstrom. 2002. "Objects and Events in the Attentional Blink." *Psychological Science* 13: 410–15.

Sherman, J. W., B. Gawronski, and Y. Trope. 2014. *Dual-Process Theories of the Social Mind*. New York: Guilford Press.

Shermer, M. 2002. *Why People Believe Weird Things*. New York: Holt Paperbacks.

———. 2003. "Psychic for a Day." *Skeptic* 10: 48–55.

Shiffrin, R. S. 2010. "Perspectives on Modeling in Cognitive Science." *Topics in Cognitive Science* 2: 736–50.

Shih, M., T. L. Pittinsky, and N. Ambady. 1999. "Stereotype Susceptibility: Identity Salience and Shifts in Quantitative Performance." *Psychological Science* 10: 80–83.

Shiota, M. N., and R. W. Levenson. 2009. "Effects of Aging on Experimentally Instructed Detached Reappraisal, Positive Reappraisal, and Emotional Behavior Suppression." *Psychology and Aging* 24, no. 4: 890–900.

Shteynberg, G. 2015. "Shared Attention." *Perspectives on Psychological Science* 10: 579–90.

Shu, L. L., N. Mazar, F. Gino, D. Ariely, and M. H. Bazerman. 2012. "Signing at the Beginning Makes Ethics Salient and Decreases Dishonest Self-Reports in Comparison to Signing at the End." *Proceedings of the National Academy of Sciences* 108: 15197–200.

Shu, S. B., and K. A. Carlson. 2014. "When Three Charms but Four Alarms: Identifying the Optimal Number of Claims in Persuasion Settings." *Journal of Marketing* 78: 127–39.

Simonich, W. L. 1991. *Government Antismoking Policies*. New York: Peter Lang.

Simonsohn, U. 2011. "Spurious? Name Similarity Effects (Implicit Egoism) in Marriage, Job, and Moving Decisions." *Journal of Personality and Social Psychology* 101: 1–24.

Sinaceur, M., and C. Heath, and S. Cole. 2005. "Emotional and Deliberative Reaction to a Public Crisis: Mad Cow Disease in France." *Psychological Science* 16: 247–54.

Sinclair, B., M. McConnell, and M. R. Michelson. 2013. "Local Canvassing: The Efficacy of Grassroots Voter Mobilization." *Political Communications* 30: 42–57.

Singer, M. T., and J. Lalich. 1995. *Cults in Our Midst*. San Francisco: Jossey-Bass.

Singh, R., S. E. Yeo, P. K. F. Lin, and L. Tan. 2007. "Multiple Mediators of the Attitude Similarity-Attraction Relationship: Dominance of Inferred Attraction and Subtlety of Affect." *Basic and Applied Social Psychology* 29: 61–74.

Slepian, M. L., M. Weisbuch, A. M. Rutchick, L. S. Newman, and N. Ambady. 2010. "Shedding Light on Insight: Priming Bright Ideas." *Journal of Experimental Social Psychology* 46: 696–700.

Slepian, M. L., S. G. Young, N. O. Rule, M. Weisbuch, and N. Ambady. 2012. "Embodied Impression Formation: Social Judgments and Motor Cues to Approach and Avoidance." *Social Cognition* 30: 232–40.

Smidt, C. T. 2012. "Not All News Is the Same: Protests, Presidents, and the Mass Public Agenda." *Public Opinion Quarterly* 76: 72–94.

Smith, C. T., J. De Houwer, and B. A. Nosek. 2013. "Consider the Source: Persuasion of Implicit Evaluations Is Moderated by Source Credibility." *Personality and Social Psychology Bulletin* 39: 193–205.

Smith, E. R., S. Coats, and D. Walling. 1999. "Overlapping Mental Representations of Self, In-Group, and Partner: Further Response Time Evidence for a Connectionist Model." *Personality and Social Psychology Bulletin* 25: 873–82.

Song, H., and N. Schwarz. 2009. "If It's Difficult to Pronounce, It Must Be Risky." *Psychological Science* 20: 135–38.

Sopory, P., and J. P. Dillard. 2002. "The Persuasive Effects of Metaphor." *Human Communication Research* 28: 382–419.

Soto, F. A., and E. A. Wasserman. 2010. "Error-Driven Learning in Visual Categorization and Object Recognition: A Common-Elements Model." *Psychological Review* 117: 349–81.

Sprecher, S., S. Treger, J. D. Wondra, N. Hilaire, and K. Wallpe. 2013. "Taking Turns: Reciprocal Self-Disclosure Promotes Liking in Initial Interactions." *Journal of Experimental Social Psychology* 49: 860–66.

Stallen, M., A. Smidts, and A. G. Sanfey. 2013. "Peer Influence: Neural Mechanisms Underlying In-Group Conformity." *Frontiers in Human Neuroscience* 7: 50.

Stanchi, K. M. 2008. "Playing with Fire: The Science of Confronting Adverse Material in Legal Advocacy." *Rutgers Law Review* 60: 381–434.

Steele, C. M., S. J. Spencer, and J. Aronson. 2002. "Contending with Group Image: The Psychology of Stereotype and Social Identity Threat." In *Advances in Experimental Social Psychology.* Vol. 34. Edited by M. P. Zanna. San Diego, CA: Academic Press, 379–440.

Stein, J. 2008. "The Swing Voter." *Time* (August 7), http://content.time.com/time/magazine/article/0,9171,1830395,00.html.

Stewart, D. W., and D. H. Furse. 1986. *Effective Television Advertising: A Study of 1000 Commercials.* Lexington, MA: Lexington Books.

Stewart, J. 2011. *Why Noise Matters.* Oxford, UK: Earthscan.

Stiglitz, J. E. 2012. *The Price of Inequality.* New York: W. W. Norton.

Stijnen, M. M. N., and A. M. J. Dijker. 2011. "Reciprocity and Need in Posthumous Organ Donations: The Mediating Role of Moral Emotions." *Social Psychological and Personality Science* 2: 387–94.

Stocco, A., C. Lebiere, and J. R. Anderson. 2010. "Conditional Routing of Information to the Cortex: A Model of the Basal Ganglia's Role in Cognitive Coordination." *Psychological Review* 117: 541–74.

Stok, F. M., D. T. de Ridder, E. de Vet, and J. F. de Wit. 2014. "Don't Tell Me What I Should Do, but What Others Do: The Influence of Descriptive and Injunctive Peer Norms on Fruit Consumption in Adolescents." *British Journal of Health Psychology* 19: 52–64.

Stouffer, S. A., E. Suchman, S. A. DeVinney, S. Star, and R. M. Williams, eds. 1949. *The American Soldier: Adjustment during Army Life*. Princeton, NJ: Princeton University Press.

Strack, F., L. Werth, R. Deutsch. 2006. "Reflective and Impulsive Determinants of Consumer Behavior." *Journal of Consumer Psychology* 16: 205–16.

Stroebe, W., G. M. van Koningsbruggen, E. K. Papies, and H. Aarts. 2013. "Why Most Dieters Fail but Some Succeed: A Goal Conflict Model of Eating Behavior." *Psychological Review* 120: 110–38.

Strohmetz, D. B., B. Rind, R. Fisher, and M. Lynn. 2002. "Sweetening the Till: The Use of Candy to Increase Restaurant Tipping." *Journal of Applied Social Psychology* 32: 300–309.

Su, R., and J. Rounds. 2015. "All STEM Fields Are Not Created Equal: People and Things Interests Explain Gender Disparities Across STEM Fields." *Frontiers of Psychology* 6: 189.

Su, R., J. Rounds, and P. I. Armstrong. 2009. "Men and Things, Women and People: A Meta-Analysis." *Psychological Bulletin* 135: 859–84.

Subra, B., D. Muller, L. Begue, B. Bushman, and F. Delmas. 2010. "Automatic Effects of Alcohol and Aggressive Cues on Aggressive Thoughts and Behaviors." *Personality and Social Psychology Bulletin* 36: 1052–57.

Sun Tzu. 2007. *The Art of War*. Bel Air, CA: Filiquarian.

Sunny, M. M., and A. von Mühlenen. 2013. "Attention Capture by Abrupt Onsets: Re-Visiting the Priority Tag Model." *Frontiers in Psychology* 4: 958.

Susman, T. M. 2011. Reciprocity, Denial, and the Appearance of Impropriety: Why Self-Recusal Cannot Remedy the Influence of Campaign Contributions on Judges' Decisions." *Journal of Law and Politics* 26: 359–84.

Swann, W. B., and M. D. Buhrmester. 2015. "Identity Fusion." *Current Directions in Psychological Science* 24: 52–57.

Sweldens, S., S. M. J. van Osselar, and C. Janiszewski. 2010. "Evaluative Conditioning Procedures and Resilience of Conditioned Brand Attitudes." *Journal of Consumer Research* 37: 473–89.

Switzer, F. S., and J. A. Sniezek. 1991. "Judgment Processes in Motion: Anchoring and Adjustment Effects on Judgment and Behavior." *Organizational Behavior and Human Decision Processes* 49: 208–29.

Szalma, J. L., and P. A. Hancock. 2001. "Noise Effects on Human Performance: A Meta-Analytic Synthesis." *Psychological Bulletin* 137: 682–707.

Szybillo, G. J., and R. Heslin. 1973. "Resistance to Persuasion: Inoculation Theory in a Marketing Context." *Journal of Marketing Research* 10: 396–403.

Tannenbaum, M. B., J. Hepler, R. S. Zimmerman, L. Saul, S. Jacobs, K. Wilson, and D. Albarracin. 2015. "Appealing to Fear: A Meta-Analysis of Fear Appeal Effectiveness and Theories." *Psychological Bulletin* 141: 1178–1204.

Tarr, B., J. Launay, and R. I. Dunbar. 2014. "Music and Social Bonding: 'Self-Other' Merging and Neurohormonal Mechanisms." *Frontiers in Psychology* 5: 1096.

Taylor, P. J., and S. Thomas. 2008. "Linguistic Style Matching and Negotiation Outcome." *Negotiation and Conflict Management Research* 1: 263–81.

Taylor, S. E., and S. T. Fiske. 1978. "Salience, Attention, and Attributions: Top of the Head Phenomena." In *Advances in Experimental Social Psychology.* Vol. 11. Edited by L. Berkowitz New York: Academic Press, 249–88.

Taylor, V. J., and G. M. Walton. 2011. "Stereotype Threat Undermines Academic Learning." *Personality and Social Psychology Bulletin* 37: 1055–67.

Telzer, E. H., C. L. Masten, E. T. Berkman, M. D. Lieberman, and A. J. Fuligni. 2010. "Gaining While Giving: An fMRI Study of the Rewards of Family Assistance Among White and Latino Youth." *Social Neuroscience* 5: 508–18.

Tesser, A. 1978. "Self-Generated Attitude Change." In *Advances in Experimental Social Psychology*. Vol. 11. Edited by L. Berkowitz. New York: Academic Press, 290–338.

———. 1993. "The Importance of Heritability in Psychological Research: The Case of Attitudes." *Psychological Review* 100: 129–42.

The Street, the Bull, and the Crisis: Survey of the US & UK Financial Services Industry. 2015. New York: Labaton Sucharow and University of Notre Dame (May). www.secwhistlebloweradvocate.com/LiteratureRetrieve.aspx?ID=224757.

Thibodeau, P. H., and L. Boroditsky. 2011. "Metaphors We Think With: The Role of Metaphor in Reasoning." *PLoS ONE* 6: e16782. doi:0.1371/journal.pone.0016782.

Thompson, E. P., R. J. Roman, G. B. Moskowitz, S. Chaiken, and J. A. Bargh. 1994. "Accuracy Motivation Attenuates Covert Priming: The Systematic Reprocessing of Social Information." *Journal of Personality and Social Psychology* 66: 474–89.

Till, B. D., and R. L. Priluck. 2000. "Stimulus Generalization in Classical Conditioning: An Initial Investigation and Extension." *Psychology and Marketing* 17: 55–72.

Tokayer, M., and M. Swartz. 1979. *The Fugu Plan: The Untold Story of the Japanese and the Jews During World War II*. New York: Paddington Press.

Topolinski, S., M. Zürn, and I. K. Schneider. 2015. "What's In and What's Out in Branding? A Novel Articulation Effect for Brand Names." *Frontiers in Psychology* 6: 585.

Trampe, D., D. Stapel, F. Siero, and H. Mulder. 2010. "Beauty as a Tool: The Effect of Model Attractiveness, Product Relevance, and Elaboration Likelihood on Advertising Effectiveness." *Psychology and Marketing* 27: 1101–21.

Trocmé, A. 2007/1971. *Jesus and the Nonviolent Revolution.* Walden, NY: Plough.

Trope, Y., and N. Liberman. 2010. "Construal-Level Theory of Psychological Distance." *Psychological Review* 117: 440–63.

Trudel, R., and J. Cotte. 2009. "Does It Pay to Be Good?" *MIT Sloan Management Review* 50: 61–68.

Tulving, E., and Z. Pearlstone. 1966. "Availability Versus Accessibility of Information in Memory for Words." *Journal of Verbal Learning and Verbal Behavior* 5: 381–91.

Turner, Y., and I. Hadas-Halpern. 2008. "The Effects of Including a Patient's Photograph to the Radiographic Examination." Paper presented at the Meetings of the Radiological Society of North America, Chicago (December).

Twenge, J. W., W. K. Campbell, and N. T. Carter. 2014. "Declines in Trust in Others and Confidence in Institutions among American Adults and Late Adolescents." *Psychological Science* 25: 1914–23.

Tyron, W. W. 2012. "A Connectionist Network Approach to Psychological Science: Core and Corollary Principles." *Review of General Psychology* 16: 305–17.

Ulrich, C., P. O'Donnell, C. Taylor, A. Farrar, M. Danis, and C. Grady. 2007. "Ethical Climate, Ethics Stress, and the Job Satisfaction of Nurses and Social Workers in the United States." *Social Science and Medicine* 65: 1708–19.

Urry, H. L., and J. J. Gross. 2010. "Emotion Regulation in Older Age." *Current Directions in Psychological Science* 19: 352–57.

Vaish, A., T. Grossmann, and A. Woodward. 2008. "Not All Emotions Are Created Equal: The Negativity Bias in Social-Emotional Development." *Psychological Bulletin* 134: 383–403.

Valdesolo, P., and D. DeSteno. 2011. "Synchrony and the Social Tuning of Compassion." *Emotion* 11: 262–66.

Van Baaren, R. B., R. W. Holland, B. Steenaert, and A. van Knippenberg. 2003. "Mimicry for Money: Behavioral Consequences of Imitation." *Journal of Experimental Social Psychology* 39: 393–98.

Van Bergen, A. 1968. *Task Interruption*. Amsterdam: North Holland.

van der Wal, R. C. and L. F. van Dillen. 2013. "Leaving a Flat Taste in Your Mouth: Task Load Reduces Taste Perception." *Psychological Science* 24: 1277–84.

Van Kerckhove, A., M. Geuens, and L. Vermeir. 2012. "A Motivational Account of the Question-Behavior Effect." *Journal of Consumer Research* 39: 111–27.

van Osselaer, S. M. J., and C. Janiszewski. 2012. "A Goal-Based Model of Product Evaluation and Choice." *Journal of Consumer Research* 39: 260–92.

Van Yperen, N. C., and N. P. Leander. 2014. "The Overpowering Effect of Social Comparison Information: On the Misalignment Between

Mastery-Based Goals and Self-Evaluation Criteria." *Personality and Social Psychology Bulletin* 40: 676–88.

vanDellen, M. R., J. Y. Shah, N. P. Leander, J. E. Delose, and J. X. Bornstein. 2015. "In Good Company: Managing Interpersonal Resources That Support Self-Regulation." *Personality and Social Psychology Bulletin* 41: 869–82.

Vogt, J., J. De Houwer, and G. Crombez. 2011. "Multiple Goal Management Starts with Attention: Goal Prioritizing Affects the Allocation of Spatial Attention to Goal-Relevant Events." *Experimental Psychology* 58: 55–61.

Vogt, J., J. De Houwer, G. Crombez, and S. Van Damme. 2012. "Competing for Attentional Priority: Temporary Goals versus Threats." *Emotion* 13, no. 3 (June): 587–98.

Volz, K. G., T. Kessler, and D. Y. von Cramon. 2009. "In-Group as Part of the Self: In-Group Favoritism Is Mediated by Medial Prefrontal Cortex Activation." *Social Neuroscience* 4: 244–60.

Wall Street in Crisis: A Perfect Storm Looming (Labaton Sucharow's U.S. Financial Services Industry Survey). 2013. New York: Labaton Sucharow (July). www.secwhistlebloweradvocate.com.

Walton, G. L. 1908. *Why Worry?* Philadelphia: J. B. Lippincott.

Walton, G. M., and S. J. Spencer. 2009. "Latent Ability: Grades and Test Scores Systematically Underestimate the Intellectual Ability of Women and Ethnic Minority Students." *Psychological Science* 20: 1132–39.

Walton, G. W., G. L. Cohen, D. Cwir, and S. J. Spencer. 2012. "Mere Belonging: The Power of Social Connections." *Journal of Personality and Social Psychology* 102: 513–32.

Wang, J., and R. S. Wyer. 2002. "Comparative Judgment Processes: The Effects of Task Objectives and Time Delay on Product Evaluations." *Journal of Consumer Psychology* 12: 327–40.

Wang, M. T., J. S. Eccles, and S. Kenny. "Not Lack of Ability but More Choice." *Psychological Science* 24: 770–75.

Warneken, F., K. Lohse, P. A. Melis, and M. Tomasello. 2011. "Young Children Share the Spoils After Collaboration." *Psychological Science* 22: 267–73.

Warner, K. E. 1981. "Cigarette Smoking in the 1970's: The Impact of the Anti-Smoking Campaign on Consumption." *Science* 211, no. 4483: 729–31.

Warrick, J. 2008. "Afghan Influence Taxes CIA's Credibility." *Washington Post* (December 26), A17.

Wasserman, E. A., C. C. DeVolder, and D. J. Coppage. 1992. "Nonsimilarity-Based Conceptualization in Pigeons via Secondary or Mediated Generalization." *Psychological Science* 3: 374–79.

Watanabe, T. 1994. "An Unsung 'Schindler' from Japan." *Los Angeles Times* (March 20), 1.

Weber, E. U., and M. W. Morris. 2010. "Culture and Judgment and Decision Making: The Constructivist Turn." *Perspectives on Psychological Science* 5: 410–19.

Weber, E. U., and E. J. Johnson. 2009. "Mindful Judgment and Decision-Making." *Annual Review of Psychology* 60: 53–86.

Wegener, D. T., and R. E. Petty. 1997. "The Flexible Correction Model: The Role of Naïve Theories of Bias in Bias Correction." In *Advances in Experimental Social Psychology.* Vol. 29. Edited by M. P. Zanna. Mahwah, NJ: Erlbaum, 141–208.

Weingarten, E., Q. Chen, M. McAdams, J. Li, J. Helper, and D. Albarracín. 2016. "From Primed Concepts to Action: A Meta-Analysis of the Behavioral Effects of Incidentally Presented Words." *Psychological Bulletin* 142: 472–97.

Wendling, P. 2009. "Can a Photo Enhance a Radiologist's Report?" *Clinical Endocrinology News* 4: 6.

Wentura, D. 1999. "Activation and Inhibition of Affective Information: Evidence for Negative Priming in the Evaluation Task." *Cognition and Emotion* 13: 65–91.

Westmaas, J. L., and R. C. Silver. 2006. "The Role of Perceived Similarity in Supportive Responses to Victims of Negative Life Events." *Personality and Social Psychology Bulletin* 32: 1537–46.

Whitchurch, E. R., T. D. Wilson, and D. T. Gilbert. 2011. "'He Loves Me, He Loves Me Not . . .'": Uncertainty Can Increase Romantic Attraction." *Psychological Science* 22: 172–75.

Williams, K. D., M. J. Bourgeois, and R. T. Croyle. 1993. "The Effects of Stealing Thunder in Criminal and Civil Trials." *Law and Human Behavior* 17: 597–609.

Williams, L. E., and J. A. Bargh. 2008. "Experiencing Physical Warmth Promotes Interpersonal Warmth." *Science* 322: 606–7.

Wilson, T. D., D. B. Centerbar, D. A. Kermer, and D. T. Gilbert, D. T. 2005. "The Pleasures of Uncertainty: Prolonging Positive Moods in Ways People Do Not Anticipate." *Journal of Personality and Social Psychology* 88: 5–21.

Wilson, T. D., and D. T. Gilbert. 2008. "Affective Forecasting: Knowing What to Want." *Current Directions in Psychological Science* 14: 131–34.

Wilson, T. D., T. P. Wheatley, J. M. Meyers, D. T. Gilbert, and D. Axsom. 2000. "Focalism: A Source of Durability Bias in Affective Forecasting." *Journal of Personality and Social Psychology* 78: 821–36.

Wiltermuth, S. S. 2012a. "Synchronous Activity Boosts Compliance with Requests to Aggress." *Journal of Experimental Social Psychology* 48: 453–56.

———. 2012b. "Synchrony and Destructive Obedience." *Social Influence* 7: 78–89.

Wiltermuth, S. S., and C. Heath. 2009. "Synchrony and Cooperation." *Psychological Science* 20: 1–5.

Winkielman, P., K. C. Berridge, and J. L. Wilbarger. 2005. "Unconscious Affective Reactions to Masked Happy versus Angry Faces Influence Consumption Behavior and Judgments of Value." *Personality and Social Psychology Bulletin* 31: 121–35.

Winkielman, P., and J. T. Cacioppo. 2001. "Mind at Ease Puts a Smile on the Face." *Journal of Personality and Social Psychology* 81: 989–1000.

Winkielman, P., J. Halberstadt, T. Fazendeiro, and S. Catty. 2006. "Prototypes Are Attractive Because They Are Easy on the Mind." *Psychological Science* 17: 799–806.

Wiseman, R. 1997. *Deception and Self-Deception: Investigating Psychics.* Amherst, MA: Prometheus Books.

Witte, K., and M. Allen. 2000. "A Meta-Analysis of Fear Appeals: Implications for Effective Public Health Campaigns." *Health Education and Behavior* 27: 591–615.

Wood, D. 2015. Testing the Lexical Hypothesis: Are Socially Important Traits More Densely Reflected in the English Lexicon?" *Journal of Personality and Social Psychology* 108: 317–39.

Wood, W., and J. M. Quinn. 2003. "Forewarned and Forearmed? Two Meta-Analysis Syntheses of Forewarnings of Influence Appeals." *Psychological Bulletin* 129: 119–38.

Wood, W., and D. T. Neal. 2007. "A New Look at Habits and the Habit-Goal Interface." *Psychological Review* 114: 843–63.

Woodside, A., G., and J. W. Davenport. 1974. "Effects of Salesman Similarity and Expertise on Consumer Purchasing Behavior." *Journal of Marketing Research* 11: 198–202.

Yang, L. W., K. M. Cutright, T. L. Chartrand, and G. Z. Fitzsimons. 2014. "Distinctively Different: Exposure to Multiple Brands in Low-Elaboration Settings." *Journal of Consumer Research* 40: 973–92.

Yang, Q., X. Wu, X. Zhou, N. L. Mead, K. D. Vohs, and R. F. Baumeister. 2013. "Diverging Effects of Clean versus Dirty Money on Attitudes, Values, and Interpersonal Behavior." *Journal of Personality and Social Psychology* 104: 473–89.

Yantis, S. 1993. "Stimulus-Driven Attentional Capture." *Current Directions in Psychological Science* 2: 156–61.

Yermolayeva, Y., and D. H. Rakison. 2014. "Connectionist Modeling of Developmental Changes in Infancy: Approaches, Challenges, and Contributions." *Psychological Bulletin* 140: 234–55.

Yopyk, D. J., A., and D. A. Prentice. 2005. "Am I an Athlete or a Student? Identity Salience and Stereotype Threat in Student-Athletes." *Basic and Applied Social Psychology* 27, no.4 (December): 329–36.

Yuki, M., W. M. Maddox, M. B. Brewer, and K. Takemura. 2005. "Cross-Cultural Differences in Relationship- and Group-Based Trust." *Personality and Social Psychology Bulletin* 31: 48–62.

Zabelina, D. L., and M. Beeman. 2013. "Short-Term Attentional Perseveration

Associated with Real-Life Creative Achievement." *Frontiers in Psychology* 4: 191.

Zebrowitz-McArthur, L., and E. Ginsberg. 1981. "Causal Attribution to Salient Stimuli: An Investigation of Visual Fixation Mediators." *Personality and Social Psychology Bulletin* 7: 547–53.

Zeigarnik, B. 1927. "Das Behalten erledigter und unerledigter Handlungen." *Psychologische Forschung* 9: 1–85.

Zell, E., and M. D. Alicke. 2010. "The Local Dominance Effect in Self-Evaluations: Evidence and Explanations." *Personality and Social Psychology Bulletin* 14: 368–84.

Zell, E., Z. Krizan, and S. R. Teeter. 2015. "Evaluating Gender Similarities and Differences Using Metasynthesis." *American Psychologist* 70: 10–20.

Zhang, M., and X. Li. 2012. "From Physical Weight to Psychological Significance: The Contribution of Semantic Activations." *Journal of Consumer Research* 38: 1063–75.

Zhong, C-B., and S. E. DeVoe. 2012. "You Are How You Eat: Fast Food and Impatience." *Psychological Science* 21: 619–22.

Zhu, R., and J. J. Argo. 2013. "Exploring the Impact of Various Shaped Seating Arrangements on Persuasion." *Journal of Consumer Research* 40: 336–49.

Zylberberg, A., M. Oliva, and M. Sigman. 2012. "Pupil Dilation: A Fingerprint of Temporal Selection During the 'Attentional Blink.'" *Frontiers in Psychology* 3: 316.

Notes

AUTHOR'S NOTE

1. W. H. Auden's line appeared in his poem "Under Which Lyre: A Reactionary Tract for the Times." James Boyle's comment comes from his book *The Public Domain: Enclosing the Commons of the Mind*, whereas the assertions of Sun Tzu and Dale Carnegie are from their classic works *The Art of War* and *How to Win Friends and Influence People*, respectively.

   An engaging question is why behavioral economics could play an accrediting role for social psychology among many decision makers. It has to do, I believe, with the high regard with which economics as a discipline has traditionally been held in business and government. When there are individuals labeled behavioral economists who have won the larger discipline's Nobel Prize (George Akerlof, Daniel Kahneman, Robert Shiller, Herbert Simon, Vernon Smith), and there are others who should win (I'm thinking principally of Richard Thaler), and when it appears that behavioral economics and social psychology share some central elements, the reputation of the second field is raised by the first.

PART 1: PRE-SUASION: THE FRONTLOADING OF ATTENTION

Chapter 1. Pre-Suasion: An Introduction

2. The restaurant name and jersey number studies were done by Critcher and Gilovich (2007); the Belgian chocolate study by Ariely,

Loewenstein, and Prelec (2003); the work performance study by Switzer and Sniezek (1991); the line drawing study by Oppenheimer, LeBoeuf, and Brewer (2008); and the wine shop study by North, Hargreaves, and McKendrick (1997).

This general result—that whatever is experienced first changes responses to what comes next, often in bizarre ways—isn't limited to communication. Recent theories have begun employing quantum probability models (as opposed to classic probability models) to explain human judgment errors of various kinds (Pothos and Busemeyer, 2013). Central to these theories is the idea that making a decision alters a person's state of mind and creates aberrations from what would logically have been expected before the decision (Busemeyer et al., Trublood, 2011; Busemeyer and Wang, 2015; Shiffrin, 2010; and Weber and Johnson, 2009).

3. The idea that success is *initiated* not so much by crashing through barriers as by removing them is represented in the instructively paired descriptors assigned to the Hindu god Ganesha, "Lord of beginnings, remover of obstacles." Other kinds of pre-suasive openers besides Jim's can remove the obstacle of insufficient trust. By first establishing similarity to an audience, even a boastful communicator increases trust and consequent persuasion (Packard, Gershoff, and Wooten, in press).

4. I am not by myself in this belief. For example, in his informative overview of the vast research into sound thinking strategies, Michael J. Mauboussin (2009, 16) steps back and concludes that "the best decisions often derive from sameness." Indeed, a notable level of sameness in a situation can often be the most instructively "different" feature of it. Jakob Dylan said as much (more eloquently than I have here) in the lyrics of his song "The Difference": "The only difference that I see / Is you are exactly the same as you used to be."

5. The concerted scientific study of persuasion began in earnest with the government communication programs that were enacted during the Second World War (Hovland, Lumsdaine, and Sheffield, 1949; Lewin, 1947; Stouffer et al., 1949). When our side was in charge, we called them information programs; when our opponents were in charge, we called them propaganda programs.

6. The physical expression of moment flows from the recognition of the operating power of leverage by the world's first great mathematical physicist, Archimedes (287 BCE–212 BCE), who declared, "Give me a lever and a place to stand, and I shall move the world." The notion of a ripe period of time (when action is called for) is even older, represented in the ancient Greek word *kairos* and the concept of the "*kairos* moment" that refers to an instant when time and circumstance converge auspiciously. Indeed, no less a teacher in the arts of influence than Aristotle advised orators of the importance of seizing the right moment when presenting an argument. It is a point of historical interest that, owing to issues of faulty translation and classification, scholars have recognized only relatively recently the significant persuasive weight Aristotle assigned to *kairos* in his *Rhetoric* (Kinneavy and Eskin, 2000).

Chapter 2. Privileged Moments

7. Several rigorous investigations of paranormal formulations for judging people have found uniform results: no credible evidence for the validity of such methods (Blackmore, 1987, 1996; Charpak and Broch, 2004; Hyman, 1989, 1996; Reichart, 2010; Shermer, 2002; 2003; Wiseman, 1997). For a humorous video take on paranormal practitioners, see www.youtube.com/watch?v=aSR-uefPmME; for a more analytic take, see www.youtube.com/watch?v=ZAI2f3vnWWU.

8. The famous exchange between Holmes and Inspector Gregory of Scotland Yard, who had gathered considerable evidence against the stranger he had under arrest, went as follows:

> **Gregory:** Is there any other point to which you would wish to draw my attention?
> **Holmes:** To the curious incident of the dog in the night-time.
> **Gregory:** The dog did nothing in the night-time.
> **Holmes:** That was the curious incident.

The spontaneous human inclination to give more attention and meaning to events than to nonevents can be seen in diverse forms of evidence. Consider that susceptibility to the bias emerges even within the intricately designed moves (and to the detriment) of chess masters (Bilalic, McLeod, and Gobet, 2010). For other examples of how this bias damages decision making and how one brilliant individual, the mathematician Abraham Wald, recognized and outsmarted it, see www.dangreller.com/the-dog-that-didnt-bark-2. Indeed, the approach that Holmes and Wald took can be seen to characterize the information gathering style of other brilliant individuals. Take for instance the founder of Facebook, Mark Zuckerberg, whose chief operating officer, Sheryl Sandberg, has observed, "When you talk to Mark, he doesn't just listen to what you say. He listens to what you didn't say." Few of us could be described likewise. Perhaps relatedly, few of us had a net worth of over $30 billion before our thirtieth birthday.

9. The Canadian college student study was carried out by Kunda et al. (1993). For reviews of many other experiments that demonstrate our widespread reliance on the positive test strategy and our almost automatic tendency for confirmatory hypothesis testing, see Klayman and Ha (1987); Lilienfeld, Ammirati, and Landfield (2009); Nickerson (1998); and McKenzie (2005).

My recommendation to refuse to answer single-chute survey questions is based on data indicating how misleading they can be. For instance, a classic study by Schuman and Presser (1981) asked a sample of Americans, "If there is a serious fuel shortage this winter, do you think there should be a law requiring people to lower the heat in their homes?" and found 38.3 percent in support. But when the researchers simply added to the question the balancing phrase "or do you oppose such a law?" only 29.4 percent of a similar sample supported the idea.

10. When I first began to study the topics of persuasion and social influence in any systematic way, I did so exclusively in a university laboratory, where I conducted careful experiments investigating why certain kinds of messages were particularly effective in changing the attitudes and actions of recipients. I still value that type of work, although not exclusively, because I've come to recognize that scientific research isn't the only worthwhile source of information about the

influence process. As I asserted in chapter 1, a vast storehouse of such information exists in the practices of influence professionals—who might be advertisers, salespeople, marketers, or fund-raisers—whose approaches I've analyzed sometimes by infiltrating their training programs to learn from the inside how they operate. But there is one intriguing type of influence practitioner, the cult recruiter, whose approaches I have never tried to explore from within. Although some researchers have pulled it off successfully (for example, Galanti, 1993), there are too many stories of individuals who entered cultic environments for reasons of curiosity and didn't come back out. So my evidence in this arena comes for the most part from interviews and reports provided by former cult members and recruiters who have been willing to discuss the persuasive devices that they used and that were used on them (Hassan, 1990, 2000; Kent and Hall, 2000; Lalich, 2004; Singer and Lalich, 1995). Information derived from such personal responses and reports on the persuasive tactics most favored by cults to recruit and retain members can be found in Almendros, Cialdini, and Goldstein (in preparation). For sources of consistently updated information in these regards, see the website of the International Cultic Studies Association (www.icsahome.com) and its scholarly publication the *International Journal of Cultic Studies*.

11. A critic might propose a different way to explain Bolkan and Andersen's results: Perhaps their subjects agreed to provide an email address not because of a momentarily magnified sense of their own adventurous natures but because they'd had a verbal interaction with the researcher (via the question-and-answer exchange) and, consequently, felt more favorable toward him and his subsequent proposals. This is a reasonable possible account, as there is evidence that requesters are more successful if they initiate even the briefest verbal dialogue before making a request (Dolinski, 2001). However, a third experiment conducted by Bolkan and Andersen indicates that this explanation can't account for the basic effect they found. In that final study, they handed out fliers to university students attending a communication class. The fliers invited students to write down an email address if they wanted to receive information on how to get

a free sample of a new brand of soft drink. For some of these students, there was no question anywhere on the flier inquiring into their adventurousness; their resultant interest was predictably low, with only 30 percent providing an address. For others in the class, the single-chute question "Do you consider yourself an adventurous person who likes to try new things?" was printed at the top of their fliers, and it made the difference: 55 percent of these students filled in their contact details, without the influence of any immediately prior verbal exchange. See Bolkan and Andersen (2009) for a full description of all three studies.

An investigation of voter turnout has uncovered a subtle factor that maximizes the impact of such single-chute questions: they should inquire about the targeted person, not the targeted act. The day before two different US elections, researchers called registered voters and asked about their intentions to vote, either with questions about their identities as voters (for instance, "How important is it for you to be a *voter* in the upcoming election?") or about the act of voting ("How important is it for you to *vote* in the upcoming election?"). Although both pre-suasive openers increased actual voting the next day, the one that put people in touch with their preferred identities as voters was the more effective in each election (Bryan et al., 2011).

12. As one example of the rapid growth of the problem, in its June 2010 issue, *Consumer Reports* magazine urged its readers toward unrelenting vigilance after detailing the results of a survey showing that a million US households are swindled annually by email scammers; three years later, the estimate had jumped to sixteen million households (Kirchheimer, 2013). Unfortunately, the fraud's growth didn't stop there. A Pew Research Center report found that the number of online America adults who reported having their personal information stolen rose by 63 percent between July 2013 and April 2014 (Madden, 2014). See Sagarin and Mitnick (2011) as well as Muscanell, Guadagno, and Murphy (2014) for harrowing stories of various ways that hackers do it. One tactic related to the Bolkan and Andersen procedure is to obtain an email address on a pretext and

then send its owner an email consistent with the pretext that includes a virus- or malware-laden attachment or Web link (Acohido, 2013; Anderson, 2013).

13. The general finding that making one concept prominent in consciousness suppresses awareness of competing concepts (Coman et al., 2009; Hugenberg and Bodenhausen, 2004; Janiszewski, Kuo, and Tavassoli, 2013; and Macrae, Bodenhausen, and Milne, 1995) plays out in a variety of specific ways. For example, stimulating a particular goal in people reduces (below normal levels) the likelihood that they'll recognize the availability of alternative goals (Shah, Friedman, and Kruglanski, 2002); leading people to focus on a particular way to find a job (practicing a job interview, for example) makes it difficult for them to recall other ways to do so, such as updating their résumé or phoning potential employers (McCulloch et al., 2008); asking people to repeatedly recall certain items that they'd learned accelerates the forgetting of other words they'd learned at the same time (Bauml, 2002; Murayama et al., 2014); and making one meaning of a word salient actively inhibits the recognition of other meanings of the word—for instance, if people are reminded that the word *prune* refers to a fruit, it then becomes significantly less likely to occur to them that the verb *prune* means "to trim" (Johnson and Anderson, 2004).

14. The one-conscious-experience-at-a-time rule applies to other information channels besides sight and sound. For instance, I've recognized that if I want to savor a particular bite of food, I'll close my eyes. On the other side of the coin, if I try to eat while watching an engrossing television program, I won't taste the food. For evidence that we're all in the same boat when it comes to the inability to register simultaneous streams of information in consciousness, see studies by Levy et al. (2006), Dijksterhuis (2004), Sergent and Dehaene (2004), Sheppard et al. (2002), Sunny and von Mühlenen (2013), and van der Wal and van Dillen (2013). Indeed, as early as 1890, William James, perhaps the greatest of all early American psychologists, asserted that owing to this cognitive shortcoming, "there is before the mind at no time a plurality of ideas" (405). It is important to note that the "mind"

to which James was referring is the conscious mind; we'll have more to say on this point later.

Our difficulty with focusing on two things at once helps explain the scary data surrounding the act of talking on a cell phone while driving. See Hyman et al. (2009) for a review of that evidence, including research showing that drivers on a cell phone show poorer performance than those legally drunk; see http://newsroom.aaa.com/2013 /06/think-you-know-all-about-distracted-driving-think-again-says-aaa for a study indicating that hands-free texting is no better. The reason that conversations with passengers in the car don't carry the same risks is that passengers know to adjust the timing and content of their remarks to the traffic situations the driver is facing (Gaspar et al., 2014).

15. For experimental evidence of the existence of the attentional blink in human perception, see Adamo, Cain, and Mitroff (2013), Barnard et al. (2004), and Shapiro (1994), as well as a review by Dux and Marios (2009); for evidence that it requires attentional focus, see Olivers and Niewenhuis (2005) and Zylberberg, Oliva, and Sigman (2012); finally, for evidence of the cortical mechanisms involved in the phenomenon, see Marti, Sigman, and Dehaene (2012). The idea that concentrated focus and shifts in such focus signal the importance of the focal entity (Mason, Tatkow, and Macrae, 2005) gains support from studies of the meaning of gaze in both infants and adults (Baron-Collins, 1995; Emery, 2000).

16. The Erickson anecdote comes from Dr. Jeffrey Zeig, the founder and director of the Milton H. Erickson Foundation. The snack food research was conducted by Labroo and Nielsen (2010, experiment 1). The general evidence that people assign more value to the things they see themselves approaching can be found in studies by Cacioppo et al. (1993), Finkel and Eastwick (2009), Neumann and Strack (2000), Priester et al. (1996), and Slepian et al. (2012). The same effect appears to apply to things people see themselves retaining. In one study, participants wrote down positive or negative thoughts about a type of diet (the Mediterranean diet) on a piece of paper and were told either to put the paper in a pocket or purse or to discard it. Even though they didn't

reread what they had written, participants' subsequent responses to the diet were most guided by their thoughts if they had placed copies of those thoughts in their pockets or purses (Brinol et al., 2013)

Chapter 3. The Importance of Attention . . . Is Importance

17. E. F. Hutton, which eventually merged with Citigroup, is no longer around, but some of the "When E. F. Hutton talks" commercials can still be found on YouTube. For example, see www.youtube.com/watch?v=SX7ZEotoFh0.

18. It is worth recognizing that work on the focusing illusion is not the scientific contribution that won Kahneman the Nobel Prize. (That is widely seen to be the development of prospect theory, which concerns the differential value people allot to prospective losses as compared with prospective gains.) Nor is the focusing illusion a topic to which Kahneman has devoted much concentrated study. So his nomination of it as the most valuable scientific concept for everyone to know is clearly not the result of the focusing illusion's effect on Kahneman himself. Support from the consumer arena for Kahneman's assertion can be seen in a study investigating why items placed in the center of an array of brands on store shelves tend to be purchased more often. It turns out that the one in the center gets more visual attention than those to the left or right. Furthermore, it is this greater attention, particularly in the moment just before a choice is made, that predicts the purchase decision (Atalay, Bodur, and Rasolofoarison, 2012).

The online discussion site to which Kahneman (among others) provided his answer is found at www.edge.org. You can read his full essay at www.edge.org/q2011/q11_17.html#kahneman. For descriptions of relevant research see Gilbert (2006), Krizan and Suls (2008), Schkade and Kahneman (1998), Wilson et al. (2000), and Wilson and Gilbert (2008). For those interested in prospect theory, the seminal article is Kahneman and Tversky (1979).

19. Eye-opening data supporting agenda-setting theory were first provided by Maxwell McCombs and Donald Shaw (1972) in a study of undecided voters before the US presidential election that brought

Richard Nixon to office in 1968. McCombs and Shaw found that voters' rankings of the importance of various political issues matched almost perfectly (a correlation of .97) with the amount of attention those issues had received in the media. Anyone trained in the social sciences can recognize one reason that this finding made a splash in scholarly circles: a correlation as high as .97 in such a study is astounding. Of equal scholarly impact has been evidence indicating that the relationship between media coverage and perceived importance of a topic occurs at least in part because the coverage causes the perceived importance, not just the other way around. For instance, in one study, subjects were randomly assigned to watch news shows that differed in issue content; after the viewings, they had significantly elevated the importance ratings of the topics that were most featured on the shows they had watched (Iyengar, Peters, and Kinder, 1982).

The Cohen quote appears on page 13 of his classic book *The Press and Foreign Policy*, published in 1963 by Princeton University Press. The source of the German illustration of media agenda setting is Media Tenor. The US 9/11 data were reported by Corning and Schuman (2013). By the way, the presumed significance of topics given recent media attention isn't restricted to political issues. Financial investment options that get short-term media coverage jump in price immediately but then decline in value as media attention wanes over time (Engelberg, Sasseville, and Williams, 2011). Of course, the subject matter of media focus affects our perceptions of importance, too. For example, media attention to grassroots citizen-based movements seems to be particularly powerful in elevating the perceived significance of the issues involved (Smidt, 2012), probably because people are inclined to believe that if a lot of others think something is important, it must be so. We'll have more to say about the primitive force underlying this kind of "social proof" in chapter 10. For a highly informed treatment of the factors that place particular stories and issues on the media agenda, see Boydstun (2013).

20. The attentional draw of monkey colony "stars" was recorded by Deaner, Khera, and Platt (2005).

Celebrities are an intriguing part of modern life. In his book *The Image*, the historian Daniel J. Boorstin described them as public figures "known for being well known" and distinguished them from past public figures known for their accomplishments. In the new form, the figure's major *accomplishment* is being known. Reality TV stars—a collection of vindictive housewives, randy twentysomethings, and preening airheads with no discernible talent except for gaining notoriety—seem to have validated Boorstin's analysis, whereas their consequent "star" standing has validated Kahneman's. For a treatment of the shifting role of celebrities in our culture, see Inglis (2010).

As regards the general rationale for and the consequences of the focusing illusion, it's easy to find evidence that what's important gains our attention and what we attend to gains in importance. For instance, in the realm of attitudes, researchers have shown that we are organized cognitively so that the attitudes we can access (focus upon) most readily are the ones that are most important to us (Bizer and Krosnick, 2001). As well, any attitude that we can access readily comes to be seen as more important (Roese and Oleson, 1994). There is even evidence that concentrated visual attention to a consumer item increases the item's judged worth by influencing sectors of the brain that govern perceived value (Lim et al., 2011; Krajbich et al., 2009).

21. The citation for the wallpaper research is Mandel and Johnson (2002). For the banner ad studies, it is Fang, Singh, and Ahluwalia (2007). Evidence of how advertising wear-out effects work can be seen in Reinhard et al. (2014). It should be clear from these studies that not all attention is conscious. Indeed, there are multiple forms of attention, some of which do not reach the level of consciousness (Marchetti, 2012; Norman, Heywood, and Kentridge, 2013); see some humorous proof at www.facebook.com/photo.php?v=10200513223453109.

The effects of elevated train noise on New York City schoolchildren was reported in articles by Bronzaft and McCarthy (1974) and Bronzaft (1981). The Munich airport study was done by Hygge, Evans, and Bullinger, (2002). For a summary of this and related research, including some demonstrating the negative health consequences of background noise on physical health, see Clark and Sörqvist (2012), Steward (2011), and Szalma and Hancock (2011). The classroom walls research was conducted by Fisher, Godwin, and Seltman (2014).

22. For evidence that greater attention to a poor or disliked idea doesn't improve its standing and often does the opposite, see Armel, Beaumel, and Rangel (2008), Houghton and Kardes (1998), Laran and Wilcox (2011), Millar and Tesser (1986), Posavac et al. (2002), and Tesser (1978).

23. The data confirming the big payoffs to brands that arrange for consumers to rate one of their strong products, alone, within a field of worthy competitors come from Dhar and Simonson (1992), Dhar et al. (1999), Kardes et al. (2002), Posavac et al. (2002, 2004, 2005), and Sanbonmatsu et.al. (1998). The data showing similar effects for singularly assessed managerial options, including data from managers at one of the world's top ten global banks, come from Posavac et al. (2010). For evidence that, in most consumer decisions, satisficing is the norm and that this tendency becomes even more pronounced when time, interest, and energy are in short supply, see Kardes (2013) and Wang and Wyer (2002). Finally, data demonstrating the debiasing power of the consider-the-opposite tactic (as well as certain variants of it) can be found in Anderson (1982), Anderson and Sechler (1986), Herzog and Hertwig (2009), Hirt and Markman (1995), Hoch (1985), Koriat et al. (1980), and Lord et al. (1984).

A report of the study on the impact of decisional debiasing strategies on ROI was produced by Lovallo and Sibony (2010). Kahneman, Lovallo, and Sibony (2011) followed up with an instructive article describing the most common decision biases and ways to combat them.

24. The media analysis findings are supported by research indicating that as individuals become psychologically closer to a matter or setting, they become more focused on "how" issues than on "why" issues (Liberman and Trope, 1998; Trope and Liberman, 2010). Descriptions of how the embedded reporter program developed and how both the print and broadcast media stories it produced were affected can be found in Aday et al. (2005), Cortell et al. (2009), Lindner (2008, 2009), and Pfau et al. (2004, 2005, 2006). Evidence that Pentagon officials screened reporters and sometimes denied them access to the

program on the basis of insufficiently favorable prior reports comes from investigations by Reed (2009) and Reed et al. (2009).

On a personal note, it is now possible to reflect on the consequences of the embedded reporter program for me while it was in place. Despite deep misgivings about the justification for the invasion, I couldn't shake the emotional sense that criticizing the war was, in a way, shameful of me. The scholarship that has since emerged helps me understand the basis for that feeling. If the prevailing media focus made the war seem principally about the actions of those who were waging it up close rather than those who had engineered it from afar, then—intellectual distinctions be damned—my opposition *was* unfair.

Chapter 4. What's Focal Is Causal

25. The waiting line study was published by Oberholzer-Gee in 2006. For evidence of the felt obligation to help, guilt for failing to help, and frequency of help associated with a vulnerable or needy other, see Berkowitz (1972), de Waal (2008), Dijker (2010), Schroeder et al. (1995), and Stijnen and Dijker (2011).

26. A summary of much of Taylor's research on the topic is published in Taylor and Fiske (1978). Subsequent research has extended the what's-focal-is-presumed-causal effect to novel contexts, demonstrating that observers give more causal status to individuals who speak louder in a conversation (Robinson and Zebrowitz-McArthur, 1982) or who are wearing attention-grabbing clothing—for example a striped shirt—in an interaction (Zebrowitz-McArthur and Ginsberg, 1981). It has even been shown that referees assign more causality to athletes wearing distinctively-colored uniforms in sports matches (Hagemann, Strauss, and Leissing, 2008; Rowe, Harris, and Roberts, 2005).

27. Although evidence of the incidence of persuaded false confessions is available from several expert sources (Davis, 2010; Kassin, 2008; Lassiter and Meissner, 2010; and Leo, 2008), readers wishing to look in one place for the details of many false confessions can do so in Drizin and Leo (2004), where 125 cases are documented. For a harrowing

account of the human consequences of one such false confession—for both the persuader and the persuaded—go to www.thisamericanlife .org/radio-archives/episode/507/confessions?act=1#play.

28. The desire on my part to avoid bringing an attorney into the matter is not to be minimized, as the action typically costs money, extends the process, and intensifies suspicions. After the murder of six-year-old JonBenét Ramsey in 1996, for instance, her parents refused to speak with Boulder, Colorado, police without their attorney when it became clear to them that the police immediately considered them suspects in the crime. As a result, many observers—in law enforcement, the media, and the public—became convinced that this act of "lawyering up" betrayed their guilt. The governor of Colorado at the time even issued a statement urging them to "quit hiding behind their attorneys." Despite the absence of any credible evidence of their criminal involvement, in many eyes, the Ramseys remained prime suspects in the never-solved murder for two decades until, finally, they were fully exonerated by DNA tests. But, even then, in a letter to JonBenét's father, the Boulder County district attorney admitted that, in spite of the new DNA evidence absolving the Ramseys of all blame, there will still be those who choose to believe the Ramseys guilty.

29. For data showing how each of these factors heightens the probability that an innocent individual can be led to confess, see Blagrove (1996), Kassin et al. (2010), Leding (2012), Loftus (2011); Mazzoni and Memon (2003), Perillo and Kassin (2011), Rajagopal and Montgomery (2011), and Shaw and Porter (2015).

The reasons that interrogators might want to use such questionable tactics to obtain a confession are several, including a legitimate desire to identify criminals. But a more discomforting reason can also apply: they get credit for obtaining a confession. As the authors of the most widely used handbook for criminal interrogators (Inbau et al., 2001) revealed about interrogator motivations, "Each investigator wants to improve his efficiency rating or otherwise demonstrate his value to the department or office. In addition, the publicity in the community is considered desirable—to say nothing of the satisfaction to the individual's own ego" (55). The authors go on to remark offhandedly, "All this is perfectly understandable and nothing more than normal human behavior" (55). Yes, but still, the cavalierly mentioned role of these factors—efficiency ratings, publicity, ego boosts—in such a high-stakes process makes me gulp.

30. The Daniel Webster quote comes from his *Argument on the Murder of Captain White* (April 6, 1830). Justice Brennan's comment was made in the US Supreme Court case of *Colorado v. Connelly*, 1986, page 182. An especially pernicious reason that false confessions lead so frequently to convictions is that the confessions corrupt other sources of evidence in the case. That is, after such a confession is registered, more errors consistent with the confession are made by forensic scientists (in ballistic, hair fiber, handwriting, and fingerprint analysis), eyewitness identifiers, and police informants. Apparently, not only does a confession—even a false one—convince judge and jury of a defendant's guilt, it convinces testifiers in the case, who then alter their testimony (perhaps unconsciously) to fit this now-installed view (Kassin, Bogart and Kerner, 2012). See Kassin (2012, 2014) for discussions of the legal implications.

Thoroughgoing descriptions of the Peter Reilly case are available in books by Donald Connery (1977) and Joan Barthel; (1976). The Barthel book, which includes the entire transcript of Reilly's interrogation, was made into a TV movie called *A Death in Canaan*, directed by Tony Richardson in 1978. My account of the case is adapted from a chapter on persuasion I've written for a social psychology textbook (Kenrick, Neuberg, and Cialdini, 2015). Arthur Miller's story of his encounter with Nien Cheng can be found, in his words, inside another Connery book (1995) on pages 89–90.

31. Lassiter has conducted multiple experiments demonstrating the potency of mere point of view in rated responsibility for observed confessions. Good summaries of much of his research in this regard are available in Lassiter (2002, 2010). That research has been acted upon in at least one country, New Zealand, which now requires that all police interrogations be videotaped from the side.

32. The overestimation of the causal role of leaders isn't limited to business organizations, although it certainly does apply there (Flynn and

Staw, 2004; Mendl, Ehrlich, and Dukerich, 1985; Pfeffer and Salancik, 1978; Salancik and Mendl, 1984; and Schyns, Felfe, and Blank, 2007). It also applies to governmental organizations (Salancik and Pfeffer, 1977), educational institutions (Birnbaum, 1989), and sports teams (Allen, Panian, and Lotz, 1979).

The data on CEO compensation versus worker compensation come from an analysis of 334 companies in the Standard & Poor's 500. (See Beck, 2011.) More recently, the discrepancy has not narrowed: a 2014 study by the Economic Policy Institute revealed that the pay of the average employee at the top 350 publicly traded firms was one-third of 1 percent of the CEO's pay, and a 2015 study showed that the difference had widened even further to close to one-quarter of 1 percent (Krantz, 2015). There are troubling societal implications of such large payment differences (Stiglitz, 2012). One study, using data from 1972 to 2008, found that unhappiness among lower-income Americans rose during years of large income inequality in the country. In a surprise, this unhappiness was not due to the discrepancy's effect on their incomes but to its effect on the amount of unfairness and distrust they were made to feel. Whenever national pay inequality was high, lower-income citizens became more troubled because they felt they couldn't *trust* people, in general, to be fair (Oishi, Kesebir, and Diener, 2011; see Twenge, Campbell, and Carter, 2014, for similar findings). The damaging effect of economic inequality on trust ramifies into academic cheating attempts. Students at schools in geographic regions characterized by large income inequality are more likely to visit online sites that provide them ways to cheat on their assignments and papers. Moreover, this greater tendency to cheat appears to be caused by the students' lower trust in people and, presumably, their associated belief that everyone else does it (Neville, 2012).

Chapter 5. Commanders of Attention 1: The Attractors

33. The French cell phone research was done by Lamy, Fischer-Lokou, and Guéguen (2010). Evidence against the liberal use of sex in advertising

appears on page 235 of J. Scott Armstrong's exceptional book *Persuasive Advertising* (2010) and in a more recent review by Lull and Bushman (2015). The data on time spent looking at photos of attractive members of the opposite sex were collected on heterosexual males and females by Maner et al. (2003, 2007, 2009) and fits with a larger literature affirming the powerful role of one's current goals on one's attention in any situation (Dijksterhuis and Aarts, 2010; Vogt et al., 2011, 2012). The finding demonstrating a connection between one's attentiveness to potential mating alternatives and the likely failure of one's existing relationship was obtained by Miller (1997).

By the way, the oft-hyped claim of a vast difference in how often men as opposed to women think about sex—for example, once a minute versus once a day (Brizendine, 2005)—appears to have no basis in reality. The best research into the question indicates that young men think about sex a little more than once every hour, whereas for young women, it's closer to once every hour and a half (Fisher, Moore, and Pittenger, 2012).

34. The evidence for an exceptional sensitivity to potentially threatening stimuli in human infants can be found in LoBue (2009, 2010) and Leppanen and Nelson (2012). This evidence aligns well with research on adults showing that, in most things, bad is stronger than good. Typically, negative (and, consequently, threatening) facts, relationships, parents, ethics, character traits, words, events, stock market changes, and consumer experiences are more memorable, impactful, and mobilizing than their positive counterparts, principally because they gain and hold our attention better (Akhtar, Faff, and Oliver, 2011; Barlow et al., 2012; Baumeister et al, 2001; Campbell and Warren, 2012; Dijsterhuis and Aarts, 2003; Risen and Gilovich, 2008; Rozin and Royzman, 2001; Trudel and Cotte, 2009; and Vaish, Grossman and Woodward, 2008).

The best analyses of the dread risk–related consequences of 9/11 can be found in Gigerenzer (2006) and Gaissmaier and Gigerenzer (2012). The single commercial plane crash in the United States during the twelve months following 9/11 took place in November 2001 and appeared to have no terrorist connection. The study of bicycle accidents in London was done by Ayton, Murray, and Hampton (2011). Yet another form of dread risk has caught the attention of medical professionals: People are overusing hand sanitizers to reduce the risk of getting colds, which is leading to more drug-resistant bacteria that pose a more significant health risk. (See www.nationofchange.org/anti-bacterial-hand-sanitizers-and-cleaners-fueling-resistant-super-bugs-1334411509 and http://healthychild.com/healthy-kids-blog/antibacterial-hand-sanitizers-unnecessary-and-risky.)

35. Summaries of many studies testing the effectiveness of fear appeals support the potent impact of such messages on attitudes, intentions, and behaviors (Tannenbaum et al., 2015; Witte and Allen, 2000). For an example of how too-threatening communications can backfire, see Nestler and Egloff (2010). Compelling evidence of the persuasive effects of strong health warnings on tobacco packaging can be found in Hammond (2010), Huang, Chaloupka, and Fong (2013), and Blanton et al. (2014). De Hoog, Stroebe, and de Wit (2008) performed the Dutch hypoglycemia research demonstrating the superiority of fear-arousing communications that contain action-step information. Other research has documented a similar effect in the arena of global warming beliefs. When climate change warnings detailed dire and catastrophic consequences, belief in climate change actually declined; but this decline was reversed when the warnings included potential solutions to the problem (Feinberg and Willer, 2011).

36. After utilizing the ads for the San Francisco Museum of Modern Art, we wanted to ensure that the effects we obtained weren't unique to museums. So we conducted the experiment twice more and got the same results, once with ads for a restaurant and once with ads for Las Vegas vacations (Griskevicius et al, 2009). Additional confidence is gained from subsequent research that has generated conceptually comparable findings (Deval et al, 2013; Zhu and Argo, 2013).

37. To read more about how Pavlov came to comprehend the nature and force of the "investigatory reflex," which he sometimes called the "What is it?" response, see Pavlov (1927) and the chapter titled "Conditioned Reflexes: An Investigation of the Physiological Activity of the Cerebral Cortex (Lecture III)." For a humorous illustration

of classical conditioning, see www.youtube.com/watch?v=nE8pFW-P5QDM. An excellent modern-day summary of research on orienting responses is provided by Margaret Bradley (2009). The doorway-induced forgetting effect was uncovered by Radvansky and coworkers (Radvansky and Copeland, 2006; Radvansky, Krawietz, and Tramplin, 2011). Newer research has shown that merely imagining passing through a doorway also produces forgetting (Lawrence and Peterson, 2014).

38. A related type of unforced error can be seen in the tendency of advertisers to bring attention to their appeals by infusing them with a plethora of vivid stimuli: quirky characters, colorful lingo, humorous plotlines, and flashy visuals. As with cuts, such an approach does bring more general attention to an ad (Hanson and Wanke, 2010; Fennis, Das, and Fransen, 2012; and Herr, Kardes, and Kim, 1991). But the approach has the potential to undermine communication effectiveness if the vivid elements are applied with a broad brush rather than reserved for the ad's crucial features or claims. For example, one study of a thousand commercials found that ads with various attention-absorbing background characters were less well understood, less well recalled, and less persuasive (Stewart and Furse, 1986). On the other hand, ads that selectively vivify information directly related to the major argument of the message are very convincing, provided that the argument is a strong one (Fennis et al., 2011; Guadagno, Rhoads, and Sagarin, 2011).

Scott Armstrong (2010, 276–77) has reviewed multiple studies demonstrating that although TV ads that contain many scene and camera angle changes attract greater total attention, they result in less persuasion. Using change to draw attention to just one appealing component of an ad has the opposite effect, though, enhancing persuasion. A more recent study is noteworthy, showing that if a single, attractive aspect of a product changes its *location* within an ad each time the ad is presented, observers automatically pay more attention to that (attractive) aspect and consequently become more likely to choose the product over rival brands when given the chance—even though they are completely unaware that the changed locations affected their attention to and preference for the product (Shapiro and Nielson, 2013).

39. I've checked with the Northwestern University researchers about their study (Hamilton, Hong, and Chernev, 2007), and they've told me they've never seen its implications put into practice by any commercial entity, which seems typical.

   The Northwestern research is not unique in demonstrating that a differentiating aspect of a product, service, or idea can win popularity by virtue of the focused attention it draws to itself. (See Boland, Brucks, and Nielsen, 2012; Chambers, 2011; Kim, Novemsky, and Dhar, 2013; and Yang et al., 2014). Sometimes the differentiation can bring enormous commercial success; Youngme Moon details several such instances in her thoughtful and provocative book *Different: Escaping the Competitive Herd* (2010). More generally, long-standing evidence of the fundamental effect of novelty on attention as revealed by the orienting response can be found in Yantis (1993) and Bradley (2009).

40. Cultural factors can also affect what naturally commands an observer's attention. For members of Western societies, attention is drawn to what is front and center within a scene, whereas for members of Eastern societies, background features have relatively greater pulling power (Masuda and Nisbett, 2001; Masuda et al., 2008; and Nisbett, 2003). Consequently, communicators seeking to convince Western audiences might want to put their strongest arguments in the foreground within their presentation; communicators addressing Eastern audiences, however, can safely present their strongest arguments within the larger context surrounding the issue under consideration.

Chapter 6. Commanders of Attention 2: The Magnetizers

41. In a related vein, there is one highly self-relevant piece of information that health communicators could use to increase the chance that a recipient would be more likely to undertake a healthier lifestyle: the recipient's birth date. For a few months after a birthday, people are

more willing to engage in healthy behaviors, such as exercise, than at other times of the year. Therefore, a personalized "Happy Birthday" message sent to individuals that urged recipients to set fitness goals for the upcoming year would come at precisely the right time. By the way, when urging such goal setting, the communicator should recommend that the recipient set a range-based goal (for instance, to lose three to five pounds) rather than a specific goal (to lose four pounds). That is because a range-based goal neatly incorporates two separate reference points that people use when deciding whether to continue to act on an intention: one that is feasible and another that is challenging (Scott and Nowlis, 2013). The birthday research was conducted by Dai, Milkman, and Riis (2014, 2015), who view birthdays as just one instance of a variety of specifiable breaking points in time (including the start of a week, month, or year) when people feel ready to make a fresh start and, thereby, are particularly inclined to act in idealized ways.

The (strong) evidence for the effects of self-referencing cues in advertising copy comes from a famous experiment by Burnkrant and Unnava (1989) and from a subsequent analysis of ninety-two existing ads (Armstrong, 2010, 193–94). Support for the idea that people are generally egocentric in their attentions can be seen in a wide variety of investigations (Burrus and Mattern, 2010; Humphreys and Sui, 2016; Kruger and Savitsky, 2009; Moore and Small, 2007; and Ross and Sicoly, 1979). For reviews of the positive effects of tailored messages on health-related action, see Martin, Haskard-Zolnierek, and DiMatteo (2010), Noar, Benac, and Harris (2007), and Rimer and Kreuter (2006). At the same time, clumsy attempts at personalization—in which the recipient's first name is inserted into the copy of a message carrying no other shred of personal relevance—are unlikely to work. See, for example http://targetx.com/when-personalization-backfires.

42. Indeed, it wasn't solely Villella's performance that I missed; you could waterboard me 183 times—but please don't—and I'd never be able to give you one accurate recollection from the talk that *followed* mine. Although it is many years later and relegated to an endnote, I want to express my gratitude to two important organizers of that conference,

Gerry and Ilse Allen, who in their kindness took pity on my predicament and invited me to return the next year in a speaking slot far from any "arts break."

Next-in-line effect studies have not only revealed a deep memory trough on both flanks of readied public pronouncements (see Brenner, 1973, for the first demonstration of the effect) but have confirmed that the deficits occur because people do not properly process the information presented on either side of their own pronouncements (Bond, 1985).

43. I've heard other somewhat different versions of where and how the Zeigarnik effect was first noticed; for example, that the restaurant was a café in Vienna. But I'm pretty confident of the relative accuracy of the account I've offered because it was told to me by one of my graduate school professors, John Thibaut, who was a student of Kurt Lewin and who reported hearing it directly from the great man.

Although the first publication of the Zeigarnik effect appeared nearly ninety years ago (Zeigarnik, 1927), support for its basic postulates has continued from soon thereafter to present day in a fairly steady stream (e.g., Ovsiankina, 1928; Lewin, 1935, 1946; McGraw and Fiala, 1982; Kruglanski and Webster, 1996; Marsh, Hicks, and Bink, 1998; Shah, Friedman, and Kruglanski, 2002; Forster, Liberman, and Higgins, 2005; Fiedler and Bluemke, 2009; Leroy, 2009; Walton, Cohen, Cwir, and Spencer, 2012; Carlson, Meloy, and Miller, 2013; Kupor, Reich, and Shiv, 2015). At the same time, some studies have failed to confirm the effect (Van Bergen, 1968). These failures can be explained for the most part in terms of a fundamental feature of the phenomenon: It applies principally to tasks, activities, or goals that individuals feel committed to accomplishing. For instance, Zeigarnik (1927) showed that her effects were stronger the further into a task people had gotten—a finding that has been confirmed by others (e.g., Jhang and Lynch, 2015); and Johnson, Mehrabian, and Weiner (1968) demonstrated that the greater memorability of incomplete tasks was especially strong among individuals who had a characteristically strong need to achieve in whatever they tried.

The study of women's reactions to men who judged their Facebook profiles was conducted by Whitchurch, Wilson, and Gilbert

(2011), whose findings comport well with earlier research showing that recipients of a kindness are made *happier* for a longer time if they are unsure of who provided it and why (Wilson et al., 2005). The studies documenting increased memory for incomplete TV commercials appeared in an article by Heimbach and Jacoby (1972), which has been almost completely forgotten. One wonders if the authors would have had better fortune in this regard if they'd taken the advice of their data and left off the last part of the article's conclusions section.

44. Dorothy Parker is often quoted as expressing the same sentiment in almost identical words: "I hate writing. I love having written." Other noteworthy authors have characterized the difficulties of their craft even more colorfully. Kurt Vonnegut, for one, declared, "When I write, I feel like an armless, legless man with a crayon in his mouth." And Ernest Hemingway famously complained, "There's nothing to writing. All you do is sit down at a typewriter and bleed."

45. I don't exclude myself from the vast majority of university instructors whose appearance is anything but au courant. For instance, I once returned from a visiting year at another school to find that my haircutters near campus had seemingly changed their approach to cater to the avant-garde. I asked for the manager (a woman I'd known from previous years) to see if she could calm my concerns that the place was no longer right for me. Those apprehensions grew when, while waiting, I began flipping through magazines featuring models exhibiting preposterous clothing and haircuts. What's more, the salon's female patrons seemed to be getting their hair colored in hues unknown to nature, whereas the men were electing "bed-head" looks that in my college days would only have been called "morning-after-a-drunk" looks. When the manager arrived, I voiced my worries, which I illustrated by opening a magazine and emphatically stating, "I don't want to look like anyone, *anyone*, in this scene." (I was pointing to a Prada ad at the time.) She was able to ease my fears in a way that supports my present point about the characteristic fashion preferences of university professors: "It's okay. I'll assign you to my stylist who cuts all the faculty members' hair. Don't worry, he's from Indiana."

46. In today's world of easily changed television channels via remote control, astute TV producers and script writers have enlisted the holding power of the need for closure to ensure that viewers won't switch away when a commercial comes on. They pose a provocative question before the commercial break and answer it only afterward (Child, 2012).

     There is no shortage of data attesting to the ability of explanation to enhance understanding. See Koehler (1991) for an early overview and Moore (2012) for more recent evidence and citations.

47. This sequence should not be approached by providing it to an audience as a set of pronouncements delivered from a pulpit. Instead, at appropriate intervals, audience members should be invited into the process of discovery. Optimally, they should be given the opportunity to offer their own speculations and explanations. They should be asked to consider how these explanations could account for all of the evidence revealed to that point and for new pieces of evidence as you reveal them. At the end of the sequence, they should be asked if they could develop an alternative explanation that fits all of the evidence. This is not an application that deserves special treatment here. It's just good instructional practice, especially with adults. And good instructional practice—getting participation, spurring critical thinking—applies to the use of mystery stories, too.

     For examples of how mystery stories have been used effectively in the fields of entertainment and branding, see www.ted.com/talks /j_j_abrams_mystery_box.html, www.ign.com/articles/2008/01/15/ cloverfield-a-viral-guide, and www.innovationexcellence.com/blog /2012/11/12/the-power-of-mystery-in-branding.

     The empirical evidence is extensive concerning the role of available counterarguments in successful attempts to blunt an opponent's persuasive arguments (Blankenship, Wegener, and Murray, 2012; Eagly et al., 2000; Killeya and Johnson, 1998; Maaravi, Ganzach, and Pazy, 2011; Petty and Brinol, 2010; Romero, Agnew, and Insko, 1996; and Wood and Quinn, 2001). That role is especially notable when a counterargument refutes an opposing claim directly (McGuire, 1961; Pfau and Burgoon, 1988; Petrova and Cialdini, 2011; and Szybillo and Heslin, 1973) and undermines the opponent's trustworthiness, as once a ruse is recognized or revealed in a persuasive appeal, individuals resist influence associated with it and its perpetrator (Eagly, Wood, and Chaiken, 1978; Sagarin et al., 2002). For example, pointing out a persuader's undue manipulative intent in a trial setting tends to render the persuader's (otherwise convincing) message ineffective (Fein, McCloskey, and Tomlinson, 1997). Similarly, in a marketing context, researchers have found that persuasive impact is severely undermined if the influence agent is perceived as using trickery (Campbell, 1995; Darke, Ashworth, and Ritchie, 2008; Darke and Ritchie, 2007; Ellen, Mohr, and Webb, 2000; and MacKenzie and Lutz, 1989).

48. There is documentation for the remarkable set of events that began in the mid-1960s when the Federal Communications Commission applied its "fairness doctrine" to the issue of tobacco advertising—decreeing that for every three tobacco ads that appeared on radio or TV, free airtime had to be given to one ad espousing opposing views—which enabled the American Cancer Society to run a series of counter-ads that satirized and parodied those of Big Tobacco. From their first appearance in 1967, the counter-ads began to undercut tobacco sales. After a quarter-century climb, per capita consumption dropped precipitously in that initial year and continued to sink during the three years that these anti-tobacco ads were aired. The majority of the decline has since been traced to the impact of the counter-ads; accordingly, when these ads ended, so for a time did the attendant decrease in tobacco consumption (Fritschler, 1975; McAlister, Ramirez, Galavotti, and Gallion, 1989; Simonich, 1991; and Warner, 1981).

Besides the self-relevant and the unfinished, there are other features of an idea that make it stick in attention and consciousness, such as a consistent history of being associated with reward (Anderson, Laurent, and Yantis, 2013). In their highly informative and deservedly bestselling book, *Made to Stick: Why Some Ideas Survive and Others Die* (2007), Chip and Dan Heath explicate several more: the simple, the unexpected, the concrete, the credible, the emotional, and the story-based. For an approach to this issue that is based on memory research, see Carmen Simon's instructive book, *Impossible to Ignore: Creating Memorable Content to Influence Decisions* (2016).

PART 2: PROCESSES: THE ROLE OF ASSOCIATION

Chapter 7. The Primacy of Associations: I Link, Therefore I Think

49. In support of this point, researchers have determined that associative (sometimes referred to as connectionist) processes are at the core of all manner of mental operations, in all manner of animals, humans included (Tyron, 2012). Among those documented association-based mental operations in infrahumans are conditioning, categorization, coordination, concept formation, and object recognition (Donahoe and Vegas, 2004; Soto and Wasserman, 2010; Stocco, Lebiere, and Anderson, 2010; and Wasserman, DeVolder, and Coppage, 1992); in humans, they are choice, learning, memory, inference, generalization, creativity, reading comprehension, priming, and attitude change (Bhatia, 2013; Helie and Sun, 2010; Hummel and Holyoak, 2003; McClelland et al., 2010; Monroe and Read, 2008; Schroder and Thagard, 2013; Seidenberg, 2005; and Yermolayeva and Rakison, 2014). Indeed, there is now credible evidence that one's feeling of personal meaning (of purpose and direction in life) derives from the experience of reliable associations among things (Heintzelman and King, 2014).

50. An early conceptualization of Semin's reformulation of language as having a principally strategic (versus descriptive) purpose can be found in Semin and Fiedler (1988). A more recent overview of relevant theorizing and evidence is available in Semin (2012). For related support, see Cavicchio, Melcher, and Poesio (2014). Other research indicates that it's not just the elements of language that can create change via the associations they activate; the *type* of language employed can do the same. When bilingual Arab-Israelis indicated their evaluations of Arabs and Jews, either in Arabic or Hebrew, the differing inherent associations within each language caused them to favor

Arabs when responding in Arabic and Jews when responding in Hebrew (Danziger and Ward, 2010).

The roots of SSM's nonviolent-language policy can be traced to the founders of the system: the Catholic congregation of Sisters of St. Mary (hence the SSM initials) that relocated to the United States from Germany in 1872 to pursue a healing mission. Constituted today as the Franciscan Sisters of Mary, the congregation has continued to exert a strong influence on the operations of SSM Health, including an abiding opposition to the glorification of violence in all of its forms.

51. The research demonstrating that exposure to hostile words increased shock intensity was conducted by Carver et al. (1983). That same general relationship has been shown in other studies too, including one in which hostile words were presented subliminally so that subjects weren't aware that they had encountered violent language; yet they became significantly more aggressive as a result (Subra et al., 2010). Besides the described studies showing the behavioral impact of stimuli such as achievement-related words (Bargh et al., 2001) and pictorial images (Shantz and Latham, 2009, 2011), comparably constructed experiments have documented similar patterns after subjects were exposed to stimuli associated with helpfulness (Macrae and Johnston, 1998), rudeness (Bargh, Chen, and Burrows, 1996), cooperativeness (Bargh et al., 2001), loyalty (Fishbach, Ratner, and Zhang, 2011; Hertel and Kerr, 2001), insightfulness (Slepian et al., 2010; disclosiveness (Grecco et al., 2013), or fairness (Ganegoda, Latham, and Folger, in press); the exposed subjects became more helpful, rude, cooperative, loyal, insightful, self-disclosive, and fair, respectively. Using individual words as openers to spur related action seems to work best when the words activate highly valued goals such as achievement (Weingarten et al, 2016). An important yet unanswered question involves whether such stimuli (for instance, when incorporated into posters) have a lasting impact or whether their effects dissipate after observers get so used to seeing them that they no longer "see" them in a functional way. Some evidence of a continuing effect comes from a follow-up to the call center study, which found that ongoing exposure to an achievement-related photo produced greater success among callers

in each of the four consecutive days they were exposed to the photo (Latham and Piccolo, 2012). Instructive additional work shows that on a task requiring a thoughtful assessment of problem-solving approaches, exposure to a photograph of Rodin's *The Thinker*, produced a 48 percent increase in correct decisions (Chen and Latham, 2014).

The self-revelatory quote from Joseph Conrad on the persuasive superiority of the right word over the right argument can be attributed to several factors. He was a writer, a participant in a profession whose members are in a constant search for the just right word. Moreover, although his first languages were Polish and then French, he wrote professionally in another (English), which must have intensified his sensitivity to the subtleties—and rewards—of locating an exquisitely correct word for the purpose of optimal communication. Finally, he was neither a reasoning-focused philosopher nor a scientist but a novelist, given to making his (narrative) case through illustrative, evocative language rather than argumentation.

52. Even more evidence that touch is enough to launch an influential metaphor is available in findings of an international team of researchers (Yang et al., 2013) who recognized that money can have either a positive or a negative metaphoric meaning. It can be *dirty* (dishonestly acquired and thereby associated with cheating and deceit) or *clean* (honestly acquired and thereby associated with fairness and decency). In seven separate studies, individuals who first handled a dirty banknote became more likely to cheat in a subsequent commercial or social interaction. For example, after vendors at a farmers' market in south China merely handled a soil-smudged banknote in an initial transaction, they became more likely to cheat by underweighting their vegetables on a scale in a following transaction. This act of dishonesty did not occur if they had first handled a clean banknote. You might want to consider, then, carrying only crisp, clean banknotes on farmer's market shopping excursions to reduce the chance of being shortchanged after paying for your purchase with a dirty bill.

The work using the beast versus virus metaphors was done by Thibodeau and Boroditsky (2011). The evidence that the experience of physical weight impacts perceptions of intellectual weight, topic importance, and the expenditure of cognitive effort comes from studies by Ackerman, Nocera, and Bargh (2010), Jostman, Lakens, and Schubert (2009), Schneider et al. (2015), and Zhang and Li (2012). In the case of the transfer of meaning from physical warmth to personal warmth, the evidence is available in Ijzerman and Semin (2009, 2010), Inagaki and Eisenberger, (2013), Kang et al. (2011), and Williams and Bargh (2008).

When taken together, recent findings and reviews of the research literature on metaphoric persuasion allow a pair of overall conclusions: first, communications employing a strong, well-placed metaphor are persuasively compelling; and, second, this effect stems from a surprisingly basic and mostly automatic process in which the associations typifying one concept simply flow to the other concept (Chernev and Blair, 2015; Gu, Botti, and Faro, 2013; Kim, Zauberman, and Bettman, 2012; Landau, Meier, and Keefer, 2010; Landau, Robinson, and Meier, 2014; Lee and Schwartz, 2012; Morris et al., 2007; Ottati and Renstrom, 2010; Sopory and Dillard, 2002; Zhang and Li, 2012; and Zhong and DeVoe, 2010).

53. There is controversy surrounding the validity of certain of the most media-favored findings from the research literature on implicit egoism—for example, that more people named Dennis become dentists and more people named Louis move to Louisiana (Pelham and Carvallo, 2011; Simonsohn, 2011). However, the results I've listed—that shared birth dates, birthplaces, first names, or initials increase liking, cooperation, compliance, helpfulness, and patronage whether encountered online (Galak, Small, and Stephen, 2011; Martin, Jacob, and Guéguen, 2013) or not (Burger et al., 2004; Brendl et al., 2005; Finch and Cialdini, 1989; Jiang et al., 2009; Jones et al., 2002; 2004; and Miller, Downs, and Prentice, 1998)—are accepted without dispute. As would be expected from a transfer of associations standpoint, implicit egoism effects are less pronounced in low-self-esteem individuals, who don't assign much value to their selves (Perkins and Forehand, 2012; Prestwich et al, 2010).

It should not be surprising that, as the connections between the self and other entities move from minor to meaningful, their force increases commensurately. Important links to the self—based on cues of common kinship, education level, or values—have produced eye-popping influences on behavior. On the first of these dimensions, French college students asked to complete and return a forty-item on-line questionnaire did so an astonishing 96 percent of the time when the requester appeared to share their last name (Guéguen, Pichot, and Le Dreff, 2005). On the second dimension, an education level similar to the interviewer's reduced refusals to participate in a face-to-face survey by half (Durrant et al., 2010). On the dimension of values, a cleaning product saleswoman describing herself as sharing customers' musical tastes tripled her sales (Woodside and Davenport, 1974). By what process? People think that similar musical preferences reflect similar values (Boer et al., 2011).

54. Data attesting to the individualistic versus communal conception of self in Western versus non-Western cultures are plentiful (Cialdini et al., 1999; Cohen, and Gunz, 2002; Hoshino-Browne et al., 2005; Markus and Kitayama, 1991; Morling and Lamoreaux, 2008; and Sedikides, Gaertner, and Vevea, 2005). The Korean-US magazine ad research was published by Han and Shavitt in 1994. The Eastern world's elevation of communal interests over those of the individual is not limited to Korea. In July 2013 China enacted a law allowing parents to sue their adult children who don't visit enough (Lawson, 2013).

It is perhaps ironic, but altogether consistent with the larger point here, that Kim Man-bok was criticized severely within his home country in the aftermath of the hostages' successful release. The disapproval stemmed from his willingness to speak about the incident in a way that seemed intended to promote his *individual* reputation and ambitions rather than those of his social collective, the nation of South Korea.

55. For a review of cognitive poetics theory and research, see Obermeier et al. (2013). The rhyme-as-truth study was done by McGlone and Tofighbakhsh (2000) and is illustrated in an instructive and entertaining video authored by Daniel Pink (http://vimeo.com/69775579).

The evidence that easy-to-process faces or names lead to heightened attraction and that such processing fluency impacts one's smiling (zygomaticus major) muscles can be found in Winkielman et al.

(2006), Laham, Koval, and Alter (2012), and Winkielman and Cacioppo (2001), respectively. The studies showing the negative effects of *disfluency* come from: on law firm advancement, Laham, Koval, and Alter, 2012; on food and food supplement descriptions, Petrova and Cialdini (2005) and Song and Schwarz (2009); on claims in general, Greifeneder et al. (2010) and Reber and Schwarz (1999); and on stock market performance, Alter and Oppenheimer (2006).

The effects of disfluency aren't always bad. Provided people are willing to take the time to stop and think deeply about your message, sending it in a hard-to-process font or form is more likely to get them to do so, which can lead to greater comprehension and retention of difficult material (Alter, 2013; Alter et al., 2007; and Diemand-Yaurman, Oppenheimer, and Vaughan, 2011). This may be one reason that poetry journal editors favor nonrhyming verses. They assume that readers are likely to reserve encounters with the material until they have the time and mental resources for full reflection. For overall reviews of the effects of fluency and disfluency on judgment and social influence, see Alter and Oppenheimer (2009), Lick and Johnson (2015), and Petrova, Schwarz, and Song (2012).

Chapter 8. Persuasive Geographies: All the Right Places, All the Right Traces

56. Some clarification may be necessary on this point. There is no suggestion here that when developing material for a popular audience, authors abandon academically derived evidence. It's only in the wide transmission of such evidence that the evolved norms of academia become unsuitable (those governing the syntax and structure of journal articles or conference presentations, for example). There's a trick I play on myself to help ensure that I don't disappoint either group when writing for an audience outside the scholarly community. I imagine two individuals over my shoulders as I compose: one, a respected academic authority on the matter at hand, and the other, a neighbor I'm confident would be interested in the topic. I don't let myself advance from a completed paragraph until I think I've

satisfied both parties. A shoulder is a terrible thing to waste; and I've got two, after all.

57. As a rule, I am reluctant to put much trust in evidence based on an anecdote or two. That is the case for the conclusion that background pictures of work-relevant individuals can change the thinking of those seeking to serve such individuals in productive ways. Fortunately, research supports the conclusion. For instance, showing radiologists a photograph of a patient alongside his or her X-ray increased the length of their reports and extent to which they conscientiously detected and registered all clinically significant aspects of the X-ray (Turner and Hadas-Halpern, 2008; Wendling, 2009).

58. Scientific evidence of the contagious character of coughing comes from an exceptional set of studies by James Pennebaker (1980), who also demonstrated that audience members who are fully engrossed in an ongoing presentation are significantly less likely to cough in response to another audience member's cough, because they have directed all their attention to the presentation. This finding gives performers yet another reason to hate the sound of coughs running through an audience: A spreading cough means they are not doing their jobs well; it tells them the audience's attention is wandering.

The insightful Ardrey quote comes from his memorable book *African Genesis*. The equally (but differently) insightful Walton quote comes from his mostly forgotten book *Why Worry?* The following documentation applies to the other mentions in this chapter segment: the editorial writers' dinner ("Coughing Fits Overcome 200," 1993); Austrian spider bites ("Eight-Legged Invasion," 2006); Tennessee gas leak (Jones et al., 2000); Canadian cancer scare (Guidotti and Jacobs, 1993); German skin conditions lecture (Niemeier, Kupfer, and Gieler, 2000); and the frequency of medical students' syndrome (Howes, 2004). It would be a mistake to assume from these examples that all, or even most, incidents of mass illness have a psychological cause; the most recent data indicate that about one in six such incidents are primarily psychogenic in nature (Page et al., 2010). Still, it's interesting to wonder whether technological advances have served to "democratize" medical students' syndrome, which might now apply to anyone with access to the internet and its many sites describing specific diseases, disorders, and other health-related problems.

59. Studies detailing the causal impact of happiness on multiple indices of health and wealth can be found in Diener and Biswas-Diener (2009), Lyubomirsky (2013), Lyubomirsky and Layous (2013), Lyubomirsky, King, and Diener (2005), and Ong (2010). Of course, like most things, the positive effects of happiness aren't invariant. For example, happiness can lead to poor outcomes when it occurs under inappropriate circumstances—a funeral would be an obvious instance—or when it isn't reflected in a person's actions (Gruber, Mauss, and Tamir, 2011; Mauss et al., 2011).

60. It's worth knowing that happy seniors don't blindly deny the existence of unpleasantness (Shallcross, Ford, Floerke, and Mauss, 2013). They accept the bad; they just don't dwell on it, choosing to concentrate on the good instead. For example, in their marriages, the thing that most distinguishes their approach to conflict from that of younger couples is the tendency to turn their focus away from partnership clashes toward other, more pleasant topics (Holley, Haase, and Levenson, 2013). This same acknowledge-the-negative-but-celebrate-the-positive orientation also allows individuals of all ages to emerge psychologically healthy after experiencing a traumatic event (Kalisch, Müller, and Tüscher, 2015; Pennebaker, Mayne, and Francis, 1997). For a sardonic commentary on the choice of some individuals to stay mired in negativity, consider the remark of the stand-up comic Marc Maron: "I think in most cases, the difference between disappointment and depression is your level of commitment to it."

Although the set of researchers who seem to have resolved the "positivity paradox of aging" has been led by Professor Carstensen (see Carstensen et al., 2011, and Reed and Carstensen, 2012, for summaries of their findings, and Livingstone and Isaacowitz, 2015, for external confirmation), others have contributed importantly as well (Gross and Thompson, 2007; Isaacowitz, Toner, and Neupert, 2009; Shiota and Levenson, 2009; and Urry and Gross, 2010). The research implicating attentional control in the elevated happiness ratings of the elderly was conducted by Isaacowitz et al. (2009), Mather and Knight

(2005), and Noh et al. (2011). Seniors with good attentional control are not the only ones who profit from possessing this trait (Cheung et al., 2014; Claessens and Dowsett, 2014; Duckworth and Steinberg, 2015; Geng, 2014; and Joorman and Vanderlind, 2014). Even creative artists, the group most thought to benefit from a tendency toward attentional flexibility, appear to do so only at the initial stages of a task or project. Those with strong-minded attentional persistence on the task are the ones who can point to greater real-life artistic achievements (Zabelina and Beeman, 2013). With such findings in mind, it shouldn't be surprising that, according to an extensive academic review, the type of intervention that has most successfully increased both short-term and long-term happiness has involved strategically effective "attentional deployment" (Quoidbach, Mikolajczak, and Gross, 2015).

The positivity paradox doesn't usually extend into the very last phases of life. That appears to be so at least in part because of the inability of the elderly to manage their internal and/or external geographies then. A reason for the disruption of *internal* management is that attentional self-control is a complex mental capability (Langner and Eickhoff, 2013; Mather and Knight, 2005) that can be drastically impaired by the rapid cognitive decline or brain-muddling medications characteristic of life's final stages. As regards the compromised management of *external* geographies, consider how relatively young seniors typically operate when in control. They upholster their living environments at every turn with cues likely to make them happy: photographs of family (no grandchild goes undeployed in this respect), souvenirs from warmly remembered trips, music from radio stations specializing in soothing sounds. Contrast that set of cues with those available to the elderly when they no longer control the powers of place within the darkened, solemn confines of home bedrooms or the sterile white walls of hospital quarters. Once again, seniors aren't alone with respect to this phenomenon. College students who are good at arranging their internal geographies through self-control do so, in part, by arranging their external geographies to allow it. That is, tactically, they spend more time with people and in

social situations that are likely to promote good self-control (vanDellen et al., 2015).

61. For experimental evidence that attention shifts can "break the sieges
of winter" even for nonseniors, consider that the moods of saddened
children could be elevated significantly by giving them a drawing task
on a topic unrelated to their sadness. Not only was this way to reroute
the kids' focus of attention simple to implement, it proved effective
for every age group in the study—from twelve years down to six years
of age (Drake and Winner, 2013).

    Accessible overviews of Lyubomirsky's findings are available in a
pair of splendid popular press books (Lyubomirsky 2008, 2013). For
the more scholarly minded, a good summary can be found in Lyubomirsky and Layous (2013). The research on the use of the Live Happy
iPhone app and its association with greater happiness was done by
Parks et al. (2012). The complete set of all twelve happiness-inducing
activities on Lyubormirsky's list can be downloaded from the link at
the bottom of the following website page: http://thehowofhappiness
.com/about-the-book.

62. I've had to speak of Alan in the past tense because of his untimely
death not far into his career, after a lifelong struggle with cystic fi-
brosis. During our years of training together in Chapel Hill, North
Carolina, I witnessed that struggle close up. It took place valiantly and
with no complaints to the fates from him. But from me, those complaints have been harsh and enduring at the loss of this fine man and
friend. Here's the latest: he isn't around to see the scientific validation
of his advice to me regarding how to do well on aptitude tests by focusing preliminarily on one's strengths and accomplishments. To wit,
one set of studies showed that—particularly among people who don't
usually do well on such tests (for example, low-income individuals)—
initially describing a personal experience that made them feel proud
and successful led to significantly better performance on intelligence
test items (Hall, Zhao, and Shafir, 2014).

63. For good reviews of the effects of the math-and-gender stereotype on
women's test performance, see Rydell, McConnell, and Beilock (2009),
Schmader, Johns, and Forbes (2008), and Shapiro and Neuberg (2007).

For research that supports my four specific recommendations, see: for number one, Inzlicht and Ben-Zeev (2000), and Sekaquaptewa and Thompson, (2003); for number two, Marx and Roman (2002), McIntyre, Paulson, and Lord (2003), Latu et al. (2013), and, relatedly, McCormick and Morris (2015); for number three, Cervone (1989) and Miyake et al. (2010); and for number four, Danaher and Crandall (2008), Rydell et al. (2009), and Shih, Pittinsky, and Ambady (1999).

Two other findings of note have appeared in the research around the math-and-gender stereotype. First, the basic psychological processes involved are not limited to the activation of that particular stereotype. For example, there is a widely held belief that athletes are not very intelligent; consequently, when student-athletes at an elite university, Princeton, were reminded of their athlete identity, their scores on a math test declined significantly (Yopyk and Prentice, 2005). In a related fashion but of much larger societal import, reminding African American students of their race just before an exam degrades their test performance (Nguyen and Ryan, 2008; Steele, Spencer, and Aronson, 2002; and Walton and Spencer, 2009). Fortunately, the procedures that buffer women students against this pernicious effect, such as self-affirmations or exposures to successful role models, do the same for African American students (Cohen et al, 2006; and Taylor and Walton, 2011).

Second, there is little or no objective basis for the belief that, on average, women are less able than men on math-related tasks (Ceci et al., 2014). Except when focused on gender, they normally score as well as men on assessments of mathematical aptitude (Lindberg et al., 2010). Why, then, are they so underrepresented in science, technology, engineering, and mathematics careers (Ceci, Williams, and Barnett, 2009)? For the most part, it seems to be a matter of preference (Ceci and Williams, 2010; Robertson et al., 2010; and Wang, Eccles, and Kenny, 2013). To do well in math-intensive fields such as astronomy, chemistry, computer science, engineering, mathematics, and physics, it's necessary to comprehend relationships among elements of inorganic numerical, mechanical, and physical systems. Women may have the same ability as men to do so, but they just don't have the same willingness. They are more interested in the operation of social systems, which are pertinent to their stronger "communal" goals that involve interacting with others rather than with things (Diekman et al., 2010; Lubinski, Benbow, and Kell, 2014; Meyers-Levy and Loken, 2015; Schmidt, 2014; Su and Rounds, 2015; Su, Rounds, and Armstrong, 2009; and Zell, Krizan, and Teeter, 2015). Indeed, this enhanced level of attention asserts itself even within infant girls, who look at human faces, including other infants' faces, significantly longer than infant boys do (Gluckman and Johnson, 2013). Anyone without access to the research I've cited can get compelling other evidence that young women are able to parse—in exquisite detail—the relationships among elements of complex systems. Simply listen to a conversation among teenage girls regarding members of their *social* networks.

Chapter 9. The Mechanics of Pre-Suasion: Causes, Constraints, and Correctives

64. Support for the general idea that an opener readies associated concepts for influence while inhibiting unassociated ones can be found in a variety of sources (Buanomano, 2011; Bridwell and Srinivasan, 2012; Gayet, Paffin, and Van der Stigchel, 2013; Higgins, 1996; Kim and Blake, 2005; Klinger, Burton, and Pitts, 2000; Loersch and Payne, 2011; Maio et al., 2008; Tulving and Pearlstone, 1966; and Wentura, 1999).

    There is strong and long-standing evidence that a concept's accessibility (ease of cognitive contact) plays a central role in subsequent attention and relevant responding (for example, Blankenship, Wegener, and Murray, 2012, 2015; Higgins and Bargh, 1987). For the research showing the effects of violent video games on antisocial behavior and aggressive thoughts, see Anderson et al. (2004), Anderson and Dill (2000), Greitemeyer and Mügge (2014), and Hasan et al. (2013). For the mirror-image findings demonstrating the effect of prosocial video games on helpfulness and prosocial thoughts, see Gentile et al. (2009), Greitemeyer and Osswald (2010), and Greitemeyer and

Mügge (2014); for evidence that the increased helpfulness occurs in players across multiple cultures and can last for years, see Prot et al. (2014). For the research indicating that violent video game play reduces aggressive behavior, provided the participants have to cooperate with one another in the game to destroy an enemy, see Jerabeck and Ferguson (2013). The explanation for this effect in terms of the decreased cognitive accessibility of aggressive thoughts comes from Granic, Lobel, and Engels (2014) and Schmierbach (2010).

65. The authors of the children's togetherness study expressed genuine surprise at "the ease with which it is possible to dramatically increase prosocial behavior in infants" (Over and Carpenter, 2009, 1192). I can understand that surprise: the individuals the children saw standing together in the photos were in the background, not the foreground of the images. The individuals were dolls, not human beings. The researcher the children helped was a virtual stranger to them, and not one they had spent time with immediately before the chance to help. Yet the effect of seeing the togetherness depictions was indeed dramatic, as 60 percent of those children spontaneously helped, compared with just 20 percent of all the others in the study. The research on the effect of togetherness cues on adult task performance was done by Carr and Walton (2014).

My littering research was conducted with Raymond Reno and Carl Kallgren (1991) and included another study that showed the potency of precisely targeted social disapproval within human behavior. Individuals who had an opportunity to litter a handbill into a parking lot did so 33 percent of the time. But if they first saw a man disapprovingly pick up someone else's litter from the ground, not one of them dropped their handbill into the parking lot, even after the man had left the scene. So to suppress the act of littering, identifying and then displaying the closely linked concept of social disapproval of littering was an exceedingly effective approach.

66. The Belgian beer results come from Sweldens, van Osselear, and Janiszewski (2010), and the mouthwash results come from Till and Priluck (2000), whereas those on soft drink consumption and worth come from Winkielman, Berridge, and Wilbarger (2005). Newer

evidence that these shifts in attractiveness can occur without conscious control over them or awareness of them can be found in Gawronski, Balas, and Creighton (2014), Hofmann et al., (2010), Hütter et al. (2012), and Hütter, Kutzner, and Fiedler (2014). A brilliant spoof of advertisers' use of the mechanisms involved can be seen at www .fastcocreate.com/3028162/this-generic-brand-ad-is-the-greatest-thing-about-the-absolute-worst-in-advertising?partner=newsletter.

67. Extensive reviews of the research literature reporting on if/when-then effects are available and compelling (Gollwitzer and Sheeran, 2006, 2009). The studies on medication regimen adherence among epileptics and job résumé production among drug addicts were done by Brandstätter, Lengfelder, and Gollwitzer (2001), and Brown, Sheeran, and Reuber (2009), respectively. The advantage that an if/when-then plan provides over ordinary intention statements is demonstrated in a study designed to encourage students to persist in trying to solve difficult logical reasoning problems. Some students were asked to indicate their willingness to do so by committing to this intention as follows: "I will correctly solve as many problems as possible! And I will tell myself, I can do this." Other students were asked to commit to the same thing but in an if/when-then sequence: "I will correctly solve as many problems as possible! And *if/when* I start a new problem, *then* I will tell myself, I can do this." Despite the seeming similarity of the two statements, the students using the if/when-then form of statement correctly solved about 15 percent more of the items (Bayer and Gollwitzer, 2007, study 2; for additional, comparable findings, see Oettinger, Hönig, and Gollwitzer, 2000; Gollwitzer and Sheeran, 2006; and Hudson and Fraley, 2015). Support for the automatic operation of if/when-then plans comes from Bayer et al. (2009). As is evident from this set of citations, the behavioral scientist Peter Gollwitzer and his associates are responsible for most of the important research and thinking on if/when-then plans.

68. Besides major goals (Dijksterhuis, Chartrand, and Arts, 2007; Klinger, 2013), examples of chronically prefetched sources of information include social roles, cultural frames, self-identities, and personality

orientations. In each case, research confirms that although they are constantly in place within an individual, these sources of information are not constantly in force. Typically, some reminder of the concept—sometimes delivered as part of a persuasive communication—is necessary to move it from ready-and-waiting mode into full-launch mode. One of the earliest descriptions of this progression occurred in the domain of gender. An extensive analysis revealed that men and women frequently behave identically, except when a gender-related cue is present—perhaps in a setting or TV show or advertising message—which then swings their responding toward prevailing masculine or feminine gender roles (Deaux and Major, 1987). We covered one such example in the previous chapter: Men and women score similarly on mathematics tests, except when reminded of their gender; only then do their scores differ appreciably (Lindberg et al., 2010). Similar evidence is available regarding the impact on behavior of culture (Oyserman and Lee, 2008; Weber and Morris, 2010), self-identity (Brown and McConnell, 2009; Oyserman, 2009), goals (Van Yperen and Leander, 2014), and personality traits (Halvorson and Higgins, 2013); each guides behavior principally after being made prominent in attention. The research applying if/when-then plans to dieting goals can be found in Stroebe et al. (2013).

69. Of course, the idea that a deftly asked question can be persuasively powerful is hardly novel. Socrates was labeled "the Great Question Master" in recognition of his signature approach to bringing about opinion shifts (Johnson, 2011). But just because the notion has ancient roots shouldn't deter us from applying it to present-day choices. For example, in the case of the effects of good moods, should we resolve never to make a large purchase when feeling happy—in the way we are admonished never to go food shopping while hungry? That's not what the research findings imply. Instead, we should ask ourselves why we are feeling elated. If the reason is irrelevant to the merits of the purchase, perhaps because the weather is glorious or the salesperson told us a funny joke or complimented us, the answer will likely be enough to cause us to correct for the bias (DeSteno et al., 2000). The same is true if we are sports fans, and our local team

has recently won a big game. Such victories increase favorability toward (and votes for) current government representatives. But if fans are asked about the outcome of the game first, and thereby reminded that the reason for their good mood is unrelated to the politicians' performance in office, this enlarged favorability toward incumbents shrinks to zero (Healy, Malhotra, and Mo, 2010). Easily the most comprehensive and well-supported conceptualization of how and when we correct our judgments comes from the Flexible Correction Model of Ohio State University psychologists Duane Wegener and Richard Petty (Chien et al., 2014; Wegener and Petty, 1997), in which they argue that correction is likely to occur when people recognize that they are susceptible to an unwanted bias, and they have both the motivation and the ability to take steps to counter it. As a general takeaway, it would be accurate to say that primitive associative processes predispose us toward certain conduct; but provided we notice the processes and have the desire and capacity to correct for them, they do not predetermine our conduct (Baumeister, Masicampo, and Vohs, 2011; Cameron, Brown-Iannuzzi, and Payne, 2012; Dasgupta, 2004; Davis and Herr, 2014; Fiske, 2004; Pocheptsova and Novemsky, 2009; Strack, Werth, and Deutsch, 2006; Thompson et al., 1994; and Trampe et al., 2010).

Research documenting the effect of mood on ratings of one's possessions was reported by Isen et al. (1978), on the effect of weather on women's willingness to provide their phone numbers by Guéguen (2013), and on the effect of sunny days on ratings of life satisfaction by Schwarz and Strack (1991). This impact of good mood on sometimes unduly positive responding is illustrated in a story told by the humorist Calvin Trillin about a friend who emerged from a coffee shop feeling great and encountered an older woman standing outside the door holding a paper cup, into which Trillin's friend deposited some spare change. The woman's response? "What on earth have you done to my tea?"

70. The product placement research was conducted by Law and Braun (2000). Evidence of the mushrooming growth of product placements in recent years is provided by Patricia Homer (2009), who obtained

results of her own indicting advertisers who overplay their hand in this domain. Audience members' attitudes toward conspicuously placed brands in movie and TV clips dropped significantly when a second form of prominence was added—that is, when the obvious placements occurred repeatedly (three times) within the clip. Yet no such drop occurred for subtly placed brands; they escaped notice as sources of potential bias even when they were shown repeatedly. In fact, observers of the clips became somewhat more favorable to a brand the more often they experienced it, provided they experienced it faintly. This finding is reminiscent of the outcomes of research (described in chapter 3) into the effectiveness of online banner ads that fly under our radar by surfacing briefly on the peripheries of e-content we might be reading. Under these circumstances the more often readers encountered an ad, the more they liked it later, even though they never remembered seeing it (Fang, Singh, and Ahluwalia, 2007). Use these links for examples—and a brief history—of product placements in movies (www.youtube.com/watch ?v=wACBAu9coUU) and TV (www.ebaumsworld.com/video/watch /83572701/). Of course, even conspicuous product placements can work, provided that they are integrated smoothly into the plotline; you can find several such successes here: http://mentalfloss.com/article/18383/stories-behind-10-famous-product-placements.

71. Besides mere reminders and signals of stealthy persuasive intent, two other kinds of cues can get us to recognize that we might be vulnerable to factors that can lead our thinking astray and, therefore, to an attempt to neutralize those influences. The first such cue involves the sheer extremity of an input (Glazer and Banaji, 1999; Herr, Sherman, and Fazio, 1983; Nelson and Norton, 2005; and Shu and Carlson, 2014). For instance, an attorney can sweep jurors in the direction of a rich settlement for a client by mentioning higher and higher monetary figures, until such time that the amount is registered by jurors as extreme—at which point, they adjust their judgments to counter the influence of large numbers (Marti and Wissler, 2000). Besides cues of extremity, our corrections can be launched by cues of a strong goal that's opposed to the direction the influence factor is taking us

(Macrae and Johnston, 1998; McCaslin, Petty, and Wegener, 2010; Monteith et al., 2002; and Thompson et al., 1994). In one study, white subjects were exposed to photos of black individuals that stimulated stereotypical responses in them toward blacks. Those subjects with a strong goal of controlling their prejudice toward racial groups reacted against these stereotypes by correcting their attitudes accordingly (Olsen and Fazio, 2004).

72. Arguments for the existence of correction mechanisms in human information processing (for example, Hayes, 2011; Klein et al., 2002) have received support from brain imaging studies that appear to have located brain sectors that are implicated in the recognition of misleading information (Asp et al., 2012) and adjustment for it (Cunningham et al., 2004; Klucharev et al., 2011). Many scholars have concluded that one of these correction mechanisms is a reasoning system differentiated in operation from more primitive systems by such terms as rational versus emotional, analytical versus experiential, deliberative versus spontaneous, considered versus impulsive, and controlled versus automatic. Extended coverage on my part would be unnecessary as excellent comprehensive reviews exist elsewhere, in Daniel Kahneman's magisterial book on the topic, *Thinking, Fast and Slow* (2011) and in an edited volume by Sherman, Gawronski, and Trope (2014).

The role of late-night fatigue in furthering the causes of infomercial producers is covered in an engaging book by Remy Stern (2009), who quotes one of the industry's forefathers, Al Eicoff, as explaining, "People are less resistant at that hour. If they're tired, their subconscious will accept without their conscious fighting it." There are two sources of the research on the effects of sleepless periods on the inability of artillery soldiers to resist clearly questionable orders, a popular one (Schulte, 1998) and an academic one (Banderet et al., 1981). Drizin and Leo (2004) provided the data on the average length of interrogations that generate false confessions. The study of the effects of limited evaluation time on camera preferences was done by Alba and Marmorstein (1987, experiment 2); for conceptually comparable results in a more recent study, see Parker and Lehmann (2015, experiment 3). We've known for a long time that, compared with written text, broadcast material such as that on TV leads viewers to give more attention to the qualities of the communicator (for example, likability and attractiveness) than to the qualities of the communication itself (Chaiken and Eagly, 1983).

PART 3: BEST PRACTICES: THE OPTIMIZATION OF PRE-SUASION

Chapter 10. Six Main Roads to Change: Broad Boulevards as Smart Shortcuts

73. Of course, a communicator who uses a pre-suasive opener to bring attention to the concept of authority before delivering a message should have strong authority evidence to present in that message. As much research has shown, drawing increased attention to any form of evidence—expertise included—is a wise practice only when the evidence is compelling. A tactic that focuses attention on weak forms of evidence will not be successful and may well backfire (Armstrong, 2010, 193–94; Burnkrant and Unnava, 1989; Houghton and Kardes, 1998; Hsee and LeClerc, 1998; Laran and Wilcox, 2011; Petty and Cacioppo, 1984; Petty and Brinol, 2012; and Posavac et al., 2002). A manifestation of this pattern can be seen in a study assessing the tendency to respond to a different one of the six major principles of influence—the principle of consistency, which states that as a rule people are motivated to be consistent with what they have already said or done. The study showed first, and unsurprisingly, that individuals who felt they had good personal evidence that consistency was a wise tendency for them were generally more consistent than people who felt that they had little such evidence. But second, and more interestingly, the study also showed that if a pre-suasive opener was used to remind them of the concept of consistency, those individuals who strongly preferred consistency became even more consistent in their responding, whereas those who didn't prefer consistency became even less consistent (Bator and Cialdini, 2006).

74. The research on young children's reciprocation-related behavior was conducted by Dunfield and Kuhlmeier (2010), whereas the candy store study was done by Lammers (1991). The Costco free sample data can be found in an *Atlantic* article that can be accessed at www.theatlantic.com/business/archive/2014/10/the-psychology-behind-costcos-free-samples/380969. Some of the big impact of free samples can no doubt be attributed to the chance consumers have to try something they then decide they like. But one study points to the important role of interpersonal factors by demonstrating that the shoppers most likely to purchase a sampled product were those most sensitive to the social aspects of the situation, not to the informational or enjoyment aspects of it (Heilman, Lakishyk, and Radas, 2011); in addition, shoppers' *overall supermarket spending* jumps significantly during their visit even when they don't get the chance to try an item in the store but just receive a surprise discount coupon for it (Heilman, Nakamoto, and Rao, 2002). For a humorous illustration of the obligations associated with receiving, see www.youtube.com/watch?v=H7xw-oDjwXQ. For examples of how the obligations are used in marketing, see www.referralcandy.com/blog/10-examples-reciprocity-marketing.

The work on campaign contributions and tax rates was performed by Brown, Drake, and Wellman (2015). Findings like these have led legal observers to be pessimistic that elected judges who receive campaign contributions can be impartial in adjudicating cases involving their supporters, despite what the judges might believe (Susman, 2011, and the American Consitution Society, at www.acslaw.org/ACS%20Justice%20at%20Risk%20%28FINAL%29%206_10_13.pdf). Although decision makers such as legislators and judges often claim to be too clear-sighted or morally upright to be biased by a gift, they would do well to heed a biblical injunction that undermines the grounds for their claims: "And thou shalt take no gift; for a gift blindeth them that have sight, and perverteth the words of the righteous" (Exodus 23:8).

75. The study of survey participation, which fits with the results of many other surveys (see Mercer et al., 2015), was published by Scherenzeel

and Toepoel (2012). The US hotel experiment appeared in an article by Goldstein, Griskevicius, and Cialdini (2011), which along with other research (for example, Belmi and Pfeffer, 2015; Pillutia, Malhotra, and Murnighan, 2003), documented the reason that giving first can work so well: it produces a sense of obligation on the part of the recipient to give back. Still, it's worth noting that in the family of factors related to reciprocity, obligation has an equally active but sweeter sister—gratitude—that operates to stimulate returns not so much because recipients of favors feel a sense of debt as they feel a sense of appreciation. Although both feelings reliably spur positive reciprocation, gratitude appears to be related to the intensification of relationships rather than just the instigation or maintenance of them.

Compelling evidence in this regard is available in the research of Sara Algoe and her associates (Algoe, 2012; Algoe, Gable, and Maisel, 2010). Nowhere are the benefits of giving first in business (and in life) presented and traced forward so convincingly as in Adam Grant's book *Give and Take: A Revolutionary Approach to Success*, which I recommend highly.

76. The New Jersey restaurant tipping study was performed by Strohmetz et al. (2002), whereas the fast-food restaurant purchase amount research was done by Friedman and Rahman (2011). For fun, an early episode of the comedy series *Seinfeld* depicts the effect of providing (and not providing) a meaningful, unexpected, and customized gift on consequent gratitude: www.youtube.com/watch?v=aQlhr-rqTQmU. The case of the appreciative Afghan tribal chief comes from the reporting of the Pulitzer Prize–winning journalist Joby Warrick (Warrick, 2008). The account of how Abu Jandal was "turned" by sugar-free cookies is provided by Bobby Ghosh (2009) in an article detailing why psychologically "soft" methods, such as reciprocity-inducing favors, can work better than coercive ones in interrogations. Research (Goodman-Delahunty, Martschuk, and Dhami, 2014) provides scientific evidence in this regard; for links to additional such evidence, go to www.psychologicalscience.org/index.php/news/were-only-human/the-science-of-interrogation-rapport-not-torture.html.

The pull of reciprocity can be both lifelong and lifesaving. As a young boy in 1938, Arthur George Weidenfeld arrived in England on a Kindertransport train taking Jewish children to safety from Nazi persecution in Europe. That train trip, and Arthur's care after he arrived, was organized by a coalition of *Christian* humanitarian societies that rescued thousands of Jewish children in this way. Arthur went on to become director of a major UK publishing house, as well as an English lord. In 2015, at the age of ninety-four, Lord Arthur Weidenfeld found a way to respond in kind. He organized and funded Operation Safe Havens, which transports Syrian and Iraqi *Christian* families out of territories where their lives are threatened by ISIS militants. When criticized for not including in the operation other religious groups (Druze, Alawites, Yazidis, and Shia Muslims) who are equally threatened, he explained in terms that reveal the prioritizing power of the rule for reciprocation: "I can't save the world, but . . . on the Jewish and Christian side . . . I had a debt to repay." A more detailed form of the story of Lord Weidenfeld and Operation Safe Havens can be found in Coghlan (2015).

77. Andrew Meltzoff (2007) collected the data on smiling infants. The findings on the effects of similar language styles have multiple sources: The evidence on romantic attraction and relationship stability comes from Ireland et al. (2011); the evidence on hostage negotiations, waitresses' tips, negotiation outcomes, and electronics sales can be found in Taylor and Thomas (2008), Van Baaren et al. (2003), Maddux, Mullen, and Galinsky (2008), and Jacob et al. (2011), respectively. Similarity's enhancement of emergency helping was documented by Kogut and Ritov (2007) and Levine et al. (2005), whereas its enhancement of mentoring program effectiveness was shown by DuBois et al. (2011).

78. Although Twain recognized the sustenance that compliments can provide, Jonathan Swift warned 150 years earlier that the calories can be empty ones: "'Tis an old maxim in the schools/That flattery's the food of fools." As regards the impact on persuasion, however, movie sexpot Mae West appears to have had the keenest observation. "Flattery," she assured her suitors, "will get you everywhere." John Seiter

was the lead researcher in the hair salon study (Seiter and Dutson, 2007), which he replicated in a restaurant by showing that waitresses who compliment diners' choices get larger tips (Seiter, 2007). Evidence that compliments can have a big effect on liking and a separate big effect on willingness to help is available in Gordon (1996) and Grant, Fabrigar, and Lim (2010). The effects of less than genuine flattery come from studies by Chan and Sengupta (2010) and Fogg and Nass (1997).

79. It's not difficult to understand why we would think that someone who praises us likes us. Less obvious is why we would think that someone who is shown to be similar to us would like us. But the evidence is clear that this is precisely what happens. Indeed, it is the belief that similar others will like us that accounts for why we come to like them so much (Condon and Crano, 1988; Singh et al., 2007). The idea that we expect those who like us, such as friends, to try to counsel us correctly is supported by Bukowski, Hoza, and Bolvin (1994) and Davis and Todd (1985).

80. The experiments showing the effect of social proof information on estimates of morality were conducted by Aramovich, Lytle, and Skitka (2012), Duguid and Thomas-Hunt (2015), and Eriksson, Strimling, and Coultas (2015). There's a heartening international quality to the evidence for the role of social proof in establishing validity: China for the restaurant menu experiment (Cai, Chen, and Fang, 2009), the Netherlands for the fruit consumption study (Stok et al., 2014), and Indonesia (García, Sterner, and Afsah, 2007) as well as India (Powers et al., 2011) for the pollution abatement research. As an aside, the impact of social proof on perceived validity gives sellers in an online auction (such as on eBay) a clear answer to the question of whether they should set their starting prices high or low. Analysis indicates that lower initial prices generate higher purchase prices. One reason: lower starting prices bring in more bidders who notice all the interest and mistakenly infer that it is due to the inherent worth of the item rather than its enticing initial price (Ku, Galinsky, and Murningham, 2006). Essentially, they apply social proof logic and think, "Wow, if there are so many bidders for this thing, it must be good."

81. The energy conservation research (Nolan et al., 2008) was conducted in middle-class neighborhoods of San Marcos, California, where our research assistants braved the dangers of backyard dogs and lawn watering systems to record actual energy usage by reading house-holds' outside power meters. Although that study examined how social proof operates in the realm of environmental behavior, the same processes apply in other arenas in which feasibility is a factor (for example, Lockwood, and Kunda, 1997; Mandel, Petrova, and Cialdini, 2006; and Schmiege, Klein, and Bryan, 2010). For instance, one of the biggest determinants of whether people will undertake healthy action is the extent to which it seems manageable (Armitage and Connor, 2001), and social comparisons help determine how manageable the action seems to any given individual. (See page 27 of Martin, Haskard-Zolnierek, and DiMatteo, 2010, for a review of the evidence.)

82. Marshall McLuhan's statement that the medium is the message comes from his 1967 book of (almost) the same title, *The Medium Is the Massage*. According to his son, Dr. Eric McLuhan, the word *massage* resulted from a printer's error, but when the author noticed it and recognized its fit with his argument that the medium manipulates the experience of the recipient, he said, "Leave it alone! It's great, and right on target!"

   The study that scanned brain activity after expert financial advice was authored by Engelman et al. (2009). It might not be surprising that an authority label can be a useful tool of influence, but it is surprising how often the tool goes unused when it could be applied suitably. For instance, programs designed to keep children from starting to smoke become significantly more effective if a doctor recommends them to the kids—something that doctors frequently don't do (Moyer, 2013). In another instance, as part of a consultation with a realty firm, my colleague Steve J. Martin recommended that upon receiving a call from a new prospect, the receptionist say honestly, "I'll connect you with our *expert* agent in your area of interest." The number of callers who turned into customers rose by 16 percent. It's instructive that the receptionist had in the past regularly connected new callers to relevant expert agents. She just hadn't previously labeled the agents as relevant experts first.

83. For confirmation that both expertise and trustworthiness lead to perceived credibility and dramatically greater influence, see Smith, De Houwer, and Nosek (2013). Evidence of the across-the-board preference for trustworthiness in many kinds of relationships comes from Cottrell, Neuberg, and Li (2007), Goodwin (2015), and Wood (2015). The effectiveness in legal contexts of the be-the-one-to-disclose-a-weakness tactic has been demonstrated repeatedly (for instance, Dolnik, Case, and Williams, 2003; Stanchi, 2008; and Williams, Bourgeois, and Croyle, 1993); the same tactic has proved effective for corporations that revealed negative information about themselves (Fennis and Stroebe, 2014). The information that politicians can increase their trustworthiness as well as their vote worthiness by seemingly arguing against self-interest was provided by Combs and Keller (2010). The advertising agency Doyle Dane Bernbach (now DDB) was the first to produce hugely successful ads admitting to a weakness that was then countered by a strength, such as the "Ugly is only skin deep" and "It's ugly but it gets you there" ads for the early Volkswagen Beetle, as well as the game-changing "We're #2. We try harder" campaign for Avis Rent a Car. Since then, similarly worded promotions for products such as Buckley's cough mixture in Canada ("It Tastes Awful. And It Works") and Domino's Pizza in the United States have also been highly effective. In fact, after Domino's "brutally honest" 2009 campaign admitting to past poor quality, sales went sky high—as did the company's stock price. Strong support for the idea that when a piece of positive information follows a piece of negative information, it will be most effective if it specifically undercuts the negativity (rather than just balancing it out with some unrelated form of positivity) can be found in Mann and Ferguson (2015) and Petrova and Cialdini (2011).

84. One person's intention to gain from others' desire to avoid losses, in this instance future losses, is proposed in this clip: www.usatoday.com/story/tech/gaming/2014/02/10/flappy-bird-auction/5358289. Aside from loss aversion (Boyce et al., 2013; Kahneman and Tversky,

1979), there are other reasons an item's scarcity drives us to want it more. For example, people automatically think that rare items have higher economic value (Dai, Wertenbroch, and Brendel, 2008); in addition, people dislike having their freedom to possess an item restricted by its scarcity, and so they will choose it to restore that freedom (Burgoon et al., 2002). The data from the automobile industry's practice of limiting production of certain models were analyzed by Balachander, Liu, and Stock (2009), whereas those from grocery store promotions were analyzed by Inman, Peter, and Raghubir (1997). For a news clip of an iPhone incident roughly similar to the one I witnessed, see www.live5news.com/story/23483193/iphone-5-release-draws-crowd-on-king-street.

85. The research demonstrating that prayer reduces the reported number of sexual infidelities was done by Fincham, Lambert, and Beach (2010), who also showed that the most effective form of prayer implored for the well-being of one's partner; simply praying daily in an unspecified way didn't have the same effect, nor did merely thinking positive daily thoughts about one's partner. So it wasn't engaging in a broadly spiritual act or thinking well of a partner that was at cause. Rather, it was a specific, active commitment to the welfare of a partner that made it difficult to then undermine the partner's well-being. The data on the consistency-producing effects of honesty pledges, prior voting action, product referrals, and intention ratifications were collected by, respectively, Shu et al. (2012), Gerber, Green, and Shachar (2003), Kuester and Benkenstein (2014), and Lipsitz et al. (1989).

86. In her book *Forcing the Spring: Inside the Fight for Marriage Equality* (2014), the Pulitzer Prize–winning journalist Jo Becker supplied a meticulously researched account of the personalities, activities, and events surrounding the twin 2013 US Supreme Court decisions favoring marriage equality. Much of the evidence I provided in my treatment comes from that account, which I recommend highly for those interested in the fascinating behind-the-scenes story. Still, the outcomes of that story in terms of the causes of Justice Kennedy's decisions—no matter how good the relevant journalism–don't have

scientific standing. Fortunately, scientific tests have confirmed the larger point that merely reminding individuals of their previous commitments is enough to spur consistent future responding. For example, asking online survey participants to reflect back on their past helping actions made them three and a half times more likely to contribute to a fund for *new* earthquake victims (Grant and Dutton, 2012).

It is worth noting that sometimes after reflecting on or performing a moral action such as helping, people feel they've earned the right to be selfish the next time they get the chance; it's as if, after contributing to the common good, they feel entitled to some "me time" in return. This phenomenon, referred to as *moral licensing* (Monin and Miller, 2001), runs counter to the normal commitment/consistency effect. To date, the best evidence indicates that enacted morality leads to continued morality when it supports one's identity as a moral person—that is, when it shows a history of moral action (Conway and Peetz, 2012), involves activity important to a moral self-definition (Miller and Effron, 2010), or requires a meaningful cost to perform (Gneezy et al., 2012); conversely, moral licensing is more likely when an incident of "good" behavior doesn't implicate an ongoing commitment to morality, isn't central to moral identity, or doesn't cost much to undertake.

Chapter 11. Unity 1: Being Together

87. Evidence for the multifaceted positive effects of in-group favoritism comes from: for agreement, Guadagno and Cialdini (2007) and Stallen, Smidts, and Sanfey (2013); for trust, Foddy, Platow, and Yamagishi (2009) and Yuki et al. (2005); for help and liking, Cialdini et al., (1997), De Dreu, Dussel, and Ten Velden (2015), and Greenwald and Pettigrew (2014); for cooperation, Balliet, Wu, and De Dreu (2014) and Buchan et al. (2011); for emotional support, Westmaas and Silver (2006); for forgiveness, Karremans and Aarts (2007) and Noor et al. (2008); for judged creativity, Adarves-Yorno, Haslam, and Postmes (2008); for judged morality Gino and Galinsky (2012)

and Leach, Ellemers, and Barreto (2007); and for judged human-ness, Brant and Reyna (2011) and Haslam (2006). This favoritism seems not only far-ranging in its impact on human action but also primal, in that it appears in other primates and spontaneously in human children as young as infants (Buttleman and Bohm, 2014; Mahajan et al., 2011). The demonstrations of how the reciprocity rule operates in holiday greeting card exchanges can be found in Kunz (2000) and Kunz and Wolcott (1976).

88. The cognitive confusion that arises among the identities of in-group members can be seen in their tendencies (1) to project their own traits onto those group members (Cadinu and Rothbart, 1996; DiDonato, Ulrich, and Krueger, 2011); (2) to poorly remember whether they had previously rated traits belonging to themselves or fellow in-group members (Mashek, Aron, and Boncimino, 2003); and (3) to take lon-ger to identify differentiating traits between themselves and in-group members (Aron et al., 1991; Otten and Epstude, 2006; and Smith, Coats, and Walling, 1999). The neuroscientific evidence for the blur-ring of self and close other representations locates their common brain sectors and circuits in the prefrontal cortex (Ames et al., 2008; Kang, Hirsh, and Chasteen, 2010; Mitchell, Banaji, and Macrae, 2005; Pfaff, 2007, 2015; and Volz, Kessler, and von Cramon, 2009). Other kinds of cognitive confusions seem to be due to the brain's use of the same struc-tures and mechanisms for distinct undertakings (Anderson, 2014). For example, the tendency of individuals who repeatedly imagine doing something and then coming to believe that they have actually done it can be explained partially by research showing that performing an ac-tion and imagining performing it involve some of the same brain com-ponents (Jabbi, Bastiaansen, and Keysers, 2008; Oosterhof, Tipper, and Downing, 2012). In another illustration, the hurt of social rejection is experienced in the same brain regions as physical pain, which allows Tylenol to reduce the discomfort of both (DeWall et al., 2010).

89. The concept of inclusive fitness was specified initially by W. D. Ham-ilton in 1964 and has remained a mainstay of evolutionary thinking since. Evidence for the particularly strong pull of kinship in life-or-death situations is available in Borgida, Conneer, and Mamteufal

(1992), Burnstein, Crandall, and Kitayama (1994), and Chagnon and Bugos (1979). Additional research demonstrated that Arabs and Israelis can be made less hostile and punishing to one another by informing them of the amount of genetic similarity between the two groups (Kimel et al., 2016). The finding that teenagers experience brain system rewards after helping family was obtained by Telzer et al. (2010). Reviews of the impressively wrought "fictive families" research can be found in Swann and Buhrmester (2015) and Fredman et al. (2015); additional research offers an explanation for these group-advancing effects—making a group identity prominent in consciousness causes individuals to focus their attention intently on information that fits with that identity (Coleman and Williams, 2015), which causes them, in turn, to see that information as more important and causal (as documented in our chapters 3 and 4). A study by Elliot and Thrash (2004) showed that the almost-total amount of parents' support of their kids in my class was no fluke. These researchers offered a point of extra credit in a psychology class to students whose parents answered a forty-seven-item questionnaire; 96 percent of the questionnaires were returned completed. Preston (2013) provides a detailed analysis of offspring nurturance as the basis for much wider forms of helping.

Although biologists, economists, anthropologists, sociologists, and psychologists know it from their studies, one doesn't have to be a scientist to recognize the enormous pull that offspring have on their parents. For example, novelists have frequently depicted the strong emotional force of the pull. A story is told of a bet made by one of the greatest novelists of our time, Ernest Hemingway, who was renowned for the emotive power his prose was able to create despite its spareness. While drinking in a bar with one of his editors, Hemingway wagered that in just six words he could write an entire dramatic story that anyone would understand completely and experience deeply. If, after reading the story, the editor agreed, he would buy drinks for the house; if not, Hemingway would pay. With the terms set, Hemingway wrote the six words on the back of a cocktail napkin and showed them to the man, who then rose quietly, went to the bar, and bought a round of drinks for all present. The words were: "For sale. Baby shoes. Never used."

90. A copy of Buffett's fiftieth-anniversary letter is available online at www.berkshirehathaway.com/letters/2014ltr.pdf as part of Berkshire Hathaway's 2014 annual report, which appeared in February 2015. Both inside and outside family boundaries, people use similarities to judge genetic overlap and to favor those high on the dimension (De-Bruine, 2002, 2004; Heijkoop, Dubas, and vanAken, 2009; Kaminski et al., 2010; and Leek and Smith, 1989, 1991). The evidence that manipulated similarity influences votes was collected by Bailenson et al. (2008). Besides physical and personality comparability, people use attitudinal similarities as a basis for assessing genetic relatedness and, consequently, as a basis for forming in-groups and for deciding whom to help (Gray et al., 2014; Park and Schaller, 2005). But not all attitudes are equivalent in this regard: fundamental religious and political attitudes toward matters such as sexual behavior and liberal /conservative ideology appear to function most forcefully to determine in-group identities. This can be seen to be so for an instructive reason: these are the types of attitudes most likely to be passed on through heredity and, therefore, to reflect the genetic "we" (Bouchard et al., 2003; Chambers, Schlenker, and Collisson, 2014; Hatemi and McDermott, 2012; Kandler, Bleidorn, and Riemann, 2012; and Lewis and Bates, 2010). Such highly heritable types of attitudes are also highly resistant to change (Bourgeois, 2002; Tesser, 1993), perhaps because people are less willing to shift on positions that they feel define them.

91. A good review of the cues that human (and nonhumans) use to identify kinship was done by Park, Schaller, and Van Vugt (2008). Strong evidence for the impact of coresidence and parents' observed care on their children's subsequent altruism can be found in Lieberman, Tooby, and Cosmides (2007). As regards Chiune Sugihara (whose first name is sometimes listed as Sempo), it is, of course, always risky to try to generalize from a single case to a broader conclusion. In this instance, however, we know that he was not the only notable rescuer of that era whose early home life incorporated human diversity. Oliner and Oliner (1988) found such a history in a sizable sample of European Gentiles who harbored Jews from the Nazis. And as would

be expected, while growing up, rescuers in Oliner and Oliner's sample felt a sense of commonality with a more varied group of people than did an otherwise comparable sample of nonrescuers at the time. Not only was this expanded sense of we-ness related to their subsequent decisions to aid people different from themselves during the Holocaust, when interviewed a half century later, rescuers were still helping a greater variety of people and causes (Midlarsky and Nemeroff, 1995; Oliner and Oliner, 1988).

More recently, researchers have developed a personality scale that assesses the degree to which an individual identifies spontaneously with all humanity. This important scale, which includes measures of the frequency of use of the pronoun *we*, the conception of others as *family*, and the extent of *self-other overlap* with people in general, predicts willingness to help the needy in other countries by contributing to international humanitarian relief efforts (McFarland, Webb, and Brown, 2012; McFarland, in press). In addition, a compassionate reaction to the plight of immigrants from other countries seems caused by perceived self-other overlap with them (Sinclair et al., 2016). Information on the situational and personal factors leading to Sugihara's helping action in the pre-WWII environment comes from histories of the circumstances in Japan and Europe at the time (Kranzler, 1976; Levine, 1997; and Tokayer and Swartz, 1979) and from interviews with Sugihara (Craig, 1985; Watanabe, 1994).

Cohen's (1972) description of the concentration camp incident came from a conversation with a former Nazi guard there who, in a bizarre association, was Cohen's roommate at the time he relayed the story. It's estimated that the people of Le Chambon-sur-Lignon, led by André Trocmé and his wife, Magda, saved the lives of 3,500 people. As to the question of why he decided to help the first of those individuals—a Jewish woman he found freezing outside his home in December 1940—it is difficult to answer with certainty. But when in custody near the end of the war, and Vichy officials demanded the names of the Jews he and his fellow residents had assisted, his response could easily have come straight from the mouth (but, more fundamentally, the heart and worldview) of Chiune Sugihara: "We do not know what a Jew is. We only know human beings" (Trocmé, 2007, 1971). As regards the question of whether his relatives or neighbors were the more likely to accede to Trocmé's requests, evidence from other sources indicates that it would have been the former: individuals for whom certainty of kinship would be stronger. For example, when, during the Rwandan genocide of the mid-1990s, attacks against Tutsis by Hutus included neighbors, those agitating for the attacks did so on the basis of tribal membership; "Hutu Power" was both a rallying cry and a justification for the slaughter.

92. The finding that people are highly susceptible to local voices has been termed "the local dominance effect" (Zell and Alike, 2010) that, when translated into electoral politics, means citizens are more likely to comply with get-out-the-vote requests of members of their own communities (Middleton and Green, 2008; Rogers, Fox, and Gerber, 2012; and Sinclair, McConnell, and Michelson, 2013). Notably, the door-to-door urgings of local field office volunteers have considerable impact on voter turnout, much more than mass media-based efforts (Enos and Fowler, in press). Accordingly, in their successful presidential campaigns, Obama organization staffers developed persuasive scripts that emphasized volunteers' local status (Enos and Hersh, 2015). For an overview of how Obama strategists employed other insights from behavioral science throughout the campaign, see Issenberg (2012).

93. The evidence of willingness to answer a survey, opposition to the war in Afghanistan, and the tendency to desert one's military unit comes from Edwards, Dillman, and Smyth (2014), Kriner and Shen (2012), and Costa and Kahn (2008), respectively. According to Levine (1997), Sugihara's visas salvaged the lives of up to ten thousand Jews, the majority of whom found asylum in Japanese territory. The events attendant to the Japanese decision to shelter them have been described by several historians (for example, Kranzler, 1976, and Ross, 1994); but the most detailed account is provided by Marvin Tokayer, the former chief rabbi of Tokyo (Tokayer and Swarz, 1979). My own account is a modified from a more academic version that appeared in a coauthored textbook (Kenrick, Neuberg, and Cialdini, 2015).

Observant readers might have noticed that when describing the murderous policies of the Holocaust, I referred to them as Nazi, not German. That is because of my view that it is not accurate or fair to equate the Nazi regime in Germany with the culture or people of that country, as is sometimes done. After all, we don't equate the culture and people of Cambodia or Russia or China or Iberia or the United States with the brutal programs of the Khmer Rouge under Pol Pot, Stalin after World War II, the Gang of Four during the Cultural Revolution, the conquistadors after Christopher Columbus, or the Manifest Destiny enactors of adolescent America (the list could go on). Government regimes, which often arise from temporary and powerful situational circumstances, do not fairly characterize a people. Hence, I don't conflate the two in discussing the time of Nazi ascendency in Germany.

Chapter 12. Unity 2: Acting Together

94. For a review of the various types of behavioral science data supporting the role of response synchrony on feelings of unitization, see Wheatley et al. (2012); additional support comes from the finding that observers witnessing synchronous movement among others use the information to infer the extent to which the individuals are, in fact, a social unit (Lakens, 2010). The case for societal mechanisms designed to foster collective solidarity is made particularly convincingly by Kesebir (2012) and Paez et al. (2015). Able and Stasser (2008) performed the research on the effects of matching choices on perceived comparability, whereas Paladino et al. (2010) did the experiment on synchronous sensory experiences' impact on perceived similarity and self-other identify confusion. Consistent with the idea that aspiring influencers might be able to benefit greatly from the unitizing effect of synchrony, consider the sweeping summary statement of the renowned world historian William H. McNeill (1995, 152): "moving rhythmically while giving voice together is the surest, most speedy, and efficacious way of creating and sustaining [meaningful] communities that our species has ever hit upon."

95. Studies of the homogenizing effects of coordinated movement via finger tapping, smiling, and body shifting were conducted by Howe

and Risen (2009), Cappella (1997), and Bernieri (1988), respectively. The water-sipping experiment was done by Inzlict, Gutsell, and Legault (2012), who also included a third procedure in the study, in which subjects were required to imitate the water-sipping actions of in-group (white) actors. That procedure produced the typical prejudice for whites over blacks to a somewhat exaggerated degree.

Interestingly, there is one form of synchronous activity that has an additional benefit: when directing attention to a piece of information, people do so with increased intensity (that is, allot it greater cognitive resources) if they see that they are attending to it simultaneously with someone else. However, this will be the case only if they have a "we" relationship with the other person. It seems that the act of paying conjoint attention to something along with a closely related other is a signal that the thing warrants special focus (Shteynberg, 2015).

96. My statement that the gold standard of social influence is "supportive conduct" is not meant to dismiss the importance of altering another's feelings (or beliefs or perceptions or attitudes) within the influence process. At the same time, it does seem to me that efforts to create change in these factors are almost always undertaken in the service of creating change in supportive conduct. The tapping study was performed by Valdesolo and DeSteno (2011), whereas the marching research was done by Wiltermuth and Heath (2009). Marching in unison is an interesting practice in that it is still employed in military training even though its worth as a battlefield tactic disappeared long ago. In a pair of experiments, Wiltermuth provides one compelling reason. After marching together, marchers became more willing to comply with a fellow marcher's request to harm members of an out-group; and this was the case not only when the requester was an authority figure (Wiltermuth, 2012a) but also a peer (Wiltermuth, 2012b).

97. As evidence for the idea grows, there is increasing acceptance of the conception of music as a socially unitizing mechanism that creates group solidarity and comes about via self-other merger (Ball, 2010; Bannan, 2012; Dunbar, 2012; Huron, 2001; Loersch and Arbuckle, 2013; Molnar-Szakacs and Overy, 2006; and Tarr, Launay, and Dunbar, 2014). Scholars aren't alone in recognizing the unitizing function

of music, sometimes to comedic extents: www.youtube.com/watch ?v=etEQz7NYSLg. The study of helping among four-year-olds was done by Kirschner and Tomasello (2010); conceptually similar results were obtained among much younger children, fourteen-month-old infants, by Cirelli et al. (2013).

98. Kahneman's book *Thinking, Fast and Slow* (2011) is the source for the most complete exposition of System 1 and 2 thinking. Evidence for the validity of the distinction between the two systems is available there but also in less fully presented form from Epstein and coauthors (1992, 1999). The wisdom of having a good match between the emotional-versus-rational basis of an attitude and a persuasive argument can be seen in Clarkson, Tormala, and Rucker (2011), Drolet and Aaker, 2002), Mayer and Tormala (2010), and Sinaceur, Heath, and Cole (2005).

99. Bonneville-Roussy et al. (2013) review and contribute data showing that young women view music as more important to them than clothing, films, books, magazines, computer games, TV, and sports—but not romance. There's solid scientific evidence that music and rhythm operate independently of rational processes (for instance, de la Rosa et al., 2012; Gold et al., 2013). However, it might be more instructive to examine what the musicians themselves have said on the topic. Take, for instance, Elvis Costello's quote concerning the difficulty of properly describing music within the structure of writing: "Writing about music is like dancing about architecture." Or, as support for the mismatch between cognition and emotion in romance, take the line from Bill Withers's 1971 song "Ain't No Sunshine" about a man agonizing over a younger woman who has left their home yet again: "And I know, I know, I know, [repeated twenty-three more times]/ Hey, I oughtta leave the young thing alone / But ain't no sunshine when she's gone." Withers makes his point in the purest form of poetry I think I've ever heard in a popular song lyric: in the throes of romantic love, what one may recognize cognitively (twenty-six times!) doesn't amend what one feels emotionally. The Costello quote comes from an interesting article by Elizabeth Hellmuth Margulis (2010), who added her own evidence to the mix by showing that giving audience members prior

structural information about musical pieces (excerpts from Beethoven string quartets) reduced their enjoyment of experiencing them.

The study of popular song content over a recent span of forty years found that 80 percent featured romantic and/or sexual themes (Madanika and Bartholomew, 2014). The French guitar case experiment (Guéguen, Meineri, and Fischer-Lokou, 2014) recorded the following percentages of successful phone number requests: guitar case, 31 percent; sports bag, 9 percent; nothing, 14 percent. Armstrong's description of the effects of music on advertising success is presented on pages 271–72 of his 2010 book.

100. The Mandy Len Catron *New York Times* piece can be retrieved at www.nytimes.com/2015/01/11/fashion/modern-love-to-fall-in-love-with-anyone-do-this.html, along with a link to the thirty-six questions. The interview with Elaine Aron is available at www.huffingtonpost.com/elaine-aron-phd/36-questions-for-intimacy_b_6472282.html. The scientific article that served as the basis for the Catron essay is Aron et al. (1997). Evidence for the functional importance of the reciprocal, turn-taking feature of the thirty-six-questions procedure is provided by Sprecher et al. (2013). The procedure has been used in somewhat modified form to reduce prejudice between ethnic groups, even among individuals with highly prejudiced initial attitudes (Page-Gould, Mendoza-Denton, and Tropp, 2008).

101. Aldo Leopold's manifesto *Sand County Almanac*, which was first published in 1949 and became a must-read primer for many wilderness groups since, is the source of my treatment of his birch-versus-pine musings. (See pages 68–70 of the 1989 paperback edition.) His strong belief that wilderness management is best accomplished through an ecology-centric approach rather than a human-centric approach is illustrated in his arguments against government predator control policies in natural environments. Stunning evidence supports his position in the case of predator wolves. A visual presentation of that evidence is available at www.distractify.com/wolves-change-rivers-1197626599.html; you'll be glad you watched it.

102. The Ikea effect research was performed by Norton, Mochon, and Ariely (2012). The study of the evaluations of one's coworkers and

co-created products was conducted in collaboration with Jeffrey Pfeffer (Pfeffer and Cialdini, 1998)—one of the most impressive academic minds I've ever encountered, especially in his remarkable ability to think simultaneously at multiple levels of analysis of a problem. Although I suppose it's possible, I'm confident that my high opinion of Professor Pfeffer is not a real-life demonstration of our experimental finding (that people elevate their opinions of their co-creators on a project), as his record of academic accomplishments before and after our collaboration justifies my appreciation of his thinking on entirely independent grounds.

The effects of collaboration on three-year-olds' sharing were demonstrated by Warneken et al. (2011). The positive results of cooperative learning techniques are summarized in Paluck and Green (2009) and in Roseth, Johnson, and Johnson (2008); educators looking for information on how to implement one such approach (the "Jigsaw Classroom," as developed by Elliot Aronson and his associates) can find that information at www.jigsaw.org. The survey study of different types of consumer feedback on subsequent consumer engagement was published by Liu and Gal (2011), who found, instructively, that paying consumers an unexpectedly high amount for their advice eliminated any increased favoritism toward the brand. Although the researchers didn't investigate why this was the case, they speculated that the unexpected payment focused the participants away from the communal aspect of giving their advice and onto an individuating aspect of it—in this instance, their own economic outcomes associated with a salient financial exchange. For some examples of how various brands are employing co-creation practices to enhance customer engagement, see www.visioncritical.com/5-ex amples-how-brands-are-using-co-creation, and a pair of links within: www.visioncritical.com/cocreation-101 and www.greenbookblog.org /2013/10/01/co-creation-3-0.

103. Despite the tongue-in-cheek status of this last line, the importance of avoiding overly simple solutions to large-gauge, knotty problems is no laughing matter. Apropos is something the prize-winning biologist Steve Jones observed about scientists of . . . let's say . . . advancing

seniority. He noted that, at about this age, they often begin to "boom about Big Issues," acting as if their acquired knowledge in a specialized sphere allows them to speak confidently on big-picture topics far outside those boundaries. Jones's cautionary point seemed to me relevant to my situation at the end of the chapter—because, first, I had entered the age category he was describing, and, second, to proceed more expansively, I would have to draw conclusions pertinent to international diplomacy, religious/ethnic conflict, and racial hostility while having no expert knowledge in any of the domains. Plainly, I'd be booming in the dark.

Chapter 13. Ethical Use: A Pre-Pre-Suasive Consideration

104. Data showing that the size of financial loss from reputational consequences can be substantial come from Bomey (2015), Karpoff, Lee, and Martin (2008), Karpoff, Lott, and Wehrly (2005), Lewis (2003), and Trudel and Cotte (2009). Studies by Rothbart and Park (1986), Herbig et al. (1994), and Nguyen and Leblanc (2001) demonstrated the difficulty of restoring trust after observed dishonesty. Much of the evidence from these scientific studies is encapsuled in an admonition to the business community from Edson Spencer, the former chairman of Honeywell Inc.: "The businessman who straddles a fine line between what is right and what is expedient should remember that it takes years to build a good business reputation, but one false move can destroy that reputation overnight." The consulting firm Ernst & Young (2013, 2014) conducted the global surveys documenting that many senior business leaders know the heavy reputational costs of recognized unethical conduct but are willing to enact or permit such conduct when it raises company fiscal outcomes. Evidence that the number of infractions remains discomfortingly large can be seen in the Ethics & Compliance Initiative (ECI) National Business Ethics Survey (2012), Ernst & Young Global Fraud Surveys (2013, 2014), and Labaton Sucharow's financial services industry surveys (2013, 2015); a glance at the business pages of your local newspaper on almost any day offers continuously updating confirmation.

The case that certain features of our economic system will push many transactors to dishonesty is made much more fully than I have in an extraordinarily well-reasoned and worthwhile book, *Phishing for Phools: The Economics of Manipulation and Deception*, by the Nobel laureates George Akerlof and Robert Schiller (2015). Scholarship showing that the likelihood of detection is a chief deterrent to punishable behavior can be found in Becker (1968), Higgins et al. (2005), Kagan (1989), Lab (2013), Nagin and Pogarsky (2001), and Paternoster (2010).

105. The analysis of health care expenses associated with workplace stress was performed by Goh, Pfeffer, and Zenios (2016), who also determined that the deleterious effects of workplace stress on health outcomes is comparable to that of secondhand tobacco smoke. Consequently, they argued that in the same way that many organizations have taken steps to reduce employee exposure to secondhand smoke, they should take steps to reduce employee exposure to management practices that create excessive occupational stress. For an accessible summary of their position, go to http://fortune.com/2015/04/13/is-your-employer-killing-you. Bischoff et al. (1999) did the study of the impact of moral stress on fatigue and burnout among financial service customer-contact personnel. It is worth knowing that the kinds of activities that most led to feelings of moral stress were those that required employees to be dishonest with customers in order to perform their job-related duties. Our research into the triple tumor structure of organizational dishonesty is reported in Cialdini, Li, and Samper (in preparation).

106. Estimates of the types and magnitudes of turnover-related costs can be found in Borysenko (2015), Boushey and Glynn (2012), and Harter et al. (2010). Analyses by Ambrose et al. (2008), Burks and Krupka (2012), De Tienne et al. (2012), Herman et al. (2007), and Ulrich et al. (2007) demonstrate that a lack of fit between the ethical values of an organization and its employees increases those employees' job dissatisfactions and intentions to quit.

107. Accounts of the heavy costs of employee malfeasance are provided in the Association of Certified Fraud Examiners (ACFE) *Report to the Nations on Occupational Fraud and Abuse* (2014), Deyle (2015),

and the PricewaterhouseCoopers (PWC) *Global Economic Crime Survey* (2014). The significant relationship between an unethical leadership approach and the occurrence of such fraudulent conduct has been shown by Gino, Norton, and Ariely (2010) and Peterson (2002). Broad support for the idea that the ethical or unethical climate of an organization is set at the top by authority figures in senior management comes from a study of 160 technology, insurance, retail, financial, food service, manufacturing, medical, and government organizations (Mayer et al., 2009), which found that ethical leadership flows down from one organizational level to the next.

Authority figures in earlier-encountered organizations such as schools and families—who can indeed foster honest conduct in young people under their supervision (Pulfrey and Butera, 2013)—might well wish to take the counsel of research indicating that ethical values predict higher life satisfaction (James, 2011), and honest conduct predicts better physical and psychological health (Kelly and Wang, 2012). One set of these researchers, Anita Kelly and Lijuan Wang, ended the presentation of their findings with a hopeful recommendation for establishing a strong honesty culture in families:

> Our 10-week experiment showed not only that participants could purposefully and dramatically reduce their lies, but also that this reduction was associated with significantly improved health. Perhaps someday parents will tell their kids that for good health:
>
> - eat your fruits and vegetables;
> - exercise; and
> - lie as little as possible.

Chapter 14. Post-Suasion: Aftereffects

108. The study of no-shows in British medical offices was conducted by Martin, Bassi, and Dunbar-Rees (2012). The American flag effects during the 2008 presidential election were reported by Carter,

Ferguson, and Hassin (2011) and were replicated in large measure for the 2012 presidential election by Kalmoe and Gross (in press). However, both sets of authors warn against the conclusion that exposure to a national flag automatically causes citizens to move toward politically conservative stances; in other countries where the flag is not strongly associated with one conservative party's position, encountering the flag does not produce such shifts to the right (Hassin et al., 2007). Indeed, even in the United States, any changes in the extent to which the flag may be associated with the Republican Party could affect whether it would move observers in that party's direction.

Pocheptsova and Novemsky (2010) performed the research showing that positive mood had an enduring impact on evaluations of art only when evaluators "locked in" their evaluations by actively registering them.

109. The impact of active, effortful/costly, and voluntary commitments on self-concept and, consequently, on lasting change can be seen in an earlier literature review I performed (Cialdini, 2009, chapter 3), as well as in more recent research showing that such commitments are most effective when they implicate self-identity (Chugani et al., in press; Gneezy et al., 2012; Kettle and Haubel, 2011; Sharot, 2010; and Schrift and Parker, 2014). What's more, they can direct subsequent responding for years afterward (Sharot et al., 2012). In that earlier review, I included a fourth factor, publicness, in the list of features that can create durable effects. There is good evidence that initial public (more than private) commitments to a cause can reach extensively into the future to spur similar conduct (Dallande and Nyer, 2007). However, newer evidence indicates that this is the case principally when individuals already feel a strong personal connection to the cause; if that personal connection is not present, then a private commitment becomes the superior vehicle for delivering lasting change (Kristofferson et al., 2014).

110. I am aware that what I have recommended in this section has an ironic element. I've contended that, in our campaign for durable change, we have to enlist our thinking-absent mechanisms in thinking-present ways. Although the irony hasn't escaped me, it hasn't deterred me

from the recommendation, as it is very much in keeping with considerable research (Marteau, Hollands, and Fletcher, 2012, and Wood and Neal, 2007) and a major theme of this book: that to be successful, the pre-work of pre-suasion must be undertaken planfully. The resultant plans should be more than worth the salvaged time and effort they require, provided they are made with an appreciation of how the automatic response system operates. If I'm sounding close to claiming, "We can do it, we can do it, we can do it, we can do it—provided we use the system," I'm willing to plead guilty. But in my defense, I'm also willing to swear there's no pyramid sales scheme involved.

111. The results of the study done by Grant and Hofmann (2011), showing that doctors increased hand washing in the presence of the sign reminding them that their patients are vulnerable to infection could be interpreted differently than I have. It could be argued that such an increase didn't reveal physicians' patient-interested concern but a self-interested concern with being sued by patients who might contract an infection owing to negligent hand hygiene during the examination. Although possible, that explanation seems unlikely. First, there is almost no legal case history of doctors being sued for that reason. Second, Grant and Hofmann (2011) reported a follow-up study in which they found that nurses showed the same increase in hand washing as doctors from the sign alerting them to the patient consequences of poor hand hygiene, even though they are rarely sued for any kinds of medical errors and never for hand-washing negligence. (Thanks are due to Gary Fadell for this legal information.) So it appears that both doctors and nurses, who made considerable commitments to their patients' welfare upon entering the medical field, were favorably affected by a simple link to that commitment years later, this time upon entering an examination room.

112. The Carnegie Mellon University study of gift taking was reported by Sah and Loewenstein (2010) in an article that also provides numerous citations of research documenting the prevalence of the activity among physicians and its problematic influence on subsequent medical decisions that favor health industry gift providers; a more recent report can be found at http://n.pr/1MmIZGk. See, as well, an earlier

article by Dana and Loewenstein (2003) that provides additional such citations and places the effects within a larger framework of evidence on the biasing effects of conflict-of-interest on other forms of human judgment and action. More recent evidence indicates that a gift of even one meal is related to physicians' rates of prescribing a drug from the pharmaceutical company paying for the meal; tellingly, the prescribing rates increase still further if the meal costs more than $20 (DeJong et al., 2016).

My final conclusion should not be interpreted as suggesting that stable tendencies, preferences, and personal traits fail to influence human behavior consistently over various settings and points in time, as I don't believe that at all. However, in keeping with long-standing evidence (for example, Bargh, Lombardi, and Higgins, 1988; Sedikides and Skowronski, 1990), I do believe that such constant, personality-based influences occur by the same process as momentary, situation-based influences—the operation of response-relevant cues that are highly accessible in consciousness. The difference is that, in the case of personality-based influences, those cues have been placed in consciousness by abiding elements such as genetic factors or life histories, which have made the cues chronically more accessible. In the case of situationally based influences, the response-relevant cues are placed into consciousness by recently encountered images, interactions, and events, which make the cues temporarily more accessible.

Index

Page numbers in *italics* refer to illustrations.